P9-DTW-821

DATE DUE

MR 13 '97			
FE 26 '98			
AG 31 '00			
NO 21 '00			
DE 28 '00			

INTERNATIONAL DIMENSIONS OF AFRICAN POLITICAL ECONOMY

Trends, Challenges, and Realities

Fredoline O. Anunobi
Xavier University of Louisiana

UNIVERSITY
PRESS OF
AMERICA

OCT '95

Lanham • New York • London

Library of Congress Cataloging-in-Publication Data

Anunobi, Fredoline O.
International dimensions of African political economy : trends,
challenges, and realities / Fredoline O. Anunobi.
p.   cm.
Includes bibliographical references.
1. Africa—Economic conditions—1960–   2. International business
corporations—Africa.   3. Africa—Foreign economic relations.
I. Title.
HC800.A77   1994   330.96—dc20   94–28281 CIP

ISBN 0–8191–9690–8 (cloth : alk. paper)
ISBN 0–8191–9691–6 (pbk. : alk. paper)

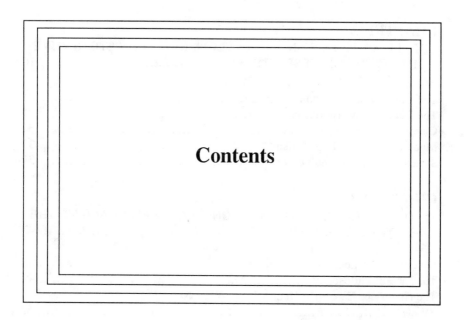

Contents

PART ONE
APPROACHES TO UNDERSTAND AFRICAN
POLITICAL ECONOMY OF EXTERNAL ECONOMIC
DEPENDENCY

CHAPTER 1

iv

PART TWO
THE ROLE OF NONGOVERNMENTAL ACTORS
IN SHAPING AFRICAN POLITICAL ECONOMY

CHAPTER 5
MULTINATIONAL CORPORATIONS: A STRATEGY FOR DEVELOPMENT OR DEPENDENCY

CHAPTER 6
SOCIO-ECONOMIC AND POLITICAL IMPLICATIONS OF MULTINATIONAL CORPORATIONS IN AFRICA

PART THREE
A CASE STUDY OF SELECTED AFRICAN STATES

CHAPTER 7
THE POLITICAL ECONOMY OF INSTABILITY IN GHANA

CHAPTER 8
POLITICAL DYNAMISM AND THE RISE OF MILITARY IN
SUDAN 215

CHAPTER 9
THE POLITICAL ECONOMY OF NEO-COLONIALISM AND THE
ROLE OF STATE IN NIGERIAN REALITY 241

CHAPTER 10

PART FOUR
INTERNATIONAL DIMENSIONS OF
AFRICAN POLITICAL ECONOMY

CHAPTER 11

CHAPTER 12

CHAPTER 13

AFRICA AND THE NORTH-SOUTH COOPERATIONS: RHETORIC OR REALITY

CHAPTER 14

AFRICA AND THE INTERNATIONAL MONETARY RELATIONS

PART FIVE
THE HISTORY AND IMPACT OF ECONOMIC AND/OR REGIONAL COOPERATIONS: STRATEGIES TO OVERCOME UNDERDEVELOPMENT AND

DEPENDENCY

CHAPTER 15
THE MYTH OF NONALIGNMENT IN AFRICA: TREND AND

CHAPTER 16
THE CONCEPT OF ECONOMIC INTEGRATION AND THE
IMPLICATIONS OF UNITED EUROPE IN 1992 AND

CHAPTER 17
CONCLUSION: THE FUTURE CHARACTERISTICS OF AFRICA

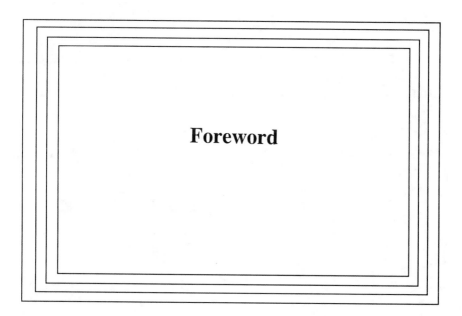

Foreword

Professor Fredoline Anunobi has written an important book about the dynamics of African political economy. His insights clearly challenge the modernization theory as inadequate in explaining and promoting economic development in Africa. He argues forcibly that the modernization theory as previously developed has omitted in its equation the critical part played by external politics in the African development scheme. The logic and illogic of the modernization theory is fully exposed in this book. Anunobi's analysis is penetrating and his insight which undermines conventional bromides makes this book a compelling book to read, especially for those interested in the development of the African economy.

Damien Ejigiri, Associate Professor
and Chairman, Public Administration
Southern University-Baton Rouge, Louisiana.

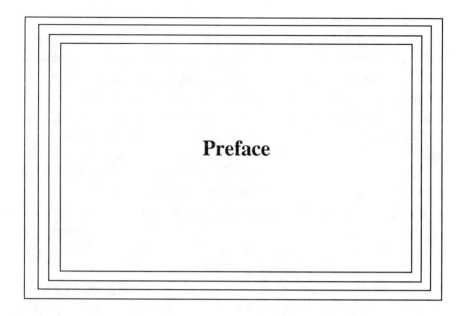

Preface

The inability of many African states to deliver the "goodies" that were expected with the attainment of independence have the citizenry of the African continent wondering what went wrong. In place of robust economy and better standard of living, most African states have provided economic stagnation and dependency, as well as encouraged foreign intervention and unprecedented large scale of human abuses. Conventional theorists have found it fashionable to blame the Africans themselves for their present economic predicament. However, African scholars are now attacking the fundamental assumptions of conventional or orthodox models of development that contribute to the unequal distribution of power and benefits in the World System.

In the early studies of African history, nationalism and development were written mainly from a conventional wisdom otherwise known as modernizaiton, or political development orientation. The fundamental assumption behind this methodology was that African economies are in the process of becoming modern rational groups in which effective and scientific reasoning replace traditional beliefs, norms and value systems. Modernization according to Economists was perceived as commensurate with mechanization, efficiency in the utilization of resources, rapid industrialization, and growth in economic and social standards. For political scientists and historians, modernization includes institution expansion, some measures of political participation, the rationalization of the government apparatus, power concentration, and the argumentation of capabilities in order to meet growing demands.

Orthodox theories of modernization originated from western social science and were mainly related to developments in American political science in the early 1950s. Its theoretical foundation assumed that a focus on transformation from traditional to modern societies would lead to a standardized theory of political development. The major theoretical concerns of many of the first works on African economic relations, however, centered on various challenges of political development that were discovered as facing nations in their effort to accomplish modernization. The first problem was defined as of identity: accelerating a common sense of concern among culturally diffuse entities.

Since the early 1960s the bulk of literature on dependency and underdevelopment in Africa and other less developed countries suggested that prosperity in underdeveloped, poor, and/or developing regions could take place mainly through the spread of modernism emerging in the industrialized nations. A major predominant line of thought portrayed undeveloped nations as "dual societies": with poverty, inequality, backwardness, feudal hinterlands and progressive capitalistic metropolitan areas. Also because the interior area was seen as having stagnated in a state of feudalism due largely to isolation from the forces of capitalism, the recommendation called for the capitalist penetration of the interior part of the same society. Prosperity was to be transferred from North America and Europe to the national urban regions, from the developed societies to the regional trading areas, and from these regions to their respective periphery societies.

However, in spite of the rapid scientific technological prosperity that characterize the post-war era, it has become generally evident that the now periphery nations in Africa have remained in a position of underdevelopment and external economic dependence. Some political economists held that there was a growing inequality among and within nation-sataes and therefore, questioned the authenticity or validity of the orthodox paradigm on backwardness. For this reason the usefulness or utility of the modernization approach was increasingly questioned, particularly in Africa frustrated by its inability to maintain previous gains, let alone progress toward the desired objectives of national betterment.

In the past, modernization theories did provide a major foundation for the analysis of post colonial African political economy. These theories helped to point out some of the major issues faced by African leaders and nurtured a series of fundamental works on the dilemmas of independence. However, by the mid 1960s, it became seriously evidence that these approaches, involved as they were on the accomplishment of ideal goals, could no longer keep up with the increase and problematic pace of events in Africa. In the early 1970s, the search for alternative theoretical and conceptual schemes became inevitable in the writings of Third World scholars.

Hence, this book is not just an academic exercise by intellectuals on Africa. It came about as a challenge and presumably as an alternative to the orthodox Western social science literature on the African continent. It is the product of our overall dissatisfaction with the general literature as well as our rejection of the orthodox view established by Western experts and scholars on Africa. Our perspective is that the theoretical foundations and analytical considerations of the conventional wisdom are in reality fallacious and inadequate in explaining African economic underdevelopment. We share the belief that a comprehensive or genuine understanding of contemporary Africa in general can only be achieved by making a radical move from the assumptions and analyses associated with the liberal economic theories.

We hope to provide the audience with an analytical and conceptual framework on contemporary Africa which is peculiar to African reality and less biased in orientation. In the same way, it is our belief that the political economy of African states cannot be comprehensively understood if we limit our analysis and orientation to internal variables within the continent as liberal theorists have done. What is needed is an international theoretical orientation that brings into perspective the interrelationship of internal and external variables, specifically the degree to which the dynamics of the international capitalist economic system result in continued exploitation and underdevelopment of the entire continent. Contrary to Western social science literature which attempts to pay more attention to internal or domestic variables, we in this book have decided to introduce a more holistic and international perspective which gives serious consideration to the external factors that have altered and continue to shape and reshape the political economy of African states.

We have proceeded on the basis of different assumptions, used different foci of analysis, and adopted different theoretical framworks and modes of analysis. In contrast to the advocates of academic specialization in the Western social sciences, we strongly hope that a genuine understanding of the problems of development in Africa requires a theoretical or an analytical perspective that transcends the disciplinary boundaries of the

Western social sciences - specifically those boundaries that divide the study of economics from the study of politics. Hence, we are concerned with the interrelationship of economic and political factors. In reality, this is the major focus of the text and it justifies to some extent our adoption of the concept "political economy" in the title.

In contrary to conventional wisdom, we not only find it impossible to separate the study of economics from the study politics, but we believe it is the nexus between what is conventionally considered economics and what is considered politics that requires our urgent concern. Only by studying this nexus can we understand in any meaningful way the causes of underdevelopment, dependence, backwardness, or poverty and the prerequisites for development in Africa. We have written this text in the hope that it will advance the study and understanding of modern Africa. Therefore, this lively and stimulating study will be an indispensable text for economists, historians, social scientists, students of all social sicence disciplines, government, international agency personnel, and others who wish to understand the issues and problems facing the African continent today.

Fredoline Anunobi is a professor of political economy at Xavier University of Louisiana. He has previously taught at Alabama A & M University, Morris Brown College in Atlanta, Georgia, Selma University in Selma, Alabama; where he served as the chair of Business Administration and Social Sciences. His previous publications include *Reforms Led To Soviet Collapse*, *The International Monetary Fund and Economic Policy in Tanzania,* and *The Implications of Conditionality*: The *International Monetary Fund* and *Africa*. The title of his forth coming text is International Political Economy in the Twenty First Century: Conflict, Competition and Cooperation.

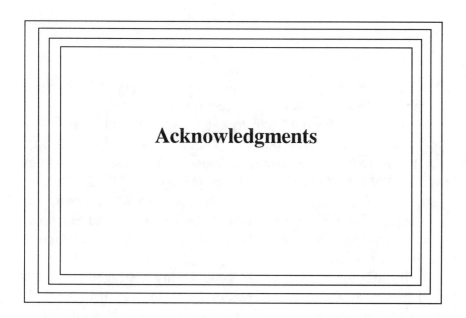

Acknowledgments

It is a great pleasure to acknowledge my indebtedness to those who have helped me shape my ideas, on the International dimensions of African Political Economy.

At this point, acknowledgments are in order. First and foremost, credit must go to my close and treasured colleague, Samuel Ubbaonu, Clark-Atlanta University. He was my prime consultant on each chapter of this research as the manuscript slowly grew. In addition, I am grateful to Ronald Slaughter, of Alabama A & M University, Richard Ajayi, of Wayne State University, Christopher Ngassam, of University of Delaware, Marcel I. Anunobi, of Howard University, Caleb Obiegbu, of Alabama A & M University, Robert G. Sherman, of American Graduate School of International Management, Marlene Ahimaz, of University of Chicago, Paul Asabere, of temple University, Rex Harawa, of State University of New York, Ayogu Melvin, of James Madison University, Smille Dube, of California State University, Green Joshua, International Monetary Fund, Janice White, of Selma University, and Mersah Sam, of University of

Michigan for carefully reading the entire chapters and offering a number of helpful criticisms, corrections and suggestions.

Furthermore, I would like to extend special thanks and deep appreciation to Kelvin Ikedum, Patience Obih, John Clifford Obih, George Ikedum, Donatus Anunobi, L.N. Ahize, Anthony Anunobi, M.A. Ozodinobi, Alphus Onyejiaku, Micah Obiegbu, Ernest Okeke, Ralph Egbuawa, Chukwemeka O. Ojukwu, and my parents for their instrumental, financial, moral and emotional supports, during those much talked about times when researchers really need such support.

I sincerely owe my special thanks to my colleagues, students and friends at Xavier University of Louisiana for their scholarly contributions and useful criticisms of this research. Although I cannot mention everyone who in one way or another has contributed to my academic success by name, I wish in particular to thank Bill Surban, Chairman of the Political Science Department, Christian Onwudiwe, Vivian A. Wilson, Ollie Christian, Chairman of the Sociology Department, Tiffany S. Bingham, C. Walker and Rebecca Domio, Janet Doucette and Laura Turnes of the Main Library and Nichole L. Wilson for their moral advice, help and encouragement. To all these I dedicate and confess my complete indebtedness and eternal gratitude, for without them this study and many of may academic endeavors would not have seen the light of the day. I would also like to thank Omega T. Major, Selma University and Harriet W. Christoff of Xavier University of Louisiana for their invaluable help in editing and typing of this work. Their overall special assistance in this research is highly appreciated.

My greatest debt; however, in this as in all my endeavors is to my wife, Eucharia Uchechukwu and my beloved children, Cynthia Ijeoma and Fredoline Uchenna•I owe all to their love and encouragement. As I continue to look to the future with hope, I dedicate this, the most recent of my collaborative effort sustained by bonds of determination, to my children, Ijeoma and Uchenna. My intellectual debt is beyond payments; shortcomings and errors in understanding, interpretation, and presentation are entirely my own.

Fredoline O. Anunobi, Ph.D.
Xavier University of Louisiana

Political Map of Africa

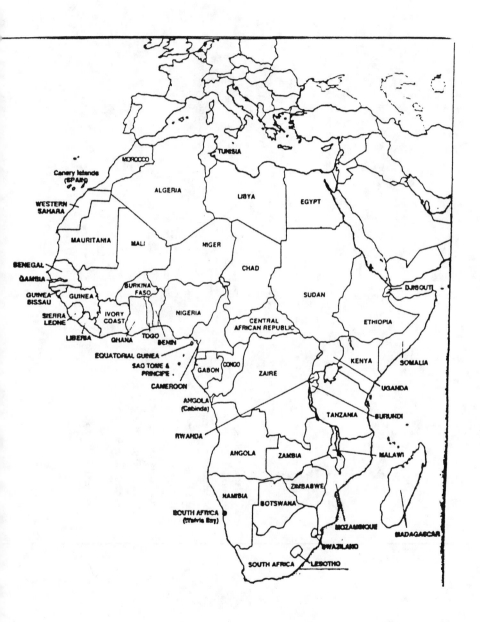

Africa: Dispelling the Myths

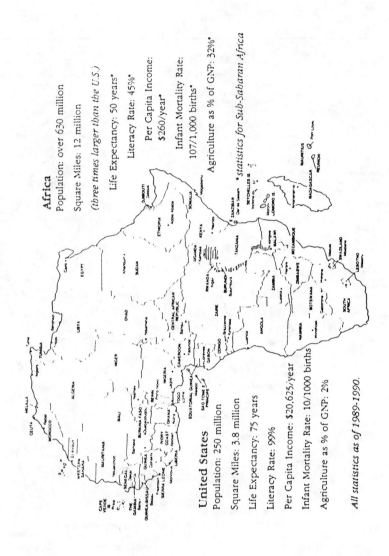

Africa

Population: over 630 million

Square Miles: 12 million

(three times larger than the U.S.)

Life Expectancy: 50 years*

Literacy Rate: 45%*

Per Capita Income: $260/year*

Infant Mortality Rate: 107/1,000 births*

Agriculture as % of G.N.P.: 32%*

*statistics for Sub-Saharan Africa

United States

Population: 250 million

Square Miles: 3.8 million

Life Expectancy: 75 years

Literacy Rate: 99%

Per Capita Income: $20,625/year

Infant Mortality Rate: 10/1000 births

Agriculture as % of G.N.P.: 2%

All statistics as of 1989-1990.

CHAPTER 1

An Overview Of The State Of Africa

INTRODUCTION

The African nations vary largely in size, in the structure of their economies, in natural resource endowment, in the level of economic, political, social and technological development. African states further differ in their political systems, in their social systems, and in the ideologies they advocate. African technological and economic diversity had become more changed in the recent years, thereby making the continent of today generally less identical than Africa of yesterday.

One of the major bonds that links African countries and their peoples together today is their desire to escape from dependency, underdevelopment, poverty, imperialism, and neocolonialism which characterize the political economy of African states. This shared aspiration is the foundation for their unity and solidarity, expressed through such an organization as the Organization of African Unity (OAU) of which all African states are members.

In international economic relations, the decision-making processes that guide global trade, technology and capital are regulated by the major industrialized capitalist countries and by the international organizations they control and dominate. The independent African countries are unfavorably placed in the international economic system as dependent satellites; they are generally powerless to influence these processes and organizations, and therefore the international economic environment which specifically affects their development. As a result, African states and other less developed countries have made a group demand for the changes of the international economic system so as to make it more equitable and universal to the needs of the large majority of these groups. However, the struggle for a better global economic system has consolidated their cohesion and strengthened their power to pursue a united front.

In the mid 1970s, there was hope that the New International Economic Order would be generally recognized and accepted as an objective test so as to narrow the North-South widening gap. However, for most less developed countries particularly African states that gap has been widening seriously. The International community is becoming, not less, but more desperate in the basic conditions and needs of human life. For many African states, the hope has faded; the prospects have become less certain than they were assumed to be only for a decade ago.

The implication of these setbacks has been serious and has been reflected in such socio-economic indicators as gross national income, per capita income, debt, debt servicing ratio, standard of living, infant mortality, level of nutrition, life expectancy incidence of disease, and school enrollment. For this reason, political unrest and social discontent have been building up rapidly, particularly among poorer groups in the population. These groups especially women have borne a disproportionate part of the impact of cuts in social services and employment.

Also, the widening gap between the less developed countries of Africa and the industrialized capitalist countries are attributable not merely to differences in economic prosperity, but also to the rapid growth of the developed countries' power vis-a-vis the rest of the international community. The leading industrialized capitalist nations of the North are now using the emerged power to further their objectives. The African fate is generally determined by the perceptions and policies of governments in the capitalist countries, of the network of private institutions that are increasingly prominent, and of the multilateral institutions over which few, if any, African governments have some degree of control. Domination and hegemonic influence have been reinforced where partnership was required and hoped for by the less developed countries of Africa. African states continue to remain economically linked generally to the market economy nations of the North-both a legacy of the colonial past sustained by the developed countries' relative economic superiority and a consequence of the North's development strategies sometimes adopted in Africa and other less developed countries.

FROM DEPENDENCY TO INTERDEPENDENCE

It is important to note that the entire global economy is linked together. However, the link is unequal between the industrialized countries of the North and less developed countries of the South. No doubt that there are links between the developed and less developed countries, but the less developed countries of African and other third world nations are politically, socially, economically, technologically and culturally dependent on the well arranged and stabilized industrial states.

It is an accepted principle that the relationship between West-West or North-North relations is interdependence; but there is, as of now, no generalized South-South interdependence. What exists between the South is dependence. This dependence generally restricts domestic and external freedom in the less developed countries. While interdependence strengthens, dependence indicates a diminution of freedom and of the ability for autonomous action for any country or any group of countries working together. Hence, after achieving political independence, the economic independence of the less developed countries of Africa has been generally hampered by its limitation. The institution conscious of the western world has not been able to give them the power to determine and control their own destiny.

There is a general belief that for African states to survive, they must seriously engage in the continuous struggle for economic independence, through self reliant developments, Africa-Africa relations, Africa-South cooperation and for equitable participation in global decision-making. The less developed countries of Africa must by their own effort free themselves from dependency, underdevelopment, poverty, imperialism and neocolonialism and have access to control their economies and peoples. This is true because history indicates that domination is never surrendered voluntarily; it has to be put to an end by the self-reliant efforts of those who are dominated. Hence, different African states have started to fight against dependence, underdevelopment and neocolonialism through economic nationalism and self-reliant development.

THE DICHOTOMY OF AFRICAN ECONOMIC NATIONALISM

There are two major reasons which have necessitated the search for self-reliance through economic nationalism in Africa and other Third World Countries. First is the desire to plan the conditions of the global economy in order to realize a better-balanced national economy. Second is the desire to be independent of sources of supply outside the nation's control not to be vulnerable in war time.[1]

For these reasons, economic nationalism is a direct response to specific circumstances in the global economy likely to be threatening to national self sufficiency. For the developing countries in general, the circumstance emerges from the peripheral duty given to it by the international capitalist division of labor, a duty which is responsible for the LDCs' relative underdevelopment vis-a-vis the advanced capitalist societies. Dependency and underdevelopment are the overriding issues facing the less developed countries in the world capitalist economy; for they threaten the total well-being of its citizens. However, these are the result of Western Colonialism and is sustained through Neo-Colonialism, the last stage of imperialism.[2]

From the viewpoint of African countries, the major strategy of economic nationalism should be constructive anti-imperialism by actions taken not just in words. This constructive anti-imperialism would include three fundamental nationalist strategic behaviors: (1) integrating the ideology of anti-imperialism in national political socialization and culture; (2) understanding the various measures or mechanisms adopted by imperialism to maintain underdevelopment and dependency; and then systematically tackling these mechanisms by all possible means.

However, in the case of African states, the problem is that effective measures or mechanisms have not been taken to systematically realize the professed national objective of economic nationalism, and the concept has not been carried out as a deliberate process or strategy for promoting autonomous development, improving the living standard of the majority of the people who are marginalized, and ending dependency, underdevelopment and imperialism which characterized the political economy of Africa.[3]

To begin with, the idea of economic nationalism is essential in both economics and political science. To the economist, economic nationalism is a driving force which enables countries to improve and accelerate economic development through nationalist control of the country's economic relations with the rest of the global community. To the political scientist, it shows an integrative ideological force which accelerates the creation of a strong and cohesive nation-state.[4]

However, nationalism is the doctrine that puts the country at the top of the scale of political values, above the possible rival values of the individual, ethnic and other internal groups, regional units,and the international community. For example, a nationalist ruling class will be more likely to practice policies of economic nationalism than a liberal ruling class of an individualistic, regionalistic, and internationalistic state.[5]

Also, nationalism played an important role in explaining African economic position. Anti-colonial nationalist movements played a serious and significant role in achieving Africa's political independence from European in the late 1950s and early 1960s. Nationalism for the nationalist leaders and for the majority of people that followed them was not a mere symbol. According to Brenton, nationalism always leads nations to invest resources in nationality or ethnicity and it encourages demand for changes in the international or inter-ethnic distribution of property and wealth of a nation. These arguments suggest that nationalist economic policies tend to emphasize activities such as manufacturing, especially in certain important industries, as iron or steel, which suggest the nation is modern and moving toward a condition of self sufficiency. In addition, nationalisteconomic policy tends to encourage too much state control over, and public ownership of economic enterprises.

However, economic nationalism is a body of economic strategies aimed at the loosening of the organic relations between economic processes taking place within the boundaries of a nation and those taking place beyond those boundaries.[6] This definition includes the idea of a nation insulating itself from the rest of the world, seeking more autonomy in its economic sphere than is available in a world system of "economic internationalism."Moreover, the pursuit of economic nationalism has been equated with the pursuit of self-reliance by many Third World Countries. While self-reliance in the fullest meaning of the term is a largely unachievable objective, this motive of nationalism rationalizes its pursuit as the basic prerequisite for an idea nation-state.

Furthermore, in the less developed countries (LDCs), economic nationalism is the foundation to the understanding of, and struggle against, the serious effect of colonialism and imperialism in their economic history. African economic nationalism is both an ideology (or state of political feeling) and an economic policy. Economic nationalism therefore indicates a preference for a number of economic policies designed to achieve national economic sovereignty or self-reliance development. In the case of many African states such economic policies include economic integration, export promotion and privatization as in The Case of International Monetary Fund Stabilization Policies, political autonomy, Indigenization and the demand for the New International Economic Order.

Furthermore, since the objective of this research is to indicate the Socio-Economic and political implication of economic nationalism in Africa, the study will be based on the evaluation and assessment of the above mentioned nationalist economic strategies. A critical examination of the degree of success and/or failure of these strategies in addressing African economic development, national autonomy, and self-reliance development will be the foundation for measuring the degree of effectiveness or ineffectiveness of these nationalist economic strategies in Africa. The aforementioned policies were chosen because the concept of economic nationalism in Africa and other developing countries emerges, as will be shown in this research, directly from the realities of the dominance - dependency relations in the contemporary capitalist world economic system, which is responsible for the Third World's structural underdevelopment and economic external dependency.

Chapter 1 of this text examines and analyzes the historical background and the overall state of Africa in general perspective. Chapter 2 provides the concept of the development of underdevelopment as a theoretical and conceptual framework to understand the dynamic nature of African political economy. Chapter 3 addresses international political economy as a means and/or approach to the study of economic nationalism. In Chapter 4, we examine the major causes of food insecurity in contemporary Africa. Also in this chapter, we review and evaluate alternative theoretical explanations as to the causes of African food crises. In Chapter 5, we provide the general features and power of the multinational corporations. We further present the arguments of the advocates and the critics of multinational enterprises. In Chapter 6, we examine, analyze, and evaluate the actual impact and socio-economic consequences of the multinational corporations on contemporary Africa. In Chapter 7, we identify the factors that cause political and economic instability in Ghana. We also provide a detailed analysis of different governments that have ruled Ghana from 1957 to present. In Chapter 8, we analyze the rise and role of military in the political economy of Sudan. In Chapter 9, we address the political economy of neo-colonialism and the nature of state in Nigerian peripheral society. In Chapter 10, we examine the essential case of racial discrimination in South Africa. We further explore and analyze various mechanisms, strategies and methods utilized by the white minority regime to oppress the blacks. We look at the specific structures and processes of this two nations in one society for a particular purpose; to understand the explosive condition in the Southern part of the continent. Chapter 11 examines and assesses the African development experience within the international capitalist economic system. Areas examined are the historical background of the African economic crisis, internal and external dimensions of the crisis. This was done to enable us to understand the role of the International Monetary Fund in Africa. Chapter 12 of this textbook provides a critical analysis and the nature of Fund conditionalities in Africa. To this end, the implications of Fund stablization policies were examined with a particular reference to Sub-Saharan Africa. Chapter 13 examines the historical foundation and theoretical perspective of the North-South cooperation. We further examined the factors which led to the demand for the New International Economic Order (NIEO) and Africa's role within the system. In Chapter 14, we provide the role of Africa in the International Monetary Relations. Variables examined include global monetary arrangement, global trade arrangement, and global monetary relations. The purpose is to find out whether international trade is a strategy for development or dependency. Chapter 15 deals with the evolution of the non-alignment movement and the role played by African states during the movements. Chapter 16 addresses the concept and evolution of regional and/or economic integration in general terms. Also examined are the factors which necessitated the formation of ECOWAS and the impact of the United Europe 1992 and beyond on West Africa. In the final analysis, we provided the failure and irrelevance of conventional theory to integration among less developed countries including African states. The final chapter projects the future characteristics of Africa toward the Twenty-First Century.

SIGNIFICANCE OF THE STUDY

This study is important for various reasons. First, it aims at offering a limited quantitative examination of the relationship between economic nationalism and self-reliance development. In this direction, the analysis emanating from the study may contribute to evaluating the relative utility of the dependency paradigm and also lead to an improved understanding of the political economy in general perspective.

Second, the problem has ramifications in Third World nations where the influences which external economic relations exercise on national development policies can be observed. It provides insight into the international political economy, which deals with the relationship of the international economic system (including political system and how it sets the limits within which national development policies in the less developed countries can move.[7] Mahler indicates in his book Dependency Approaches to International Political Economy the implications of the interplay of politics and economics, which shows the asymmetrical nature of international economic relations. On the one hand, according to him:

> Politics largely determines the framework of economic activity and channel it in directions intended to serve the interests of dominant groups; the exercises of power in all its forms is a major determinant of the nature of an economic system. On the other hand, the economic process itself tends to redistribute power and wealth; it transforms the power relationships among groups. This in turn leads to the transformation of the political system, thereby giving rise to a new structure of economic relationships. Thus, the dynamics of international relations in the modern world is largely a function of the reciprocal interaction between economics and politics.[8]

Third, economic nationalism was selected for this study because it narrows the concern of the Third World countries in pursuit of economic autonomy or self-reliance development. Also, Africa was chosen for this study for many reasons. First, Africa is a good example of an independent Third World continent, where, at least in terms of natural resources and size, shows a promise of successful regional or indigenous capitalist development. As a majority of African states are members of the Organization of Petroleum Exporting Countries (OPEC), the continent possesses an international strategic resource which gives it scope for initiative in the exercise of public policy as well as the financial means of developing through states, regional or indigenous private enterprise its enormous internal market.

Second, the neo-colonial nature of the African economy is relevant to the major tenents of the dependency paradigm. For example, at independence Africa was left with both political, social, and economic structures created after and by the former colonial masters. When political independence was achieved,

Africa's efforts at continental building and economic development were influenced largely by the colonial governments.

While African states, like other Third World Countries, experience economic problems associated with dependency, it is not protol typical of the latter in the periphery of the international economic system. This is due to the fact that African countries unlike the majority of the less developed countries are endowed with a strategic resource which has increased their bargaining leverage in the international economic environment. In reality, many scholars describe African states as semi-periphery nations, which in essence means newly industrialized countries within the international economic system.

The goal of this study is to point out the disparity between the concept and practice of economic nationalism by putting it in a clearer perspective in the context of African political economy. Our hypothesis is that economic nationalism has failed because it has not been applied systematically as a strategy against Western imperialism and imperialist relations that underdeveloped the entire continent. Also, our position here is that in order to be successful as a strategy, African economic nationalism must first be clearly articulated as a concept. Policy makers will then fully implement these economic nationalist policies.

The test of this hypothesis will be important to the advancement of research within the development of underdevelopment or dependency paradigm because it is derived from a major premise of the framework. That is external economic dependency leads to the suppression of autonomous policies in the less developed countries. Support of the selected hypothesis will encourage other scholars to pay more attention to the utility of the dependency framework in general. Withspecific reference to the political economy of African, any support, given, to the selected hypothesis will alert scholars to consider more seriously the policy measures as will be discussed in this research. In addition, further studies would be needed to focus on the outcomes of the policies pursued during the period under study.

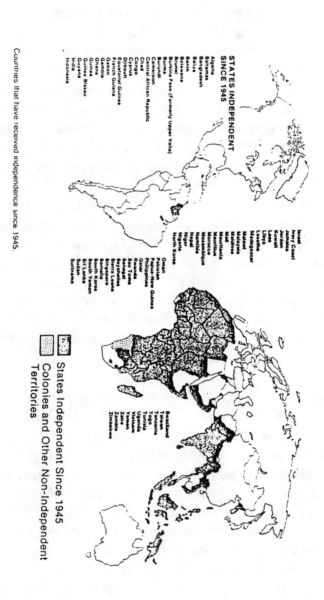

STATES INDEPENDENT
SINCE 1945

Algeria
Bahamas
Bangladesh
Belize
Benin
Botswana
Brunei
Burkina Faso (Formerly Upper Volta)
Burma
Burundi
Cameroon
Central African Republic
Chad
Congo
Cyprus
Djibouti
Equatorial Guinea
French Guinea
Gabon
Gambia
Ghana
Guinea
Guinea Bissau
Guyana
India
Indonesia

Israel
Ivory Coast
Jamaica
Jordan
Kenya
Laos
Libya
Lesotho
Madagascar
Malawi
Malaysia
Maldives
Mali
Mauritania
Mauritius
Morocco
Mozambique
Namibia
Niger
Nigeria
North Korea

Oman
Pakistan
Rwanda
Papua-New Guinea
Philippines
Qatar
São Tomé
Senegal
Seychelles
Sierra Leone
Singapore
Somalia
South Korea
South Yemen
Sri Lanka
Sudan
Suriname

Swaziland
Taiwan
Tanzania
Togo
Tunisia
Uganda
Vietnam
Yemen
Zaire
Zambia
Zimbabwe

States Independent Since 1945

Colonies and Other Non-Independent
Territories

Countries that have received independence since 1945.

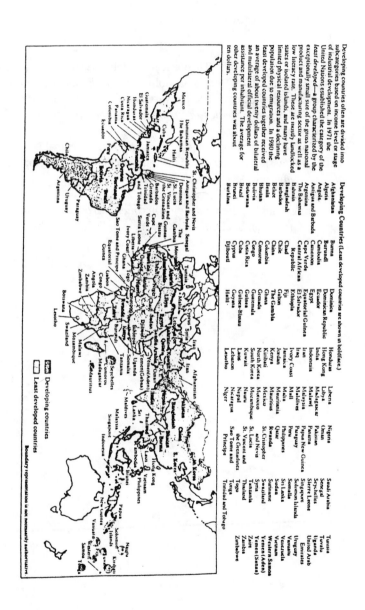

Notes

1. Chibuzo Nwoke, Africa Today, (October 15, 1987), p. 57.
2. Ibid.
3. Ibid.
4. See Harry G. Johnson, "A Theoretical Model of Economic Nationalism in New and Developing States", in H. G. Johnson, ed., *Economic Nationalism in Old and New States* (Chicago: The University of Chicago Press, 1967), p. 1.
5. See M.A. Heilperis, *Studies in Economic Nationalism* (Geneva: Libraurei E. Droz, 1962), p. 18.
6. Henry Johnson, *Economic Nationalism Old and New*, p. 27.
7. Thomas Weisskopf, "Imperialism and Economic Development," *The Political Economy of Development of Underdevelopment*, ed. by Charles Wilber (New York: Random House, 197), pp. 22-23.
8. Vincent A. Mahler, *Dependency Approaches To International Political Economy*: A Cross National Study (New York: Columbia University Press, 1980), p. 143.

CHAPTER 2

Development of Underdevelopment: An Alternative Theoretical Perspective

This chapter is not just an academic exercise by intellectuals on Africa. It came about as a challenge and presumably as an alternative to the orthodox Western social science literature on the African continent. It is the product of our overall dissatisfaction with the general literature as well as our rejection of the orthodox view established by Western experts and scholars on Africa. Our perspective is that the theoretical foundations and analytical considerations of the conventional wisdom are in reality fallacious and inadequate in explaining African economic underdevelopment. We share the belief that a comprehensive or genuine understanding of contemporary Africa and other less developed countries in general can only be achieved by making a radical move from the assumptions and analyses associated with the liberal economic theories.

However, we hope to provide the audience with an analytical and conceptual framework on contemporary Africa which is peculiar to African reality and less biased in orientation. In analysis and orientation to internal variables within the continentas liberal theories believed. What is needed is an international theoretical orientation that brings into perspective the interrelationship of internal and external variables, specifically the degree to which the dynamics of the international capitalist economic system result in continued exploitation and underdevelopment of the entire continent. Hence, contrary to Western social science literature which attempts to pay more attention to internal or domestic variables, we in this chapter have decided to introduce a more holistic and international perspective which gives serious consideration to the external factors that have altered and continue to shape and reshape the political economy of African states. Thus, in order to achieve these goals and objectives, it is usually advantageous to criticize or refute the liberal theory of development and underdevelopment and introduce an alternative analytical and conceptual scheme more consistent to address, examine, analyze and evaluate the socio-economic and political realities of modern Africa.

It is important to note that every discussion of African economic dependency and underdevelopment centered around the question of the proper role of colonialism and neocolonialism. To understand the African economic predicament, it is important to examine and analyze the role of the international capitalist system which is responsible for Africa's economic underdevelopment and external dependency. And the only way to understand the dynamic nature of international capitalism is by using the theoretical and conceptual scheme of development of underdevelopment as perceived by the dependency paradigm.

The new wave of economic nationalism in the less developed countries was provoked by the historical process which led to their structural underdevelopment. It would be necessary at this point to put the crucial phenomenon in proper perspective.

The basic issue faced by African states arose from the fact that many years of political independence from European colonial masters have left many Africans wondering what happened to the promised fruits of that independence. Economic stagnation and dependency, foreign military intervention, and in many cases the wholesale debasement of human rights have characterized large areas of the African continent in recent years. Conventional theorists have found it fashionable to blame the African themselves for their present economic predicament. However, African scholars are now attacking the fundamental assumptions of conventional or orthodox models of development that contribute to the unequal distribution of power and benefits in the world system.

Karl Marx (1818-1883) was the father of modern communism. His work as a philosopher, political thinker, and economist has made him one of the single most influential thinkers of all time. Born in Germany, Marx spent much of his life in England studying contemporary society and actively working for revolution. In association with Friedrich Englels (1820-1895), he published their famous call for revolution, *Manifesto of the Communist Party* in 1848. He published the first volume of his study of contemporary economic, *Capital*, in 1867; Engels undertook the publication of the other volumes. Today, every word that Marx wrote is carefully studied by a wide range of scholars and revolutionists for clues to his thought. *(Library of Congress)*

According to radical scholars, industrialization, first of Britain and then of other advanced industrial societies of Western Europe and North America in the nineteenth century, would not have been possible without the creation of an international division of labor which turned other areas of the world into sources of primary products and markets for the advanced industrial societies' surplus of manufactured commodities. Karl Marx addresses this tendency toward colonization in the development of capitalism. Referring to the result of the industrial revolution, Marx had observed that as soon as the general conditions requisite for production by the modern industrial system have been established, this mode of production acquires a capacity for sudden extension by leaps and bounds that finds no hindrance except in the supply of raw materials.[1] To quote Marx:

> By ruining handcraft production in other countries, machinery forcibly converts them into fields for the supply of its raw materials. In this way, East India was compelled to produce cotton, wool, hemp, jute, and indigo for Great Britain. By constantly making a part of the hands "supernumerary", modern industry, in all countries where it has taken root, gives a spur to emigration and to the colonization of foreign lands, which are thereby converted into settlements for growing the raw material of the mother country; justas Australia for example, was converted into a colony for growing wool. A new and international division of labor, a division suited to the requirements of the chief centers of modern industry springs up, and converts one part of the globe into a chiefly agricultural field of productions, for supplying the other part which remains a chiefly industrial field. This revolution hangs together with radical changes in agriculture.[2]

Also, the advanced capitalist countries, following the rapid exhaustion of their industrial raw materials, have succeeded in replacing these goods by shaping periphery nations of the world capitalist market into resource-colonies. The importance of the periphery as supplier of agricultural raw materials has thus, from the standpoint of metropolitan capital, been superseded by its importance as supplier of industrial raw materials, for example minerals and fuels.

Today, the situation which Marx had observed is thus

found in the relations between the industrialized and Third World countries whether the latter are outright colonies or formally independent. Their economies are shaped to cater to the needs of the raw materials-consuming countries of the Western World. Third World nations were underdeveloped as primary producers, meaning that they lack the instruments of production, that is, capital and technology, which are essential for capitalist industrialization but which are monopolized by the industrialized countries.[3] It is the resulting, deliberately shaped structural condition of dependence that has enabled the advanced industrial societies to continue to exploit, to their own advantages, the primary resources of the underdeveloped countries, including African states.

THE CONVENTIONAL WISDOM PERSPECTIVE

There are two major theoretical and conceptual frameworks to understand the dynamic of underdevelopment and external economic dependency in Africa, Asia, and Latin America. One is called the neoclassical approach and is generally known as the developmental or modernization school. The other is known as the dependency school. The neo-classical school emerges from the orthodox textbook economics based on the teachings of conventional or orthodox theorists such as Adam Smith, John Stuart Mill, David Ricardo, and Keynes. These theorists emphasized the importance of free market economy, comparative advantage, direct foreign investment and foreign trade as the bases for growth and development.

There was a general agreement that certain deficiencies accounted for African economic underdevelopment and external dependency. Prominent among them are inadequate infrastructures, lack of diversity in the economy, inadequate savings and capital formation, lack of managerial skills and International Relation:

Neo-Classical analysts argued that the removal of these deficiencies would be enough to assure development. Foreign technical assistance and foreign private investment were seen as a partial, if not critical, solution to the problem of inadequate savings, lack of capital and lack of entrepreneurial skills and technical know how. Economic planning was seen as a partial solution to integrating and diversifying the economy and a means of inculcating achievement motivation.[4]

John Stuart Mill (1806-1873) was the most influential philosopher in the English-speaking world in the nineteenth century. His major political works were *On Liberty* (1859), *Considerations on Representative Government* (1861), *Utilitarianism* (1861), and *The Subjection of Women* (1869). Mill developed and modified the philosophy of utilitarianism of Jeremy Bentham (1748-1832, but Mill is best known today for his defense of freedom in On Liberty and for his defense of representative government. With his wife Harriet Taylor (1807-1858), Mill began to explore the subordinate role of women in contemporary society, and he became an advocate of women's rights. *(Library of Congress)*

In the early studies of African history, nationalism and development were written mainly from a conventional wisdom otherwise known as modernization, or political development orientation. The fundamental assumption behind this methodology was that African economies are in the process of becoming modern rational groups in which effective and scientific reasoning replace traditional beliefs, norms and values systems. Modernization, according to economists was perceived as commensurate with mechanization, efficiency in the utilization of resources, rapid industrialization, and growth in economic and social standards. The objectives and goals of modernization were defined as increasing citizen mobility, establishing methods for universal resources allocations, and controlling the political significance of communal characterististics. For political scientists, modernization includes institutional expansion, some measures of political participation, the rationalization of the government apparatus, and augmentation of capabilities in order to meet growing demands, and power concentration.[5] Orthodox theories of modernization originated in the Western World and were mainly related to development in American political science in the early 1950s. Its theoretical foundation assumed that a focus on transformation from traditional to modern societies would lead to a standardized theory of political development. The major theoretical concerns of many of the first works on African economic relations, however, centered on a varieties of the challenges of political development that were discovered as facing nations in their effort to accomplish modernization.[6] The first problem was defined as of identity: accelerating a common sense of concern among culturally diffuse entities.

In the orthodox perspective, the task of politics was to establish the necessary and sufficient conditions for equitable growth by encouraging social quiescence and stable governmental structure. However, if African and other developing countries faltered in this approach, then specifically these shortcoming could be recommended either to mistaken ideologies, to poor judgement, to an inability to overcome cultural obstacles deeply in Third World societies including African and/or to the conflicts between competing objectives of modernization.[7] As Ake indicates in his book *Social Science As Imperialism*:

> When Western scholars turned their attention to the study of Africa and the other Third World regions, they did so not by inventing new

analytic tools, but by using the tools already in vogue especially those which were conducive to the comparative study of Western countries and the Third World societies. The comparative studies which emerged from this concern with the Third World tended to use the topologies of Western social science to characterize the evolution and development of societies. They represented the societies of the Third World as being approximations of the topologies of the lower ends of the developmental continuum and offered the Western societies as approximations of the topologies of the higher and advanced stages of the development continuum. Examples of the type of Western scholarship in question are: Apter, The Politics of Modernization; Black, The Dynamics of Modernization; Almond and Coleman, Politics of the Developing Area.[8]

Ake further comments that:

> The second major bias of Western social science is a tendency to equate contemporary Western society with the ideal society. This bias is closely associated with the first one for the implication of putting contemporary European society at the pinnacle of evolution, is a commitment to the view that Western European society is the best possible historical society. This tendency to equate the society that ought to be, with the one that is, was a distinctive feature of Western social science in its classical age. But is also persists today, and underlines the conservatism and optimism of Western social science.[9]

Since the early 1960s the bulk of literature on dependency and underdevelopment in Africa and other less developed countries suggested that prosperity in underdeveloped, poor, and/or developing regions could take place mainly through the spread of modernism emerging in the industrialized nations. A major predominant line of thought portrayed underdeveloped nations as "dual societies: with poverty, inequality, backwardness, feudal hinterlands and progressive capitalist metropoles".[10]   Also, because the interior area was seen as having stagnated in a state of feudalism due largely to isolation from the forces of capitalism, the recommendation called for the capitalist penetration of the interior part of the same society. Prosperity was to be transferred from North America and Europe to the national urban regions, from the developed societies to the regional trading areas, and from these regions to their respective periphery societies. The following definition and explanation of modernization by S.N. Eisenstadt is a classic example:

> Historically, modernization is the process of change toward those types of social, economic, and political systems that have developed in Western Europe and North America from the seventeenth century to the nineteenth and have then spread to other European countries and in the nineteenth and twentieth centuries to the South American, Asian, and African Continents.[11]

Another fundamental assumption according to the proponents of the orthodox paradigm is that while modernization of the Third World countries has been encouraged and supported by the industrialized societies, it has been prevented by several impediments and factors within each of the less developed countries.

Also, a closely related orthodox line of thought on underdevelopment believed that every society passes through a process of economic growth showing five successive historical stages, mainly " the traditional society, the pre-condition for the take-off, the drive to maturity, and the age of high mass consumption".[12] However, the concept of growth and development was generated by the intrusion--generally in the form of new and advanced technology--of more advanced countries at the "pre-condition for take-off" stage.

Furthermore, orthodox theorists believed that there are number of domestic obstacles to modernization in Africa, Asia and Latin America. These obstacles include, among others traditionalism, rapid population growth, political instability, capital scarcity, lack of social integration, and inappropriate technology. As the two quotes from an article by J.J. Spengler and the other from a work by Mutton Esman put it:

In the underdeveloped world, per-capita income, capital equipment, and capital formation are very low; inferior technologies predominate; enterprise is lacking; accessible natural resources are badly exploited; natality and (usually) natural increase are relatively high....[13]

In virtually all these societies, the stability of political authority is impaired by a limited capacity to provide satisfaction or output demanded by the impatient elites themselves or by other mobilized groups. This disproportion between expectation and performance is aggravated by (1) clashes of interest beyond the capacities of the elites to resolve; (2) shortages of physical and financial resources and of technical and managerial skills; and (3) the persistence of ethnic, sectional, or kinship loyalties and power structures and the absence of substitute institutions which can perform the integrative functions essential to the effective performance of tasks to which the governing elites are increasingly committed.[14]

However, inspite of the rapid scientific technological prosperity that featured the post-war era, it became generally evidence that the now periphery nations remained in a position of underdevelopment and external economic dependence. Hence, some political and economic analysts held that there was a growing inequality among and within nation-states and therefore, questioned the authenticity or validity of the orthodox paradigm on backwardness. For this reason, the usefulness or utility of the modernization approach was increasingly questioned, particularly in an Africa frustrated by its inability to maintain previous gains, let alone progress toward the desired objectives on national betterment.[15]

One major criticism of modernization in Africa and other developing areas has related to the priorities built into these models. First, the emphasis on economic growth or development without a concomitant delineation of beneficiaries of this economic activity was subjected to serious examination by the mid-1960s. The bias toward dynamic equilibrium and harmony was generally challenged. while the tendency of some development theories to encourage and support the status quo perspective and elitist was found to be particularly troublesome.[16] Also, the prepposition that the orthodox and capitalist theories of development were both feasible and desirable resulted in a type of arrogance not easily acceptable in nations that had only recently emerged from a period of colonial administration.

THE DEPENDENCY APPROACH

In addition to these views, Raul Prebisch, one of the major pioneers of the dependency paradigm, argued that long term weaknesses in raw material prices neglected positive results that were hoped to emerge from the principle of comparative advantage. After showing how the global system was divided into a developed center and an underdeveloped periphery, Prebisch indicated that the centers still retain the benefits of technological prosperity and expropriate increase in output in exporting areas of less developed countries through the decreasing terms of trade method. The negative implications of this relationship exchange resulted in external economic dependency and subordination to foreign interest that the less developed countries had to overcome in order to achieve industrialization and development. However, the alternative model prescribed by Prebisch and his colleagues at the United Nations Economic Commission for Latin America (ECLA) centered around three variables: Industrialization through import substitution, the promotion of exports of manufactures and institutional transformations in favor of periphery nations at the global level.[17]

However, in the mid-1960s Latin America and other Third World nations experienced the emergence of a new direction of writings that resulted in a qualitative approach toward the discussion of underdevelopment and dependency. As Heraldo Munoz stipulates:

> The works of Fernado H. Cardoso, Andre' Gunder Frank, Theotonio Dos Santos, Osvaldo Sunkel, and others went beyond

Prebisch's perspective and interpreted the phenomenon of dependencia in a holistic fashion and in terms of the capitalist mode of production. These writers saw a structural link between domestic and external factors, with transnational capitalism as the common denominator. In their works the key unit of analysis was not the nation-state alone, but also social groups, classes and multinational corporation.[18]

Right now, there is a massive proliferation of imperialism, underdevelopment, and dependency writings, specifically in America and other industrialized states. A major variation between these new scholars and the older dependencia analysts is that the former are more often than not interested in explaining global relations whereas the latter are generally and always interested in addressing and providing solutions to the problems of underdevelopment and external dependency. For many analysts, underdevelopment or dependency is generally an inequality inherent in the power structure between two or more global actors, principally nation-states.

Furthermore, a series of criticisms centered around the proper tools of analysis generated by scholars of political development. Less than enough tools were designed to examine and analyze how changes could take place or to evaluate the effects of ongoing processes. Hence, many analyses were seriously static in nature. Also, the external context of African political economy was virtually overlooked. Problems critically important to Africans, such as negritude, socialism, racial justice, and pan-Africanism, were not treated with the degree of seriousness that they need.[19]

In the past, modernization theories did provide a major foundation for the analysis of post colonial African political economy. These theories helped to point out some of the major issues faced by African leaders and nurtured a series of fundamental works on the dilemmas of independence.[20] However, by the mid 1960s, it became seriously evident that these approaches, involved as they were with the accomplishment of ideal goals, could no longer keep up with the increase and problematic pace of events in Africa. In the early 1970s, the search for alternative theoretical and conceptual schemes became inevitable in the writings of Third World scholars. As Ojo states:

On analysis, it is soon clear that the things offered... as cause of underdevelopment are in fact symptoms of underdevelopment. Moreover 'the explanation is highly biased in that it suggest that development presupposes capitalism'. In so far as capital accumulation, commodity exchange (external trade in this context), acquisitive drive (achievement motivation) and skills (technological and entrepreneurial) have an organic unity in a distinctive capitalist mode of production, the explanation is a tautology in a second sense, 'because it amounts to suggesting that a society is not developed because it does not have characteristic of a developed society.' In the second place, the explanation begs the question of why the identified deficiencies in African developmental process are prevalent in Africa but no where else. Certainly it is not by sheer coincidence that such differentials exist between Africa and the rest of the world, particularly in the industrialized part of it. It is because of these inadequacies of the neoclassical school and the empirical failings of the policies it inspired that academicians and some political leaders have turned attention to alternative explanations and strategies.[21]

Theories of underdevelopment and dependency came into vogue as a reaction to the premises and the avenues of political development theory and were dependent on the opposite assumptions that African prosperity has been, and continued to be, prevented by forces (internal and/or international bent on the ongoing exploitation of the continent and its natural resources.[22] Chazan and Mortimer further comment that:

These primarily capitalist, interests could only be held at bay if the global system underwent a fundamental change that would alter the structural relations between the Third World and the industrialized world (underdevelopment) or between the masses and the dominant classes within Africa (dependency). Thus, in stark contrast to the moderinization approach, these theorists have focused not on the process of development but on the roots of underdevelopment. They have shunned what they claimed to be empty objectivity in favor of an avowedly committed and activist approach and have rejected the seeming benevolence that underlay modernization analysis. They have asserted that if Africans have remained impoverished, then this condition is a result of circumstances that have enabled other to benefit at their expense.[23]

Over the years, one major concept which comparative politics and international relations scholars have been wrestling with is "dependency". The concept of dependency has provoked a great deal of disagreement between and among scholars concerning its definition and scope. Although the conflict and controversy still persist, there is a widely cited definition that has gained ground. That is the definition offered by Theotonio Dos Santos:

> By dependence we mean a situation in which the economy of certain countries is conditioned by the development and expansion of another economy to which the former is subjected. The relation of interdependency between two or more economies, and between these and world trade, assumes the form of dependency when some economies (the dominant ones) can expand and be self-sustaining, while other countries (the dependent ones) can do this only as a reflection of that expansion, which can have either positive or negative effect on their immediate development.[24]

Hence a country is relatively dependent if it does not have control over major decisions affecting its economy. Development of underdevelopment theorists believe among other things, that international economic dependence lead to the suppression of autonomous policy in the less developed countries, exploitation of the periphery nations in the international economic system and the development of underdevelopment in the Third World countries.[25] Dependency scholars stress that the less developed countries leaders really do not have any choice; either they are very weak to cope with the powerful industrialized countries and their multinational corporations (MNCS) or they are coopted by being taken in as partners in effect of the multinational enterprises. As a result, their policies and development efforts are compromised.[26]

Third World leaders are further controlled in another form because of their dependent position in the international capitalist economic system. As one writer indicates, "The level of dependency may define the opinions open to a dependent nation in the areas of both economic and political decisions."[27] This is to say that, when a Third World nation is heavily dependent upon external resources for its development aspirations, it becomes vulnerable to external manipulations. Hence, national institutions (including private business and interest groups) are forced to give up rights, capacity and power to take and implement decision affecting their national economy and its component parts. A corollary of the foregoing discussion is that the power given up by the national institutions is usually held by the transnational organizations or foreign government.

Monopoly and dependence are control and exploitation in simple terms. According to Walter Rodney, "all countries named as underdeveloped in the world exploited by others and the underdevelopment with which the world is now preoccupied is a product of capitalist, imperialist, and colonialist exploration.[28]

In addition to this, Ojo shows that less developed countries in Africa, Asia and Latin America are poor because Western Imperialism has exploited their natural resources, human wealth and economies. He further shares the belief that Western progress was built on the exploitation of the underdeveloped nations. To quote Ojo:

> Underdevelopment was and still generated by the exploitations attendant upon the incorporation of African countries into the world capitalist system via imperialism and colonialism. It can therefore be understood only as an aspect of imperialism past, present and future. This explains why the political kingdom which Kwame Nkrumah thought would lead to economic freedom and development has proved to be a pious hope. In his book, Neocolonialism: The Last Stage of Imperialism (1966) the first President of Ghana adopted in virtually identical terms the definition of neocolonialism

adumbrated by the 1961 All-African Peoples Conference at Cairo as an explanation of the dashed hopes.[29]

In support of the above viewpoint, Harry Magdoff also argues that what matters to the business unit, and to the business environment as a whole, is that the option of global investment (and foreign trade) should remain available. For this to be meaningful, the business environment requires, as a minimum, that the political and economic principles of capitalism should operate and that the door be fully open for global capital at all times. Even more, it seeks a privileged open door of the capital of the home country in preference to capital from competing industrial societies.[30]

For many years the countries of Western Europe, and later North America had exploited the wealth of Africa, Asia and Latin America. However, this forceful appropriation of one nation's land, labor, resources and markets by another is what we meant by imperialism. Capitalism is generally younger than imperialism in its stage of development. Neither the emperors of Rome nor Alexander the Great were capitalists. They did not systematically accumulate capital through rationalized exploitation of free human labor and the expansion of private markets. But these earlier plunderers all had one thing in common with capitalists: the desire to expropriate the wealth of other peoples' land, labor and markets for their own advantage.

Theotonio Dos Santos agreed that in order to understand the system of dependent reproduction and the socio-economic institution created by it, we must see it as part of a system of global economic interactions based on monopolistic regulation of large-scale capital, on control of certain economic and financial centers over others, on a monopoly of a complex technology that leads to unequal and combined development at a national and international level. Attempts to analyze backwardness as a failure to assimilate more advanced models of production or to modernize are nothing more than ideology disguised as science. The same is true of the attempts to analyze this international economy in terms of relations among comparative cost which seeks to justify the inequalities of the global economic system and to conceal the relations or exploitation on which it is depended.[31]

Michael Parenti argues that the nature and structure of underdeveloped economies motivated capitalist, imperialism and exploitation. According to Parenti:

> The attractions of Third World investments are evident: a relative lack of competition, a vast cheap labor pool, the absence or near absence of environmental and safety regulations and corporate taxes, and the opportunity to market products at monopoly prices. As the practical limitations of investment are reached in one country and the margin of profit narrow, outlets are sought in other less advantaged and more vulnerable lands.[32]

CLASSICAL THEORY OF IMPERIALISM

It is essential to note that dependency theorists draw on two theoretical perspectives: The structuralist theories of development and the Marxist theory of imperialism.[33] However, classical theories of imperialism deal with many themes. The first discussed by Spero refers to the relationship of the hegemonic state to peoples or countries under its control.[34] In this direction, imperialism connotes relationship at any time or place-from the Roman to British Empire. For Karl Deutsch, Imperialism in the foregoing sense represents the idea that the capability for external domination is ultimately biological-instinctive, and geographic strategic.[35]

Also, another theme refers to imperialism as a result of forces which are mainly structural. Scholars holding this notion disagree with the idea that the course of history can be explained in terms of power drives, love of war, desire for glory and the influence of understanding personalities.[36] What is evident among these scholars is a narrower sense of imperialism in which the expansion of Western dominance globally since the 1800s is seen as the result of the economic pattern found in Western nations.[37]

Thus, imperialism or colonialism was designed to maintain the position of the European countries. In this sense, imperialism is seen as an instrument used to secure trade and markets, as well as to ensure high employment levels and high exports levels for the European countries. To Hobson, imperialism was instigated by the evolution of Western capitalism into a system firmly dominated by a relatively small number of monopoly interests. The theory of imperialism pioneered by Hobson postulates that under-consumption and over-production led the European nations to expand abroad. In essence, maldistribution of wealth denied the poor majority the means to purchase over-produced goods. Consequently, the rich were unwilling to invest in productive activities and their income began to diminish. Investors were forced to seek more profitable opportunities for their capital in underdeveloped countries. As one writer puts it, "The flag followed investment in this case, as monopolist interests encouraged political control that would solidify control of their foreign investment".[38]

However, this line of thought reflects the idea that capitalism will usually produce surplus goods, which must be placed abroad either through capital export or through sales. The point to make here is that the competition generated by capitalism may lead to war among the European nations in the process of acquiring markets and colonies. Hence, only special groups within the colonial economy would benefit from the competition instead of the economy as a whole.[39] According to Ake in his book, *Social Science as Imperialism*:

> The term imperialism is used in two senses here, one broad, the other narrow. According to the broader usage, imperialism is the subordination of one country to another or at any rate the attempt to subordinate one country to another in order to maintain a relationship of unequal exchange. The subordination may be military, economic, political, cultural, or some combination of

these. Hence we talk of political, cultural, military and economic imperialism.[40]

MODERN THEORY OF IMPERIALISM

Conversely, traditional theories of imperialism emphasize its modernizing and civilizing influence upon the colonies.[41] The available literature on modern imperialism represents the work of Karl Marx and V. I. Lenin. According to Lenin the condition of imperialism was important for the wide spread of the capitalist economic system. In other words, imperialism was a necessary condition to sustain capitalism. Overseas possessions were used as the outlets for surplus capital accumulated in the capitalist states. European hegemony was a result of economic expansion consistent with the international capitalist system. Lenin further re-emphasized the danger of war, which capitalist expansion is likely to bring about. Thus, Lenin was primarily concerned with the conditions that gave rise to imperialism and its role in the domestic political economy of industrialized countries.

Lenin viewed imperialism as a function of the internal development of advanced capitalism, and argued that as such, it will eventually lead to war among the colonial powers. Lenin identified five characteristics of imperialist expansion as follows:

I The concentration of production and capital so that it creates monopolies;

II The fusion between banking capital and industrial capital which occurs as the result of concentration of production in monopolies. This merger gives rise to the finance capital dominated by financial oligarchies and financial traders;

III The exportation of capital, which is more important than the export of commodities into other countries, thanks to foreign investment;

IV The formation of international capitalist monopolies that share the world among themselves;

V The territorial division of the whole world by great powers.[42]

Modern dependency and development theories stress informal economic structures of dominance and control rather than direct political military.

In more recent writings, Paul Baran and Andre Frank argue that the dual process of imperialist-capitalistic expansion is the cause for the underdevelopment prevalent in most Third World societies today.[43]   Other proponents of the Marxist-Leninist theme are equally concerned about the fact that a vast majority of the less developed countries do not gain from their inclusion in the global capitalist system.   They observe that only a handful of the elite class (the compradores in the Third World countries) enjoy the benefits of the international capitalist system.[44]   In support of this position, Ojo has this to comment:

> There is yet another class. It comprises the relatively recent class of urban factory workers under colonialism as well as those such as-peasants and craftmen engaged in traditional occupations. Together, these might be labelled the proletarian class. In Marxist terms a dual contradiction and dual class struggle arise from this class structure. On the one hand the contradiction between the metropolitan international bourgeoisie who own the means of production and the comprador national bourgeoisie results in a class struggle as the latter seeks to overthrow the former and acquire for itself control over the means of production. This aspect of the struggle was reflected symbolically in the struggle for independence and, since then, in the struggle for what is now termed a New International Economic Order (NIEO).[45]

In addition to the above shared view, Fanon, however, supported the idea that colonial modes of production were instrumental in the formation of a comprador class which would look after the interests of the metropolitan power once it formally departed its colonial outpost. Such a class does not establish deep roots in the indigenous community, but rather establishes linkages to various elements in the international system. Since its interests naturally diverge from the national interest, it is unable to engender enduring support and loyalty from large segments of the population. As a system of privilege within an underdeveloped countries, the comprador class faces continual challenge to the role. Lacking significant political and economic resources, harsh suppression become the typical political capital of the regime.[46]

Nkrumah, like Fanon and others, perceives that the indigenous, bourgeoisie is the immediate enemy of the African people. According to him:

> In Africa, the internal enemy-the reactionary bourgeoisie-must be exposed as exploiters and parasites, and as collaborators with imperialists and neo-colonialists on whom they largely depend for the maintenance of their positions of power and privilege. The African bourgeoisie provides a bridge for continue imperialist and neocolonialist domination and exploitation. The bridge must be destroyed. This can be done by worker-peasant solidarity organized and directed by a vanguard socialist revolutionary party.[47]

Nkrumah's analysis coincides with Fanon and Frank's analytical framework in that both perceive the indigenous bourgeoisie to be the immediate enemy of the impoverished masses and, therefore, the primary target of their struggle for genuine liberation and material well-being.

In addition to what has already been said about the structure of underdevelopment and neo-colonialism in Africa, it should be clear that the people of Africa cannot hope to achieve both genuine independence from foreign control and meaningful socio-economic development without a radical transformation of the present structure of their societies. In other words, the development of Africa is contingent upon a comprehensive social revolution which will replace the present social order with a new order based on totally different political and economic relationships. In the words of Thomas Hodgkin, "The basic problem of the African people cannot be solved by self-seeking bourgeois administrations, supported by neo-colonialist interest, within a framework of petty states."[48] What is needed is a new structural configuration serving the basic interests and needs of the African people, rather than the special interests of a privileged few and the needs of international capitalism. However, a structural configuration of this type must be based on Africa's disengagement from the international capitalist system and the elimination of the present class structure and political regimes which presently divide and oppress the African citizens.

In support of this position, Giovanni Arrighi and Jolin Saul, in The Journal of Modern African Studies, set the problem of Africa's development in clear focus. they state that Africa must disengage from international capitalism for two fundamental reasons: (1) because of the capital drain which the present dependency on foreign capital engenders; and (2) because of the distorted growth which foreign investment encourages by its choice of capital intensive techniques and its concentration in the export and extractive sectors of African economies. Also, they further argue that disengagement from international capitalism must be followed by a change in the power structure of the existing African states:

> The emergence of a labor aristocracy, with considerable political power, was brought about not only by the pattern of foreign investment but also by the acceptance of a colonial salary structure on the part of independent African governments. The labor aristocracy will therefore continue to use its power in a state-controlled modern sector in order to appropriate a considerable share of the surplus in the form of increasing discretionary consumption. Under these conditions 'perverse growth' would continue notwithstanding state ownership of the means of production. In order to achieve 'real' long-term development, disengagement from international capitalism will have to be accompanied by a change in the power base of the African governments.[49]

As far as Africa's disengagement from the international capitalist system is concerned, the question usually arises as to whether Africa can realistically achieve economic development and development in general without the capital and aid of the Western capitalist-societies. According to Frank, the development of both the Soviet Union and Japan shows that development can occur though disengagement from international capitalism and isolation from foreign investment and control. Frank stipulates:

Japan is the crucial example among the capitalist economies, as the Soviet Union is among the socialist, of a country which, in order to achieve the take-off into economic development in a world already industrialized and imperialist countries, began by isolating itself substantially from foreign trade and totally from investment and control. Neither country found it necessary, let it be noted, to permit such foreign investment in order to take advantage of the technology of the industrially more advance countries. Only after they had forged an economic structure and their own control of it, which permitted them to take advantage of more intimate economic ties with already advanced countries, did Japan and the Soviet Union enter into such relations.[50]

However, Frank is not suggesting that underdeveloped countries of Africa, Asia, and Latin American follow the Japanese or Soviet patterns to development. Instead, he is suggesting that the general experience of these two nations shows that an underdeveloped country can isolate itself from foreign investment and direct foreign involvement in its economy and achieve the take off into self-sustained economic development.

The most annoying fact is that foreign investors and their governments always tend to work together to exact as favorable conditions as possible from the African countries. As Green and Seidman put it:

The resulting pattern is one of joint investor and government pressure on the African states. High rates of profits are a usual symptom, and a drain on capital needed for economic reconstruction. But probably the most crippling results are the determination of structural change, the warping of economic plans to suit foreign investors or governments, and the thwarting or blocking policies designed to secure African control over African economies.[51]

It is important to note that under such situations, the individual country find it next to impossible to formulate and execute development programs which do not have the approval of the foreign private interest involved in their economies. A good example of this circumstance is Nigeria under Buhari's regime. In other words, foreign interests tend to exercise a dominant power over development planning of the African states. Furthermore, it is likely that under these conditions, foreign financial pressure can be used to coerce these states to pursue domestic and foreign policies compatible with foreign interests.

The negative effects of foreign investment upon the economies and development efforts of the developing countries are increasingly being recognized by these nations. For instance, Octaviano Salas, former minister of industry of Mexico, has shown the results of foreign investment as follows: A) Private international capital takes over high profit zones permanently, expelling or not permitting the entry of domestic capital, by relying on the ample financial resources of its home office and on the political power which it sometimes exercises. B) The permanent takeover of important sector of economic activity impedes domestic capital formation and creates problems of balance of payments instability. C) Private direct world investment interferes with anti-cyclical monetary and fiscal policy-it comes when there are expansions and withdraws during depressions. D) The demands by private international investors for concessions to form a 'favorable climate' for investment in the receiving countries are unlimited and excessive. E) It is much cheaper and more consistent with the underdeveloped countries' aspirations to economic independence to hire foreign technicians and to pay royalties for the use of patents than to accept the permanent control of their economies by powerful consortia. F) International private capital does not adapt itself to development planning.[52]   However, the aforementioned quote shows that the unfavorable results of foreign investment are many and pose serious obstacles to the development of the less developed countries. In Africa, as elsewhere in the LDCs, efforts to maintain a favorable climate for foreign investment continue to make it possible for foreign investors and firms to monopolize the high profit sectors of their economies.

STRUCTURAL ANALYSIS AND ORIENTATION

The theory of structuralism from which dependency scholars also borrowed is an attempt to explain the underdevelopment in many countries of the world. This school of thought shows that the global system is structured in a way unconducive to the development potential of the less developed countries. Furthermore, structuralists point to the fact that technological progress tends to reduce the importance of primary products in the overall production process. Therefore, Third World countries, whose many exports are primary products, are generally worse off in the scheme of the global economy. This is because the prices of primary products tend over the long run to deteriorate relative to prices of the manufactured goods that Third World countries import. Thus, less developed countries are more likely to suffer chronic balance of payment difficulties.[53] Prebisch observed that the terms of trade between developed industrial nations of the world and the underdeveloped poor countries have skewed in favor of the former. He noted that even though the underdeveloped countries are exporting more raw materials than ever before in their history, the reward is at best the same or even less for those similar raw materials. Unfortunately, these countries are compelled by market forces to pay more for the manufactured goods they must import from industrialized countries. Furthermore, foreign trade has other dimensions that must be pointed out.

> The unequal development of the world goes back to the sixteenth century with the formation of a capitalist world economy in which some countries in the center were able to specialize in industrial

production of manufactured goods because the peripheral areas of the world colonized provided the necessary primary goods, agricultural and mineral, for consumption in the center. Contrary to some assumptions in economic theory, the international division of labor did lead to gain at the expense of the periphery. But, just as significantly, the different functions of center and peripheral societies had a profound effect on the evolution of internal social and political structures. Those which evolved in the periphery reinforced economies with a narrow range of primary exports. The interdependent nature of the world capitalist system and the qualitative transformations in that system over time make it inconceivable to think that individual nations on the periphery could somehow replicate the evolutionary experience of the now developed nations.[54]

A study by Albert O. Hirschman on German economic penetration of Eastern Europe prior to World War II illustrates some of the potential consequences of external economic dependence.[55] Hirschman found that international trade could be used as an instrument of a state's power. In this fashion, one country has the capacity to influence and control another country. According to Hirschman, international trade produces two effects; the benefit of trade and dependence on trade. Trade benefit is derived from the fact that goods will be available to the parties involved. Dependence on trade gives the more powerful partner the ability to interrupt commercial and financial activities with less damage to itself than the damage that may result in the economy of the less powerful trading partner. The implication is that the dependent state is vulnerable to the actions of its more powerful trading partner and it is also subject to its control. The notion of dependence as manifested in the above discussion also forms the cornerstone of the dependency paradigm.

Also, Myrdal made the following observations about foreign trade which are relevant to dependency formulation. According to him, global trade will generally tend to breed inequality, and will do so the more strongly when substantial inequalities are already established. Unregulated market forces will not work toward reaching any equilibrium which could imply a trend toward an equalization of income. By circular causation with cumulative effects, a nation superior in productivity and income will tend to become more superior, while a nation on an inferior level will tend to be held down at that level or even to deteriorate further--as long as matters are left to the free unfolding of the market forces.[56] Myrdal saw the inability of the free market to regulate itself. He supported governmental intervention to effect national economic integration. He firmly believed in comprehensive rational state planning as an essential requirement for the solution of Third World underdevelopment.

The contribution of John Galtung to the literature on structuralism is hailed as classic. Galtung's formulation postulates that center countries have a high level of economic development. Second, those countries have a low level of internal disharmony. Third, center countries provide processed or manufactured goods for what Galtung calls the periphery countries-which provided primary, or unprocessed, goods for the center. This system, as discussed above, is generally referred to as an international division of labor. Structuralists claim that global division of labor perpetuates a vast inequality between the center and the periphery. In the center of the system, the production of processed goods with the aid of high technology generates " spin off" effect. As a result, extensive linkages occur across the economy which lead to development. On the other hand, periphery countries whose main products are raw materials-involving little or no technology experience "distorted development" or " growth without development" or "enclave economy" which lacks integration of sectors, but is externally oriented.[57] Galtung postulates that interactions (whether based on economic, political, cultural, communications or military) among the countries of the world reflect a feudal structure characterized as follows: a) center to center countries experience high interactions; b) center to periphery countries experience medium interactions; c) periphery to periphery countries experience low or in some case no interaction.[58] In essence,

Galtung's emphasis is on how inequality between the center and the periphery countries is maintained due to vertical interaction and the international division of labor.

The contemporary dependency paradigm has brought to the fore historical events consisting of colonial government policies, and transnational economic activities that shaped the present global system. Dependency theorists claim that those activities have established a structure that is disadvantageous politically, economically and socially to periphery countries. The historical linkages of the current international system under the dependency paradigm have led to new formulations in theories of economic and political development. Other pursuits within the dependency perspective relate to theories that explain global hegemony, the role of transnational actors, foreign trade, technological transfer, foreign direct investment, foreign aid and military as well as educational relations.[59]

Dependency and underdevelopment are the primary results of the international division of labor in a developing country. They should constitute the fundamental bases of the country's grievance about its exploitation in its international economic relations with the advanced capitalist societies. Our position is that for economic nationalism to be a viable and successful strategy in Africa and elsewhere, it must aim to redress this exploitation. Furthermore, the preposition argued in this research is that the rejection of the conventional orthodox model of development in its several varieties is now widespread throughout the less developed countries, and that there are many new and exciting efforts on the part of intellectuals and political elites throughout these regions to assert a new indigenous model of development. Also, these efforts represent serious and fundamental challenges to a cherished social science assumption and understanding and even to the presumption of a universal social science of development. Hence, we underestimate or continue to disregard such changes at the expense of both perpetuating or malcomprehension of the developing areas and retaining a social science of development that is parochial and enthnocentric rather than accurate and comprehensive.

NOTES

1. Karl Marx, *Capital: A Critique of Political Economy* (New York: International Publishers, 1977), Vol. 1, pp. 450-451.

2. Ibid. p. 451.

3. "Orthodox or Traditional Theories", here refer to scholars such as Adam Smith, David Ricardo, Alfred Marshall down to economist like John M. Keynes, Arthur Lewis, Paul Samuelson, and other capitalist--oriented economists.

4. Olatunde Ojo, *African International Relations* (London: Longman Publishers, 1985), p. 56.

5. For some overall analysis of the literature, see Richard A. Higgot, *Political Development Theory: The Contemporary Debate*, (London: Coom Hlem, 1983), and Samuel P. Huntington, "*The Change to Change*: *Modernization Development and Politics,*" *Comparative Politics*. Vol 4 no. 3 (1973), p. 55079. for a critical discussion of modernization, see Irene L. Gendzier, *Managing Political Change: Social Scientist and the Third World* (Boulders, Colorado: Westview Press, 1985).

6Leonard Blinder et al., *Crisis and Sequences in Political Development* (Princeton, NJ: Princeton University Press, 1977).

7. Naomi Chazan, Robert Mortimer, John Ravenhill, and Donald Rothchild, *Politics and Society in Contemporary Africa* (Boulder, Colorado: Lynne Rienner Publishers, 1988), p. 15.

8. Claude Ake, *Social Science As Imperialism:* The Theory of Political Development (Ibadan: Ibadan University Press 1982), p. 127.

9. Ibid.

10. For a general study of dualistic economic see Gerald M. Meiser (3d), *Leading Issues in Economic Development: Studies International Poverty* (New York: Oxford University Press, 1970), pp. 126-128.

11.S.N. Eisenstadt, Modernization Protest and change (Englewoods Cliffs, NJ: Prentice Hall, 1966), p. 1.

12. W. W. Rostow, *The Stages of Economic Growth* (New York: Cambridge University Press 1960), p. 4.

13. J. J. Spengler, "Economic Development: Political PreConditions and the Political Consequences of Economic Development", *Journal of Politics*, Volume 22, (August 1960), p. 387.

14. Mutton J. Esman, "The Politics of Development Administration From Approach to Development", ed. by John Montgomery and Williams Siffin (New York: McGraw-Hill, 1968), p. 71.

15. Chazan, *Politics and Society in Contemporary Africa*, p. 15.

16. For detail explanation of this theory, see Samuel Huntington, *Political Order in Changing Societies* (New Haven: Yale University Press, 1968).

17. For details analysis, see Raul Prebisch, *The Economic Development of Latin American and its Problem* (New York: United Nations, Department of social and Economic Affairs, 1950).

18. Heraldo Munoz, *From Dependency to Development: Strategies to Overcome Underdevelopment and Inequality* (Boulder, Colorado: Westview Press, 1982), p. 2.

19. Richard Handbook, "The Crisis in Political Development Theory", The *Journal of Development Studies*, Volume 12, No. 2 (1976), p. 165-185.

20. Some of the major notable examples of these early studies include: Aristotle Zolberg, One Part Government in the Ivory Coast (Princeton, NJ: Princeton University Press, 1964); James S. Coleman, *Nigeria: Background to Nationalism* (Berkeley: University of California Press, 1958; Rath Schachter Morgenthau, *Political Parties in French Speaking Africa* (London: Oxford University Press 1964).

21. Ojo, *Africa International Relations*, p. 57.

22. Chazan and Mortimer, *Politics and Society in contemporary Africa*, p. 16.

23. Ibid.

24. Theotonio Dos Santos, "The Structure of Dependence", *American Economic Review*, Vol. 60, (May 1970), p. 232.

25. Fernando H. Cardoso and E. Faletto, *Dependency and Development in Latin-America* (Mexico: Siglo Veintiuno, 1969), Osvaldo Sunkel, National Development Policy and External Dependency in Latin America", *Journal of Development Studies*, Vol. 6, (1970). Also, see Frank's Capitalism and *Underdevelopment in Latin America* (New York: Monthly Review Press, 1969) and Walter Rodney, *How Europe Underdeveloped Africa* Washington, DC: Howard University Press, 1981.

26. F.H. Cardoso, "Imperialism and Dependency in Latin America", *Structure of Dependence*, ed. by P. Bonilla and R. Girling (Stanford: Stanford University Press, 1973), p. 114-123.

27. Reginald Green and Ann Seidman,? *Economic of Pan Africanism* (Baltimore: Penguin, 1968).

28. Walter Rodney, *How Europe Underdeveloped Africa* (Washington, DC: Howard University Press, 1974), p. 21-22.

29. Olatunde Ojo, *African International Relations*, p. 58.

30. Harry Magdoff, quoted in The Third World Opposing View Points, p. 19.

31. Theotonio Dos Santos, "The Structure of Dependence" in Charles K. Wilber, ed., *The Political Economy of Development and Underdevelopment* (New York: Random House, 1973), p. 116.

32. Michael Parenti, "Imperialism Causes Third World Poverty" ed by David Bendr and Burno Leone, *The Third World Opposing View Points* (San Diego: Greenhaven Press, 1989, p. 19.

33. Karl Deutsch, "Theories of Imperialism and Neocolonialism", *Testing Theories of Economic Imperialism*, ed., S. J. Rosen and J. R. Kurth (Washington, DC: Lexington Heath 1974), pp. 15-17.

34. Joan E. Spero, *The Politics of International Economic Relations* (New York: St. Martin's Press 1990), p. 150.

35. Deutsch, p. 21.

36. Vincent A. Mahler, *Dependency Approaches to International Political Economy: A Cross National Study* (New York: Columbia University Press, 1980), p. 48.

37. Charles W. Kegley and Eugene R. Wittkopf, *World Politics: Trend and Transformation* (New York: St. Martin's Press, 1985), pp. 75-77.

38. Mahler, *Dependency Approaches to International Political Economy*, p. 73.

39. John Hobson, *Imperialism: A Study* (Michigan: University of Michigan Press, 1965), Chapter 1.

40. Ake, *Social Science As Imperialism*, p. 137.

41. Deutsch quoted in Rosen and Kurth Book, *Testing Theories of Economic Imperialism*, pp. 18-22.

42. V.I. Lenin, *Imperialism: The Highest Stage of Capitalism* (New York: International Publishers, 1939), pp. 29-30.

43. Paul Baran, "On the Political Economy of Backwardness," *The Political Economy of Development of Underdevelopment*, ed. by Charles E. Wilber (New York: Random House, 1979), pp. 91-102.

44. Gunnar Myrdal, *Economic Theory and the Underdeveloped Regions* (London: Gerald Duckworth, 1957). Raul Prebisch, *Toward A New Trade Policy for Development* (London: Metheun, 1975), pp. 131-151. See also the work by Kwame Nkrumah, *Neocolonialism The Last Stage Imperialism* (New York Publisher, 1966). Neil R. Richardson, *Foreign Policy and Economic Dependence* (Austin University of Texas Press, 1978).

45. Ojo, African International Relations, p. 59.

46. Frantz Fanon, *The Wretched of the Earth* (New York: Grove Press, 1963), pp. 165-166. See also the work of the following authors: A. G. Frank, *Capitalism and Underdevelopment in Latin America* (New York:

Monthly Review Press, 1969). Kwame Nkrumah, *Neo-Colonialism - The Last Stage of Imperialism* (New York: New York Publishers, 1966).

47. Kwame Nkrumah, *Class Struggle in Africa* (New York: International Publishers, 1970), p. 84-85.

48. Hodgkin in the *Unity or Poverty? Economic of Pan Africanism*, Green and Seidman ed (Baltimore: Penguin, 1969), p. 18.

49. Giovanni Arrighi and Jolin Saul, "Socialism and Economic Development in Africa," *Journal of Modern African Studies*, Vol. VII, No. 4 (1970), pp., 150-151.

50. Frank, *Capitalism and Underdevelopment in Latin America*, p. 159.

51. Green and Seidman, p. 131.

52. Quoted in Frank, *Capitalism and Underdevelopment in Latin America*,k p. 53.

53. Prebisch, Toward a New Trade Policy for Development, p. 139.

54. Samuel Valenzula and Arturo Valenzuela, "Modernization and Dependency: Alternative Perspective in the Study of Latin American Underdevelopment" ed., in Heraldo Munzo, *From Dependency to Development*, p. 26.

55. Albert Hirschman, *National Power and The Structure of Foreign Trade* (Berkeley: University of California Press, 1945).

56. Gunnar Myrdal, *The Challenge of World Poverty* (New York: Vinlage, 1970), p. 297.

57. Mahler, *Dependency Approaches To International Political Economy*, p. 51-53.

58. John Galtung, "A Structural Theory of Imperialism," *Journal of Peace Research*, Vol. 8, (1971, p. 81-117.

59. Fernando H. Cardoso and E. Faletto, *Dependency and Development in Latin America*, (Mexico: Siglo Veintiuno, 1969). Andre Gunder Frank, *Latin America Underdevelopment or Revolution,* (New York Monthly Review Press, 1970). Osvaldo Sunkel, "Big Business and Dependencia," *Foreign Affairs*, Vol. 50, (1970) pp. 517-534.

CHAPTER 3

Economic Nationalism: An Approach To The Study of International Political Economy

For a century and a half, the ideologies of Liberalism, Marxism and Economic Nationalism have shaped the entire international political economy. In this chapter, "ideology refers to systems of thought and belief by which individuals and groups explain how their social system operates and what principles and laws it exemplifies.[1] These three ideologies differ on a wide range of questions they raise such as: what is the importance of the market mechanisms for economic growth and distribution of wealth between and among nation-states? What ought to be the functions of market structures in the institution of domestic and international systems? What is the implication of the market structure on issues of war and peace. These and other similar questions are central to discussions for international political economy.

However, these ideologies have basic differences in their perceptions of the relationships between nation, state or market. It may not be an overstatement to mention that every controversy in the area of international political economy is ultimately unbelievable in differing perceptions of these relationships. The ideology that is relevant to our study in this chapter is economic nationalism.

DIVERGENCY OF ECONOMIC NATIONALISM

Economic nationalism has undergone a series of changes over the past many centuries. Its names have also changed: mercantilism, statism, protectionism, the German historical school, and more recently new protectionism. Its main concept is that economic activities are and should be dependent to the objectives of state building and the interests of the state. Almost all nationalists prescribe to the primacy of the state, of national security, and of military hegemony in the institution and functioning of the international system.[2]

> The fact that economic nationalism should be perceived as a primary commitment to state building, the precise objectives sort and the strategies advocated have differed in different times and in different places. Jacob Vinver argues that practically all mercantilists, whatever the period, country, or status of the particular individual, would have subscribed to all of the following propositions: (1) wealth is an absolutely important means to power, whether for security or for aggression; (2) power is essential or valuable as a means to the acquisition or retention of wealth; (3) wealth and power are each proper ultimate ends of national policy; (4) there is long-run harmony between these ends, although in particular circumstances it may be necessary for a time to make economic sacrifices in the interest of military security and therefore also of long-run objective.[3]

Although liberal theorists primarily view the pursuit of power and wealth as a trade off, nationalists tend to regard the two objectives as complementary.

Also economic nationalism emphasizes the role of economic factors in the international economic system and views the struggle between states-capitalist-socialist for economic resources as pervasive and indeed inherent in the nature of international system. As one scholar indicates, since economic resources are essential for national power, every conflict is at once both economic and political.[4] Nations at least over the long run generally pursue national power and wealth. As Stiles and Akaha puts it:

> In the first place, nationalists believe that industry has spillover effects (externalities) throughout the economy and leads to its overall development. Second, they associate the possession of industry with economic self sufficiency and political autonomy. Third, and most important, industry is prized because it is the basis of military power and central to national security in the modern world. In almost every society, including liberal ones, governments pursue policies favorable to industrial development.[5]

Stiles and Akaha further argue that economic nationalism in the early modern period and today, emerges in part from the tendency of market mechanisms to concentrate wealth and to create dominance - dependency relations between the strong and weak societies. In more defensive form, economic nationalism attempts to protect the economy against external economic and political forces. However, defensive economic nationalism generally exists in the Third World countries or in those industrialized countries that have experienced a decline in their economic power and wealth. Such governments pursue protectionist and related strategies to protect their nascent or falling industries and to safeguard national interests.

THE LIBERAL PHILOSOPHY

The Liberal Theory on political economy is embodied in the field of economics as it has emerged in Britain, the United States and Western Europe. From Adam Smith to its contemporary supporters, liberal thinkers have shared a coherent set of assumptions, prepositions, and beliefs about the nature of humanity, economic activities and societies. Liberal economic theory has assumed many forms-Classical, Neo-classical, Keynesian, Monetarist, Austrian, Rational Expectation and so on. These variants range from those giving preference to equality and tending toward social democracy and government intervention to achieve the goal, to those emphasizing liberty and non interventionism at the expense of social equality.

Adam Smith (1723-1790) is best known as the author of *An Inquiry into the Nature and Causes of the Wealth of Nations* (1776-better known under the short title *The Wealth of Nations*), in which he presented a history of economics in Europe, a description of manufacturing in his day, and, most important, a set of recommendations. Smith argued that the greatest social benefit would be produced by each individual pursuing his or her own self interest. He applied this idea to the operations of the economic system and, thereby, he became famous for providing the moral justification and part of the intellectual foundation of capitlaism. *(Library of Congress)*

All forms of economic liberalism are committed to market and price strategy as the most effective avenues for organizing national and international economic relations. For this reason and other similar reasons, Liberalism is nothing but a doctrine and set of principles for regulating, directing, organizing, managing, and controlling a market economy in order to achieve maximum efficiency, economic growth and individual welfare. Liberal theory believes that a market emerges spontaneously in order to satisfy human wants and that once it comes in operation, it works in accordance with its philosophy. Man is by nature an economic animal, and therefore markets originate naturally without specific direction. To quote Adam Smith, it is inherent in mankind to "truck, barter and exchange". To facilitate exchange and improve their well being, people create markets, money, and economic organization.

The brain behind a market economic system is that it accelerates economic efficiency, maximizes economic growth and development, and henceforth enhances citizens' welfare. Although liberal economic theorists assume that economic operation also improves state power and national security, they argue that the major aim of economic operation is to benefit individual consumers. Therefore, their ultimate defense of free trade and open market is that they increase the range of goods and services available to the people. According to Stiles, the basic premise of liberalism is that the individual consumer, firm, or household is the basis of society. Individuals behave rationally and attempt to maximize or satisfy certain values at the lowest possible cost to themselves. Rationality applies only to endeavor, not to outcome. Thus, failure to achieve an objective due to ignorance or some other cause does not, according to liberals, invalidate their premise that individuals act on the basis of a cost/benefit or means/ends calculus. Finally, liberalism argues that an individual will seek to acquire an objective until a market equilibrium is reached, that is, until the cost associated with achieving the objective are equal to the benefits. For many centuries, liberal economic theorists have derived the laws of maximizing behavior, such as these of the theory of comparative advantage and the theory of marginal utility function.

Stiles finally explains that, In reality, liberals believe that trade and economic intercourse are a source of peaceful relations among countries because the mutual benefits of trade and expanding interdependence among national economies will tend to foster cooperative relations. Whereas politics tends to divide, economics tend to unite peoples. A liberal international economy will have a moderating influence on international politics as it creates bonds of mutual interests and a commitment to the status quo. However, it is important to emphasize again that although everyone will, or at least can, be better off in absolute terms under free exchange, the relative gains will differ. It is precisely this issue of relative gains and the distribution of the wealth generated by the market system that has given rise to economic nationalism and Marxism as rival doctrines.[6]

Also, in a world of competing interests, the nationalist will consider relative gain to be more essential than mutual gain. Hence, states continually trying to change the rules of the game guiding international economic relations in order to benefit themselves at greater potential with respect to other economic powers. To quote Adam Smith, "everyone wants to be a monopolist and will attempt to be one unless prevented by its rivalries."

As we mentioned earlier, economic nationalism has taken several dimensions in the modern era. In response to the commercial revolution and the expansion of world trade throughout the century, financial mercantilism or classical liberalism emphasizes the promotion of international trade and a balance of payment equilibrium. With the emergence of the industrial revolution, industrial mercantilists like List and Hamilton emphasize the supremacy of industry and manufacturing over agriculture. During the First and Second World Wars these earlier concerns have been the increasing significance of advanced technology, the desire for domestic control over the commanding heights of modern economy, and the emergence of policy competitiveness have become the major characteristics of modern mercantilism. However, at every stage of development, the desire for power, wealth and independence have been the overriding concern of economic nationalism.

THE HISTORY OF ECONOMIC NATIONALISM: WESTERN VIEW

The history or practice of economic nationalism is as ancient as political philosophy. For example, Aristotle was said to have regarded self-reliance as a prerequisite of the ideal nation state.[7] Also, "mercantilism", that came into effect in sixteenth to eighteenth century Europe brought about for the first time what could be explained as doctrines of economic nationalism, stated in official government pronouncements explaining and justifying state action to control, regulate and restrict various elements of international economic interactions.[8]

Furthermore, the industrial revolution which first emerged in Great Britain and then spread to other parts of the industrial societies espoused free trade and economic internationalism, heralded in 1776 by Adam Smith's Wealth of Nations. But a new wave of economic nationalism, "liberal protectionism", soon began to emerge. Alexander Hamilton laid its intellectual background and practical foundation in his work *Report on the Subject of Manufactures*, published in 1791, which was the most essential early challenge against Adam Smith's free trade doctrines.[9] However, Hamilton emphasizes the use of government policies for the support of domestic industries, much like the protection of infant industries argument advanced by today's less developed countries.

In addition, the infant industries doctrine was developed and given its most perfect formulation and serious consideration by the German early classical economist Friedrich List whose main work, *The National System of Political Economy*, appeared great in 1840.[10] In contrast to Hamilton's, List was anxious in outlets for surplus population and advocated the need for the establishment of colonies. According to List, economic nationalism far from being a mere adjunct of political nationalism, appeared as a measure that welcomed even war as a means of achieving strategic economic objectives.

In spite of the emergency of protectionism, World War I, which occurred in a fairly well-integrated international capitalist economy of free enterprise, disrupted global economic relations and restated economic nationalism. However, the exchange controls and import restrictions it encouraged soon disappeared. But economic nationalism, at least as a consciousness, remained fairly strong both in the old created nations and in those that either achieved their political independence or were newly formed at the Paris Peace Conference of 1919. Again, it is important to note that the "new" nations were largely inspired by the infant industries doctrine, and the older countries by the protection of vested interests.[11] After World War II, the most strict form of economic nationalism were limited to the Soviet bloc, but many other nations continued to pursue strict payments trade regulations.[12]

ECONOMIC NATIONALISM FROM THE THIRD WORLD PERSPECTIVE

Contemporary economic nationalism, although present elsewhere, is most generally associated with the less developed countries. During the colonial period these nations were given their functions in the existing global economic order; that of providing cheap raw material for the industries of the developed countries and cheap food for their factory employees.

More recently, world-system analysts have argued that imperialism, specifically the expansion of the British Empire in

Africa in the last quarter of the Nineteenth Century, was encouraged by the need of the hegemonic core state to maintain its privileged position in the international division of labor in the face of growing competition from the newly emerging core states of Germany and the United States.[13]

Also, as the European nations competed for power and prestige, not in Europe, but in Africa and Asia, their political domination led to economic domination and exploitation. According to Spero: As in the days of mercantilism, colonies were integrated into a global economic system which was designed to serve the economic interest of the metropolis {colonial power}. The political victors controlled investment and trade, regulated currency and production, and manipulated labor, thus creating structures of economic dependency in their colonies which would endure far longer than their actual political authority.[14]

Furthermore, Wallerstein argues that the European powers' geographic expansion resulted in the creation of a capitalist world-system characterized by an international division of labor among three strata or stages: Core, semi periphery, and periphery.[15] Northwest Europe first emerged as a core, and as the industrial revolution proceeded, it exchanged manufactured commodities for agricultural and mineral products produced in the colonial territories at the periphery. According to this view-point, the world-economy is overlaid by a political system of competitive states, and state power is sometimes used to perpetuate the international division of labor.[16] According to Chase-Dunn:

> In the competitive state system it has been impossible for any single state to monopolize the entire world market and to maintain hegemony indefinitely....success in the capitalist world-system is based on a combination of effective state power and competitive advantage in production.[17]

Thus, by the 1800s, Great Britain emerged as the latest dominant core state in a succession of hegemonies.[18]   As the hegemonic power in politics and economics, Britain became the chief promoter and advocator of free International trade, which had the effect of promoting disproportionate economic growth in the core state relative to the periphery.

By 1870, a new wave of imperialism washed over the world. The Western European countries (joined later by the United States and Japan) once more carved the world into a series of overseas empires.   By the outbreak of World War I in 1914, nearly all of Africa was under the control of only seven European powers; in all of the far East and the Pacific only China and Japan remained outside the direct control of Europe or the United States.   But China to a certain degree had been divided into spheres of influence by foreign powers, and Japan had joined the imperialist wave with the acquisition of Korea and Fomosa now Taiwan.   In the Western Hemisphere the United States expanded across its continent, acquired Puerto Rico from Spain, extended its colonial reach westward to Hawaii and the Philippines, leased the Panama Canal Zone and came to exercise considerable political leverage over several Caribbean lands, mainly Cuba.[19]

Again, in contrast to classical Imperialism, the new imperialism of the late nineteenth century was marked by extraordinary competition among the imperial powers, for whom colonies became an important symbol of national power and prestige. In the course of this competition, the local inhabitants of the conquered lands were often ruthlessly suppressed. As Myrdal Gunnar addressed in his book, *The Economic Theory and The Underdeveloped Regions.* According to him the capitalist nations and the imperial powers typically pursued their various interests overseas in a blatantly aggressive way. Bloody, one-sided wars with local citizens of contested territories were commonplace; "sporting wars," Bismarck once called them. The powers themselves rarely came into direct military conflict, but competition among them was keen, and they were perpetually involved in various diplomatic crises. In contrast to the preceding years of comparative political calm, the period after 1870 was one of unaccustomed hostility and tension.[20]

THE EVOLUTION OF NEW IMPERIALISM

Many explanations of the cause of the new imperialism have been offered. They include Marxist interpretations, such as V.I. Lenin's famous work, *Imperialism: The Highest Stage of Capitalism,* which viewed imperialism as the "monopoly stage of capitalism." In general, these interpretations saw capitalism's need for profitable overseas outlets for surplus capital as a cause of Imperialism from the Marxist perspective, the only way to end imperialism was to abolish capitalism. For Lenin, the control of capital by capital, that is of industrial capital by financial capital represented the dominance and highest stage of capitalist development. Capitalism, Lenin argued, had escaped its three fundamental laws of acceleration through international imperialism. The possession of colonies had helped the capitalist states to dispose of their unconsumed goods, to acquire cheap raw materials, and to invest their surplus capital. The exploitation of these colonies hence provided an economic boom with which the industrial societies could purchase off the leadership (labor aristocracy) of their own workers. Colonial imperialism, Lenin argued, had become a necessary characteristic of advance capitalism. As its productive forces emerged and matured, a capitalist society had to expand overseas, capture colonies, or otherwise suffer internal revolution or economic stagnation.

However, the importance of Lenin's theoretical argument is that capitalist global economy does develop the world, but does not develop it equally. Some capitalist states grow at different rates and this differential growth of national power is generally responsible for capitalist imperialism, global political transformation, and possibly war. Responding to Kautsky's position that capitalist societies' were very rational to fight over colonies and would ally themselves in the joint exploitation of colonial citizens, (in the doctrine of ultra imperialism), Lenin indicated that this was impossible because of what he called the principles of unequal development:

> This question [of the possibility of capitalist alliances to be more than temporary and free from conflict] need only be stated clearly enough to make it impossible for any other reply to be given than that in the negative, for there can be no other conceivable basis under capitalism for the division of spheres of influence than a calculation of the strength of the participants in the division, their general economic, financial, military strength, etc.   And the strength of these participants in the division does not change to an equal degree, for under capitalism the development of different undertakings, trusts, branches of industry, or countries cannot be even. Half a century ago, Germany was a miserable, insignificant country, as far as its capitalist strength was concerned, compared with the strength of England at that time. Japan was similarly insignificant compared with Russia. Is it "conceivable" that in ten or twenty years' time the relative strength of the imperialist powers will have remained unchanged? Absolutely inconceivable.[21]

Vladimir Ilyich Lenin (1870-1924, born Vladimir Ilyich Ulyanov) was a follower of Karl Marx. He is remembered primarily as the leader of the successful Bolshevik section of the Communist Party of the Soviet Union and as the first leader of the USSR, which he headed from the time of the Russian revolution in 1917 to his death. He was a major theorist of revolution as well as one of its successful practitioners. His books *What Is to Be Done?* (1902) and *One Step Forward, Two Steps Back* (1904) presented the case for a highly disciplined body of revolutionists as the only approach to a successful revolution. His *Imperialism: the Highest Stage of Capitalism* (1916) and *State and Revolution* (1918) were his major contributions to Marxist theory. *(Library of Congress)*

In his attempt to show that a global capitalist system was inherently unstable, Lenin added another law to the original Marxist laws of capitalism. According to his law, as capitalist economies mature, as capital accumulates, and as profit expectations fall the capitalist states are forced to seize colonies and create dependencies to serve as investment outlets, markets, sources of raw materials and food. In competition with one another, they divide up the colonial regions in accordance with their strengths and capabilities. Hence, the most advanced capitalist state, generally Britain, had appropriated the largest share of colonies. However, the Marxists' explanations of imperialism differed from those of the classical or liberal economists. Conventional orthodox economists regarded the new imperialism not as a product of capitalism as such, but rather as a response to certain maladjustments within the contemporary capitalist system which given the proper will, could be corrected. Nonetheless, the Marxist and Liberal economists both believed that the new imperialism was based mainly on economic considerations.

> The fundamental problems was in the presumed materials needs of advanced capitalist societies-the need for cheap raw materials to feed their growing industrial complexes, for additional markets to consume their rising levels of production, and for investment outlets to absorb their rapidly accumulating capital. The rush for colonies was supposed to be the response of these capitalist societies to one or another of these materials needs.[22]

Also, following World War II, a global economic order marked by profound and growing inequalities was fully established in the non-communist world. At one end of the system were the centers of advanced capitalist-states, characterized by sustained economic growth and technological development, almost full-employment, structurally transformed and flexible economic systems and a considerable amount of international economic, political, financial, and military power. At the other were found the less developed countries, the periphery of the international capitalist economy, characterized by dependent and underdeveloped economic systems and by a low standard of living for the majority of their population. During this period, however, the development and underdevelopment dichotomy of the international economic system had been strongly formed and most of the periphery states had completed their adaptation to the needs and benefits of the advanced capitalist societies.

It is not surprising that the development of such a system according to Girvan, has been fraught with conflict and tensions. Until World War II, relations between colonial masters and colonial subjects were marked by wars and other forms of conflicts. During the post war era, while it seemed that a relative stability had been accomplished, this apparent stability (sometimes called the Pax Americana) only served to conceal certain fundamental and unresolved conflicts in the twentieth century (just as the Pax Britannica had in the nineteenth).[23]

Moreover, according to Girvan, the Organization of Petroleum Exporting Countries (OPEC) offensive of 1970-1973, which was long in the making, indicated the vanguard of the new wave of LDCs economic nationalism. However, the origins of the OPEC offensive lay not in the creation of the organization in 1960 nor even in the Arab Petroleum Congress or in the policy discussions within Arab League in the late 1940s, but ultimately in a growing need to respond directly to the structure of unequal power relations that persisted, and continue to persist, in the contemporary global capitalist system.[24] The OPEC reaction was only the most visible strategy and dramatic symbolism of an evolving and larger less developed countries economic nationalism against Western imperialism and neocolonialism in the contemporary global economic relations. It is therefore very surprising that development planners and economic policy-makers in the developing countries have not paid adequate and sufficient attention to the important concept of economic nationalism.

NATIONALISM AND ECONOMIC NATIONALISM:
THE THIRD WORLD AGAINST GLOBAL LIBERALISM

The drive for equality, however, extends beyond economics to politics; equality of dignity and equality of influence are also at issue. In view of this therefore, Wriggins argues that many LDCs leaders are tired of being ignored, of never being invited to the global high table, or of pressing their views and having them regularly rebuffed. More substantially, many are hostile to the notion that the state system should be organized in its present sharply hierarchical manner, in which a few with wealth, industrial and technological strength, and the capability to apply force regularly and make decisions that so profoundly affect the conditions and well-being of even distant states. They are coming to insist upon participating in the making of decisions that affect them.[25]

Closely related to the drive for equality is the objective of autonomy or independence. Each state, it is held, should be able to manage its own political and economic affairs without interference from outside. Each should be in a position to decide for itself how its resources should be utilized, and what policies industrial and agricultural enterprises operating within its borders should follow.

As we mentioned earlier in our introduction, the concept of economic nationalism is significant in both political science and economics. To the political scientist, economic nationalism represents an integrative ideological force which facilitates the creation of a visible and cohesive nation-state. To the economist, it is a driving force which compels countries to accelerate economic development through nationalist-control of the nation's economic relations with the rest of the world.[26]

Nationalism has been defined by many scholars in the Third World in different ways. Abiola in his book, *The History of West Africa*, sees nationalism as a means to eliminate foreign domination in Africa or desire to eradicate neo-colonialism and imperialism. According to him, nationalism is defined as an opposition against foreign rule or an avenue to eliminate colonialism.[27] Abiola further attacks the entire foundation of the colonial political, social, and economic systems. He strongly maintains that imperialist domination brought about the fragmentation and destruction of the pre-colonial African economy. He explains how funds were denied to potential African businesses and technical training limited to those selected individuals who could protect colonial masters' interest. He indicates how social welfare schemes were developed to keep African workers healthy and productive and traditional institutions were destroyed or retained on the basis of their utility to the colonial regime. He also shows how the indigenous African economy was destroyed by the imperial powers of Europe and replaced it with capitalism not competitive capitalism as a rule but monopoly capitalism. And how the commercial system which emerged during that period sought to exploit in a systematic way Africa's resources and raw materials at the expense of the native population. He finally concludes that it was the system which took away our raw materials at low price and sold them to us at a very high price that is responsible for African economic underdevelopment and external dependency.

From the standpoint of Abiola this scenario is essential in strategic thinking because the concept of economic nationalism arises, as will be shown in this study, directly from the realities of the dominance-dependency relations in the contemporary capitalist world system which is responsible for the Africa's structural dependency. According to Abiola, the primary aim of economic nationalism should be "constructive anti-imperialism" by action. For him, economic nationalism should be geared toward eliminating all forms of colonialism, neo-colonialism and imperialism in Africa.

Added to this was the view shared by Nnamdi Azikiwe, the first President of Nigeria. According to Azikiwe, foreign oppression and domination were the prime reasons for African economic backwardness. To quote him: "Colonialism interrupted normal African economic development, capitalism denied Africa of its wealth and imperialism deprived Africa of its birthright."[28]

Nnadi Azikewi

However, with respect to contemporary underdeveloped countries, nationalism is, according to Harry Johnson:

> The motivation for their formation, the key to their policies, and also an objective of their development, in the sense that the cultivation of feelings of nationalism, i.e., of attachment to the nation, is essential to the formative processes, and a means for the integration of the nation and the differentiation of from other nations." and, he continued, "from a psychological point of view, nationalism is concerned with establishing the self-respect of members of the nation in comparison with members of other nations, and with creating a distinctive national identity...Nationalism involves hostility toward other nations and a tendency to adopt a double standard of morality with respect to them.[29]

At this point, this double standard of morality colors every part of the behavior of nation-state in contemporary global arrangements. In a world divided into sovereign states interacted in global relations, all policies are first and foremost national. Even policies resulting from an international agreement are essentially national policies. As *Africa Today* put it:

> "International policy" is at best a set of coordinated national policies, the ends and means of which are combined into an allegedly harmonious whole. We can then describe this composite of individual national policies and "internationalism". The difference between internationalism and nationalism thus lies in the fact that the latter, not the former, would subordinated the state of international relations to the realization of purely national objectives.[30]

Africa Today further commented that:

> while all policies are national, they can either be guided by a nationalist concept like interdependence compromise or cooperation. In its international economic relations, a government may adopt policies of autarky, insulation, or protectionism on the one hand, or policies of international cooperation and of free trade on the other. The former would be an expression of economic nationalism.[31]

Also, economic nationalism comprises a body of economic measures aimed at the loosening of the organic links between economic processes taking place within the boundaries of one nation and those taking place beyond those regions.[32] This fundamental definition includes the idea of a country isolation itself from the rest of the international community, autonomy in its economic life than is available in an international system of economic relations. The search for economic nationalism has been equated with the pursuit of self-reliance. One writer has provided a useful general definition of this concept:

> a strategy of national self-reliance can be defined as 1) a deliberate policy of selective disengagement from international transactions trade aid investment, technology, information, and manpower capabilities; 2) a conscious restructuring of basic economic and political relationships, values, and institutions: (a) internationally,

between the country pursuing self-reliance and the other countries in the international system and (b) domestically, with the country pursuing self-reliance; and 3) reassociation, or partial reestablishment of previous economic and political international transactions with industrial countries on a [more equal] basis.[33]

Although self-reliance or economic independence, in the fullest sense of the concept, is an illusive and unattainable objective, this spirit of nationalism rationalizes its pursuit as the basic historical foundation for an ideal nation-state. For this and other similar reasons, economic nationalism is fundamental to the understanding of, and struggle against, the brutal effect of colonialism, neocolonialism, and imperialism in the less developed countries. For the African countries, economic nationalism is both an ideology and an economic policy. Economic nationalism however includes a preference for a number of economic policies created to realized national economic sovereignty or self-reliance economic development. Such policy measures would include:

I   Taking over, through confiscation or nationalization, existing strategic facilities that are not controlled by the nation, e.g., the idea behind the nationalization of the oil sector in Nigeria and in the Third World at large..

II   Creating strategic facilities that the nation lacks which are considered important to the national economy, e.g., the idea behind the iron and steel and petrochemical projects in Nigeria, Ghana and Sudan.

III   Attaching high value to having property owned and economic functions performed by nationals, e.g., the idea of indigenization policies in Nigeria and other African Countries.

IV   Promoting the domestic production of all essential commodities, which is the commendable idea behind the unsuccessful "import substitution industrialization" strategy in most Third World countries today.

V   Strongly opposing the investment of many types of foreign capital, and the employment of foreign scientific, technological and managerial personnel, an opposition which is still mostly at the level of rhetoric in most Third World countries today.

VI   Limiting the nation's consumption to those goods that are the fruits of its own soil and labor, e.g., the message behind the on-going radio slogans in Nigeria about boycotting "oyibo" food and foreign goods.

VII   Securing a favorable balance of payments in a nation's international economic relations, still a largely elusive measure for the most Third World countries.

VIII   Expanding transaction and cooperative efforts with other underdeveloped countries, e.g., the idea behind membership in organizations like the Organization of Petroleum Exporting Countries (OPEC), Economic Community of West African States (ECOWAS), and very recently, African Petroleum Producers Association (APPA).[34]

CONCLUDING EVALUATION

The Third World countries are integrated into an international system that is in essence very different from the world in which the industrialized capitalist countries emerged. One of the most obvious changes is the existence of the modern industrial capitalist nations themselves. One major hurdle for the less developed countries, then is to compete with mature industrialized economies that have a running head start in manufacturing, finance, and technology.

The notion of economic nationalism reflects to a frame of mind that endorses a set of national policies aimed at controlling the economic relations between and among nations. In the overall history, sovereign constituted governments (whatever their form of arrangement, their underlying philosophy, their political objective, and the size of the territory over which they exercise control) have wanted to regulate international trade and finance relations. A major primary objective of policies of economic nationalism has been the achievement and maintenance of economic independent.

Regardless of its relative strengths and weaknesses as an ideology or economic policy of global political economy, the nationalists emphasis on the geographic location and the distribution of economic activities provide it with powerful and potential appeal. For the period of contemporary history, states have pursued strategies promoting the development of industry, commercialization, advanced technology, and other economic operations with the highest profitability and creation of employment opportunity within their own domains. As a result of these, nation-states try to create an international division of labor favorable to their political and economic objectives. Thus, economic nationalism is more likely to be an important factor in international relations as long as the state system still persists.

NOTES

1. Kendall W. Stiles and Tsuneo Akaha, *International Political Economy* (New York: Harper Collins Publishers, 1991), p. 3. See also the work by Jeffry A. Frieden and David A. Lake, International Political Economy: Perspectives on Global Power and Wealth, Second Edition, (New York: St. Martin's Press, 1991). Stephen Gill and David Law, *The Global Political Economy: Perspectives, Problems and Policies* (Baltimore: The John Hopkins University Press, 1993). Robert Keohane, *After Hegemony* (Princeton: Princeton University Press, 1984). Robert Gilpin, *The Political Economy of International Relations* (Princeton: Princeton University Press, 1987). Hans J. Morgenthau,

Politics Among Nations (New York: Knopf, 1948, 1954, 1960, 1967);
Frederick L. Schuman, *International Politics: An Introduction to the Western State System.* 4th and 5th eds. (New York: McGraw-Hill, 1948, 1953); Robert Strausz-Hupe and Stefan T. Possony, *International Relations* (New York: McGraw-Hill, 1950, 1954); Norman D. Palmer and Howard C. Perkins, *International Relations* (Boston: Houghton Mifflin, 1953, 1957, 1969); Norman J. Padelford and George A. Lincoln, *The Dynamics of International Politics* (New York: Macmillan, 1962); Ernst B. Haas and Allen S. Whiting, *Dynamics of International Relations* (New York: MccGraw-Hill, 1956); Harold and Margaret Sprout, *Foundations of National Power* (Princeton: Van Nostrand, 1945, 1951) and *Foundations of International Politics* (Princeton: Van Nostrand, 1962).

2. Stiles and Akaha, p. 8.

3. Viner, p. 286; Charles P. Schleicher, *Introduction to International Relations* (Englewood Cliffs, N.J.: Prentice-Hall, 1954) and *International Relations: Cooperation and Conflict* (Englewood Cliffs, N. J. Prentice-Hall, 1962); Frederick H. Hartmann, *The Relations of Nations* (New York: Macmillan, 1957, 1962); A.F.K. Organski, *World Politics* (New York: Knopf, 1958); Lennox A. Mills and Charles H. McLaughlin, *World Politics in Transition* (New York: Holt, Rinehart and Winston, 1956); Fred Greene, *Dynamics of International Relations* (New York: Holt, Rinehart and Winston, 1964); W.W. Kulski, *International Politics in a Revolutionary Age* (Philadelphia: Lippincott, 1964, 1967).

4. Hawtrey, p. 103.

5. Stiles and Akaha, *International Political Economy*, p. 9.

6. Ibid., p. 8.

7. See M.A. Helpein, *Studies in Economic Nationalism*, p. 46.

8. Ibid., p. 38.

9. Ibid.

10. Ibid., pp. 58-60.

11. Ibid., p. 62.

12. Ibid., p. 64.

13. Indeed, within the European Subsystem itself, the trend was more toward the disintegration of political units into smaller ones that their integration into larger ones, as was occurring elsewhere in the world. (The unification of Germany and Italy are principal exception).

14. Joan E. Spero, *The Politics of International Economic Relations* (New York: St. Martin's Press, 1981), pp. 7-8.

15. Immanueal Wallerstein, "The Rise and Future of the World Economy," in Terrence K. Hopkins and Immanuel Wallerstein, eds., *Processes of the World*

System (Beverly Hills, Calif.: Sage Publications, 1980). Wallerstein's theory is to be found in two volumes: *The Modern World Economy in the Sixteenth Century* (New York: Academic Press, 1974), and *The Modern World System II: Mercantilism and the Consolidation of the European World-Economy, 1600-1750* (New York: Academic Press, 1980). See also his *Capitalist World-Economy* (Cambridge: Cambridge University Press, 1979). Furthermore, see the work by A. G. Frank, *Capitalism and The Underdevelopment in Latin America* (New York: Monthly Review Press, 1969). Victor A. Adams *Inequality In International Economic System* (London: Hicks Publishers, 1963).

16. Wallerstein, p. 418.

17. Christopher Chase-Dunn, "Interstate System and Capitalist World Economy: One Logic or Two?" *International Studies Quarterly*, (March 25, 1981), pp. 14-42. See the other articles in this special issue on "World System Debates," edited by W. Ladd Hollist and James N. Rosenau. Cf. also William R. Thompson, Christopher Chase-Dunn, and Joan Sokolovsky, "An Exchange on the Interstate System and the Capitalist World-Economy," ibid., 27 (September 1983).

18. George Modelski, "The Long Cycle of Global Politics and the Nation-State, "*Comparative Studies in Society and History*, (April 20, 1978), p. 217.

19. See Stewart Easton's Background Note, *The Rise and Fall of Western Colonialism* (New York: Praeger Publishers, 1964). For further reference, see Johnson Chijioke, *The Decline of European Empire in Africa* (New York: International Publishers, 1965). Rita C. Anderson, *The Causes of European's Imperialism* London: Oxford University Press, 1970). See, for example, Jeffrey A. Frieden and David A. Lake, eds., op. cit., esp. pp. 1-17; Paul R. Viotti and Mark V. Kauppi, *International Relations Theory, Realism, Pluralism, Globalism* (New York: Macmillan, 1987); Kenneth Waltz, Theory of International Relations (Reading, Mass.: Addison-Wesley, 1979); and the works by Stephen Krasner, Immanuel Wallerstein.

20. Myrdal Gunnar, *The Economic Theory and The Underdeveloped Regions* (London: Gerald Duckworth, 1968), p. 120. An excellent analysis of the Evolution of Contemporary Imperialism was done by Charles Robert and Susan Easton, *The Future of Imperialism* (New York: Hickson Publishing Company, 1973). Also see the work done by Scott Williams, *The Nature and Structure of New Imperialism* (N.J.: Cooks Publishers, 1980). Martin Brown, *The Golden Age of Imperialism* (London: Kentson and Sons Company, 1983). Roca Jamison, *World of Imperialism* (New York: Holmes and Sons Inc., 1978). Kenneth E. Boulding has reiterated Schumpeter's view that imperialism was a form of social lag and, from an economic standpoint, unprofitable to the point of being a fraud. "Reflections on Imperialism," in David Mermelstein, ed.,

Economics: Mainstream Readings and Radical Critiques, 2nd ed. (New York: Random House, 1970), Joseph A. Schumpeter, op. cit., pp. 89-96. Schumpeter's own analysis of imperialism did not go unchallenged. Murray Greene, "Schumpeter's Imperialism-A Critical Note," Social Research (An *International Quarterly of Political and Social Science*), XIX (December 1951). Green took issue with Schumpeter's thesis that because capitalism is nationalistic, it is antithetical to imperialism, militarism, and armaments.

21. Lenin, *Imperialism: The Highest Stage of Capitalism* (New York: International, 1939), p. 119.

22. Mydral Gunnar, *The Economic Theory and The Underdeveloped Regions* (London: Gerald Duckworth, 1968), pp. 34-35.

23. Norman Girvan's work is probably the only exception to this observation. But his treatment was not primarily aimed at conceptualizing the idea of economic nationalism, and it was limited to the oil sector. See Norman Girvan, "Economic Nationalism", in Raymond Vermon, ed., *The Oil Crisis*, (New York: Norton Co., Inc., 1976), and "Economic Nationalist vs. Multinational Corporations: Revolutionary or Evolutionary Change", Carl Widstrand, ed., *Multinational Firms in Africa*, (New York: African Publishing Co., 1975), p. 25-56.

24. Ibid., p. 148.

25. Howard Wriggins, "Third World Strategies for Changes: The Political Context of North-South Interdependence", ed. in Howard Wriggins and Gunnar Alder Karlsson, *Reducing Global Inequities*, (New York: McGraw-Hill 1978), p. 39.

26. Johnson, *Economic Nationalism in Old and New States*, p. 1.

27. Abiola, *The History of West Africa* (Ibadan: Ibadan University Press, 1971).

28. Ibid., p. 143.

29. Johnson, *Economic Nationalism in Old and New States*, p. 126.

30. *Africa Today* (4th Quarter, 1986), p. 55.

31. Ibid., p. 56.

32. Ibid., p. 27.

33. See Thomas J. Biersteker, "Self Reliance in Theory and in Practice in Tanzanian Trade Relations, *International Organization*, Vol. 34, No. 2, Spring 1990, p. 236. For a recent study that analyzes self-reliance in Nigeria as an illusion see Olantude Ojo, "Self-Reliance as a Development Strategy" in Claude Ake, et. al., *Political Economy of Nigeria*, (London: Longman Group Ltd., 1985), Chapter 8).

34.*Africa Today*, pp. 56-57.

CHAPTER 4

The Political Economy of Food Insecurity and Agricultural Backwardness in Sub-Saharan Africa

It is generally perceived that the main focus of a food program, and particularly in Sub-Saharan Africa, should be to increase food production. Again, it is commonly believed that malnutrition is simply a product of peoples's inability to purchase food which is available. Hunger is the most serious problem facing the African continent. The issue of food insecurity has now become so common that it cannot be explained any more as the outcome of specific political or climatic events such as wars, drought or political instability. Sub-Saharan Africa is one of the regions in the world where food production per capita has declined during the past two decades. As a result, the average calorie intake per capita has now fallen below minimal nutritional standards in a majority of African states. By current estimates, approximately 150 million out of Africa's 450 million people suffer from some form of malnutrition originating in an inadequate supply of food stuff. This abysmal picture is further highlighted by the fact that the Food and Agricultural Organization of the United Nations recently indicated that no fewer than 28 African countries were faced with food shortages so critical that further famine might occur imminently.   This stark reality challenges basically our earlier assumptions about the possibility of economic development.[1] However, there is a strong evidence that scarcity of food supplies will become more rather than less severe in the next 10 years. Before 1983, Africa in general and Sub-Saharan Africa in particular had already become strongly dependent upon food imports at a period of time when wheat and grains prices were increasing and African nations suffered from shortages of foreign reserves.

Furthermore, food scarcities on such unprecedented scale are a sobering entry level for Africa's thirty years of independence. The crisis is much deeper than the failure of a agricultural continent to feed itself.   This can be found in the environmental degradation that afflicts not only the semi-arid zones of Western and Eastern Africa, but also the high rainfall areas of Zambia, Zaire, and the West Africa regions.   However, desertification - that is, the conversion of once arable region to desert like infertility, can be seen in every state in Africa across the equatorial region from Senegal to Somali.   Soil depletion on so appalling a scale reflects both the pressure of increasing population to land ratios and the imprudent use of capital intensive temperate region techniques on tropical soils.

CAUSES OF FOOD INSECURITY IN AFRICA

The majority of African states are by nature disadvantaged since they were located in an arid area that places physical constraints on the development efforts.   In addition to physical and structural restrictions, the majority of these states are also prone to floods, earthquakes drought, deforestation, desertification, crop failure and animal diseases.   The impact and scale of these devastating natural variables in Sub-Saharan African are greater than in the

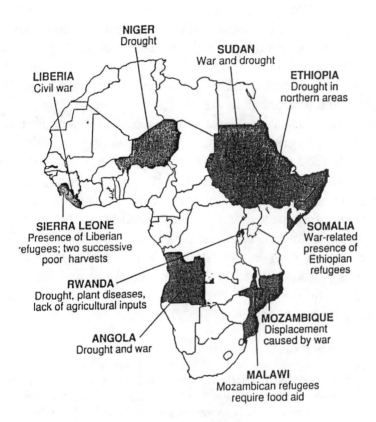

Figure 4:1
Countries affected by drought in Africa

other parts of the world (see figure 4:1 for countries affected by drought in Africa). There, calamitous weather conditions in a score of nations threatened food shortages approaching in severity the famine of 1973-1974, when starvation, hunger and death became daily events in Sahel areas such as Ethiopia, Somalia in the East and Mauritania in the West.

However, Africa is one of the continents in the world where T. R. Malthus's grim prediction that population growth would supersede food production has become a reality. In the 1970s, food production in Africa increased at only 1.8 percent annually, while the population grew at 2.8 to 3 percent annually. At the same time, food production per person fell by approximately one percent a year over that decade, so that in 1980 it was actually 11 percent lower than in 1969-1971. Per capita food production over this period declined in thirty-five countries and increased in only six nations.[2] In further explanation of African food crisis, Helleiner comments:

> By far the single most devastating plague on African countries is the drought, which has been persistent and severe and is rapidly spreading to hitherto unaffected areas. In addition, desertification is said to be spreading at a pace that spells disaster for the continent if it is not checked. It is estimated that 44 percent of the land in Africa has been affected by drought and desertification, which together have reduced agricultural production by more than one half. The United Nations Disaster Relief Coordinator's Office reported that between 1970 and 1981, because of natural disasters, over one million people in Africa lost their lives, while material damages were put conservatively at $46 million. In addition to the loss of human life, outbreaks of disease and pest infestation also took their tolls on crops and livestock on a large scale in various parts of the continent.[3]

Another serious problem that faces African society is population explosion. Population growth is a general factor in the persistence of poverty in the world. According to Wayne McWilliams and Harry Piotrowski, the population of the global

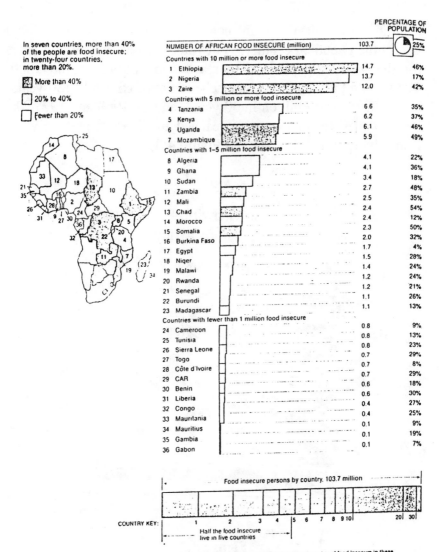

Figure 4:2

Figure 4:2
Africa's food insecure

community has grown at an increasing and particularly alarming rate in the twentieth century. For it took about five million years for the world's population to reach one billion, around 1800. The second billion mark was reached in approximately 130 years, by 1930, the third billion in 30 years, and by 1960 and 1975, the fourth and fifth billions were reached in 15 years and 11 years respectively (see Table 4:1 and Figure 4:3).

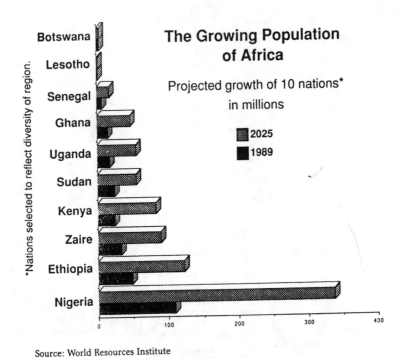

Source: World Resources Institute

Figure 4:3

The implication of over population is much greater in the Sub-Saharan Africa and other less developed countries of the south. The industrialized countries had experienced to a certain extent a steady decline in population compared with Third World countries, particularly African states. Figure 4:3 best illustrates this phenomenon in a proper perspective. During and after World War II, the African population has grown at a historically unprecedented fashion, especially Sub-Saharan Africa. The majority of Sub-Saharan African states have growth rates of more than 3 percent, and some have increased to more than 4 percent. On the contrary, the advanced industrial societies have a much lower rate of population growth, and even some of them have a fairly stable growth. Furthermore, rapid population growth rates, according to Helleiner, have impose pressure on arable land, therefore forcing marginal lands to be brought into cultivation, which in turn dramatically reduced agricultural productivity, incomes, economic growth, and employment and has exacerbated inflation. To these critical issues are added the prevalence of subsistence production, which renders Africa's food production prone to adverse weather conditions, pests, and diseases.

> The situation has been further exacerbated by the "international demonstration effect" that shifts tastes away from traditional African staples in favor of imported foods. (This is especially true for manufactured food products.) These influences have led to a sharp rise in the total food import bill for the region and a worsening of the external payments position. A growing dependence on imported foods has reduced the possibility of using trade, specifically imports, for economic growth and development.[4]

However, chronic food insecurity is the product of a continuing lack of a nation's ability to grow or purchase the minimum significant quantity of food necessary to sustain the population.. As was said earlier, the main causes are many, varying from nation to nation and from region to region. Prominent among these are again inequalities in land ownership and distribution, especially in some Asian, Latin American and African countries, leading to landlessness or lack of enough land of reasonable quality for smallholder farmers. This problem not only affects employment and income opportunities for both the rural and the urban poor but also it leads to underinvestment in basic rural infrastructural development and lack of credit and capital for further expansion. In many states, these conditions are perpetuated as the rural poor have little or no weight in political structures and therefore limited influence on national and state policies.

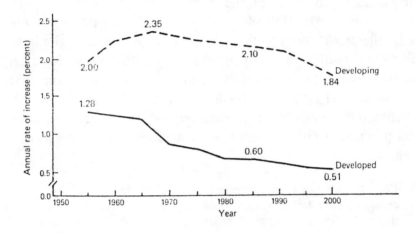

Figure 4:4
Population Growth Rates in Developed and Developing
Countries, 1950-2000.

According to the World Bank's current estimate, more than a billion people in the Third World countries are too poor to purchase sufficient food to sustain their living. Although more than 50 percent of them live in East and South Asia. Approximately, one third are in Sub-Saharan Africa. Earlier projections by The Food and Agriculture Organization (FAO) for the year 2008 show a further increase in the number of people without sufficient food supply. The condition is even worse in Sub-Saharan Africa where drought, wars, environmental damage, deforestation, desertification, earthquakes, and inappropriate policy measures have caused food productivity to decline, leading to a mark rise in dependence on food imports.

Inequality of land distribution as we mentioned earlier is a serious and prolong problem in Africa and other less developed countries. Throughout the less developed countries, agricultural production suffers because the majority of the peasants have little or no land to farm and majority are tenants burdened with large rent payments. The impoverished, debt-owned peasants are some times forced to become landless laborers. As one international study puts it in Latin America 80 percent of the farmland was owned by 8 percent of landowners, while the poorest of the poor peasants 66 percent of all owners were squeezed on to only 4 percent of the land.[5] In a majority of African states, the richest land with the best irrigation belongs to bourgeoisie landowners or to multinational enterprises who grow cash crops-cocoa, cotton, coffee, peanuts, wheat, grain, etc. for export rather than food for domestic consumption. African states have been misled by The International Monetary Fund and The World Bank to produce more of cash crops for exports in order to generate sufficient hard currency to pay off their debts and import the products that they can not produce. Meanwhile, African leaders and policy makers have accepted the "dogma" that the success of their nation largely depends upon what they can produce for sale to the advanced industrialized societies.

In many Northern industrial countries food producers enjoy preferential political treatment, farm prices have been supported at a high level, and food production has been artificially stimulated. As a result, imports have been discouraged, at times a surplus has accumulated, and exports have been subsidized. Meanwhile, in many Southern nonindustrial countries,...rural development and food abundance have been slighted by skimpy public investments in agriculture and by artificially low farm prices, so that production has lagged and imports have grown. By controlling the food policies of their respective governments, a powerful minority in the North (rural producers) has joined in a curious alliance with a powerful minority in the South (urban consumers), the result being a "North-to-South" flow of food that misrepresents production efficiencies and drags against the urgent task of agricultural development in poor countries.[6]

A worried Somalia mother comforts her starving child

An Ethiopia woman and child.

TABLE 4:1
ESTIMATED WORLD POPULATION GROWTH THROUGH
HISTORY

Year	Estimated Population	Estimated Annual increase in the intervening period
Circa 10,000 B.C.	5,000,000	
A.D.1	250,000,000	0.04
1650	545,000,000	0.04
1750	728,000,000	0.29
1800	906,000,000	0.45
1850	1,171,000,000	0.53
1900	1,608,000,000	0.65
1950	2,486,000,000	0.91
1970	3,632,000,000	2.09
1980	3,995,000,000	1.76
1990	5,286,000,000	1.70

SOURCE: Based on V. Carr-Saunders in W. S.Thompson and D. T. Lewis, Population Problems, 5th ed. (New York: McGraw-Hill, 1965), p. 384 United Nations, Demographic Yearbook for 1971; and Population Reference Bureau, 1988 World Population Data Sheet.

TABLE 4:2
CRUDE BIRTHRATES, 1950-2000 (PER 1000 POPULATION)

	1950–1955	1960–1965	1970–1975	1980–1985	1990–1995	1995–2000
World Total	35.6	34.0	30.3	26.1	25.4	23.8
Developed Countries	22.7	20.3	16.7	15.9	15.2	14.9
Developing Countries	41.8	40.0	35.5	32.1	28.3	26.2
Africa	48.1	47.6	46.1	45.0	40.1	36.9
Middle East	47.9	48.0	46.3	44.2	40.0	36.9
Latin America	41.4	39.9	36.3	43.4	31.3	29.6
China	39.8	33.8	26.0	20.1	18.0	17.4
East Asia	36.6	38.3	30.1	26.1	22.4	20.3
South Asia	43.2	44.1	40.5	36.9	31.0	27.8

SOURCE: UN, World Population Trends and Prospects, 1955-2000 (New York: United Nations, 1979), Tables 2-A and 2-B.

The implication of the maldistribution of internal political power in Third World nations as perceived by Robert Paarlberg is "leading relentlessly to deeper dependence upon an unstable and ever less dependable, world grain market". Also, the political influence of urban consumers in the less developed countries points toward one dimension of the agricultural mismanagement. This, along with rapid population growth and urbanization, helps to explain the LDCs growing dependence on the industrialized countries for food assistance. However, dependence on one or few cash crops for export put the less developed African states at a mercy of the global market where prices fluctuate generally. This has proven disastrous for African states in recent years when prices of their agricultural exports have declined rapidly while prices of necessary imports-fertilizers, petroleum and finished goods have increased steadily. MeWilliams and Piotrowski argue that majority of Third World leaders have neglected the needs of the majority of the farmers, that is, the food-producing peasantry in favor of support for the cash crop farmers. In many instances these leaders have purposely kept food prices artificially low to the benefit of the growing number of city dwellers and to the disadvantage of the food-producing peasantry.[7]

Also, in the early 1960s the world food regime was characterized by fairly stable prices and a comparatively small volume of total food production. However, this condition changed drastically during the 1970s. In the early 1970s, the volume of food entering international trade increased rapidly, prices became unstable, and national sensitivities to international food productivities multiplied. The rapid increase in the price of oil between 1973 and 1974 and again in 1979 accentuated the global food crisis by increasing the cost of petroleum and fertilizers used in agricultural production. The economic implication of these variable factors was a 300 percent rise in the price of grain. The aftereffect was that increasing food prices added as much to world inflation as did increasing petroleum costs.[8] The world food regime today can be described by Charles Kegley and Eugene Wittkjopf as comparatively more interdependent but much less dependable. A number of tightly interrelated variable factors explain this including:

> (1) the vagaries of weather and excessive exploitation of natural systems; (2) the internationalization of American agriculture; (3) the growing dependence of other nations on food imports, notably from the United States; and (4) the effects on the world's food regime of choices made in individual nations for essentially domestic political reasons.[9]

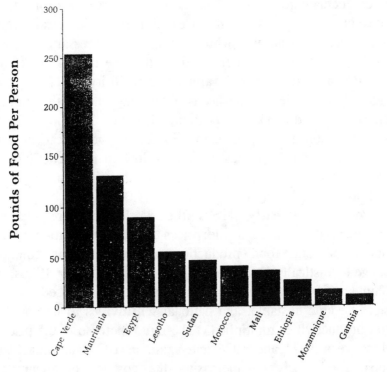

Source: United Nations and USDA Economic Research Service.

Figure 4:5
1985 International Food Aid to Selected African Countries

As mentioned above, the clearly optimistic global picture changed rapidly in the early 1970s. For example, between 1971 and 1972 food production decreased, but the global demand for food increased through a combination of population growth in the Third World countries and increasing influence of industrialized capitalist countries. Also, a number of weather calamities in the Soviet Union, Africa, Asia and China shifted the global food situation to the crisis zone, as global food reserves in 1974 reached their lowest level in twenty years.[10] As indicated in Table 4:3, global grain reserves defined in terms of the equivalent number of days of global grain consumption, dropped from 81 days in 1965 to only 41 in 1974.

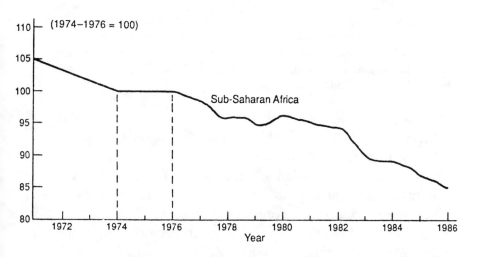

Figure 4:6
Per Capita Food Production in Africa, 1971-1986. Source:
International Institute for Environment and Development, World
Resources 1987.

However, the decrease in Africa's per capita food production is closely associated to the Africa's over increasing population. Other major variables are also responsible. These include according to Lester R. Brown, President of the World Watch Institute and an expert on world resources, inadequacy of basic social and extension services in rural areas, inefficient systems for food distribution and marketing, government policies that tend to discriminate against the agricultural sector, specifically food production, lack of capital and credit for small holders, under investment in agriculture, and physical deterioration of the countryside. Brown further states that:

> Trends in Africa since 1970 are a harbinger of things to come elsewhere in the absence of some major changes in population policies and economic priorities...The forces that have led to the [the per-capita grain production] decline in Africa are also gaining strength in the Andean countries of Latin America, in Central America, and in Indian continents. Whether the declining food production now so painfully evident in Africa can be avoided will be determined in the next few years.[11]

Also, in the majority of African states according to McWilliams and Piotrowski, we find the World's worst poverty, lowest economic growth rates, highest infant mortality rates and highest rates of population explosion. The population of the African continent is growing at approximately twice the rate of increase in food production in the last ten years (see figure 4:3). Persistent malnutrition, hunger and starvation become more clear in contemporary time. To quote McWilliams and Piotrowski:

> Perhaps as many as 200,000 people succumbed starvation in the Ethiopian famine in the early 1970s', and another famine a decade later, more publicized than the earlier one, took an equally large toll. Media attention focused on Ethiopia diverted attention from the hundreds of thousands of people malnourished and on the verge of starvation in Sudan, Chad, Niger, and Mali. These nations as well as Ethiopia are most affected by the relentless expansion of the Sahara desert. Further south, such countries as kenya,

TABLE 4:3
INDICATORS OF WORLD FOOD SECURITY, 1960-1963

Year	World Carry-Over Stocks of Grain	Grain Equivalent of Idled Cropland	Total	Reserves as Days of World Consumption
1960	200	36	236	104
1965	142	70	212	81
1970	164	71	235	75
1971	183	46	229	71
1972	143	78	221	67
1973	148	25	173	50
1974	133	4	137	41
1975	141	3	144	43
1976	196	3	199	56
1977	194	1	195	53
1978	221	22	243	62
1979	197	16	213	54
1980	183	0	183	46
1981	221	0	221	56
1982	260	13	273	66
1983	191	92	283	68

SOURCE: Lester R. Brown, et al., State of the World 1984 (New York: Norton, 1984), P. 187. Reprinted with the permission of the World Watch Institute and the authors.

Uganda,Gabon, and Mozambique are also drought-stricken.   The Economic Commission for Africa, a UN agency, reported that from 1960 to 1975 there was no significant improvement in most African ations' economies and it suggested that, if trends continued, Africa will be even worse off in the year 2000 than it had been in 1960. In 1960, Africa was about 95 percent self-sufficient in food, but twenty-five years later every African country except South Africa was a net importer of food.[12]

Among the African states, Ivory Coast is the only state that has had economic progress and better a standard of living since her political independence.   Nigeria, burdened with Africa's largest population and blessed with large deposits of mineral resources such as, coal, oil, limestone, gold, tin, columbine, silver, lead-zinc and asbestos, has progressed to a certain extent since independence, only just to find its economy in total break down as a result of mismanagement, political corruption and declining global oil prices in the early 1980s.

A review of per capita gross national product and per capita income in the early 1970s indicates that African states are either struggling to maintain marginal economic progress, marking time, and/or in reality decline.[13] According to World Bank data on gross national product and per capita income, those nations experiencing marginal growth include Botswana, Cameroon, Benin, The People Republic of Congo, Rwanda and Ivory Coast. Those countries in Africa that are marking time include Ethiopia, Angola, Guinea, Kenya, Namibia, Malawi, Zimbabwe, Mali, and Niger.   While those nations with falling per capita GNP growth rates include Chad, Gabon, Central African Republic, Ghana, Guinea-Bissau, Nigeria, Liberia, Mozambique, Senegal, Tanzamia, Sierrra Leone, Uganda, Zambia and Zaire.[14] Most surprising are those countries that have the brightness and potential for economic growth and development and that really made remark progress in the first ten year of their political independence only fall backwards after sometimes. Nigeria, Kenya, Zaire and Ghana are very fresh in my mind.

The main causes and solutions of food deficiency in Africa have been a matter of strong debate in both national, continental, and international forum. However, this chapter examines some of the major schools of thought which engage in this debate, and evaluates the strategies to solve the problem suggested by each one of them. Our primary aim is to identify some of the prevailing theoretical and analytical perspectives and to recommend a theoretical paradigm within which future research on food insecurity in Africa could be fruitfully proceed. It is necessary to begin our analysis with a discussion of two dominant theoretical schemes. These can be best identified as the Theory of Dependency and the Law of Comparative advantage profounded by different intellectual precursors such as, Paul Baran and Adam Smith respectively.

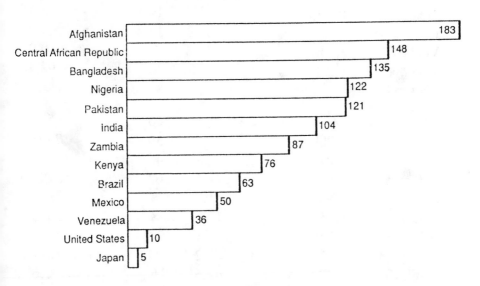

Table 4:7
Infant Mortality Rates in Selected Countries, 1988 (Per 1,000 Live Births). **Source:** **Population Reference Bureau, 1988 World Population Data Sheet**

TABLE 4:4
HERE POPULATION BELOW THE POVERTY LINE IN 35
DEVELOPING COUNTRIES, 1988

	Per Capita gross national product, 1986 ($)	Population, 1988 (millions) in poverty*	Percentage of population	Number of people in poverty (millions)
Latin America (All Countries)	1,720	429.0	19	81.5
Argentia	2,350	32.0	3	1.0
Brazil	1,810	144.4	8	11.5
Chile	1,320	12.6	9	1.1
Colombia	1,230	30.6	14	4.3
Guatemala	930	8.7	10	0.9
Mexico	1,130	83.5	10	8.3
Peru	1,130	21.3	15	3.2
Venezuela	2,930	18.8	5	0.9
Asia (All Countries Except Japan)	1,020	2,995.0	40	1,198.1
Bangladesh	160	109.5	60	65.7
Burma	200	41.1	56	23.0
India	270	861.8	46	375.7
Indonesa	500	177.4	62	109.0
Iran	N/A	51.9	8	4.1
Malaysia	1,850	17.0	8	1.3
Pakistan	350	107.5	34	36.5
Phillippines	570	63.2	29	18.3
South Korea	2,370	42.6	6	2.6
Sri Lanka	400	16.6	10	1.7
Taiwan	2,650	19.8	4	0.8
Thailand	810	54.7	23	12.6
Turkey	1,110	52.9	11	5.8

TABLE 4:4 CONTINUED HERE
POPULATION BELOW THE POVERTY LINE IN 35 DEVELOPING
COUNTRIES, 1988

Africa (ALL Countries)	620	623.0	33	205.6
Egypt	660	53.3	14	7.5
Ethiopia	660	48.3	62	29.9
Ghana	390	14.4	19	2.7
Ivory Coast	740	11.2	14	1.6
Kenya	300	23.3	48	11.2
Morocco	590	25.0	16	4.0
Nigeria	640	111.9	29	32.4
Senegal	420	7.0	29	2.0
Sudan	320	24.0	47	11.3
Tanzania	240	24.3	46	11.2
Tunisia	320	7.7	9	0.7
Uganda	180	16.4	45	7.4
Zaire	160	33.3	49	16.3
Zambia	300	7.5	7	0.5
ALL DEVELOPING COUNRIES	640	3,391.0	35	1,375.8

HINT: The poverty percentages in column 3 are for 1975 as estimated by Ahluwalia et al. they are then applied to the 1988 population figures to calculate the 1988 poverty number estimates of column 4. SOURCE: Columsn 1 and 2: Population Reference Bureau, 1988 World Population Data Sheet (Washington, D. C.:1988); column 3: M.S. Ahluwalis, N. Carter, and H. Chenery, "Growth and Poverty in Developing Countries,"Journal of Development Economic 6 (September 1979), Tables 1 and 2.

THE DYNAMIC NATURE OF DEPENDENCY THEORY

During the early and mid 1960s, less developed countries experienced bulk of writings that constituted a qualitative and quantitative approach in the discussion on dependency and underdevelopment. The works by Paul Baran, Paul Sweezy, Andre Gunder Frank, Fernando Cardoso, Sunkel, Samir Amin, Arrighi Emmanuel, Walter Rodney, and Immanuel Wallerstein explained and interpreted the phenomenon of dependencia in a holistic fashion and in terms of the capitalist mode of production.[15] Since we have done what we considered to be accepted intellectual work on dependency theory, we will briefly but concisely state the major points to enable us to convey our message. It often suffice to extract from this bulk of literature a general core of presuppositions which bears most directly on the issue of food crisis and on the failure of food-producing area of African agriculture to provide sufficiently for the continent's inhabitants. Dependency theorists saw a structural link between domestic and external with multinational corporations or transnational capitalism as the general denominator. Caporaso and Zare advocate a provisional definition of dependency as "a structural condition in which a weakly integrated system cannot complete its economic transition except by an exclusive reliance on an external complement." Dependency is understood as the process by which less developed countries of Africa are incorporated or integrated into the international capitalist system over a period of centuries.

The point of fact from the theory of dependency is the perception that the root causes of Africa's economic crisis, like those of other Third World countries, lie in the nature and structure of the Africa's relationship with the international capitalism. Dependency analysts usually begin their analysis with the argument that the international capitalist system can be divided into the center and the periphery. The center comprises those few nations, mainly in Western Europe, North America and Japan, which during the past 500 years have been able to develop advanced capitalist economic systems. While periphery nations are those countries in Africa, Latin America and Asia, generally known as the Third World countries, whose economies are in reality under developed. Therefore, the theory of dependency or underdevelopment argues that the center-nations have been able to accomplish advanced stages of capitalism at least in part because of their ability to exploit the peripheral nations's economic surplus. The peripheral nations, in other words, are poor and underdeveloped because their wealth has been drained off to sustain the process of economic growth and development in the center. In a summary form, the economic surplus which might have been used to generate growth and development in peripheral regions is used instead to finance further enrichment of already wealthy societies.[16]

For this reason and other similar reasons, peripheral countries find it exclusively next to impossible to change their status in the international capitalist economic system. The foregoing discussion suggests that the widening gap between the developed and less developed countries must be caused by a combination of variable factors indigenous to the less developed societies and inherent in their relationships with the industrialized capitalist states. African states and other LDCs depend on the industrialized capitalist societies not only for capital, technology and manufactured products but also for markets in which to sell the raw materials and agricultural commodities that for many are their main source of foreign reserves needed to purchase imported goods necessary for their industrialization and development.

Also, the plight of the less developed countries is tied not only to the persistenty of their domestic economic and social crises according to Kegley and Witticopf, but also to their relationships with the rich countries of the North. However, what is essential to note is that many theorists, specifically from the less developed countries themselves, have argued that the very dependence of their economies on the North is totally responsible for their persistence economic and social crises. This view of the plight of the poor attributes the causes of dependency and underdevelopment to the dominance and dependence that typifies the present structure of global economic relations between the rich and the poor, rather than to the indigenous characteristics of African states. Dependency theorists argue that the unequal distribution of wealth between the North and South by the global economic system further helps to explain and perpetuate the differences between the center and peripheral nations. They further argue that the poverty of the poor is the product of their exploitation by international capitalism which make other countries developed at their expense.

After the periphery has been integrated into the center, the inherently exploitative linkages that bind them together are sustained by the local elites within the periphery, whose own successes depend on the center and who are coopted by their desire to maintain privileged positions in their countries. One major critic of underdevelopment theory explains the role that the less developed countries's local elites play in the politics of dominance and dependence as follows:

> Have almost invariably structured their domestic rule on a coalition of internal interests favorable to the international connection. Thus, it is not the sheer economic might of the outside that dictates the dependent status of the South, but the sociological consequences of this power. The result, as most dependency theorists see it, is that the basic needs of the international order must be respected by the South if this system is to continue to provide the services that the local elites need in order to perpetuate their rule in their turn. In other words, a symbiotic relationship has grown up over time in which the system has created its servants whose needs dictate that its survival be ensured, whatever the short-term conflicts of interests may be.[17]

The belief that the world is divided between "center", "semi periphery" and "periphery" is necessary to this argument. Hence, world-system theorists, such as Immanuel Walterstein argue that there is only one world-system with a top (the center) and a bottom (the periphery) usually connected in a single international division of labor. From this perspective, dependency or underdevelopment is not a stalled form of linear development, a matter of precapitalism, retarded and/or backward development, but rather a structural position in a hierarchial international division of labor.[18] This view rejects the idea that development generally passes through a process of economic growth involving five stages, such as from traditional stage to the high mass-consumption. [19]

The majority of African states have emerged in the latter part of the twentieth century from a past in which either political colonialism, economic imperialism, neocolonialism, or both predominated their economies. Perhaps all Western industrial economies including Japan experienced some problems in the transition from traditional to modern economies. For a majority of them, the process has been gradual and phased over a longer period.[20] However, many African countries quickly caught up in rapid social change have experienced revolutionary pressures as a product of the modernization process. James E. Dougherty and Robert Pfaltzgraff summarize the whole incident in this way:

> Most of them manifest glaring inequities in patterns of accumulated wealth and annual income distribution. Most suffer from high or above-average rates of population growth, infant mortality, malnutrition or hunger, contagious disease, and illiteracy, as well as inadequate programs of education, health, and welfare. Throughout the Third World, planning for coherent economic development is hampered by shortages of technical-administrative expertise, political instability, inflation, unfavorable terms of trade (because of dependence on the export of a few primary products and the import of costly capital and manufactures, plus large-scale indebtedness to foreign banking institutions, whether national or international), and pressures for consumption that more often than not outstrip domestic productivity.[21]

Dependency theory emerged during the 1970s as one of the major schools of thought representing the views of the less developed countries. The fundamental thesis of the "dependentistas" is that dependency differs from the dependence that the majority of intellectuals have in mind when they refer to an economic interdependent between and among nation-states.   For this reason, James Caporaso differentiated the two theoretical and conceptual schemes in this fashion:

> The dependence orientation seeks to probe and explore the symmetries and asymmetries among nation-states. This approach most often proceeds from a liberal paradigm which focuses on individual actors and their goals and which sees power in decisional terms. The individual actors are usually internally unified states which confront the external environment as homogenous units. The dependency orientation, on the other hand, seeks to explore the process of integration of the periphery into the international capitalist system and to assess the developmental implications of this peripheral capitalism. This approach proceeds from a structuralist paradigm which focuses on the class structure and international capital, and the role of the state in shaping and managing the national, foreign, and class forces that propel development within countries. The dependency framework, in other words, explicitly rejects the unified state as actor as a useful conceptual building block of theory.[22]

Also, the radical political economy theorists, according to Dougherty, argued that the relationship between the Northern "center" and the Southern "periphery" far from being a relationship of mutual interest cooperation, result in the subordination of the latter to and exploitation by the former. Hence, in the view of the radical political economy theorists, the less developed countries do not lack capital behind the advanced industrialized capitalist nations because they lie outside or on the edge of the capitalist economic system, but, rather, because they have incorporated into the international class structure of the capitalist system. In this way, dependency or underdevelopment theory is importantly a variant of the Neo-Marxist view on the condition confronting the erstwhile colonial areas. With the above view in mind, Tony Smith comments that:

> Put briefly, it holds that economic processes are the basic structural force of history, and that over the last several centuries it has been northern capitalism (first in its mercantile, then in its free trade, later in its financial, and today in its multinational guises) that has been history's locomotive. Those lands and peoples are "dependent" that are not "autonomous" (a favorite word of many of these writers that is never rigorously defined) in the face of these external economic forces. The major criticism to be made of dependency theory is that it exaggerates the explanatory power of economic imperialism as a concept to make sense of historical change in the south. Too much emphasis is placed on the dynamic, molding power of capitalist imperialism and the social economic forces in league with it locally; too little attention is paid to political motives behind imperialism or to the autonomous power of local political circumstances in influencing the course of change in Africa, Asia and Latin America.[23]

At this point, however, J. Samuel and Arturo Valenzuela criticized the modernization theory that many Political Scientists, Economists, Sociologists and Anthropologists had established during The World War II to explain the failure of new states to accomplish the economic take-off stage with a diffusion of Western capital and technology. Such an idea, in their own perspective, was an outgrowth of the tradition-modernism dictonomy of nineteenth-century European sociology that perceived culture and tradition as resistant to change and as the major hinderance to economic modernization. Modernizationists according to Dougherty and Pfaltzgraff, believed that traditional societies are marked by ascription, not achievement; by social status and not individual endeavor; by extended family structure rather than the nuclear family. By the same token, the characteristics of modern economy are conceptually quite different-however, typically opposite: high rates of social mobility, a complex occupational system, a predominance of secondary over generally primary economic operations, distinguished political, legal, and social structure, etc. Conventional wisdom was faulted for perceiving that unless traditional economies could learn to innovate and implement liberal ideas, techniques, incentives, organizational models and institutions, they will continue to remain poor, underdeveloped and dependent.

However, radical theorists of underdevelopment often acknowledge a degree of mutual interdependence between the center and periphery nations, they perceive this as clearly unequal and exploitation because the center nations have far greater bargaining power over the terms of their participation in the international economic relations. Therefore, the periphery nations, because they are very poor, are economically and politically weak must usually accept whatever terms of trade they are faced with as a set of given over which they have little or no access.

For these reasons, the theory of dependency attempts to justify the reasons for the failure of the agricultural sector of African economies to generate a sufficient supply of domestically needed foodstuffs. Radical political economy theorists believed that since the economies of the less developed countries of Africa are basically shaped by their dependence upon the international economic system, there is a pronounced tendency to favor export led agriculture over the production of food for local consumption. As Lofchie and Commins stipulate:

> Dependency gives rise to a pronounced dichotomy between the export sector and the food-producing sector; the striking contrast between the two has given rise to the concept of 'agrarian dualism'. For export production is often carried on in large, plantation-sized farms which are highly favored in terms of agricultural inputs, whereas food crops for local consumption are grown on peasant farms which are badly deprived of needed agricultural supports. The export-oriented plantations have benefitted from a host of supportive inputs not typically available to peasant farmers. They have access

to agricultural-extension services which can help to introduce and sustain scientific methods of production, including high-yield seeds, pesticides, and advanced irrigation technologies. They also benefit from the availability of highly developed infrastructures to deal with the transportation, packaging, and storage of their products.[24]

African food producing farmers need better equipment, chemical fertilizers, storage facilities, irrigation network, and effective transportation lines. Unfortunately, none of these they can provide nor have their government been willing and able to provide the capital needed for them. Peasant agriculture is further starved of other important inputs. Agricultural-extension services are insignificant by their inadequacy, with the result that there is little or no provision of scientific and technical inputs needed for efficient production. Therefore, the scarcity of food productivities in Africa South of Sahara can be perceived directly to the systematic structural neglect of the food producing areas.

THE LAW OF COMPARATIVE ADVANTAGE

The main alternative theoretical perspective to underdevelopment or dependency paradigm is explained by the law of comparative advantage. The idea that trade is a stimulus to growth is based also on the theory of comparative advantage, which dates back to David Ricardo famous work on international trade in his 1817 book, "The Principles of Political Economy and Taxation". According to this trade theory, in the absence of barriers in trade, nations will specialize in the production of the commodities they produce relatively cheaper (that is, engage in the production of those commodities in which they have the greatest comparative advantage and least comparative cost over others) and will import the commodities in which other nations have a comparative advantage. This will result to increase in consumption and real income which would otherwise not have been possible in the absence of foreign trade. For Ricardo, the idea of comparative advantage was a powerful argument for free trade since an unrestrained flow of goods between and among nations would help them to utilize their productive resources most effectively:

> It is quite important to the happiness of mankind that our own enjoyment should be increased by the better distribution of labor, by each country producing those commodities for which by its situation, its climate and its natural or artificial advantages, it is adapted, and by their exchanging them for the commodities of other countries, as that they should be augmented by a rise in the rate of profit.[25]

However, this type of specialization, according to Ricardo, would not only lead to more wealth for all countries, but to the sufficient improvement in the standard of living between nations and their people. Ricardo strongly believed that comparative advantage must work to the advantage of all parties, and that the poorer nations would only accentuate their economic problems by withdrawing from the global market activities. Meanwhile, there is strong consequence in Ricardo's argument that the less developed countries would be specifically well encouraged to specialize mainly in their primary commodities. Since this would help them to trade in global markets on the most beneficial terms of trade.

Intellectual precursors who supported Richardo have expanded and altered some of his theoretical concepts, but the basics of his argument still remained unchanged.[26] Sometimes, the most essential addition has been the expansion in the number of variables of production which need to be taken into consideration in determining a nation's comparative advantage as viewed by Ricardo. Ricardo exclusively emphasizes on labor as the only measuring yard stick of effectiveness in any area of production possibility procedure. Meanwhile, recent writings have argued the need for land and capital to be taken into consideration, as well, before a nation's comparative advantage inclusively comptemplated. As of this writing, two of the main premises of Ricardo's thought have remained unquestionable in economics or related subjects. Contemporary theorists of comparative advantage tend not to question the legitimacy of his assumption of the movement of labor between areas of production, or his conviction that the developed and less developed countries alike would improve their economic condition by engaging efficiently in international trade.

Even the agricultural economists who believe in the principle of comparative advantage tend to see no basic problem in countries which are characterized by agrarian dualism. These scholars perceive the heavy structural emphasis on export cash crops as the natural and advantageous implication of the operation of free enterprise interactions. As William Jones puts it:

> The great African production of coffee, cocoa, tea, peanuts, palm oil, and cotton occurred because these crops could be sold; that is, because consumers in Europe, North America, and elsewhere manifested an economic demand for these commodities, and because a marketing system was developed to communicate the character and magnitude of this demand to African farmers. As a consequence, African producers were able to enjoy more nonfarm goods such as textiles and utensils, than they had before.[27]

In view of this concept, it would be a serious mistake to shift away from export crops to food production as an avenues of providing solutions to food problems in Africa or other less developed countries. If the factors of production, such as land, capital, and labor are more efficiently used when distributed to the production of export crops, it would from the argument of comparative advantage, be economically imprudent to shift these resources to food production. The income realized from the sale of export crops, such as cocoa, cotton, coffee, and/or tea would make it advantageously possible to buy for larger quantities of 96 wheat, grain, and/or corn than would have been produced locally with the same amount of inputs.

The most significant advocate of the theory of comparative advantage for the less developed nations is Hollis Chenery, a trained economist who works with the World Bank.   His authority and influence have been based specifically on his capability to challenge some of the unnecessary assumptions often advocated by the classical economic theorists in the area of foreign trade. In practical reality, Chenery questions the validity of the orthodox economic assumption that specialization based on the division of labor of production for international trade promotes economic growth and development.   Chenery differentiates between analyses of comparative advantage (trade theory) and of economic development (growth theory).   He finally integrates himself with a number of intellectual economists, such as Joseph Schumpeter, who believed that the law of comparative advantage is a static concept that ignores a majority of dynamic equilibra.[28]

However, for the government of Africa and other Third World nations who need practical guidance in making decision concerning how best to allocate Third World's scarce resources, growth theory would appear to have realistic advantages. The theory is far more concerned than is the theory of comparative advantage with changing relationships over time between producers, consumers and investors in related areas of the society. Growth theory also emphazes more in multiple areas of the economy more than trade theory. For this reason, Chenery has this to say:

> Development requires much more emphasis on the sequence of expansion of production and factor use by sector than on the conditions of general equilibrium. Growth theory either ignores comparative advantage and the possibilities of trade completely, or considers mainly the dynamic aspects, such as the stimulus that an increase in exports provides to the development of related sectors...With this different point of view, growth theorists often

suggest investment criteria that are quite contradictory to those derived from considerations of comparative advantage.[29]

According to Hollis Chenery, it is very wise that the less developed nations's best long-run economic interests lie in a balanced, multi-area development strategy. The recent market mechanisms, which the law of comparative advantage would rely on to promote this objective, are inefficient, because they do not reflect future patterns of consumption, demand and exchange. Despite the above criticism, it is rather surprising that Chenery still continues to support a positive role for the principle of comparative advantage in the development process. He believes that if comparative advantage can be modified by taking into consideration some of the essential differing perspectives of growth theory, it can best serve as a dominant strategy of planning. Some of these assumptions, according to Chenery include:

> (a) factor prices do not necessarily reflect opportunity costs with any accuracy; (b) the quantity and quality of factors of production may change substantially over time, in part as a result of the production process itself; (c) economies of scale relative to the size of existing markets are important in a number of sectors of production; and (d) complementarily among commodities is dominant in both producer and consumer demand.[30]

CRITICAL THINKING! WHICH WAY TO GO? CRITICISMS OF DEPENDENCY AND COMPARATIVE ADVANTAGE THEORIES

The dependency and/or underdevelopment literature has been subject to a great deal of criticisms by professionals in international political economy, international relations, and comparative politics. Most of the criticisms are centered around dependency and world system theory profounded by Immanuel

Wallerstein. Some critics of dependency theory question whether dependency creates economic, technological and social backwardness that actually lead to a condition of underdevelopment and/or dependency. In reality, there is no general agreement or consensus on causality. That is, there is no clear evidence to prove whether dependency is the main cause of backwardness, poverty, and/or inequality in the international economic relations or whether it is the impact of this situation.

Furthermore, critics of underdevelopment theory have argued that some radical theorists have reduced the activity of international economic system down to the process of capital accumulation and related changes. They have failed to explain non economic variables of imperialism and relations between nation-states. For instance, how can one justify for nineteenth century European states scrambling for economically low value pieces of terrain such as present day chad?[31] According to Viotti, the economic factors critics argue, cannot carry the very great explanatory weight assigned to it.

One of the concerns of main disagreement in the underdevelopment theory is how to overcome or reverse underdevelopment and dependency. As Heraldo Munoz argues, the issue is not that this is a highly controversial ideological problem, but also that there are different ways of conceptualizing underdevelopment. For instance, those scholars who perceive dependency essentially as a problem of unequal power relations among nations might consider a strategy of negotiating with the cores to capture a proportionate share of the world's resources enough, while for those who view underdevelopment in transnational perspective and as a function of the capitalist mode of production mainly call for abandoning the international capitalist economic system.[32]

However, in spite of radical theorists references to internal dynamics, critics claim that there is an extensive radical theorists reliance on external variables in explaining backwardness, poverty, dependence and underdevelopment in the periphery and that internal variables or domestic factors are down played. Also, blaming almost every less developed countries' economic, political, social, technological problem on the industrialized Northern countries is itself biased.

ATTACK ON THE BOLD AND THE BEAUTIFUL OF COMPARATIVE ADVANTAGE

Conventional wisdom embodies a set of analytical instruments and policy prescriptions that assist a nation to maximize its economic return from scarce resources. Radical theorists reject the modernization assumption that accurate development can result only through an appropriate response to external stimuli from exogenous variables according to the uniquely successful western mechanism, as if development and westernization were same processes. Underdevelopment theorists further reject the idea that the national economy is the only proper unit of analysis in the global context. However, Valenzuela argues that different degrees in the transition from tradition to modernism can not explain differences in levels of economic growth and development accomplishment. He finally believes that nations and/or regions can be analyzed only with reference to their locus in the international political economy perspective whether they are closer to the center or the periphery countries. Liberal commitment to efficiency and the maximization of total wealth provides much of its strength and power capability. The market determines the most efficient means for arranging economic interactions, and the price mechanism operates to ensure that mutual benefit and thus aggregate social gain tend to result from economic exchange. For this reason, conventional economics convey to a given economy, whether domestic or international, if you wish to be rich, this is what you must carry out.

It is important to note that economic development or growth theory, like every given aspect of social theory is greatly influenced by the time in which it is conceived. Therefore, the economists of the mid-eighteenth and early nineteenth centuries were very much interested in the conditions conductive to industrial economic prosperity. Most of these theorists lived through the period of the industrial revolution in Europe, and hence witnessed the take off of sustained urban-centered in industrial growth and development there. Their observations should be of considerable interest to us, since what occurred in nineteenth century Europe is what is sometimes prescribed as a model for the less developed nations of Africa, Asia, and Latin America.

Adam Smith, the father of the classical school, was the first to outline the general nature of economic development. In *The Wealth of Nations*, Smith advocated the general preposition that the growth of national wealth depends on the productivity of labor associated with the technologically determined "division of labor" and on the accumulation of wealth in the form of capital. Smith further referred to trade as an exchange of surpluses of goods in excess of domestic consumption and emphasized that international trade, by increasing the level market structure, improves the division of labor and hence increases output within the exporting nation and specialization between nations:

> Between whatever places foreign trade is carried on, they all of them derive two distinct benefits from it. It carries out that surplus part of the produce of their land and labor for which there is no demand among them, and brings back in return for it something else for which there is a demand. It gives value to their superfluities, by exchanging them for something else, which may satisfy a part of their wants, and increase their employments. By means of it, the narrowness of the home market does not hinder the division of labor in any particular branch of an art or manufacture from being carried to the highest perfection. By opening a more extensive market for whatever part of the produce of their labor may exceed the home consumption, it encourages them to improve its productive powers, and to augment its annual produce to the utmost, and thereby to

increase the real revenue and wealth of the society. These great and important services foreign trade is continually occupied in performing, to all the different countries between which it is carried on.[33]

Global trade theorists such as Jacob Viner, Gottfried Haberler, Peter Bauer, Alex Cairncross, and many others expanded and reinforced the classical and neoclassical economic philosophies. These scholars share the neoclassical belief that trade can promote the growth of the rest of the world economy, and that the expansion of trade in any kind of commodity produces spillover effects that are favorable to the other areas. For this and other similar reasons, Cairncross puts his point across as follows:

I confess to some skepticism about the supposed ineffectiveness of foreign trade in producing innovation and development. it does not strike me as entirely plausible to speak as if foreign trade could becontained within and enclave without transmitting its dynamic influences to the rest of the economy.[34]

In support of the above view, Haberler clearly indicates that global trade have many indirect and dymanic advantages, despite static benefits to the trading partners. In his observation, world trade has made a large contribution to the development and growth of the Third World nations (as well as developed countries) in the 19th and 20th centuries and can be expected to make further contributions in the future, if it is permitted to proceed.[35]

For Haberler, global trade has several advantages:

First, trade provides material means (capital goods, machinery and raw and semi-finished materials) indispensable for economic development. Secondly, and even more important, trade is the means and vehicle for the dissemination of know-how, skills, managerial talent and entrepreneurship. Thirdly, trade is also the vehicle for the international movement of capital especially from the developed to underdeveloped countries. Fourthly, free international trade is the best anti monopoly policy and the best guarantee for the maintenance of a healthy degree of free competition.[36]

In addition to the free trade argument advanced by classical and neoclassical economists, Michael P. Todaro summarizes the theoretical answers to five fundamental questions about trade and development derived from the neoclassical free trade mechanism:

1. Trade is an important stimulator of economic growth. It enlarges a country's consumption capacities, increases world output, and provides access to scarce resources and worldwide markets for products without which poor countries would be unable to grow.

2. Trade tends to promote greater international and domestic equality by equalizing factor prices, raising real incomes of trading countries, and making efficient use of each nation's and the world's resource endowments (e.g., raising relative wages in labor-abundant countries and lowering them in labor scarce countries).

3. Trade helps countries to achieve development by promoting and rewarding those sectors of the economy where individual countries possess a comparative advantage whether in terms of labor efficiency or factor endowments.

4. In a world of free trade, international prices and costs of production determine how much a country should trade in order to maximize its national welfare.

5. Countries should follow the dictates of the principle of comparative advantage and not try to interfere with the free workings of the market.

5. Finally, in order to promote growth and development, an outward-looking international policy is required. In all cases, self-reliance based on partial or complete isolation is asserted to be economically inferior to participation in a world of free unlimited trade.[37]

However, the classical comparative advantage theory of free trade is a static approach based restrictively on one variable factor of production (labor cost) for its analysis. At least in the short run, the array of consumer demands, the organizational framework, and the technological environment are accepted as constants. These are assumed to be a set of restrictions and opportunities within which economic decisions and tradeoffs are made. Therefore, questions about the historical backgrounds of, or the directions taken by, economic organizations and the technological mechanisms are for the classical theorist a secondary point.

Orthodox economic theorists are further restricted according to Robert Gilpin by these assumption that exchange is often free and occurs in a competitive market between and among equals who possess full information and are hence able to gain mutually if they choose to exchange of one item for another.[38] However, Charles Lindblom believed that exchange is rarely free and equal. Instead, the terms of an exchange can be seriously influenced by coercion, differences in bargaining power (monopoly, monopsony), and other importantly political and social factors. Hence, since liberalism neglects both the implications of non economic variables on exchange and the implications of exchange on politics, liberal economic theory lacks a true sense of political economy.

Also, orthodox economic theory of comparative advantage can be criticized on the ground of providing insufficient information as regards market mechanisms. As a means to understand economy and particularly its dynamics, liberal economics is limited. It cannot serve as a comprehensive model to political economy. However, orthodox economic theorists have tended to forget this inherent short coming, to address economics as the master social science, and to allow economics to become hegemonic stability.   When this happens, the nature and fundamental claims of the economics discipline can lead economists astray and limit its utility as a theory of political economy.[39]

Another major criticism labelled against orthodox economic theorists is that its fundamental claims, such as a competitive market structure, the existence of rational economic actors, the maximization of equal benefits, and the like, are unrealistic assumptions. In reality, Posner perceived that this claim is unfair in that liberal theorists knowingly make these simplifying claims in order to accelerate scientific research which would not have been possible without the simplification of these assumptions.

African states have relied on the western definition and explanation of development to address their economic crises. Yet one of the main characteristics of the present day international economic order is the unequal relationship between the advanced industrialized capitalist countries and the less developed periphery nations.   The less developed countries of Africa have relied heavily on the law of comparative advantage (a classical theory of international trade) often initiated by the western societies, without favorable results.   According to this theory, countries should specialize in the production of those goods in which they have greatest comparative advantage and least comparative cost over the other nations. In this process, classical theorists argue that there would be proper international division of labor and technological diffusion between countries.[40] As it turned out the benefits of the comparative advantage of global trade accrued disproportionately to the developed countries at the expense of the African states.

In summary, we have tried to distinguish between the modernization and dependency theoretical paradigms to explain development and underdevelopment.   However, Valenzuelas believe that modernization and dependency are two different perspectives seeking to explain the same reality. These two approaches emerged in different area with different evaluative judgements, different assumptions, different methodologies and different explanations.[41] Through a comparative study of modernization and dependency in Latin America, Valenzuelas allow us to compare and weigh the relative utility of these competing theoretical and conceptual frameworks in explaining underdevelopment in the less developed countries including African states. In reviewing a large bodies of literature in modernization and dependency, we have come to the conclusion that the dependency approach concentrates on a richer body of empirical evidence and a broader range of phenomena and that it is also methodologically more promising than modernization in explaining the dynamic nature of underdevelopment and/or vulnerability of the Third World nations.

One of the major problems facing the LDCs in the world market, is the long-run decline in the terms of trade for the exchange of primary goods for industrial goods. That is, the value of primary commodities has declined relative to the value of manufactured goods in international trade. There are a number of features that account for the decline in the terms of trade between African states and developed countries which classical or liberal economists have neglected or treated implicitly. Prominent among them, as perceived by Prebisch, is the fact that productivity advances in industrial societies lead to wage and other input cost rises that keep prices relatively constant. In contrary, in the less developed countries of Africa productivity advances do not result to wage rises because of weak labor unionism and disguised unemployment. This particular situation lead to price declines that are distributed among consumers located in the advanced industrialized capitalists nations.

Added to this is the relative lower income elasticity of the demand for primary commodities, as compared with manufactured goods. This indicates that the forces operate to dampen rises in demand for primary goods as income rises: the amount of money spent on food as a percentage of income decreases, and primary goods as a percentage of total factor inputs required to produce manufactured goods also decrease. These variables, in combination with the development of synthetic alternatives, serve to influence demand and prices for primary commodities in international trade relative to industrial products, for which demand and input prices rise as a proportion of income as income rises.

The above variables are perceived by advocates as evidence of a structural bias in international trade that relegates producers of primary commodities to a valid second class status in the world economy, even though all barriers to free trade were to be eliminated. As many constraints on trade continue to exist in reality, as we have perceived they make it specifically difficult for African states to change themselves from exporters of primary commodities to exporters of manufacture and semi processed products as an avenues of overcoming the problem posed by the terms of trade in international economic exchange.

This theoreticalization of the manner in which less developed countries of Africa are denied their own special "cake" of trade benefits is quite unfair with conventional liberal economic theory. For this reason and other similar reasons, we find the liberal policy recommendation for free trade as inadequate solution to the trade and development problems of African states. Instead, many African states have united together and called for a complete transformation of the international economic order designed to eliminate the structural inbalances that produce disproportionate benefits from trade for advanced nations and to compensate poor African states for any resulting inequalities as we indicate in Chapter 12.

SOLUTIONS TO FOOD CRISES

After the achievement of political independence from Europe, African states started to blame their economic underdevelopment, poverty, backwardness, and other similar economic problems on their former colonial powers. African states also looked forward to rapid prosperity as independent political entities, believing to narrow the gap that divided them from the economically, politically, socially, and technologically industrialized societies. The leaders and policy makers of African states generally perceived industrialization and development as the means to economic modernization. However, by giving priority and preferential arrangement to industrialization and economic growth, African states tended to neglect agriculture and its function in economic development. Even in the area of agriculture, African leaders encouraged the production of export crops, such as cotton and coffee at the expense of food crops. These circumstances resulted in the food crises in almost all African states. This proceeding section focused on the nature and strategies to overcome food insecurity in Africa South of Sahara.

Broad-based agricultural prosperity and sustained improvement in the productivity and income of the rural poor, according to the South Commission are central to achieving food sufficiency in predominantly agrarian societies.[42] An alternative mechanism based on modernizing the small and middle size peasant area that aimed at achieving food sufficiency is also the best avenues by which the agricultural area can specifically contribute to equitable and sustainable growth and development in modern Africa. At this point, however, The South Commission indicates that:

> Experience shows that treating peasant agriculture merely as a source of 'surplus extraction' or 'primitive accumulation', through manipulation of the agricultural terms of trade, forced sales of farm products at low prices to the State, or agricultural taxation, can in the end be highly counter-productive. Such treatment of the agricultural sector amounts to an unfair distribution of the gains of economic growth between urban and rural areas. The consequential

stagnation in rural income in turn impedes efforts to speed up industrialization, whose success depends on an expansion of the markets for what industry produces.   The end result is the retardation of the growth process as a whole, while food insecurity persists or becomes worse.[43]

The harmful effect of agricultural neglect is serious for Africa. Agriculture provides employment for half of the continent's labor force. Its decline since the early 1970s has been followed by a large fall in Africa's labor force participation rate. In 1960, the ratio of labor in agriculture was 80 percent. However, by 1970 it had declined to 62 percent. Meanwhile, during the same time, the proportion of the labor force in industry increased from 28 percent to 41 percent. On the average, the continent's total labor force participation rate reduced from 61.4 percent in 1960 to 40.5 percent in 1982.[44] Despite providing food for the population and raw material for the industrial zone, agriculture has primarily generated most of the revenues and foreign exchange from exports. The decline in this sector not only has generally affected the export receipts but also has led to increase in food imports. This significant shift has also in part been hastened by the policy measures of advanced societies, whose heavy subsidies to their own agricultural farmers have influenced international food prices, thereby preventing the drive to expand food productivity in many African states.   However, African development experience seriously shows that a diversified economy with a large industrial area can hardly be accomplished without a modern broad-based and highly productivity agricultural establishment.

Furthermore, alternative agricultural development will also have to put more emphasis on environment regulation or sustainability. In the 1970s, fears have been expressed about the possibility of further African food scarcity due largely to accelerating environmental stress in agricultural area. In many parts of Africa, the degradation of natural resources such as drought, desertification, deforestation, deterioration of soils, and falling water-tables are contributing to lower agricultural productivity and hence malnutrition of the continent's inhabitants.

Land Reformation

General disequilibrium in land ownership have often imposed obstacles to widespread agricultural prosperity and to the accomplishment of food sufficiency. The large concentration of land ownership always results in a slow expansion of cultivated land, prevents the rapid growth of agricultural production, and distorts the method technical prosperity, resulting in ineffective use of the resources of the rural sector. As The South Commission puts it:

> When agricultural modernization occurs in these conditions, it fails to upgrade the economic and technological capabilities of small farmers and agricultural workers. The result is a shrinking peasant-economy and an increase in technological dualism, rural underemployment, and demographic pressure on land. Agricultural modernization needs to be broad-based if it is to make its full contribution to achieving people-centered development goals.[45]

Land reforms and land tenure methods need to be adapted to the dual purposes of increasing food productivity and promoting a broader distribution of the gains of agrarian prosperity. Land reforms leading to more equitable distributions of ownership and more effective or efficient land use are indispensable for rising agricultural productivity and food sufficiency.

Agricultural and rural development that benefits many citizens can survive only through a joint endeavor by the government and all the local farmers, not just the large peasants. The first step in such an effort in Africa and other less developed countries, according to Todaro, is the provision of secured tenure rights to the individual farmer. When he is driven off his land or gradually impoverished through accumulated debts, not only is his material well being damaged but, more significant, his sense of self-worth and his desire for self and family improvement can be permanently dimished.[46] For these reasons as well as for reasons of enhancing agricultural productivity and the simultaneous accomplishment of both greater efficiency and more equity that land reform is always recommended as a necessary first step for agricultural development in the Third World nations including African states. Since in most African countries the largely unequal pattern of the land ownership is probably the most significant determinant factor of the existing largely unequitable distribution of rural income and wealth. It is therefore the basis for the structural feature of agricultural development in Africa. Hence, when land is highly unequally distributed, rural farmers can have little or no future for economic progress.

There is a general consensus between and among economists and development economists on the need for land reformation. To Myrdal, land reformism holds the pillar to agricultural development in Asia and/or Africa. The Economic Commission for Latin America (ECLA) has steadily identified land reformism as a necessary if not a sufficient precondition for agricultural and rural prosperity. In the 1970s, FAO report confirmed that in many less developed countries including Africa land reformation remains a precondition for industrial development. The report believed that such reformation was more urgent today than before, mainly because (1) rapid population explosion threatened also to worsen existing inequalities, (2) unequal distribution of wealth particularly income and unemployment in rural sectors have deteriorated, and (3) current and potential technological break through in agriculture, such as (The Green Revolution or Operation Fed The Nation) can be misused generally by large and powerful rural landowners and this can lead to an increase in power, income, wealth, and ability to resist future land reformation.

Therefore, if policies of land reformation can be legislated and effectively adopted by different governments in Africa, then the basis for enhanced productivity outputs and a higher standard of living condition for the masses will be established. Meanwhile, the majority of land reform endeavors have failed to materialize in Africa and other Third World countries because their government bowed to political pressures from dominant land-owning peasants and refused to adopt the most simple land reforms.

Since an egalitarian land reform policy alone can no longer guarantee successful agricultural and rural development, it becomes necessary for strong and active government participation in land reform process. Government can do that by providing the necessary incentives, economic opportunities, access to needed inputs to enable small peasants to expand their levels of operation and increase productivity. As Todaro summarizes:

> While land reform is essential in many parts of Asia and Latin America, it is likely to be ineffective and perhaps even counterproductive unless there are corresponding changes in rural institutions that control production (e.g., banks, moneylenders, seed and fertilizer distributors), in supporting government services (e.g., technical and educational extension services, public credit agencies, storage and marketing facilities, rural transport and feeder roads), and in government pricing policies with regard to both inputs (e.g., removing factor price distortions) and outputs (paying market value prices to farmers). Even where land reform is not necessary but where productivity and incomes are low (as in the whole of Africa and much of Southeast Asia), this broad network of external support services along with appropriate governmental pricing policies related to both farm inputs and outputs is an essential condition for sustained agricultural progress.[47]

For food sufficiency to be achieved, the government's investment and promotional measures will further need to be reoriented in favor of small land cultivators and cooperatives. However, this method will require enlarged expenditure on infrastructure and technological enhancements. Transportation and irrigation have to be effectively and rapidly expanded.   Also research and development have to be channelled to the generation and dissemination of agricultural techniques that serves and meets the demands for small peasant farmers.

In Africa, the preparation of land for cultivation through leveling, irrigation, and drainage and such supporting infrastructure as road, electricity, storage, and effective market strategies, are useful in promoting agricultural productivity.   In many African states, programs that would make it possible to start farming on large areas of specifically rich land would largely stimulate agricultural growth and development.

Africa, in reality, needs an effective agricultural research system to carry out specific studies in different areas, such as scarcity of irrigation water, diversity of crops, conditions of fragile soils, and vagaries of weather conditions.   However, majority of these countries can not afford such a dynamic system on their own, and its introduction therefore requires joint effort between and among them.   Such cooperation may also make it possible to create an effective link with the global agricultural research centers.

Integrated Rural Development Strategies

As we mentioned earlier, rural development, while dependent specifically on small subsistence agricultural prosperity, indicates much greater.   It consists of (1) endeavors to increase both farm and nonfarm rural real incomes and wealth through employment expansion, rural industrialization, and the raised establishment of education, health and nutrition, urban and rural housing opportunities, and general social and welfare services, (2) a declining equitable distribution of rural incomes/wealth and a reducing of urban-rural disequilibrium in incomes and economic opportunities, and (3) the ability of the rural area to withstand and increase the pace of these improvements in the near future.

However, this assumption is self explanatory in nature. We need only add that the accomplishment of the above stated objectives is important to national economic development. This is true, not only that the majority of African states are located in the rural zones but also because the burgeoning crisis of urban unemployment and population congestion must discover their primary solution in the improvement of the rural surrounding. Also by creating a strong balance between rural and urban economic opportunities and by establishing the conditions for large mass participation in national development endeavors and reinforcements, African states will have taken a proper step toward the achievement and realization of true and meaningful economic development.

Price Incentive Techniques

Furthermore, the agricultural terms of trade are a essential determinant in the distribution of incomes and wealth between and among rural and urban sectors. There is again considerable evidence that there is a small farmer agriculture with positive reactions to price incentives within the limits of its technological capability. Previously, measures on tariffs, domestic prices and exchange rates have always discriminated against agricultural producers, particularly subsistence farmers. Efficient and sufficient protection for agriculture has been low and sometimes negative in many African states because of high protection for industries, firms, overvalued exchange rates and domestic price measures have reinforced this bias against farming and disencouraged the production of food crops. Therefore, any policy measure that provides peasant agricultural farmers enough incentives toincrease production is central for agricultural prosperity and food security in Africa.

NEW THOUGHTS AND WESTERN RESPONSIBILITIES

It is important to note that breaking the backbone of the farming trap in Africa requires a fundamental shift in how we perceive development and how we look at Africa too. The first approach is to understand that development is something done by citizens, and not to them. As we see it now, development policies in Africa and other LDCs are formulated by experts who sit at capital cities of the Western World. To transform the always destructive effect of these macro-policies, the industrialized capitalist countries of the North has to listen to, and support, Africa's preferential arrangements for its own growth and development. A case by case review on African strategy for development gives self-reliance the first priority.

Primary to economic self-reliance is food productivity aimed not at external markets but at domestic consumption. This looks like common sense statement, yet during 1986-1987 famine, Ethiopia and similar countries in Africa were exporting green beans, coffees and cotton to Western World, particularly Great Britain. To eliminate famine in these areas, Ethiopia and other similar states have to shift away from the capital intensive, import dependent agricultural development promoted and supported by the industrialized states toward producing rice, maize, grains, and vegetables for their own citizens.

The instruments needed to make this change are not difficult. Most of them are available within Africa, based on traditional agricultural mechanisms. However, this change would further require western donors both public and private to extend credit opportunities to local or domestic rather than commercial producers, and to make seeds, fertilizers, and other instruments of production largely available to small, poor peasant farmers, especially women.

Also, agreeing that Africans should be the ones to establish their development strategies shows that the West will have to shift its own strategies too. For example, dumping food assistance on Africa would no longer be a means to solve the problem of over production resulting from domestic under consumption. International aid programs would have to be uncoupled from political machinations and re-directed toward development. Western governments, financial institutions, and international organizations would have to accept some radical debt relief approaches. For instance, in 1988 France canceled the $170 million debt of the twenty poorest African nations even if such an amount is as too small compared with $230 billion owned by the continent, it indicated to other western countries that debt cancellation is a possible strategy to eliminate African economic crisis. However, chances are that unless western development preferences change, new debts will continue to accumulate.

Finally, eliminating the cycle of famine would include abandoning the charity mentality that prevails in the arena of foreign aid. Western aid donors should insist that foreign aid go for rehabilitation programs, not only for emergency food.

NOTES

1. Michael F. Lofchie and Stephen K. Commins, "Food Deficits and Agricultural Policies in Tropical Africa", ed. in Charles K. Wilber, *The Political Economy of Development and Underdevelopment* (New York: McGraw Hill Publishing Company, 1988), p. 303. See B. M. Bond *Agricultural Responses to Prices in Sub-Saharan Africa*, Washington, D.C.: IMF Research. Diana Callear, "Who Wants to be a Peasant? Food Production in a Labor Exporting Area of Zimbabwe" (*Metheuson*, 1983). Edwin Harris, *The Political Economy of Food Crisis in Sub-Saharan Africa* (London: Histin Co., 1978). H. Muhtar, *Agricultural Policy in Developing Countries: Groundnut in Northern Nigeria Cambridge:* (Cambridge University Press, 1983).

2. Kegley and Wittkopf, *World Politics: Trend and Transformation*, p. 284.

3. Gerald K. Helleiner, *Africa and The International Monetary Fund* (Washington, DC IMF, 1987), pp. 54-55.

4. Helleiner, *Africa And The IMF*, p. 55.

5. For detail analysis see Paul Harrison, *Inside The Third World* (New York: Perguin, 2nd ed. 1984) pp. 414-415.

6. Kegley p. 291.

7. McWilliams and Piotrowski, *The World Since 1945*. For further analysis see World Bank, *The World Bank Critical Analysis* (New York: New York Monthly Review, 1982). Kin Peterson, *The Politics of Food and Health Administration in Zambia, South Africa Labor Bulletin* (1984). A. Singh, "The Basic Needs Approach to Development versus the New International Economic Order: The Significance of Third World Industrialization", *(World Development June* 1979). C. Stevens, *Food Aid and the Developing World* (London: Croom Helm, 1979). *Thomas Johnson, Food Dependency and Industrial Transformation in the Less Developed Countries: A Critical Analysis* (London: Croom Helm, 1980). H. Wagstaff, "Food Imports of Developing Countries: Trends and Dilemmas' *(Food Policy*, Autumn 1981). M.G. Weibatum, "Food and Political Instability in the Middle East," Studies in *Comparative International Development*, No. 15, Summer, 1980.

8. John W. Sewell, "Can the North Prosper Without Growth and Progress in the South?", ed. in Martin M. McLaughlin, *The United States and World Development Agenda* (New York: Praeger, 1979), pp. 45-77).

9. Kegley and Wittkopf, World Politics: Trend and Transformation, p. 283.

10. Ibid.

11. Lester R. Brown, Edward Wold, Linda Starke, Williams Chandler, Christopher Flavin and Sandra Postel, *The State of the World* (New York: Norton, 1984), p. 192.

12. McWilliams and Piotrowski, *The World Since 1945*, p. 242.

13. Ibid., p.244.

14. World Bank Atlas, 1985. Jeffrey A. Hart, *The New International Economic Order: Cooperation and Conflict in North-South Economic Relations* (New York: St. Martin's Press, 1983); Craig N. Murphy, "What the Third World Wants: An Interpretation of the Development and Meaning of the New International Economic Order Ideology," *International Studies Quarterly*. 27 (March 1983); and Stephen D. Krasner, *Structural Conflict: The Third World Against Global Liberalism* (Berkeley: University of California Press, 1985). Stephen D. Krasner, "Transforming International Regimes: What the Third World Wants and Why," *International Studies Quarterly*, 25 (March 1981). For additional discussions of North-South economic relations and the obstacles to achieving the NIEO, see Roger D. Hansen, *Beyond the North-South Stalemate, for the Council on Foreign Relations* (New York: McGraw-Hill, 1979); John Gerald Ruggie, ed., *The*

Antinomies of Interdependence (New York: Columbia University Press, 1983); Robert O. Keohane, *After Hegemony: Cooperation and Discord in the World Political Economy* (Princeton, N.J.: Princeton Univerity Press, 1984); and David A. Lake, "Power and the Third World: Toward a Realist Political Economy of North-South Relations," *International Studies Quarterly*, 31 (June 1987).

15. Heraldo Munzo, *From Dependency to Development*, Chapter One. See Commission on Transnational Corporations, "Supplementary Material on the Issue of Defining Transnational Corporations," *United Nations Economic and Social Council*, March 23, 1979, pp.8 and 11; *Transnational Corporations in World Development: A Re-Examination* (New York: United Nations, 1981). Joan Edelman Spero has concluded that more than 95 percent of recorded direct foreign investment flows from countries that are members of the Organization of Economic Cooperation and Development (OECD), and that about three-quarters of this total is invested in other OECD countries. *The Politics of International Economic Relations*, 3rd ed. (New York: St. Martin's Press, 1985). John R. Oneal and Frances H. Oneal, after comparing the rates of investment return in two groups of countries -LDCs and industrialized-that dependence results in systematic exploitation. "Hegemony, imperialism and the Profitability of Foreign Investments," *International Organization*,42 (Spring 1988).

16. Wilber, *The Political Economy of Development of Underdevelopment* (New York: McGraw Hill Publishing Company, 1988); Heraldo Munoz, *From Dependency To Development: Strategies To Overcome Underdevelopment and Inequality* (Boulder, Colorado: Westview Press, 1982), chapter one. Samir Amin, *Unequal Development* (New York: Monthly Review Press, 1976); Cardoso Fernanda, *Dependency and Development in Latin America* (Berkeley University of California Press, 1978; and Fredoline Anunobi, *The Implications of Conditionality: The International Monetary Fund and Africa* (Lanham, Maryland: University Press of America, 1992).

17. Tony Smith, "The Underdevelopment of Development Literature: The Case of Dependency Theory" *World Politics* (31 January 1979), pp. 247-288.

18. Kegley and WittKopf, *World Politics Trend and Transformation*.

19. Rostow, *Stages of Economic Growth*.

20. James E. Dougherty and Robert Pfaltzgraft, *Contending Theories of International Relations A Comprehensive Survey* (New York: Harper Collins Publishers, 1990); E.M. Winslow, *The Pattern of Imperialism* (New York: Columbia University Press, 1949); V.I. Lenin, *Imperialism: The Highest Stage of Capitalism* (New York: International Publishers, 1939; James Caporaso "Dependence and Dependency in The Global System" *International Organization*, 32 (Winter 1978). Fredoline Anunobi, *The Implications of*

Conditionality: The International Monetary Fund and Africa
(Lanham,Maryland: University Press of America, 1992).

21. Dougherty and Pfaltzgraff, *Contending Theories of International Relations*. p. 249.

22. James Caporaso, "Dependence and Dependency in The Global System" *International Organization*, 32 (Winter 1978) p. 2.

23. Tony Smith, "The Logic of Dependency Theory Revisited," 1bid 35 (Autumn 1981) pp. 736-737.

24. Lofchie and Commins, *The Political Economy of Development of Underdevelopment*, p. 307.

25. Works and Correspondent of David Ricardo, edited by Pierro Staff, Volume I, (Cambridge, 1962, On *The Principles Of Political Economy and Taxation*, p.132.

26. Payne Rhys, *Economic Development and The Principles of Comparative Advantage* (Los Angeles: University of California Press, 1980).

27. William O. Jones, *Marketing Staple Food Crops in Tropical Africa* (Ithaca, 1972), p. 233.

28. Lofchie and Commins, *The Political Economy of Development of Underdevelopment*.

29. Hollis Chenery, *Structural Change and Development Policy* (Oxford: Oxford University Press, 1979), p. 275.

30. Ibid.

31. Viotti, *International Relations Theory*.

32. Munoz, *From Dependency To Development*. For a detailed examination of this concept, see Gustav A. Wetter, *Dialectical Materialism: A Historical and Sysematic Survey of Philosophy in the Soviet Union* (New York: Praeger, 1963). Karl Marx and Friedrich Engels, *Manifesto of the Communist Party* (New York: International Publishers, 1932), See Karl Marx, *Capital: A Critique of Political Economy* (New York: Random House [ModernLibrary], n.d.), especially chs. 1, 7, 9, 11, and 12. Marx's most ectensive treatment of the concept of surplus value. Karl Marx and Friedrich Engels, *Manifesto of the Communist Party*; See Robert C. Tucker, *The Marxian Revolutionary Idea* (New York: Norton 1970) and *Philosophy and Myth in Karl Marx* (Cambridge: Cambridge University Press, 1972); Vendulka Kubalkova and Albert Cruickshank, *Marxiam and International Relations* (Oxford: Clarendon Press, 1985).

33. Adam Smith, *An Inquiry into The Nature and Causes of The Wealth of Nations* (New York: Modern Library, 1776, 1937) p.415.

34. Alex K. Cairncross, "International Trade and Economic Development" *Economist* (August 1962), p. 240.

CHAPTER 5

Multinational Corporation:
A Strategy For Development Or
Dependency

The problems, concerns or issues of managing and controlling the multinational corporations are of greater important in the Third World nations than in the industrial societies. Multinational Corporations have greater authority and influence in the less developed countries than in the developed countries of the western world. For these reasons, it is necessary to examine, analyze, and evaluate the activities of multinational corporations in the less developed countries with a particular reference to African States. In this section, we briefly examine the role of MNCs. We also provide the general characteristics and power of the multinational corporations in the LDCs. In addition, the positions taken by the advocates and critics of multinational corporations were presented. In Chapter 6, efforts are made to examine and evaluate the Socio-economic and political implications of Multinational Corporations in poor and developing countries of Africa.

THE ROLE OF MULTINATIONAL
CORPORATIONS IN AFRICAN STATES

This section begins with a general discussion on how development theorists justify what is assumed to be the benevolent function of the multinational enterprises in the development of the less developed countries. This is accompanied by a discussion on how this function has been safeguarded and accelerated in the development policies of Various African States.

Foreign businesses strongly and adversely militate against all endeavors by the less developed countries to accomplish take-off into sustained growth. Multinational firms also invest capital and technology in extractive or distributive industrial sectors, and to a certain extent in productive sectors. Because of this, the Lion share of the economic surplus generated from the extractive industries goes into the states of foreign monopolies. Since investment is not in productive industries, the by-product of industrial resources are virtually non-existent. Hence, the effort of the less developed countries of Africa to have industries that will create forward and backward linkages in their economies is generally frustrated.[1]

However, the production functions of the extractive industries according to Arthur Nwankwo are "fixed technical co-efficient" (highly capital intensive) and thereby have a low employment creating effect. The less developed states of Africa have endemic unemployment and underemployment problems, and the means to alleviate this is not by a production function of this type. The monopolization of certain Sectors in African economy by multinational enterprises is not the main issue, but the behavior and practices of international monopolies. Some industries by their nature according to Nwankwo may require certain amount of "bigness" in order to be able to sufficiently and effectively reap the advantages of economy of scale and the inherent mass production and standardization of products. In advanced industrial societies such as United States, Canada, Great Britain, Japan and France, there are heavily monopolized industries that are classified as oligopoly. These industries cannot be economically effective by division or fragmentation. Despite the economies of scale advantage inherent in multinational corporations, there are also costs to the capitalist economies for allowing the existence of International Corporations. Multinational enterprises in advanced industrial societies when left unchecked can take the advantage of their powers to restrict output and raise prices of manufactured goods seriously. This behavior creates scarcity and robs individual consumers of some portion of their consumer surplus.

As we mentioned above, if this type of behavior or practice goes unchecked, the cost to the nation may off-set the advantage inherent in "bigness". For this reason, the advanced industrial societies have adopted series of measures to reduce the powers and influence of large corporations. Such measures or laws enacted to check the activities of MNCs include Antitrust Laws, laws against price- fixing, restrictive practices, and the like. However, these type of laws are not available in the less developed countries.

In the developed market economies, multinational firms invest heavily in productive ventures which further cement and encourage the already established forward and backward linkage of the economy. To quote Nwankwo:

> Multinational corporations in advanced industrialized countries invest heavily in productive ventures which further cement and augment the already existing backward and forward linkage of the economy. As a matter of policy, the lion share of undistributed profits which are re-invested generally go into productive industries with very minute and infinitesimal portions going to extractive industries. Multinational corporations have double standards. One standard is to concentrate on productive investments in their countries of origin and the other standard is to invest mainly in extractive industries in the developing countries; and instead of re-investing profits productively, they ship them away to their

respective countries. The practice of double standards has raised serious questions as to their usefulness in developing countries.[2]

As a result, some economists in less developed countries, particularly those of Latin America, have taken a strong and unbiased examination of the function of international corporations in the Third World. These scholars discovered a great deal of exploitation, and believed that the multinational firms take more from the LDCs than they provide for development. This situation forced the United Nations specialized agents, particularly the United Nations Conference on Trade and Development (UNCTAD) and the Economic Commission For Latin America, to examine and evaluate the role of multinational corporations in the development process of the less developed countries. These scholars argued that the actions of MNCs are generally supported by their home governments which give them strong assurances for their investments in the LDCs. Therefore, the MNCs preach for economic development theories that are indispensable of the multinational enterprises in the development effort of the LDCs.

However, indigenous policy makers in Africa and other less developed countries, because of lack of or limited experience, adopt these theories without justification, interpretation and/or recognition of their after effects to their economies. In addition, the advanced industrialized nations export experts and managers whose primary responsibility is to propagate the economic development theories of western capitalist countries and thereby strongly cement the role of multinational enterprises in the development process.

Moreover, the behavior and actions of the western world are more often than not justified on the grounds that economics is a science, and as such, has universal application. Western orthodox theorists refused to understand that theories are means, but not ends by themselves. Ends, however, should take into consideration the socio-economic reality and circumstances of the environment where the theory is to be applied. There are few factors of economic theory which should not be applicable, at least in part, to the less developed countries of Africa but which have justified and accelerated the role of direct foreign investment and of multinational enterprises in Africa.

THE IMPORTANCE OF CAPITAL IN DEVELOPMENT THEORY

There are four major factors of production in economic theory: land, labor, capital, and management. However, land, labor, and management are available in African countries but capital which is available in advanced industrial societies, is scarce in relation to demand in Africa and other LDCs. Hence, the advanced industrial states should help the Third World countries by supplying the scarce capital required for production either as foreign aid or in the form of direct private investment. It is argued that once this scarce factor of production is supplied, economic growth and development will be promoted in Africa and other LDCs. As it turned out, this has not happened in the history of Africa's development experience.

Also, in order to accelerate the transfer of resources from the advanced capitalist countries to the less developed countries, the latter should generate enough foreign exchange through the production of export crops and other primary goods. Hence, the less developed countries of Africa were educated and encouraged by the western economists to produce primary products which they have to exchange for manufactured goods, machinery and capital equipment. In this way, an international division of labor has been established. Therefore, the multinational firms which are responsible for the production of manufactured goods and equipment in the less developed countries have been brought into a central position in the economic development of LDCs-economies.   Capital is only a means of supporting man in production process. Cairncross believed that expansion goes with market opportunity and effective management, and that where these are available, financial problems can be overcome. This type of approach has not been applied to the Third World countries where technological know-how, should be replaced by effective management. Instead, the less developed countries have been encouraged and made to demand for the scarce factor of production from the advanced capitalist societies. The formation of subsidiary firms in the LDCs by the parent corporations in developed countries has thus, becomes a convenient and efficient means of exploiting the global division of labor that has been created by the classical economic theorists.

INCENTIVES TO ENCOURAGE FOREIGN INVESTMENT IN AFRICA: NIGERIA AS A CASE STUDY

Since capital and technology are considered crucial for economic development, the promotion of foreign investment was, in reality, made the central issue for economic development in majority of African states. Various policy prescriptions were implemented to this end, and efforts were made for political stability. Therefore, foreign investment conditioned economic measure and largely influenced the political atmosphere. This generally   exacerbated   economic   imperialism   and/or neocolonialism in today's African economies.

In Nigeria, the government measures for promoting direct foreign private investment is explained in the National Development Plans. In the recent Plan, under the heading "A new Industrial Charter," it stipulates that:

> In order to harness the tremendous potentials of the manufacturing
> sector and to realize the particular advantages which a dynamic
> private sector has in this area of economic activity, the government

has decided to further open the doors to both indigenous and foreign private investors of manufacturing.[3]

In the same plan, political stability and availability of infrastructure were particularly believed to have much influence in attracting foreign investors. So, Nigeria's policy prescriptions were summarized in the plan in this way:

> In the attempt to aid the industrialization process, efforts have been made to attract desired industries through the granting of tax concessions to pioneer industries, the granting of relief from import duties and the imposition of tariff to protect infant industries. These policies have been pursued since the 1950s. As early as 1952, Aid to Pioneer Industries Ordinance was enacted. This law granted tax relief and similar concession to the industries prevailing at that time which were subsequently declared to be pioneer industries. A pioneer industry was defined in Industrial Development (Income Tax Relief) Ordinance, 1958 which superseded the 1952 Ordinance to mean "any industry which is not being carried on in Nigeria on a scale suitable to economic requirements of Nigeria, or at all and there are favorable prospects of further development of any (such) industry.[4]

For this reason, the tax relief granted to such industries in Nigeria was for at least the first two years of production operation. When such industries really become subject to taxation, they had capital allowances and allowance for variety of losses. Some of their dividends were further exempted from tax. In addition to these reliefs, all the imported inputs - machinery and capital equipment needed for production were exempted from import duty under the Industrial Development (Import Duties Relief) Ordinance of 1957. Also, majority of these industries were granted infant industry status. Therefore, protective import duties were place on the imported goods that competed with the goods such industries produced. At this point, however, the Industrial Development (Income Tax Relief) Ordinance, which became an act according to Nwankwo, was replaced by the Industrial Development (Income Tax Relief) Decree of 1971.

The decree further extended the initial tax - free period from two to three years.

Direct foreign investment was also supported through the granting of approved status to the industrial establishments in which international capital was invested or utilized for an approved objective. Also, the granting of approved status was an acceptance by the Federal government that approval in principle had been given for the repatriation of the investment capital at a future date by the foreign monopolies. Furthermore, approval was granted in practice for the repatriation of profits and dividends resulting from direct foreign investment. As Nwankwo states:

> Manufacturers in general also benefitted from the approved user scheme, from the Companies Income Tax Act of 1961 and the Companies Income Tax (Amendment) Decree, 1971. With the approved user scheme all imports used in the manufacturing at a concessionary rate of duty for a period of three years. The Companies Income Tax Act and Income Tax (Amendment) Decree permitted companies, both private and public, to effect a quick write-down of their capital assets in their early period of operation by granting them a high initial amortisation allowances as well as a high rate of subsequent annual amortisation. By this, mining and plantation capital assets and machinery could be written off within 6-7 years.[5]

Also, these concessions and allowances resulted in loss of revenue by the Federal government and much benefits to the business monopolies who are mainly consisted of foreign investors. Furthermore, those industries and firms that were granted the infant industry status were able to increase the prices of their goods to the level of prices of imported competing goods on which protective duty had been paid. This in the final analysis generated inflation in the economy. Moreover, with such an opportunity to receive excessive profits, a condition that did not exist in their respective home countries, the multinational firms and other foreign investors found Nigeria as a viable place for their economic operations.

THE AUTHORITY AND INFLUENCE
OF MULTINATIONAL CORPORATIONS

The significance of direct foreign investment in Africa and other LDCs varies from nation to nation.   In some countries, the activity of multinational corporations is generally low, whereas in others, it plays a significant role.   Multinational corporations more often than not tend to concentrate in a relatively few Third World nations.   For instance, only eighteen nations account for 86 percent of all direct foreign investment in the less developed countries.[6] In these nations, the power and influence of multinational corporations emerge out of their structural influence within the relatively poor and underdeveloped societies.

However, given the fact that agricultural and service areas still contribute more to gross national product of African states, the multinational corporations play little or no role in their total gross national product.   Meanwhile, foreign investment primarily accounts for a large share of important areas.   In reality, multinational corporations controlled African extractive area, necessary for development. Multinational corporations according to Spero:

> controlled oil in the Middle East, copper in Chile and Zambia, and bauxite in Jamaica and Guyana. In many cases, even when the ownership and control of production have been transferred from multinational corporations to state-owned companies, the developing countries remain dependent on the multinationals for processing, shipping, marketing, and distributing their raw materials. For example, in 1980, despite widespread nationalization of the petroleum industry in the developing countries, 43 percent of all crude oil produced outside North America and the socialist countries was either produced or purchased by the seven major international oil companies, and 24 percent was produced or purchased by

smaller international oil companies, or trading companies. In 1982, 46 percent of the world's bauxite capacity, 50 percent of its alumina capacity, and 45 percent of its aluminum capacity were owned by six large multinational corporations.[7]

Also, since 1945, African states have sought to expand their industrial area as a strategy for development and have provided attractive incentives for investment in manufacturing sector. However, multinational corporations have taken the lead in these areas. Foreign investment is increasing more rapidly than ever in manufacturing sector and is hence accelerating to dominate specific areas of the new African industries. In Africa today, foreign companies control more than 31 percent of export, 42 percent of production, and 28 percent of employment in manufacturing sectors.

Furthermore, multinational corporations stand for a significant percentage of the largest if not the most powerful businesses in African economies. For one thing, foreign investment in Africa primarily is found in industries dominated by a small number of large multinational corporations. For instance, American foreign investment is centered on industries such as chemicals, insurance, transportation, machinery, food products, petroleum and electronics. The predominant corporations that dominate such industries have strong power to control supply and regulate price than those in competitive industries. Hence, the oligopolistic structure of international investment indicates that important economic power is controlled by few large multinational corporations.

WHAT IS GOOD FOR THE GOOSE IS NOT GOOD FOR THE GANDER: THE OPPOSING VIEWS OF MNCS

The rapid increase in the international activities of firms whose parent corporations are located elsewhere and their increasing hegemony of the world economy are the main reasons that the multinational corporations have merited attention. However, the word multinational corporations often evoke strong emotional responses, suggesting that the multinational corporations have become more than simply the agents of the international system of production and exchange. The expected cost and benefits analysis of the multinational corporations are usually great as we shall see in the later part of this chapter. Sometimes we may ask whether the multinational corporations have become so powerful as to undermine the ability and capability of countries to control their own destiny. Perhaps, it seems possible that multinational corporations are seriously undermining the structure of the present international economic foundation. The concept of multinational corporation is generally used to describe the instrumentality of this transnational phenomenon, which has led to the internationalization of production. The implication of this development is suggested by estimates that by the year 2020 more than three quarters of industrial production in the world will be produced by a handful of multinational enterprises. Table 5:1 provides the changing profile of the top multinational corporations in 1980. This Table indicates the leading multinational corporations according to the value of their 1980 sales. Exxon heads the list with $103 billion. This amount was larger than the gross national product (GNP) of all but twenty-two countries. No single African state, and only two Latin American states (Brazil and Mexico) and three Asian states (Japan, China, and India) had a gross national product greater than Exxon's sales. Also, in addition to Exxon, Mobil, Texaco, Standard Oil of California, Royal Dutch Shell, General Motors, and Ford had more than $30 billion of sales each year. The above table further suggests that majority of the MNCs are in the oil industry of which eight of the top ten MNCs are oil corporations mainly owned by the U.S.

With reference to one analyst, about 250 of the largest multinational manufacture and extractive businesses are located in

America, 150 in various European nations, 70 in Japan, and 20 in the rest of the world. In the same token, the United States is the home nation for 20 of the largest multinational banks compared with 13 for various European nations, 9 for Japan, and 3 for Canada.[8]

As of this writing, Concern about and attention to the multinational enterprises have continued to be greater among the LDCs, since Multinational enterprises are of primary important to the LDCs overall gross national product and to their most advanced economic areas. The less developed countries' perceptions of the multinational firms have also been more charged emotionally, since these predominantly industrialized countries'-based economic giants are perceived through nationalistic eyes of newly independent states as promoters of neocolonialism and subimperialism.

Given the fact that discussions on multinational enterprises are done by observers who start quite often from different ideological points of view and with quite different sets of facts, observers have clearly arrived at different conclusions about the implications of direct foreign investment by multinational enterprises in Third World countries.[9] Supporters of multinational corporations argue that the MNCs are not only important but also beneficial to the survival of the capitalist system. They argue that the operations of MNCs bring a lot of advantages to the Third World countries, especially technological training and knowledge resulting from the large capital expended on research and development.[10] Proponents of direct foreign investment believe that such investment helps to promote rapid economic development in Africa and other less-developed countries, because, they claim, that foreign firm provides: technological assistance, "hard-to-find" capital, managerial, and organizational skills. These proponents contend that foreign investors are usually able to mobilize both foreign and local capital which otherwise could have been invested elsewhere. They point out that MNCs provide specially qualified personnel

TABLE 5:1
LEADING MULTINATIONAL CORPORATIONS, 1980

Company	Nationality	Sales Millions U.S.$)	Income (or Loss) (Millions U.S.$)	Industry Group
Exxon	U.S.	103,143	5,650	Oil
Royal Dutch Shell	Dutch-British	77,114	5,174	Oil
Mobil	U.S.	59,510	3,272	Oil
General Motors	U.S.	57,729	(763)	Auto
Texaco	U.S.	51,196	2,643	Oil
British Petroleum	British	48,036	3,337	Oil
Standard Oil of California	U.S.	40,479	2,401	Oil
Ford Motor	U.S.	37,086	(1,543)	Auto
ENI	Italian	27,187	98	Oil
Gulf Oil	U.S.	26,483	1,407	Oil
International Business Machines	U.S.	26,213	3,562	Electronic
Standard Oil of Indiana	U.S.	26,133	1,915	Oil
Fiat	Italian	25,155	N/A	Auto
General Electric	U.S.	24,959	1,514	Electrical
Francaise des Petroles	French	23,940	947	Oil
Atlantic Richfield	U.S.	23,744	1,651	Oil
Unilever	British - Dutch	23,608	659	Consumer
Renault	French	18,979	160	Auto
Petroleos de Venezuela	Venezuelan	18,819	3,451	Oil
International Telephone & Telegraph	U.S.	18,530	1,378	Electronic
Elf Acquitaine	Frence	18,430	1,378	Oil

TABLE 5:1 CONTINUED
LEADING MULTINATIONAL CORPORATIONS, 1980

Company	Nationality	Sales (Millions U.S.$)	Income (or Loss (Millions U.S.$)	Industry Group
Philips' Gloeilampenfabrieken	Dutch	18,403	165	Electroni
Volkswagenwerk	West German	18,339	171	Auto
Conoco	U.S.	18,325	1,036	Oil
Imens	West German	17,950	332	Electrica
Daimler-Benz	West German	17,108	605	Auto
Peugeot	French	16,846	(349)	Auto
Hoechst	West German	16,481	252	Chemica
Bayer	West German	15,881	351	Chemica
BASF	West German	15,227	198	Chemica

SOURCE: The World Almanac and Book of Facts, 1982 edition, copyright Newspaper Enterprise Association, Inc., 1981, New York, NY.

that is able to train both local labor and management personnel.[11] They argue that the multinational businesses are capable, as a result of their production, marketing and control systems facilitate exports from the developing nations. These advocates of the MNCs believe that without the direct foreign investments of the multinational firms, it would have been almost impossible for the less-developed countries to develop their mining and agricultural exports. They claim that multinational enterprises provide socio-economic advantages and benefits such as increased revenues to boost national income, provision and development of modern amenities such as recreational facilities, pipe-borne water, roads, health centers and so on which in turn "quicken" political and economic development. The advocates of foreign investments argue that the presence of MNCs breaks down monopolies of domestic businessmen and exposes domestic producers and businessmen to strong competition thereby resulting in lower prices for consumers. In the view of these advocates of MNCs, the large foreign corporations and their direct investments are indispensable to Africa and other less-developed countries if they are to develop at all. For example, in his analysis of the impacts of MNCs, John Fayeweather comments that:

> Multinational corporations which have evolved as the central institution in the tremendous post-war expansion of the international capitalism have two basic roles: Transmission of resources, especially technological and managerial skills, and organization of unified multinational economic activities, notably in fields where there are advantages from the global integration of research and development, logistics, and financing. In pursuit of these roles the multinational corporations encounters fundamental obstacles in nationalism and the structure of the nation state. Nationalistic resistance to outsiders (including the multinational corporations) is aroused by the MNC which penetrates host nations, exercising control and extracting profits. Its global approach to economic decisions that is often at odds with the nation-oriented criteria of governments. Furthermore, its control of critical economic elements, notably technology and investment weakens the ability of national elites to control their own national affairs. This situation generates periods of tension and mutual suspicion between the multinational corporations and the nation-state. [12]

Fayeweather supports strongly the view that LDCs have "benefits" to derive from allowing the multinational corporations' "free hand" in the host countries.

The critics of Multinational enterprises have a different perspective. In relation to governments of both developed and less developed countries that lament that they cannot control the activities and actions of multinational enterprises, labor unions criticize the multinational businesses for their ability to relocate in areas where labor is unorganized and/or inexpensive. By building plants and equipment with excessive capability, multinational corporations can insulate themselves from Labor's most useful weapon, the strike.

In addition, nationalists generally criticize multinational corporations and their economic philosophy. As we have already mentioned earlier in this chapter, most multinational firms are based in America, Western Europe, and Japan, and this led many LDCs to reject MNCs as agents of western imperialism and neocolonialism as well as the promoters of International Capitalism.

In reality, the best evaluation of these and other critical assessments of multinational enterprises appeared in Global Reach, a book written in 1974 by Richard J. Barnet and Ronald Muller. In this book, Barnet and Muller argue that the multinational corporations utilize managerial capability and technical know-how available only in the Western World and cheap labor and inexpensive resources available specifically in the less developed countries to maximize and increase their profits without making essential contributions to the countries where they operate. In addition, Barnet and Muller proceed, multinational enterprises do not bring in large quantities of external capital but rather use available capital that could be utilized for other purposes within LDCs. With their superior capital-intensive techniques, MNCs drive other labor-intensive local market competitors out of business operation, hence seriously accelerating unemployment in a host state. Also, multinational enterprises are accused of destroying traditional cultures by idealization of sophisticated advertising mechanisms, and replacing them with local versions of Europeans and North

American consumer societies. Because profit on the international levels is the primary objective of MNCs, the Multinational Corporations are primarily accused of ignoring local questions such as health, nutrition, environmental quality, resource conservation and preservation.

The classic example is the 1980s' endeavors of the Nestle Corporation and other global distributors of powdered dry baby formula to market their product to the less-developed countries including African states. The multinational corporations, at this point argued that dry baby formula was as good or even better than mothers' natural milk in providing the nutritional needs of infants. However, they refused to consider the quality of the LDCs water supplies, which are often undrinkable. By mixing formula with water, mothers in Third World countries would in reality be exposing their little babies to a variety of diseases that they could otherwise prevent by drinking their mother's milk. Another danger to infants occurred when, in endeavors to economize, mothers use too little formula into each measure of water. This will result to malnutrition between and among infants.

According to Barnet and Muller, continued unbridled operation of multinational firms in the less-developed nations will inevitably lead to more unemployment, poor nutrition and health standards, more environmental degradation, and more inequitable distribution of wealth in the LDCs.

In a position different from those of advocates of MNCs, Barnet and Muller ask whether MNCs can adapt to a radically revised concept that growth is not enough; that it is more essential to ask who gains and who loses in a nation's development activity, and whether growth without internal reform inevitably ignores--and even exacerbates the plight of the impoverished majority in the underdeveloped world who were left behind during the so-called "Decade of Development" of the 1960s. Contrary to the arguments of supporters of foreign investments, studies have shown that large firms invest in African states primarily to exploit special benefits. The question then is whether while the MNCs are exploiting special benefits, the host countries are actually receiving adequate benefits. For example, in the study by one of the scholars on multinational corporations it was indicated that:

> With the development of large capitalist monopolies in the leading capitalist countries, the capitalists of those countries lost interest in developmental investment in the less developed countries because such investment threatened their established monopolistic positions-- (developmental investment: investment which can actually lead to development such as investment in infrastructure, manufacturing etc. which will also threaten the established monopoly position of the developed capitalist nations and reduce their profits)-- Consequently, investment in underdeveloped countries of capital from the highly developed countries acquired a specific character. it went chiefly into the exploitation of natural resources to be utilized as raw materials by the industries of the developed countries; and into developing food production in the under-developed countries to feed the population of the developed capitalist countries. It also went into economic infrastructures...needed to maintain economic relations with the underdeveloped countries.[13]

According to these scholars, the profits which were made by foreign capital were exported back to the country in which the capital came from. Or if used for investment they were not used for industrial development on any major scale, which, as we know from experience, is the real dynamic factor of modern economic development.

Furthermore, the majority of capitalist powers encouraged the feudal [and bureaucratic elite] elements in the less developed countries as an instrument for maintaining their economic and political influence. This provided another obstacle to the economic development of these countries. In his study of the situation, Arrighi stipulated that the origin of the large-scale corporation was the typical unit of production in advanced capitalist societies which has momentous effects for the process of development in the still Third World area.[14]

Scholars on MNCs such as Roger believe that influencing governments is legitimate while influencing them through corruption, undue pressures, and unethical practices, is wrong and objectionable.   To him, what matters, therefore, is the purpose, the method, and the manner of exerting influence. Roger acknowledged that national and international economies may be in conflict at certain times, on certain issues, or even on certain broad philosophies. According to Roger, if MNCs are to carry fully their functions, they must pursue the internationalization of financing, production, distribution, and organization as a whole to the greatest possible extent. This aim and modus operandi may be in conflict with contingent policies of one government or another. There is no escape. There is also, the possibility of alleviating the conflict by adopting flexible criteria and adjusting to local social, political, and economic conditions, without departing from an international approach. If the conflict between the global economy and a given national economy or between the aims and objectives for a multinational enterprise and a given national economy is not reconcilable, then that economy is not suited to the operations of a multinational enterprises, and the latter should go elsewhere in the world for its investment.

Roger believes that what he had stated is becoming the case increasingly in certain countries "where nationalism is taking the upperhand and where a majority or even higher proportion of equity participation must be by local businesses or where other restrictive provisions impede the fulfillment of multinational duties and objectives." He explains:

> Taken as a whole and apart from certain temporary and even explosive crisis, the world is open to the operations of multinational corporations. If there are some spots here and there where they are incompatible with local conditions and policies, companies should not insist on trying to sew a land which is not fertile...This writer firmly believes that there is no case for an irremediable conflict between sovereignty and multinationalism. The alleged tensions between them are neither basic nor permanent, but they are rather

the result of psychological reactions to spotty instances. The so-called tensions between nation-states and multinational corporationsare not very often different from those confronting government and business in normal course of their mutual relations.[15]

Also Charles P. Kindleberger (one of the leading authorities in the U.S. on international economics states that, "the international corporation has no country to which it owes more loyalty than any other nor any country where it feels completely at home."[16] The governments in LDCs are almost always ill-equipped to deal with the giant corporations which often present them with seemingly beneficial and highly attractive investment strategies.

In contrary to this argument, Prebisch, another observer of the operation of foreign firms, emphasizes that the terms of trade between the "industrial cores" and the "periphery" of the global economic system have behaved in the opposite way than one would expect from the competitive model. Prebisch's position is that in that model the faster technical progress in the industrial cores, relative to the "periphery", ought to result in increasing prices of industrial products relative to primary products.[17] He further showes that as a result of stronger power of workers and oligopolist in the industrial cores than the power of workers and capitalists in the "periphery," in the cores the incomes of entrepreneurs and of productive factors increase relatively more than productivity, whereas in the "periphery" the increase in income is less than that in productivity. [18] In support of this view Michael Manley, Prime Minister of Jamaica, in his demonstration on foreign investments stated that:

That relationship {the one between the producing and the manufacturing countries/simply stated involved a manufacturing country paying token recognition in the form of a royalty to a host country for the privilege of extracting its natural resources and then removing these raw materials to its home-base for refining and other processing. Normally the host country rarely participated in even the primary stage of the manufacturing process. Thus it was denied the benefits (whether in employment or expertise) of rudimentary technology. The rationale from the point of view of the multinational corporations--that is, IBM, ITT, oil companies, and others--involved in this exploitation, was simple: It was cheaper and more economical to transport the raw material to its own refineries at home. It was also probably considered safer, both from the profit and, in some cases, the military or strategic point of view.[19]

Furthermore, Manley argues that the growth of the multinational enterprises in the last twenty years poses major dangers to the international community in two ways. He believes that first, MNCs conspire against the free enterprise ethic by invisible forms of price-fixing, and second, MNCs are regarded as being sacred and representative of the best of the American (and capitalist) way of life. In explaining these two points, Manley points out that because MNCs control all stages of production from raw material to the finished and packaged product, few areas exist in which its operations are either an object of scrutiny or competition, hence their oligopolistic and monopoly practices. To quote Manley:

> In a sense they have taken over the imperialist or "colonizing" role of earlier days in the Third World without any of the accompanying benefits of direct occupation (preferential economic treatment and educational facilities), guided only by the profit ethic and accountable only to their stockholders.[20]

In a similar fashion to that of Manley, one scholar on multinational corporations argues that international firms backed by their parent countries perpetuate the underdevelopment of the LDCs through monopoly controls over the utilization of its resources. According to O'Connor, indirect control of local capital in Asia, Latin America, and Africa is pervasive; the mobilization of local capital, control of subcontractors, and other suppliers, "management contracts" which afford foreign capital day-to-day control of joint ventures, and licensing agreements which restrict the use of technology by prohibiting "fundamental investigation and research" extend the way of foreign capital still further, and multiply the quantitative impact of the international corporations on the misutilization of resources abroad.

In a nutshell, raw material investments tend to make less developed nations mere appendages of advanced capitalist states, depriving them of any opportunity for autonomous, ongoing economic development, and thwarting the development of industry and an industrial bourgeoisie. The companies provide the institutional framework for many Third World countries, particularly the smaller, more vulnerable societies. Integrating more and more resources into their own structures, the international businesses are able to mobilize, transform, and dispose of capital on a regional or even world-wide scale--in effect, constituting themselves as extraterritorial bodies.

Production objectives and techniques, investment measure, labor relations, prices, profit allocation, purchasing, distribution, and marketing policies are all decided from the standpoint of the profit objectives of the international business "whether or not these objectives are consistent with local economic development." The corporations are the channels for the diffusion of technology and consumption patterns; again, profits come first, local needs second. Supporters of big businesses have even occasionally agreed that the profit maximization objectives of foreign firms may not be compatible with the interests of the host countries.[21]

Also, Giovanni Arrighi has related the situation to Africa. He described foreign firms operating in tropical Africa as: The typical expatriate business operating in tropical African States is more and more what has been called the multinational enterprise for the "great inter-territorial unit", i.e., an organized ensemble of means of production subject to a single policy-making center which controls establishments situated in several different national territories.[22]

Arrighi provided the conclusion that centralized decision making policy used by MNCs is detrimental to the national interests of the less developed countries. In support of the above view, Richard Barnet and Ronald Muller have demonstrated that the international approach to management used by the MNCs is quite often incompatible with national or local interests. They remarked that the most revolutionary aspect of the planetary enterprise is not its size but its world view. The men who run the international businesses are the first in history with the organization, technology, money, and ideology to make a try at managing the world as an integrated unit.[23]

Barnet and Muller clearly point out how "international corporations are integrating the global economy into a single unit in which resources are deployed so as to rationalize worldwide production in accordance with economic efficiency. They wonder if the nationalists who seek to impose restrictions on the activities of MNCs by imposing limitations on their free movement of capital, technology and managerial skill are actually sabotaging corporate international economic progress and efficiency. These scholars challenge the feeling that MNCs are engineering worldwide economic rationalization, promoting rapid economic progress and plenty including world peace. They argue that in Third World countries, the operations of the MNCs in trying to influence economic growth have often been accompanied by massive unemployment, wider gap between the rich and the poor, and a wider gap between the developed and the underdeveloped countries as well as increased inequality for the citizens of the host countries, especially between the local elites and the polities.[24]

CONCLUDING COMMENTS

Multinational corporations, as we have seen, claim to have the experience, expertise and resources to structure and restructure a more effectively productive world, and hence improve world living standards. According to MNC specialists, only the unique blend of size, centralization and internationalization peculiar to multinational enterprises, they believe, can bring about the world reality of comparative advantage. As envisioned by British economists David Richardo and John S. Mill during the nineteenth century, the idea of comparative advantage states generally that commodities should be produced wherever they can be produced at least cost per unit, and that goods produced at one place should be imported and paid for with excess internal commodities. However, as an economic theory, the law of comparative advantage has been operationalized by multinational enterprises.

Furthermore, multinational corporations do not stop their argument on their corporations with their assertions that multinational enterprises will improve the global living standards. They also believe that multinational enterprises help the Third World countries to modernize, industrialize and develop by transferring technology, providing employment opportunities, and expertise to restructure the less developed economies. The advantages and benefits of economic surplus would therefore not be restricted to the advanced industrial societies but would be extended throughout international community and all human societies.

Generally, the most ardent proponents and the most vocal critics of the multinational enterprise are separated by a wide chasm. Both agree that the size, centralization of decision-making and international flexibility of MNCs give them an almost unprecedented power and opportunity to act in the global community. The advocates and critics, however, disagree as to the end results of their actions. The advocates of multinational corporation see improved living standards, more employment, and a less conflict world, if they are only allowed to operate in a global community without governmental intervention and more generally accepted set of world standards. Hence, when multinational corporation proponents specifically speak of regulation of MNCs, they mean international control that would enhance the operating environment and capability for the multinational enterprises.

Conversely, the critics of MNC see higher unemployment, poor living standards, and a more elitist world with largely unequal distribution of wealth if multinational corporations continue to operate without increased subnational , supranational and/or national control.   Therefore, when critics of MNC generally speak for the control of multinational firms, they seriously mean control that would reduce the capability of multinationals to make decisions on their own without government regulation at some point.

Thus, as the debate among advocates and critics of MNCs should make clear, the function of multinational enterprises in contemporary global relations is essential.   However, the more extreme claims of both advocates and critics of multinational firms can perhaps be safely ignored, it is somehow true that a conflicting body of evidence exists concerning the function of multinational corporations in today's international community. Therefpre, for students and scholars of international relations, multinational corporations must still remain a body of inquiry for years ahead.

NOTES

1. Arthur A. Nwankwo, *Can Nigeria Survive* (Enugu: Fourth Dimension Publishers, 1981).
2. Ibid., p.5.
3. Ibid., p. 25.
4. Ibid., pp. 25-26.
5. Ibid., pp., 28-92.
6. For detailed analysis of Multinational Corporation Action in LDCs, See United Nation Center on Transnational Corporations (hereafter UNCTC), Transnational Corporations in the World Development: Trends and Prospects (New York: United Nations, 1980), p. 18. The States are Brazil, China, Chile, Egypt, Argentina, Nigeria, Taiwan, Oman, Mexico, Indonesia,

Malaysia, Colombia, Hong Kong, Singapore, Trinida and Tobago, Venezuela, Thailand and Tunisia.

7. Spero, *The Politics of International Economic Relations*, p. 237.

8. Steve Chan, *International Relations in Perspective: The Pursuit of Security, Welfare, and Justice* (New York: Macmillian Publishing Company, 1984), p 271.

9. See among other works: Norman Girvan, *Foreign Capital and Underdevelopment in Jamaica*, Institute of Social and Economic Research, University of West Indies, Jamaica, 1971; Louis Turner, *Multinational Companies and the Third World* (New York: Hill and Wang, 1973). Charles K. Wilber, ed. *The Political Economy of Development and Underdevelopment* (New York: Random House, 1973), and Norman Girvan, "Making the Rules of the Game: Country-Company Agreements in the Bauxite Industry" *Social and Economic Studies*, Institute of Social and Economic Research, Univ. of the West Indies, Vol. 20, No. 4, Dec. 1971.

10. See for example, John Kenneth Galbraith, *The New Industrial State*, Boston: Houghton Mifflin, 1973, and also his *Economics and the Public Purpose* (Houghton Mifflin, 1973). See also Joseph Schumpteter, *Imperialism and Social Classes* (New York, 1951). Among the earlier assessments of the pros and cons of MNCs, see Samuel Huntington, "Transnational Organizations in World Politics," *World Politics*, 25 (April 1973), and John Diebold, "Multinational Corporations-Why Be Scared of Them?" *Foreign Policy*, No. 12 (Fall 1973).

11. For extensive and divergent views on multinational corporations and the impact of their investments and operations in the less-developed countries see Annals of American Academy of Political and Social Sciences. The Multinational Corporation, Vol. 403, (September 1972). Samuel P. Huntington, "Transnational Organizations in *World Politics*," World Politics, XXV (April 1973); Joseph S. Nye, Jr., "Multinational Corporations in World Politics," *Foreign Affairs*, 53 (October 1974); Robert Gilpin, U.S. *Power and the Multinational Corporation* (New York: Basic Books, 1975); David E. Apter and Louis Wold Goodman, eds., *The Multinational Corporation and Social Change* (New York: Praeger, 1976); Raymond Vernon, *Storm over the Multinationals: The Real Issues* (Cambridge, Mass.: Harvard University Press, 1977).

12. John Fayeweather, "The Internationalization of Business" in Annals of American Academy of Political and Social Sciences: *The Multinational Corporation*, Vol. 403, (September 1972), p. 1. See also John Fayeweather, "Nationalism and the International Firm" in A. Kapoor and Phillip Grub, eds. *The Multinational Enterprise in Transition* (Princeton, N.J.: Darwin, 1972).

13. Oscar Lange, *Economic Development, Planning and International* Corporation (New York, 1963), pp. 10-11.

14. Ibid.

15. Ibid.

16. Charles P. kindleberger, quoted in Barnet and Muller, *Global Reach*, op. cit., p. 16.

17. Giovanni Arrighi and John S. Saul, *Essays on the Political Economy of Africa*, pp. 105-110. George Modelski, ed., Transnational Corporations and World Order (San Francisco: Freeman, 1979); Charles W. Kegley, Jr., and Eugene R. Wittkopf, eds., "The Rise of Multinational Corporations: Blessing or Burse?" in chap. 5 of their *World Politics: Trend and Transformation* (New York: St. Martin's, 1981); Joan Edelman Spero, *The Politics of International Economic Relations*, 3rd ed. (New York: St. Martin's, 1985), chaps 4 and 8; and Robert T. Kudrle, "The Several Faces of the Multinational Corporation," in Jeffrey A. Frieden and David A. Lake, eds., *International Political Economy* (New York: St. Martin's 1987).

18. R. Prebisch American Economic Review Papers and Proceedings (May 1959).

19. Michael Manley, "Jamaica's White Gold" in Encore, (November 1974), pp. 18 and 19.

20. Ibid.

21. James O'Connor, The Corporation and The State op. cit.

22. Giovanni Arrighi citing from "Multinational Companies, a Special Report," *Business Week,* (April 20, 1963). See also Giovanni Arrighi, "International Corporations, Labor Aristocracies, and Economic Development in Africa" in Giovanni Arrighi and John S. Saul, Essays on the Political Economy of Africa, op. cit.

23. Richard J. Barnet and Ronald E. Muller, *Global Reach*, op. cit., p. 179.

24. Ibid., pp. 179-189.

The Physical geography of Africa

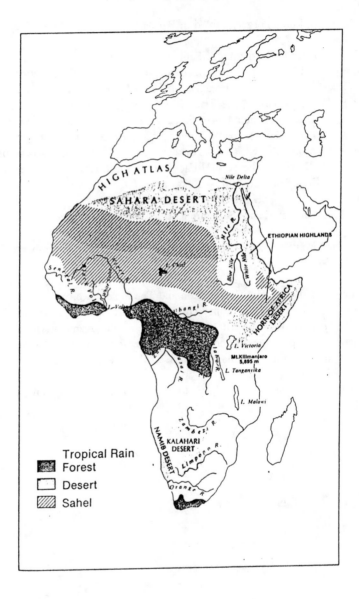

CHAPTER 6

Socio-Economic and Political Implications of Multinational Corporations in Africa

In chapter five, the general features and power of the multinational corporations were provided. Also, the arguments of the advocates and the critics of multinational firms were presented. In this particular chapter, efforts were made to examine, analyze, and evaluate the actual impact and socio-economic implications of the multinational corporations in contemporary Africa.

The function and implications of foreign capital investment in the less developed countries of Africa form one of the most controversial and sensitive issues in development policy measure. The realities concerning this issues may be seem in this way: There is the perspective of orthodox "pure economics, which perceives the problem as the need for external financial resources and the transfer of technology. This perspective attributes almost exclusively positive effects to the import of foreign capital and personnel. It is deeply rooted in the orthodox apologetic concept of "underdevelopment," which asserts that the present state of third world nations is simply an earlier and lower, but natural, stage of growth, compared to that of the developed countries; it does not search for origins of the problem in the historical development of the international capitalist division of labor.[1]

> The political recommendation following from this concept is quite simple: Even if there be some relatively negative side effects temporarily, such as the demonstration effect, real development (breaking into the "vicious circle") depends on the inflow of foreign capital and personnel, which creates a "hospitable climate of investment" for foreign investors. This in fact means giving the latter a free hand, retaining at most and indirect influence on their activity via monetary and fiscal policy.[2]

One of the most disastrous effects of direct foreign investment is the peculiar socio-economic structure itself which it has brought about. This structure is characterized by the lack of internal integration, which, manifests itself in the dualism of capitalist and procapitalist socio-economic areas. The wide and long-lasting co-existence of export economies side by side, and the distortion of the sectoral arrangement of economy and the weakness of inter sectoral linkages.[3]

The distortion and dualism of the economy are generally the products of the historical reality that, instead of the internal self evolution of economy, it was the colonial penetration of international capital which gave rise in certain manners to the capitalist mode of production and linked the economies of Africa to the international market. Eventually, these changes which would have been positive purse, as well as their conditions and results, were not determined by the internal laws of development, but instead by an external variable, the interests of international monopolies.

MULTINATIONAL STRATEGY
AND FOREIGN EXCHANGE EARNINGS

Now majority of African countries are working seriously to industrialize, nearly all developing African states are making serious shift away from raw-material exporting to import-substituting manufacturing industries. The importation of capital goods from the advanced capitalist societies for industrialization and development objectives causes serious balance of payments disequilibria for almost all African states .

The high prices paid for capital and consumer goods, including military equipment ammunition from the multinational enterprises and their subsidiary businesses drain further the foreign reserves of the less developed countries of Africa. This is one of the main reasons why majority of African countries turn to foreign loans which again require debt-servicing. It is not surprising that most, if not all, African nations are seriously in trouble over servicing their international debts (see chapter 11 table 11:8).

In addition, Barnet and Muller have demonstrated how the expansion of U. S. based multinational banks, unconstrained by any governmental regulations, has led to a concentration of financial assets in 20 or 30 banks, characterized by interlocking directorates. They further point out how these banks are exercising a critical influence on corporate policy, especially that corporations have come to rely increasingly on debt financing for capital expansion. What results as Barnet and Muller, among others, have shown is a clear picture of oligopolistic corporate and financial power merging together to create a dominating and an imperialist power for the multinational corporations. This is in conformity with Marx's and later Lenin's analysis of the characteristic features of capitalism. Through interlocking, directorates, and organizational techniques multinational corporations have come to rely on internal sources as well as debt financing for capital expansion. The multinational banks are exercising profound influence on corporate policy of the giant companies. What emerges from this relationship is an oligopolistic corporate domination of capital resources with little or no attention to external or non-corporate financial resources. This situation has adverse effects on local capital market and financial sources. Branch plants or subsidiaries of MNCs usually practice discriminatory policies against local products, discourage import-substituting efforts of national governments and encourage importation of foreign products, especially from their parent companies and other subsidiaries abroad. As a result of very powerful marketing and advertising mechanisms which foreign firms are able to employ in the less developed countries, the consumption pattern in the poor countries have been geared towards the "tastes" and consumption patterns of the industrialized nations. The multinational corporations have thus succeeded in homogenizing world demand for both capital and consumer goods. James O'Connor commented on the situation as follows:

> The present built-in bias toward importation of supplies from parent corporations inhibits import-substitute industrialization programs....At best, import-substitute industrialization under the auspices of the international corporation merely changes the composition of import, leaving the dynamic of expansion with the traditional export section. The profitability of the parent corporation is assisted by every influence which eliminates cultural resistance to the consumption patterns of the metropolis. The corporation thus has a vested interest in the destruction of cultural differences and homogenization of the way of life, the world over. For one thing, the lack of integration of foreign investments into the local economy, especially branch plants which exist only to provide a market for the parent corporation, places heavy pressures on foreign exchange reserves.[4]

The changed consumption pattern and mode of living of nationals of less developed countries of Africa caused by the imported style of living and mode of production of the advanced capitalist societies constitute a big drainon the revenues of the

TABLE 6:1
AFRICA: SELECTED ECONOMIC INDICATORS, 1973-84

	1973	1975	1977	1979	1981	1983	1984
Economic growth	2.39	2.75	2.30	2.00	1.70	0.80	3.20
Inflation	9.86	15.84	24.30	22.90	28.00	26.50	17.00
Term of Trade	8.30	-12.19	18.10	2.70	-3.00	-0.10	3.50
Ratio of external debt to GDP	4.90	27.50	36.00	37.90	43.40	54.60	57.70
Debt service ratio		9.50	11.90	15.50	18.70	22.60	24.90
Current account	-4.50	-7.20	-6.60	-9.60	-14.40	-10.20	-9.40
Net official transfers	1.10	1.7	2.30	3.00	3.40	3.30	3.40
Net capital inflows	3.80	4.90	5.00	6.40	8.40	5.40	5.10
Overall balance of payments	0.50	-0.60	0.70	-0.20	-2.30	-1.50	-0.90
Total outstanding debt	11.60	18.40	31.00	45.10	56.30	62.20	69.30

SOURCE: International Monetary Fund, Current Studies Division, Research Department, and World Economic Outlook (Occasional Paper No. 27, 1984).

African countries. The development of 1) a petty-bourgeoisie, 2) technocrats, 3) local bureaucrats, and 4) local capitalist and industrial labor class equally increase the problem of class formation and division in less developed countries of Africa. The new elite class quickly becomes supporters of the "status quo" and very resistant to change. Their new consumption pattern leads to importation of expensive luxury goods for the local affluent to the detriment of local products and the scarce foreign exchange earnings of African states. The very low and unsatisfactory regional economic cooperation between the less developed countries of Africa also constitute an unnecessary drainage on their foreign exchange resources. Using Africa as an example, Nwankwo proceeds: "Since the period of about twelve years (1970-1982) profit remittances, debt service, royalties and other invisible financial services alone accounted for nearly 50 percent of the regions foreign exchange earnings."[5]

By usually understating the true profits on their earnings, and by keeping the prices of imports high, foreign companies are able to deprive their host countries of large revenue. Apart from inflating their real costs of operating and making questionable and complex claims and deductions to reduce actual levels of profit, multinational enterprises specifically extract large additional income from interlocking relationships with their associate-and other intra-company sales and operations within a given nation. According to Dale R. Weigel, several occasions of overcharging by foreign companies have been documented in Colombia, where subsidiaries in the pharmaceutical industry were said to have paid 155 percent more than the C.I.F. price of intermediate drugs imported from their parent firms. Weigel also pointed out that over-charging of 40 percent was also found in the rubber industry, 26 percent in the chemical industry, and 16-20 percent in the electronic industry. Commenting on the situation, Weigel has this to say:

> While it is possible to dispute these figures, there can be little doubt that multinational corporations sometimes do use intra-firm sales to transfer profits out of developing countries, particularly when the host country limits dividend repatriation.[6]

One major reason for intra-firm manipulations by multi-national enterprises is their desire to reduce local taxes to host countries and to circumvent the restrictions by the host countries on dividend repatriations. A comparison of the balance of trade of the advanced capitalist and the developing countries shows clearly the impact of corporate practices upon the less developed countries. The developing non-industrialized countries were virtually the dumping grounds for the exports of developed countries.

In his study on multinational corporations, James O'Connor has pointed out that the MNCs overcharge their manufactured products to less developed countries and underprice the raw materials from the poor countries. According to O'Connor, "the large businesses seek to buy the output of small independent producers at depressed prices; second, that low prices discourage the development of new independent producers and hence potential competition; third, that depressed prices reduce foreign exchange risks when local governments attempt to reduce profit remittances; and last, that low buying prices mean that the corporations pay fewer taxes and lower royalties and wages."[7] In general, the foreign firm mechanism is; an effective instrument for maximizing the appropriation of surplus from satellite economies by metropolitan economies. On the one hand, the parent corporation charges its branch plants (in both the raw materials and manufacturing sectors) the highest price possible, in order to maximize profits on exports, and as a hedge against local government restrictions on profit remittances. However, the parent corporation's interests are best served by keeping final product prices in the Third World Nation as high as possible, consistent with the role of the branch plant as the parent's export market. On the other hand, the parent company purchases raw materials from its branches and subsidiaries at the lowest possible price. Bauxite, iron ore and copper--among other minerals [including crude oil until recently]--all tend to be undervalued.[8]

The overpricing of imports and the underpricing of raw materials in the less developed countries cause the poor nations balance-of-payment problems. The effects of the same policy for the industrialized nations are large profits and relatively low prices compared to those in the less developed countries.

TECHNOLOGICAL CONSEQUENCES OF MNCS IN THE POLITICAL ECONOMY OF AFRICA

It is a well-known reality that although the much vaunted technology of foreign business may be employed in the less developed countries, it is not actually transferred to nationals of the host country. This is so because the key technical and managerial positions are almost always reserved for expatriates except where the host country is able to impose effective quota system on the foreign monopoly. The package of capital, technology, managerial skill and other benefits are often provided by the multinational enterprises to the less developed countries of Africa at expensive cost. Also, the multinational enterprises sell advanced technology to the less developed nations and fail to adapt it to local situation.

Furthermore, the transfer of technology to the less developed countries of Africa generally attributed to the multinational enterprises has not been as beneficial to the citizens of African states as has often been believed. The type of technology transferred to Africa is not the kind that can be readily purchased or learned by indigenous businessmen. The multinational corporations have more often than not kept the most essential technology which can actually lead to development exclusively to their own technocrats. As Alavi puts it:

> Typically, strict control is sought over the use to which the techniques imported are put...The supplier of the new technique is often protected from imparting a complete technology by clauses which specially exclude fundamental investigation and development...The Indian concern is often effectively prevented from adopting products or processes to local ancillary industries and

so becomes even more dependent on imported supplies.-- Imperialism.[9]

Also, multinational corporations do very little to adapt their production processes and technology which are designed and developed specifically for use in the advanced capitalist societies. The primary reason generally given for this poor performance in actually transferring appropriate technology to the African economies is that the African states lack skilled and highly trained indigenous experts capable to handle the highly technical management and operations of modern business enterprises which are by their nature very difficult.

Transnational corporations usually ensure that in the contracts they sign with the African governments, restrictions are placed upon local control of technology. These corporations do everything possible to discourage (and ensure that their branches in the Third World countries do not apply) technological resources to local technological problems beyond or above what international businesses consider to be desirable for their limited interests of profit maximization, loss minimization and domination of the industry and the available resources. This is one of the main reasons why many industries or firms in Africa and other less developed countries find it difficult to compete effectively or efficiently with the international business and have not been able to capture the benefits and advantages of economies of large scale production. Also, the technology made available to such locally-owned industries are usually obsolete and inadequate. This is true because multinational corporations are very often unwilling to release important technological information for fear that it may lead to rapid development of local competitions and strong rivalry from the Third World countries.[10]

Therefore, multinational firms effectively and efficiently regulate the diffusion of foreign technology. The international monopoly businesses make technological decisions with concern for the effects upon the resources base and export market of the foreign monopolists rather than concern for the effects upon the Third World nations. For example, in the case of Nigeria, the multinational corporations are not ready to transfer technology of capital goods. There have been several studies for the establishment of an iron and steel industry in Nigeria. However, only the highly sophisticated and capital-intensive projects have been adopted. Such projects will take Nigerians decades to master the processes. At the same token, Nigeria will still largely depend on the nations that are supplying the technology for the spare parts maintenance. Given the importance of such an industry in the economy, the domination of the Nigerian economy by the supplier of the required technology is being affirmed.

EMPLOYMENT IMPLICATIONS AND THE DICHOTOMY OF MNCS IN AFRICA

The implications of multinational enterprises in Africa are many and vary. The investment measures of these multinational firms are biased against the development and expansion of capital goods industries in Africa, and biased in favor of the use of capital inventive technique in their extractive and export-oriented operations. However, both of these biases prohibit the balanced development of Africa. For example, capital-intensive methods demand less labor per level of output than labor-intensive methods. Capital intensive methods further require a small labor force made up of specialized management professionals and semi-skilled workers, whereas labor-intensive methods tend to require a much larger labor force composed largely of skilled and unskilled workers.

Despite the scarcity of highly skilled or trained professionals in Africa and other less developed countries, the monopoly advantages and/or benefits of multinational enterprises insulate them from the need of really exploring and using local labor and available sources. The adjustment processes that the multinational corporations make in Africa are made in the non-skilled, low paying jobs-such as that of laborers, cooks, house-keepers, domestic-servants, road-menders, and other menial workers. In many occasions, multinational corporations have insisted on importing from their home countries their own clerks, typists, secretaries, and other employees whose jobs cannot strictly be viewed as being skilled or highly professional. The reason of the foreign firms is, also, lack of skilled and experienced professional in less developed countries of Africa. The reality is that international firms are mainly able to withstand the diseconomies arising from failure to minimize costs. However, this is true not only because of their monopoly advantages but also because multinational enterprises more often than not charge uncommercial use of land and other resources to costs of operating which are tax deductible and exempted from the payments that are paid to the host nations.

Furthermore, by exporting the so-believed "experts" and experienced clerks, typists, secretaries, small machine operators, cooks, drivers, welders, cleaners, and many others to the less developed countries of Africa and paying them salaries far above local rates for local workers of the same status, international businesses provide employments for more of their own citizens than they would have done if they had hired local citizens in the host country.

As a result of this, policy makers and leaders of African states have been very sensitive to this situation and have responded to it by placing restrictions on the type of workers that international companies can bring from their home nations. The African states have demanded to have lion share of their citizens employed by the multinational corporations rather than a wholesale importation of employees from the advanced capitalist societies.

Given the distortions by international firms in the cost of labor and capital which they employ in Third World countries, the incentive for the multinational enterprises operating in the Third World countries to utilize more labor from local sources and less capital intensive techniques is largely minimized. Meanwhile, this is not to deny the fact that in some industries or firms, alternative labor intensive techniques do not exist or that in many circumstances local expertise is scarce or simply not available. The point to make here is that because of the monopoly advantages of multinational enterprises and the benefits that they receive from tax concessions and other arrangements, they do not specifically pay more attention to utilizing local resources, particularly labor. International companies do not however, feel enough enthusiasm to function at optimal costs by fully making use of local resources.

Therefore, since labor-intensive techniques are prone to be slower and less sophisticated in terms of productivity, though not necessarily ineffective, inefficient, or inferior in terms of quality of good, locally-owned businesses in Africa and other less developed states follow the international owned industries in implementing capital-intensive technologies. The main reason behind such a behavior is simply the importance and need for domestic industries to be able to compete for survival with the internationally-owned businesses.

Although, multinational enterprises are aware that they are engaged in investment operations in which their sustained profits largely depend upon persistent replenishment of technological advantages, they have clearly done very little to change the technology or the goods which they exports to the underdeveloped world either through local research and development or through intensive and massive training for citizens of the underdeveloped countries in order to be of better employment service to the host nations. It is a fact that international companies have been, as a result of pressures from the host countries of underdeveloped world, engaged in scholarship and other training programs for citizens of the Third World countries.

Meanwhile, the type of technological "know-how" provided to these trainees are not in any fashion changed to meet the conditions in the Third World countries.   As a result of production methods used by the international firms, additional employment and/or jobs for local citizens of the less developed nations has been very low.   For instance, in Venezuela, petroleum production provides employment for only 3 percent of the labor force; in Zambia and Chile, the copper industry employs only 4 percent and 5 percent of the labor force respectively.   However, for the period 1950 - 1960, while industrial production compared with total production for the entire Latin American countries rose by 16.5 percent, industrial employment in relation to total employment fell by 10 percent.[11]

SOCIO-ECONOMIC IMPACT OF MNCS ON DOMESTIC MARKETS

A more specific, and probably more realistic, concern is that, within a given state in Africa foreign investment always dominate the most profitable, the most technologically advanced, the most growth-oriented, and the economic trend-setting firms.   For instance, Norman Girvan has examined, analyzed and evaluated some of the major consequences of the collective characteristics of international conglomerate.   He discovers that in any single industry or firm, production is dominated by a small number of giant corporations operating across the whole special spectrum of the global economy.   "The implications," he believes, "is an enormous oligopolistic market power on a global scale."   Girvan also believes that since the corporations in any industry "almost always fix their own prices in sympathy with one another, what is oligopoly in form becomes monopoly in reality."

Furthermore, he demonstrates specifically that in pursuing their corporate and ologopolistic policies, multinational corporations have come to adopt the formation of mergers and consortia for specific projects.   Such mergers and consortia, Girvan points out,

1) benefits of hugh size, 2) technological superiority, 3) diversified production, and 4) collective market power. This type of merger and consortia have become a common practice of large firms both within nation-states and globally between firms from different nation-states.[12] Although small competitive firms still exist, they exist in a subordinate position with respect to the large manufacturing or distributing corporation.[13] The latter, on the other hand, are increasingly able to get their investment needs from internal financing (especially depreciation allowances), thus freeing themselves from outside financial regulations.[14] The reciprocal recognition of strength and retaliatory power on the part of competitors, suppliers, and customers, enables the corporations to protect their profit positions through adjustments in prices, techniques and employment. Very often than not, the multinational enterprises absorb local capital, drive local firms and competitors out of business and divert consumers from local firms through powerful advertising method. However, they use their oligopoly (and monopoly) advantages to exploit the host countries through excessive profits, high import prices, repatriation of revenues, tax exemptions, and also through the wide disparity between the wages paid to nationals and the expatriates employed.[15]

Although multinational enterprises may effectively break local monopolies, they do so only to impose stronger monopolies from abroad thereby effectively tying the economy of the host country to the international activities of the multinational firms. Richard J. Barnet and Ronald E. Muller have this to say:

> In the process of developing a new world, the managers of firms like GM, IBM, Pepsico, GE, Pfizer, Shell, Volkswagen, Exxon, and few hundred others are making daily business decisions which have more impact than those of the most sovereign governments on where people live; what work, if any, they will do; what they will eat, drink, and wear; what sorts of knowledge, schools and universities will encourage; and what kind of society their children will inherit.[16]

Multinational enterprises operate in Africa and other LDCs along standards set by their parent firms or by other metropolitan institutions rather than by local standards. This means that the new enterprise places demands which cannot be met by the local people. As MNCs make decisions on basis of cost-efficiency and cost-benefit considerations such decisions can be impediments to local development and the imposition of external values from the capitalist societies. The international corporations carry their value systems with them when they invest in the Third World Nations and use western expectations about production and efficiency, which may not be compatible with local cultures and needs of less developed societies. Furthermore, the MNCs are more anxious to get their business under way than they are willing to cultivate local inputs necessary for development.

The long-run horizon in investment decisions that the financial independence of the corporations makes possible, and the greater calculating rationality of corporate managers enables the MNCs to approach new developments with care and circumspection and to calculate more accurately the risks involved.[17] The vast financial resources available to the corporations favor further vertical integration, while their oligopolistic behavior encourages the formation of consortia. By this practice, multinational corporations are able to dominate domestic markets.

Norman Girvan has been quite articulative in his criticism of the situation, especially with regard to mineral-exporting companies. He explains:

> It is not clear, for example, why the mineral-export industry does not exert any pressure for the establishment of national supplying industries, such as capital goods industries for the supply of the materials used in such refining as is carried out locally. Nor is their any full explanation for the virtual absence of any tendency for the industry's factor proportions to adjust to the relatively capital-short, labour-plentiful situation in these economies. Capital shortage as an explanation of total foreign ownership looks weaker in the face of the emergence, in countries such as Venezuela and Chile, of a class of domestic capitalists eager to put their money to work. Finally, if

the objective of imperialist capital is to extract a surplus from the country as such...why is the surplus not invested in their other sectors after having made a killing in the mineral-export sector.[18]

Foreign investors are always quick to argue that their expertise, their technology, and their investment facilities are limited to particular industries and that investments which they consider as not being too important for foreign investments (but which in the real sense form the nucleus of development for the local people) should be properly regarded as the task of the host government and local people. This might hold some element of truth. However, the large profits generated locally by international firms can be reinvested in the host country in such sectors as fishing, agriculture, handicrafts and other locally-owned industries and economic activities without the domination and control of the multinational firms.

Moreover, the mineral export industry has been the most obvious target of those who want to see profits of international firms reinvested in local activities. There are other sectors of the economy which could benefit from foreign investment under effective control and supervision of host governments. Such sectors include agriculture and service industries.

As a result of the large profits which multinational enterprises have been able to make in the Third World nations and allowed to repatriate to their home countries, prices have been kept very low in the metropolitan states while they are kept very high in the Third World nations. Barnet and Muller described the situation in this way:

To put it simply, the extraordinary profits which global companies by virtue of their superior power have been able to make in poor countries have represented a kind of subsidy for the American consumer. When the "profit faucet" from poor countries--is flowing at full force, it is possible for a company to show only modest world-wide profits which hide the extraordinary rates of return from poor countries--that make it possible to keep consumer prices in the United States relatively low. But when the oil-producing countries, for example, begin closing the faucet by demanding and getting a higher price for crude and the companies wish to maintain their profit levels, visits to the local gas station in the United States must become more expensive.[19]

Foreign firms are usually able to effectively control both the foreign market and the foreign sources of raw materials even in the face of high tariffs and other regulations by the host nations. In addressing the implication of branch-plant of MNCs upon the local industry in less developed countries, David Felix argues that "foreign capital throughout competes with local capital partly because of its ability: to self-insure against risk and to inflate the capital base of subsidiaries by transferring to them already depreciated equipment and designs from their more advanced home plants. O'Connor carried the argument further and maintains that "local capital thus tends to be either co-opted by foreign capital or confined to especially risky undertakings." He summarizeds the whole problems in this way:

> Further branch-plant industrialization fragments the local capital market; branch-plant savings are not ordinarily available to other sectors of the local economy, being reinvested, used to purchase facilities from local capital, or repatriated. All in all, branch-plant investments promote the misutilization of capital, and generate sever immobilities in the local capital market.[20]

In order to use its international capacity to the fullest extent, the giant corporation places great emphasis on intra-company activities between the parent and the subsidiary companies regardless of the differences in location or territory. Hence, oil companies will produce crude oil in Nigeria for processing in their refineries in the Unites States or Britain. Bauxite companies will prefer to produce their raw output in Jamaica or Guyana and export it to their parent or subsidiary aluminum smelting plants in the United States to processing it in the smelting in either country. This practice is common with multinational firms particularly if the processing plants in the raw material producing country are owned by a different corporation. By feeding its own parent company or its subsidiaries regardless of distance, a multinational enterprise is able to avoid paying some of its profits to a different corporation and it is also able to spread its overhead costs of operation. The result of this practice for the less developed countries is higher import costs. Another detrimental result of such a practice of the less developed countries is regional economic disintegration caused by needless rivalry between states and poor national economic integration within the nation-state. Girvan and Jefferson, in their study of the bauxite industry in Jamaica and Guyana, indicated that the policies of the bauxite companies in the Caribbean could not lead to national or regional economic integration.[21] A study by Sterling Brubaker in 1967 concluded that national or regional integration in aluminum is highly unlikely because the prospects for the development of smelters and processing capacity in the underdeveloped countries are little.

CLASS STRUCTURE AND POWER CONFIGURATION IN AFRICA

Frank's position that the internal class arrangement and socio-political structure of the less developed countries is the result of their incorporation within the international capitalist economic system is supported by the African experience. Given the fact that antagonistic social variations had already emerged in African states before European involvement, the effect of European trade followed by colonial administration usually transformed the fabric of African political economy and produced new and more persisted social cleavages. Hence, Samir Amin, in his study on the class struggle in Africa, stipulates that:

> The complete colonization of West Africa had two principal social effects: The acceleration of the decadence of the primitive community and the reinforcement of traditional class differences on the one hand, the introduction and development of new class

differences linked to the capitalist exploitation of the country on the other hand.[22]

That is to say, colonialism created a class structure in Africa in which some traditional groups were reinforced and new groups were established as a result of the imperialist exploitation cemented by colonial administration. Where possible, the colonial master recruited their local agents from the traditional ruling class, and as Amin indicates, they even endeavored to introduce traditional class relationships from the more feudal regions into less differentiated regions which no formal foundation for such relationship occurred. To quote Amin:

> The artificial creation of "district chiefs" in the French colonies, and "headmen" in the English colonies derived from the desire to create an auxiliary class of privileged people to exploit the peasants. The descendants of the traditional elements favored under colonialism today constitute a segment of the privileged sectors of the contemporary African states.[23]

Furthermore, the emergence of varieties of new class configurations resulting from the metropolitan capitalist transformation of African Political economy was by far the most essential development during the colonial era. As Kwame Nkrumah indicates in his work on class struggle in Africa, the colonial era has given rise to the development and growth of "capitalist social configurations" in Africa. Nkrumah further comments that:

> Although feudal relics remained, the colonial period ushered in capitalist social structures. The period was characterized by the rise of the petty-bourgeoisie consisting in the main of intellectuals, civil servants, members of the professions, and of officers in the armed forces and police. There was a marked absence of capitalist among the bourgeoisie, since local business enterprise was on the whole discouraged by the colonial power. Anyone wishing to achieve wealth and status under colonialism was therefore likely to choose a career in the professions, the civil service or the armed forces, because there were so few business opportunities. Foreigners

controlled mining, industrial enterprises, banks, wholesale trade and large-scale farming.[24]

Nkrumah further shows that, the class configuration which resulted during the colonial administration was composed of: a ruling class of European colonial officials and businessmen; a petty bourgeoisie of non European functionaries, professionals, merchants, and in some cases large farmers and other similar in nature. In the same direction, Fanon characterizes the group as an "underdeveloped middle class" since it has little or no independent economic power and no capacity, authority and/or inclinations to play the historical role performed by the bourgeoisie in Western world. Therefore Fanon indicates that the national bourgeoisie:

> lacks something essential to a bourgeoisie: money. The bourgeoisie of an underdeveloped country is a bourgeoisie in spirit only...Consequently it remains at the beginning and for a long time afterward a bourgeoisie of the civil service....it will always reveal itself incapable of giving birth to an authentic bourgeois society with all the economic and industrial consequences which this entails.[25]

In the same manner, Fanon perceives what Nkrumah, Amin, Ledda and many others have clearly perceived that this new ruling class configuration has no independent economic power apart from its regulation and control of the state apparatus and its ties to international capital. It cannot, however, be correctly described as a national bourgeoisie, since it is dependent for its privileged positions upon the intermediary function which it plays in the neo-colonial arrangement. Therefore, that the post-independence configuration of African political economy is best described as neo-colonial cannot be serious questioned for the idea of "neocolonialism" as Thomas Hodgkin has so seriously argued, generally describes the nature of the relationship that emerges between the African economies and the major core of western capitalism. Hodgkin further explains that:

'neo-colonialism' tends to be regarded as something of a dirty word, to be used-if at all-in inverted commas, reflecting the shocking lack of gratitude of the former colonial powers, and from the West in general. But in fact it is an entirely necessary way of describing the situations arising out of false decolonization-the preservation of the basic relationship of Western dominance and African dependence by other means, after the transfer of formal power. This is evident not only in the field of economic relations. This neo-colonial relationship is the product of the transfer of formal political power to a class created by, and dependent upon Western capitalism.[26]

Moreover, according to Amilcar Cabral, decolonization has given western capitalist imperialism a new lease on life by allowing the continued economic exploitation of the less developed nations of Africa through invisible hands. That is to say, decolonization has made possible an agreement between and among the local bourgeoisie and the bourgeoisie of the capitalist societies-an agreement which allows on the one hand the local bourgeoisie to participate in the sharing of the benefits derived from the continued exploitation of the economies by western capitalist and on the other hand frees the imperialistic metropolitan societies from the onus of direct domination of these nations.

Also, Ledda was able to differentiate certain distinct classes as follows a) local entrepreneurs who are either associated with international capital, b) the bureaucratic bourgeoisie composed of top management and administrative military official and government ministers; c) a comprador groups (present during the colonial era) which serve as intermediaries for the foreign import-export businesses; and d) rural bourgeois groups such as local planters, large farmers who are engaged in the production of cash crops for export and feudal landlords.[27] These emerged elements-entrepreneurial, bureaucratic, comprador, and rural bourgeoisie-are to use Ledd's word "tied body and soul to foreign capital" upon which their privileges and livelihood are dependent.

In addition to the transformation character of the local bourgeoisie, the nature and structure of the agreement between this class and international capital has been changing rapidly. Nkrumah further indicates that the agreement has been also cemented by the increased participation of the African bourgeoisie in the local activities of the giant multinational enterprises. As for Nkrumah:

> The Alliance between the indigenous bourgeoisie and international monopoly finance capital is being further cemented by the growing trend towards partnership between individual African governments, or regional economic organizations, and giant, imperialist, multinational corporations. African governments, some of whom claim to be pursuing a socialist path of development and "nationalizing"key industries, are in fact merely "participating" in them. They are combining with collective-imperialism in the continuing exploitations of African workers and rural proletariat. The African government shields the corporations from the resistance of the working class, and bans strikes or becomes a strike-breaker; while the corporations strengthen their stranglehold of the African economy, secure in the knowledge that they hold government protection. In fact, the African governments have become the policemen of imperialist, multinational corporations. There thus develops a common front to halt socialist advance.[28]

Instead of creating a strong and efficient national bourgeoisie, imperialism creates just a dependent "comprador" bourgeoisie which is a mere appendage of the international bourgeoisie of the metropolis. The "comprador" dependent bourgeoisie becomes an ally and a defender of international capital. It services international capital for the "benefits" it derives from such alliance. The international capitalist in return for such a "cooperation" affords "protection" of a "privilege position" to the local bourgeoisie.

NATIONALISTS, RADICALS AND GOVERNMENT RESPONSE

The rapid growth of indigenous "techno-bureaucratic" class and a fairly organized and growing state bureaucracy in the Third World countries has helped to strengthen the influence and stability of the international bourgeoisie and the multinational corporations in the developing countries. In his analysis of the situation Norman Girvan wrote:

> in most Third World countries there has been the rapid development and maturation of a techno-bureaucratic class based on the state apparatus. Where this occurs together with the additional leverage represented by the possession of strategic export commodities, it creates the possibilities for the techno-bureaucratic class, in alliance with the traditional comprador bourgeoisie, to attempt to transform itself into a class of state capitalists in a project for national industrialization and development using the additional surpluses from the industry, with the mass of the population more-or-less coerced or mobilized into the so-called "struggle against imperialism."[29]

Paul A. Baran and Paul M. Sweezy usually correctly perceived the issue when they commented:

> The alliance of foreign interests with conservative elements in the periphery (feudal elements, landowning classes, some sections--or the whole of the national bourgeoisie, upper ranks of the armed forces, corrupted bureaucrats, etc.), is usually thought to be the most powerful factor determining the stability of center periphery relations.[30]

Nationalists and local capitalists in African countries have contended that they are involved in a struggle against western imperialism. A close examination of what is actually happening in most of these countries reveals that only modifications in the power of international capitalism, in terms of role and powers of local elites and capitalists have occurred without necessarily causing any significant and fundamental changes in the relative power of international corporations. This development has led to the current powerful ideological debate existing in almost every African country as regards the most appropriate strategy for development. The most noticeable or articulative group is the group of nationalist. This group argues from Marxist and Leninist point of view and insists that capitalist system can not lead to development in the less developed countries. They see foreign investments as the tool for modern imperialism.

However, the domination by multinational corporations of global market, global demand and global consumption pattern is compatible with Marxist theory of consumption. Marx has demonstrated in his economic analysis of the theory of consumption that production creates the materials which satisfy man's economic needs as well as the economic needs that are satisfied by the materials produced. In short, Marx argued that production determines consumption just as consumption determines production.[31] Nationalists in many less developed countries have taken a highly critical perspective of capitalist mode of development and the role of foreign investments especially in the developing nations. The critical view and rejection of foreign investments as a road to development in the less developed countries presented by the nationalist emanate from many areas. University professors, staff and students, labor unions, and the militant groups-all of who believe that foreign control or regulation of local economies has been and continues to be, a serious impediment to prosperity, political freedom, economic growth and stability.

Majority of African states now perceive multinational firms as threat to their well being, sovereignty and development. African nationalists complain that the increased financial power of the multinational corporations and their domination of national and global economies have helped the multinational firms to concentrate economic power in the hand of a very few percentage of the population in the nation-states. They argue that the large companies have been effective obstacles to equitable distribution of national and international wealth. Also, the nationalists indicate that multinational enterprises have developed and continued to service an international class configuration, a structure in which a numerically ineligible but economically and financially very powerful control of the economy. African nationalists have pleaded with leaders and policy makers in the Third World countries to prevent a pattern of development in which the few control and dominate the economy and politics of nation-states to the disadvantage of the large majority, the poor and peasants. Unfortunately, that arrangement which the nationalists criticism is the one that is rapidly growing in almost all Third World countries.

Furthermore, radical scholars of political economy see national participation as exploitation of Africa and other less developed states; in a new arrangement under the guise of equality and sovereignty. The major contradictions between the multinational enterprises and the nationalists center around few key issues. Nationalists perceive the physical presence and involvement of foreign investors in the major sectors of the economy and social life of the host nation as direct encroachment on national sovereignty, national culture and societal values.

Also, the nationalists criticize joint-venture between foreign investors and government and argue that when government invests in oil, copper, diamond or any other business with international corporations, the government is mainly wasting money to finance the pillars of imperialist capitalism. They believe that international firms operate on the basis of what is to their corporate interests. The nationalists further argue that "all the arrangement" about establishing boards with local directors and chairmen are simply expensive joke-playing because none of the essential decisions are made or will be made in the host less developed countries any well. Nationalists argue that what the LDCs want and need is ownership and control, not ownership only by mouth.

The radical political economists tend to perceive development in terms of effective improvement of the human condition and they are thus concerned with the wide gap between governmental rhetoric and the every day living conditions of the poor. Therefore, they perceive a collusion between government and large corporations in the less developed nations as one which results in little benefit to the laborer or to the masses of unemployed. Some groups explain this situation in terms of the inherent or implied corruption of imperialistic capitalism. For intellectual radical political economists, the lack of development is seen to be the product of neocolonialism and its exploitation. International firms are perceived as "white conspirators" whose primary motives and attitudes are thoroughly imperialistic and empirically exploitative. Their actions and behavior are aided by the domestic elites, national bourgeoisie, comprador bourgeoisie, and government bureaucrats.

However, it is not a surprise that the threat to contemporary capitalism (and its catalyst multinational corporations) has come mainly from radical movements and elements both in the less developed countries and in the advanced capitalist countries. Such movements and elements have been sparked by a deep-seated yearning for true national independence - political as well as socio -economic. These radical movements are engineered by an increasingly urgent need for economic development and political stability, which in regards to LDCs' experience is proving to be unattainable except on the basis of domestic control of the factors of production, particularly capital. A mere replacement of foreign imperialists with domestic capitalists cannot bring egalitarianism to the less developed countries of Africa. International imperialism and domestic capitalists can only result in indigenization of capital in Africa and other LDCs.

In Africa, cries of the so-called radical political theorists are often heard with skepticism by government officials and business elites alike. They argue and believe that radicals can afford to be reckless in their development rhetoric because they bear no responsibility for wrong decisions.

The radical elements have argued in favor of nationalization of foreign investments. In a number of instances, the more radical nationalists have gained support and have successfully nationalized foreign investments. In almost every instance where these has been done, the MNCs, often with the support of their home governments, have shown their wrath and attempted, sometimes successfully, to create political and economic turmoil in the nationalizing nation. A second perspective on development can be found among the local elites and the businessmen. Many expatriate and local businessmen tend to think that development goals are served through the active recruitment of foreign capital and expertise. They favor this because such an approach would restrain government involvement and control in the economy and would encourage a more "competitive", capitalist approach to development.   They argue that stringent policies on the operations of multinational corporation and foreign investors would slow down growth of domestic trade and development. As a result, local businessmen in African countries are likely to, and actually do, tolerate the penetration of the local economy by MNCs. Local businesses in Africa are enthusiastic about foreign-owned businesses and would rather cooperate with them than "fight" against them. In many instances, local businessmen find that they can do better by cooperating or joining the big corporation as junior partners. Quite often local firms find that they do not have any other alternative than to sell their businesses to the large foreign-owned firms.

The high priority and level of cooperation given to the MNCs by people from Africa can be illustrated with the enthusism and desperate efforts of many individuals (including government leaders and officials) and students from Africa to join big corporations based in the industrial centers and thereby becoming the representative of the corporation in Africa. Foreign students who study in the industrial countries are the most hungry seekers of such "opportunities". The same situation is seen in the strong efforts of economic advisers in the foreign offices (embassies, consulates, etc.) of African countries to attract multinational corporations to invest in their respective countries.

Despite the fact that government officials and local businessmen agree with nationalists on many aspects of development, such as what the human needs are or that unemployment is the main issue, they disagree intensely on approach. Local businessmen and government officials embrace national participation as being the best way to obtain optimum national income and control of national economy without scaring away foreign investors. It is a common pronouncement by leaders and policy makers in Africa that in order to increase their country's income from foreign trade, the government must pursue a policy which will significantly attract private foreign investment, with meaningful national participation. They believe that African countries must have adequate knowledge of international marketing arrangements and increase their share of benefits that will accrue from international economic operation.

African governments do not deny that real development needs local resources and investments. However, the initial concerns of officials are the ways and means of increasing local revenues necessary for implementation of their development programs. It seems that African governments see national participation in joint ventures with foreign investors as the most immediate way to increase the financial resources of the host government. Many leaders of government in African nations argue that in exporting industries, the nation must be competitive in world markets while at the same time increasing their national control at home. In this area of concern government spokesmen always complain that "radical" programs are "lacking in patience and planning."

In conclusion, therefore, the policy of most African states in dealing with foreign investors and multinational enterprises are mainly ones designed to replace foreign capitalist class with domestic one. Such a policy cannot lead to a desirable egalitarianism in Africa. What is needed in Africa is an effective public control of the national economy. Ordinary nationalizing of industries and other factors of production will not alleviate the evils of capitalism. Nationalization of foreign industries and investments in African countries may be a necessary step but the main impact of such an action may be the dependence of the national economy upon domestic capitalists and the local comprador bougeoisie controlled in a disguised form by the international corporations and foreign investors.

It is important to note that, it is the role given to capital in economic theory and in development planning that has made international investment and the multinational enterprises very significant for the development economies of the less developed countries. The real constraint has been hidden and, along with it, the most effective path for economic growth and development of the less developed countries. Thus, the multinational corporations take series of measures to ensure that this situation is maintained and their role preserved. This is the most preserved function of the multinational enterprises in Africa and other LDCs. It is a role which has been neglected or overlooked because the educated elites and policy makers in the less developed countries have implemented without questioning the theoretical constructs put forward to them by multinational enterprises. It is a role which directly militates against economic independence, self-reliance development and/or economic autonomy of the less developed countries.

NOTES

1. Peter C. W. Gutkind, and Emmanuel Wallerstein, *The Political Economy of Contemporary Africa* (Beverly Hills: Stage Publication, 1976).

2. Peter C. W. Gutkind, and Emmanuel Wallerstein, *The Political Economy of Contemporary Africa* (Beverly Hills: Stage Publication, 1976), p. 261.

3. Ibid., p. 267.

4. James O'Conner, The Corporations and the State op. cit., p. 208.

5. Nwankwo, p. 100.

6. See Dale R. Weigel, "Multinational Approaches to Multinational Corporations," *in Finance and Development*: A Quarterly Publication of the *International Monetary Fund and the World Bank Group*, Vol. 11, No. 3, (September 1974), p. 27-29 and 42.

7. James O'Connor. The Corporations and the State, p. 206-207.

8. Ibid.

9. Hamza Alavi, "Indian Capitalism and Foreign Imperialism", *New Left Review*, No. 37 (May-June 1967), p. 83. Alavi has also argued that informal economic control exercised by the advanced capitalist countries can be as effective and as profitable, as formal political rule--See Hamza Alavi, "Imperialism Old and New," in Ralph Miliband and John Saville, eds., *The Social Register*, (London, 1964), p. 108-109.

10. When this issue was raised in a Conference on Multinational Corporations in February 1990 in Washington, D.C. at least one Exxon representative present agreed that multinational corporations have on occasions found it necessary to withhold and keep to themselves certain crucial technological "know-how" which they feel can be too vital for their own continued security in business and should not be made readily available to competitors. The Conference was one of several conferences attended during this research work. The Conference cited here was held at Shoreham Americana Hotel (in Washington, D. C. on February 20 and 21, 1990). It was a regional meeting of the American Society of International Law co-sponsored by the American University Law Review and International Law Society.

11. See Edward Carrington, "Industrialization by Invitation in Trinidad and Tobago since 1950," *New World Quarterly 4*, No. 2, 1968. See also James O'Connor, The Corporations and the State, op. cit., p. 208.Kendall W. Stiles and Tsuneo Akaha, *International Political Economy: A Reader* (New York: Harper Collins Publishers, 1991). Stephen Gill and David Law, *The Global Political Economy* (Baltimore: The John Hopkins University Press, 1993).

12. Norman Girvan, Nationalist vs. Multinational Corporations, op.cit., p. 11.

13. See C. Wright Mills, *White Collar* (New York, 1956), p. 23-38.

14. Baran and Sweezy, *Monopoly Capital*, p. 102-105.

15. See James P. Grant, *Multinational Corporations and the Developing Countries: The Emerging Jobs Crisis and Its Implications* (Washington, D.C: Overseas Development Council, January 1972) and Charles K. Wilber, ed. *The Political Economy of Development and Underdevelopment*, op. cit. Also Techsee Robert B. Stobaugh, *The International Transfer of Technology in the Establishment of the Petrochemical Industry in Developing Countries* (New York, UNITAR (United Nations Institute for Training and Research) 1971. UNITAR Research Reports No. 12).

16. Richard J. Barnet and Ronald E. Muller, *Global Reach: The Power of the Multinational Corporations* (New York: Simon and Schuster 1974), p. 15. See also Stobaugh, Robert B. *The International Transfer of Technology in the Establishment of the Petrochemical Industry in Developing Countries*, op. cit. 17Ibid., p. 50. See also Raymond Vernon, "The American Corporation in Underdeveloped Areas" in E.S. Mason, ed., *The Corporation in Modern Society* (Cambridge, Mass., 1959, 0. 238-239. Fredoline Anunobi, *The Implications of Conditionality: The International Monetary Fund and Africa* (Maryland: University Press of America, 1992). Glenn Hastedt and Kay Knickrehm, *Toward The Twenty-First Centruy* (N.J.: Prentice Hall, 1994). 18Norman Girvan, "Multinational Corporations and Dependent Underdevelopment in Mineral Export Economies", *Social and Economic Studies*, Vol. 19, No. 4 (Dec. 1970), p. 490.

19. Barnet and Muller, *Global Reach*, op, cit., See also "Offshore Bonanza: Foreign Ventures Fetch More Profits for Firms Located in United States," *The Wall Street Journal,* (November 1, 1973), p. 1 and U.S. Department of Commerce, Special survey of U. S. Multinational Companies 1970. Washington, D.C.: National Technical Information Service, (November 1972). James E. Dougherty and Robert L. Pfattzgraff, *Contending Theories of International Relations: A Comprehensive Survey* (New York: Harper Collins Publishers, 1990).

20. David Felix, quoted in James O'Connor, The Corporations and the State, p. 202.

21. Norman Girvan and Owen Jefferson, "Corporate vs. Caribbean Integration," *New World Quarterly 4*, No. 2 (1968), pp-52-54, cited in O'Connor, The Corporations and the State, p. 205.

22. Samir Amin, "The Class Struggle in Africa" *Revolution*, Vol. 1, No. 9, 1970, p. 38.

23. Ibid.

24. Kwame Nkrumah, *Class Struggle in Africa* (New York: International Publishers, 1970), pp. 55-56.

25. Frantz Fanon, *The Wretched of The Earth* (New York: Grove Press, 1963), pp. 178-179.

26. Thomas Hodgkin's Forward to Green and Seidman's *Unity or Poverty* op. cit., p. 14.

27. Ledda, p. 563.

28. Nkrumah, p. 63.

29. Norman Girvan, Economic Nationalist vs. Multinational Corporations, op. cit., Section III.

30. Cited in Giovanni Arrighi and John S. Saul, "International Corporations" in giovanni Arrighi and John S. Saul, eds., *Essays on the Political Economy of Africa,* op. cit.

31. Today consumption in both the developed and the less developed countries has been greatly diffused. Consumption in the less developed countries has come to be determined increasingly by the production in the industrialized countries. The result of this situation has been that real economic needs of the less developed countries have been distorted and therefore poorly or inadequately satisfied.

CHAPTER 7

The Political Economy Of Instability In Ghana

It is important to note that the study of Ghana in Western academic circles has been hopelessly biased by the influence of government funding on academic research, grants from the large private institutions, the bureaucratization of knowledge by disciplines, the prevailing social and political idealogies, and the general ethnocentricism of Western scholars, experts and policy makers. To resolve the deficiencies resulting from this situation, a great deal of intellectual effort and research needs to be concentrated on the real barriers to development and the manner in which these barriers can be overcome. This simply means that Ghana's economic dependence and subordination to foreign interests must be openly recognized and, along with the failings and short comings of the present administrations, analyzed in depth. In addition, attention must be focused on those strategies of development and configurations of power which will lead to a political economy of "rapid, self sustained expansion, controlled and directed by and for the Ghanian people themselves."[1]

The primary aim or objective of this chapter is to identify the factors that may lead to economic instability in the developing nations, by using Ghana as a case study. Ghana, a former British colony, got her independence on 6 March, 1957. Ghana was the first black country in Africa South of the Sahara to achieve political independence. The country has an area of about 92,000 square miles with a population of about 12,531,000 in 1981.

Ghana, since 1957 has experienced seven changes of government, administration and numerous foiled coup d'etats. Out of eight regimes that ruled Ghana since her political independence, three were constitutionally elected Civilian regimes and five have been military rules (see Table 7:1). Based on this table, one finds that the eight regimes have ruled Ghana in succession over a period of Thirty-five years. However, each regime, on the average, ruled Ghana for four years and three months. As a result of this no meaningful economic program of any country can be accomplished within a short period of time particularly as Ghana is a developing country with series of problems usually associated with less developed countries.[2] It is even worse if the country has no continuity of development programs as a result of the abrupt successions of governments that it has experienced. In this section, Agbango's unpublished research paper provided a useful background for indepth analysis.

The socio-politico-economic study of Ghana is examined taking into account some economic variable indicators such as gross domestic product, per capita income, price indices, the level of social services available, unemployment rate, and the rate of inflation-which have influenced the economic state of Ghana from regime to regime.

Ghana has been chosen for this study of the effect of political instability on its economic development because it was at the time of independence a pace setter for the newly independent countries of Africa. As Nkrumah (the first President) pointed out, "The independence of Ghana is meaningless unless it is linked up with the total liberation of Africa."[3]   Actually, Ghana did play her

TABLE 7:1
CHANGES OF GOVERNMENT IN GHANA FROM 1957-1981

From	To	Name of Government	Head of Government	Type of Government	Nature of Change	Dominant Ideology
March 6, 1957	February 24, 1966	Convention Peoples Party (CPP)	Nkrumah	Civilian	Elected	Socialist
February 24, 1966	September 1969	National Liberation Council (NLC)	General Ankrah	Military	Coup	Pro-West
September 1969	January 13, 1972	Progress Party (PP)	Busia	Civilian	Elected	Pro-West
January 13, 1972	November 1978	National Redemption Council (NRC)	General Acheampong	Military	Coup	Neutral
November 1978	June 4, 1979	Supreme Military Council (SMC)	General Akuffo	Military	Coup	Neutral
June 4, 1979	September 24, 1979	Armed Forces Revolutionary Council (AFRC)	Ft. Lt. Rawlings	Military	Coup	Neutral
September 24, 1979	December 31, 1981	Peoples National Party (PNP)	Dr. Limann	Civilian	Elected	Neutral
December 31, 1981	Present	Provisional National Defense Committee	Ft. Lt. Rawlings	Military	Coup	Communist

Source: George Agbango's Table on Changes of Government in Ghana, Unpublished Research, Atlanta University, 1988.

Nkrumah

leadership role effectively but today, her economy is in trouble and economic development has become stagnant. On the other hand, the economies of other African Nations which were very far behind Ghana's economy, have today surpassed that of Ghana.[4] What is the cause? This is what this chapter attempts to find out. How well we are able to accomplish this objective will be seen in the later part of this chapter.

THE POLITICAL ECONOMY OF GHANA AND NKRUMAH'S EXTERNAL ECONOMIC DEPENDENCY

In 1957, Nkrumah, under the banner of the Convention Peoples Party, became leader of government business in the then Gold Coast (now Ghana). The British colonial office was preparing the Gold Coast for independence. Nkrumah came to the scene when the Gold Coast, under nearly a century of colonial administration has a very high illiteracy rate, few roads, poor health facilities, high rate of unemployment, and lack of means of communication. Most of the roads and railway lines available linked only to the sources of supply of primary export products such as gold, cocoa, manganese bauxite, and timber. Development planning was extremely very low and coupled with this, was the post World War II inflation. The poor economic conditions of Ghana led to the boycotts and civil riots and social unrest of 1948.[5]

Nkrumah as the leader of Government Business, drew up the first Development Plan for 1951-1956.[6] The purpose of this development plan was to provide skilled labor force through education and better health facilities. To provide better social services such as transport system, communication, and the necessary infrastructure towards preparing Ghana for political independence. On March 6, 1956, the Gold Coast was granted her   independence   and   received   the   name   Ghana.

Ghana was then one of the richest, most successful and politically mature states in black Africa. Per capita income was reportedly the highest, real growth was so excellent, her sterling reserves were substantial, and development plans were completed.[7] At the end of the first five year Development Plan, a consolidated Development Plan was launched in 1957 through 1959 in order to buttress the gains of the first development plan. The second five year Development Plan which was launched in 1959 also aimed at transforming Ghana into a modern industrial state with a primary emphasis on the export of manufactured goods rather than primary products. The program also aimed at making the country self-sufficient in food supply. However, by 1960 when Ghana became a republic, the results of earlier development plans were positive.

TABLE 7:2
ENROLLMENT IN EDUCATIONAL INSTITUTIONS IN GHANA

Type of Educational Institution	1951	1961	Percentage Increase
Primary School	154,361	481,500	211.8
Middle School	66,176	160,000	141.6
Secondary Technical School	3,559	160,000	437
Teacher Training	1,916	4,553	137.4
University	209	1,206	478.9

SOURCE: Adapted from Panaf, Kwame Nkrumah 1973, pp. 110-112 and developed by the writer.

By the same token, the number of students enrolled in schools, colleges or universities had recorded high as shown in Table 7:2. Also, basic social services such as medical care, electricity supply, pipe borne water, transport system and the like had improved. Between 1964-1965 school year there were about 9,987 primary and middle schools with an enrolment of 1,287.581 and 89 secondary schools with 32,980 pupils.[8] The number of teacher training colleges had also increased up to 47 with a population of 10,169 students. Before and by the time of independence, Ghana had only the University of Ghana which was affiliated to London University; but by 1965, the University of Cape Coast and Kumasi had been opened along with 11 technical schools.[9] At this time Ghana had one of the highest literacy rates in Africa, the best public services and the highest standard of living per capita in Africa. Ghana's educational standard consumption per population is compared with other Third World nations such as Nigeria, Ivory Coast, Zambia, Mexico, and South Africa. It must be noted that in the case of South Africa, much of their educational and utility services are not readily available to all sectors of the population because of her apartheid policy. Whereas countries like Mexico, unlike Ghana has been an independence country in over a long period and hence was higher than Ghana by about 2.6 according to Abangwo.

There is no doubt that development projects were remarkably visible in Ghana by 1965. The Akosombo Dam was at its final stage of construction and was to supply and provide electricity to the country's numerous growing industries as well as being exported to the neighboring countries such as Togo, Benin, upper volta and Ivory Coast. The Aluminum Smelter was constructed at Tema to process alumina extracted from bauxite (a mineral which Ghana has in abundance) Tema Harbor was built and became the largest in Africa.[10] The Accra International Airport was constructed during the same period. Many local airports were also built in different major regional capitals such as

Sunyani, Kamasi, Takoradi and Tamale.   And these however, improved transportation systems in Ghana.   In addition, more roads were constructed during this period which include the Tema-Accra motor-way and many modern buildings were erected. Generally speaking Ghana's economic development plan was very positive.

Furthermore, a Third development plan, the Seven-Year Development Plan, was launched in 1964.   This plan was designed to transform Ghana into an industrialized socialist country within the planned period 1967-1971. State participation in commerce within this period had increased. For example, there were more than sixty three state enterprises in 1964. Nkrumah as the opponent of private ownership of means of production, supported the state ownership of means of production in Ghana. Private investment was strongly discouraged except where it was with the joint participation of the state. A para-military workers brigade was also introduced with the primary emphasis to mobilize for agricultural production. Many state farms were established in all districts. It was programmed to become collective farms along similar lines as the Chinese communes. Ghana was on her road to becoming an economically independent nation. Inflation reported very low, and with the creation of numerous state farms, workers brigades, factories, and many other construction and semi-construction works, unemployment was taken care of. Local food supplies were good enough for the entire society.

The question is, was Nkrumah able to achieve economic independence in Ghana? The fourth coming explanation will provide the answer. After Nkrumah and the CPP had achieved political independence from the British in 1957, the economy still depends upon the export of cocoa and other primary products revenue for her survival. Six months before the coup, the world cocoa price fell to half of which it had been the previous year. The resulting drop in export earnings meant that Ghana was unable to obtain necessary imports, the country's foreign

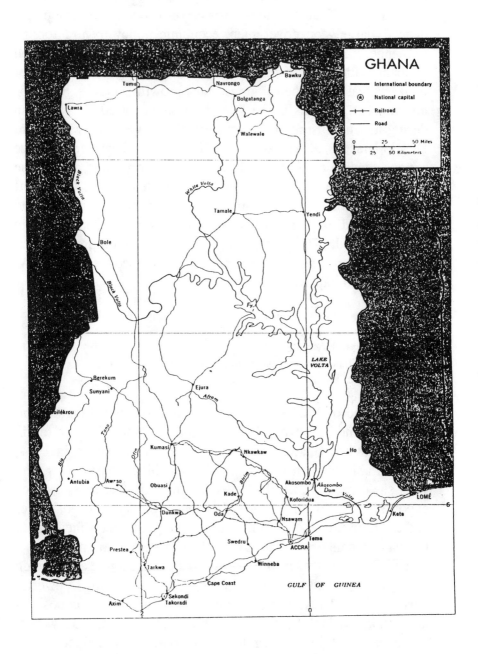

exchange reserves have almost disappeared. As Ukandi Goodwin pointed out "That the most aspect of economic development depends largely on government economic policy toward foreign exchange". If a country has not enough foreign exchange as well as loans with which to buy imports of capital goods needed for industrialization, then industrial growth may well be unattainable.[11] This is the kind of problem faced by Nkrumah during his administration. So, by 1965 (two years after the Third Development Plan had taken off) Ghana was beginning to face serious economic problems. The $250 million reserve at the time of independence was almost exhausted. Revenue from her export of cocoa which serves as a major source of national income had fallen beyond expectation that the seven year Development Plan was threatened. The plan was heavily dependent on projection on the possible revenue to be realized from cocoa exports. As Dennis Austin puts it:

> If you want to send your children to school, it is cocoa, If you want to build your house, it is cocoa, If you want to marry, it is cocoa, If you want to buy cloth, it is cocoa, If you want to buy a lorry, it is cocoa, Whatever you want to do in this world, It is with cocoa money that you do it.[12]

By the end of 1964 the price of cocoa in the world market had fallen tremendously from $467 a tone in 1954 to $87.10 a ton in 1964.[13] When Ghana exported 500,000 tons of cocoa in 1964, she was able to earn only $77 million which was far less than what she earned in the mid 1950s for only 250,000 tons of cocoa exported.[14] Nkrumah, however, attributed the fall of cocoa prices and the refusal of the western countries to grant credit facilities to Ghana as a deliberate effort to kill the socialist program.

Also, Nkrumah's self pronounced radical economic and foreign policy position had irritated the military as well as other powerful Ghanaians, and his excessive attacks on his political opposition had weakened his claim to democratic government.[15] However, it was his inability to regulate and control external economic variables that resulted to his downfall. The historical background of Ghanaian political economy can be understood only in the context of Ghana's colonial past. The colonial condition created a situation of economic dependence which plagued Nkrumah's developmental strategies, and the colonial legacy continued to ensnare the new administrations which have succeeded him. In spite of political independence gained in 1957, Emily Card proceeded:

> Ghana exhibits continuing, albeit modified, colonial economic relationships. Nkrumah denounced neo-colonialism and pursued some socialist programs in an effort to free political and economic relationships from their colonial inheritance; yet his efforts suffered from contradictions inherent in any attempt to achieve economic independence while remaining almost completely dependent upon the same foreign, capitalist nations to which the country was attached before independence.[16]

Furthermore, Card indicated in his writing about Nkrumah perception of development. Nkrumah's solution to the issue of development was twofold. In the economic sphere, agricultural productivity was to be accomplished through large-scale mechanized farming rather than through increased productivity of small-scale peasant agriculture. But, development was to depend primarily on industrialization rather than agriculture and state enterprises were considered essential to guarantee rapid and significant results. Both in agriculture and industry, development would be based upon direct state investment in the means of productions. The main objective was a socialist economy freed from control by external forces, but during a preceding transitional period, the economy was to be mixed. Paradoxically, while Nkrumah denounced the forces of Western imperialism, he believed that new investment capital for the development of Ghana would be received from Western public and private sources.[17]

The political element of the development endeavor was guided by the belief that with Ghana's persistent economic underdevelopment and dependency on the western capitalist states, the identification of the citizens with the socialist objectives of the state was necessary.   Moreover, the administration was against of the growth of a class of Ghanaian entrepreneurship who could potentially undermine socialist strategies through their own identification and cooperation with external economic interests.   However, as a result of the predominance of political over economic preferential arrangements, Nkrumah succeeded in achieving neither.   To this situation, Card argued that preserving party power became an end in itself rather than a means to socialist development.   In reality, the presence of foreign capital did militate against the rise of a national bourgeoisie.   Meanwhile, the continued presence of external influence undermined Ghana's transition from a capitalist to a socialist society.

> The necessity for rapid economic development was manifest. Political independence brought with it rising expectations on the part of the population which the nationalist government was increasingly hard-pressed to fulfill.   Steady,   rapid growth meant providing more consumer goods for the population at the same time that the government needed its scarce foreign exchange to support its increasing share of capital investment.   A study for potential foreign investors noted in 1959 that "such steady development is counted on to support the political ascendancy of the CPP.   The party's survival became tied to the growth of the economy, which reinforced the emphasis on the necessity for a concentration of power in the party.   The successful military coup in February, 1966 - which occurred when consumer prices were rising rapidly and shortages of consumer goods were critical - only provides the final example of the extent of the party's dependence upon its ability to deliver the economic goods."[18]

To understand the dynamic developmental challenge that Nkrumah faced, it is necessary to understand the conditions under which he and his political party came to power.   The major concern was that the CPP won political independence not by prolonged struggle but through a period of electoral political process which extended over a period of six years.[19] Between 1951 through 1957, Nkrumah's administration, shared power with the British, and to a certain extent both the party and Nkrumah were dependent on the British for their continued power. As Card puts it:

> The fundamental economic and political decisions made during the dyarchy continued to impose their parameters upon Nkrumah's action long after nominal political independence was achieved. These decisions were made mostly by the British themselves, either directly or indirectly. The economic decisions determined the direction of the developmental effort; and the CPP's political reliance upon elections, and, later, legal control, deprived the party of any potential organizational base for an effective national challenge to continuing economic imperialism.[20]

The acceptance of the conditions imposed by the British government during the dynarchy presupposed basic challenges to the existing political and socio economic order. Between 1951, when Nkrumah became leader of government business, and 1957, when Ghana became the first black African state to achieve its political independence; Nkrumah was, in reality, completely dependent on the British for his power.

> This sharing of power during the dyarchy served the British in several ways: they could "assist" in the determination of major economic policies; they could educate African leaders to their political ideology and they could prevent a revolution from taking place under "communists" thus allaying their Cold War fears. The British administration retained control over crucial sectors, including defense, external affairs, justice, and finance during the early years Nkrumah was in office.[21]

Furthermore, this particular arrangement clearly served the interests of the nationalists, at least in their own efforts. As Fanon indicates "the will to break colonialism is linked with another quite different will; that of coming to a friendly agreement with it."22   Also, the nationalists believed that economic assistance would be realized through cooperation; the legitimacy of authority of the CPP would be reinforced through association with the British; and party leaders gained time to rebuild their power viv-a-vis both their opponents within the party and opposition parties.23   One may even argue that Nkrumah's political victory would not have been possible without extensive British support.

Although, the CPP's ideology continued to be channelled toward mobilizing the people for the responsibility of national development, through its efforts at rigid control it sometimes served in Fanon's language "to mobilize the people."   The Nkrumah's administration did not make a strong distinction between reducing public and/or private consumption.   The administration had to continue to permit private consumption to increase in order to retain its political support.   Hence, capital continued to flow out of Ghana at a faster rate.   Also, during this period, the planners overestimated the government's ability to attract foreign direct private investment while at the same time underestimated the rate at which recurrent spending from previous programs would consume reserves.

Meanwhile, the prices of imported capital and manufactured goods needed for industrial and agricultural projects under the plan rose during the same period by 25 percent.24   By early 1966, Ghana's average import bill was 264 million cedes (local currency) as apposed to 245.4 million cedes which was the export earnings for cocoa, timber, diamonds, manganese, and gold.25 This gives a trade deficit balance of 8.9 million cedes.   The above mentioned problems had resulted to political instability in Ghana.   Many attempts to kill the president had been made by several people and in many areas of Ghana-notably Kulungungu, in the upper region, Kumasi, in Ashanti region and also in Accra, the capital city.   There were widespread political detention and many ministers, and party functionaries used this as an opportunity to settle disputes between and among their political opponents. That there was some level of corruption and nepotism in high places cannot be disputed. Nkrumah realized this and in one historical broadcast (the Dan Broadcast) on April 8, 1961 had to say that, "I am aware that the evil of patronage finds a good deal of place in our society. I consider that it is entirely wrong for person placed in positions of eminence or authority to use the influence of office in patronizing others, in many cases wrong persons, for immoral favors. I am seeing to it that this evil shall be up-rooted, no matter whose ox is gored. The same thing goes for nepotism, which is, so to speak, a twin brother of evil of patronage."[26]

As the economy was shaky by early 1966, austerity measures had to be used to save the situation. It is possible that Ghana would have over come her economic problems with time. However, experience has shown that whenever a country experiences economic problems in addition to political tension and social vices such as corruption and nepotism, instability can easily set in. Ghana is not an exception. So on 24 February, 1966 while president Nkrumah was enroute to Hanoi on a peace mission, the military cum police seized power. This marked the fall of the first republic of Ghana and the end of Nkrumah's administration as well.

GHANA UNDER THE NATIONAL LIBERATION COUNCIL

The new military cum police government called itself the National Liberation Council (N. L. C.) under the leadership of General Ankrah labelled charges against Nkrumah and the Convention Peoples Party. The charges include the following: (1) mismanagement of the economy, nepotism, corruption, massive unemployment, oppression and suppression of the people. The N.L.C. after taken over the government, immediately abandoned the Seven-Year Development Plan.

Many of the state enterprises were shut down for allegedly not being productive and in most cases they were sold to private investors who were mainly foreign Multinational Corporations. These investors inturn transferred some of the machineries to neighboring countries where they deemed desirable. Most of the state farms were closed down. The workers brigade was abolished. Other important projects, such as the building of an International Airport was halted. Some fishing travelers belonging to the state Fishing Corporation were sold to private companies and the expansion of the fleet of the National Shipping Line (called Black Star Line) was stopped. However, in reality, it seemed apparent that the new government was not going to pursue the socialist policies of the Nkrumah era. In fact, it was a capitalist government with close ties with the West. Loans, immediately after the coup, began to pour into Ghana to help her solving her economic problem. However, the terms of agreement for these loans were not critically examined in this text.

As a result of political instability which hindered economic development, many schools, colleges and universities were closed down "for lack of high enrollment." As these state enterprises were sold out or closed down, many employees were thrown out of jobs and Ghana for the first time since independence recorded the highest unemployment figure of 105,000.[27] Between 1966 and 1969 of N.L.C. rule, the Labor Department officially recorded 70,500 layoffs. Again, with the abandonment of Seven Year Development Plan and after having dismantled the existing economic order, the economic problems of Ghana worsened. Despite the rise in cocoa prices and the loans contracted for Ghana by the assistance of the western industrialized countries through the International Monetary Fund (IMF) and the International Bank for Reconstruction and Development (IBRD), Ghana's economy deteriorated to a peak where the N.L.C. had to devalue the national currency by 44 percent on July 8, 1967.[28]

However, the N.L.C.'s policy of trade liberalization resulted to high rate of inflation. Corruption had reached its zenith and in October 1967, the West African Magazine in an article wrote that bribery and corruption in "both high and low places... has become inevitably a feature of our national life."[29] Unfortunately the head of state, General Ankrah had to resign from both the government and army for having admitted of receiving bribes amounting up to 30,000 cedes from Foreign firms through an intermediary.[30]

By 1968, it was apparent that there was great disaffection towards the N.L.C. whose membership had rapidly promoted themselves to higher military and police ranks. This disaffection was manifested even much earlier in a coup attempt on April 17, 1967, which claimed the life of Lt. General Kotoka the leader of the 1966 coup d'etat which toppled the Nkrumah government. The only solution to this situation was to hand over the government to civilian regime. They did this in September, 1969 to Prime Minister K.A. Busia whose political party (The Progress Party) won the election.

Many documented evidences available indicated that Ghana did not experience any economic development during the three year rule of N.L.C. As mentioned earlier, inflation and unemployment were widespread. National debt had also increased beyond limit. Thus, by the time Busia inherited the Office in 1969, Ghana's indebtedness had increased up to one billion dollars as estimated by the New York times; as against a national debt of 805.3 million cedes inherited from Nkrumah regime.

BUSIA AND THE POLITICAL ECONOMY OF GHANA

Given the above information, one can see that the Progress Party under K.A. Busia had inherited administration with many economic, social and political problems. There was low rate of economic growth, high rate of inflation, high rate of unemployment and tremendous fall in the prices of cocoa. Added to these points was the debts increased. Most of the debts borrowed by his predecessor governments had become matured for repayments. And that alone added more pressure on the K.A. Busia's administration. Despite all of these problems, the Busia's government still pursued a trade liberalization policy under an open general licensing system. Under such policy option, every capable financial person could import any goods without the prior consent of the government. This system similar to the present Nigerian policy increased the national debt. Many austerity measures were under taken to remedy and restore the state of the economy to its normal position.

The decline in the price of cocoa in the world market led to the general decrease in the standard of living. Lack of incentives for agricultural farmers and cocoa industry resulted in shortage of food supply and employment opportunity for the citizens. The smuggling of crops to neighboring countries such as Togo and Ivory Coast for better prices and a stronger currency definitely affected the export figures and earnings respectively. Furthermore, Ghana's position as one of the largest producers of cocoa was also threatened. The government's expulsion of about two million aliens from Ghana most of whom worked in the cocoa farms had some economic repercussion. It further weakened Ghana's cocoa production and hence resulted in the decline of government revenue.

There is no evidence that the Progress Party Government under Busia pursued a continuity of any economic program introduced by the N.L.C. The only visible continuity was found in the field of trade and the development of a capitalist economy in Ghana. Busia's government, however,did make effort to stabilize the economy as a means to achieve economic development. By the end of 1967, the foreign exchange reserves were at its low level of about $40 million. To prevent any economic obstruction, the Prime Minister, Busia on December 27, 1971 devalued the nation's currency by 73 percent.[31] The devaluation came as a shock to the entire nation and it was not taken lightly. On January 13, 1972, Lt. Col. I.K. Acheampong seized control while Busia was in London for medical treatment. Following Ghana's second coup in six years, an editorial in the government owned Ghanaian Times proclaimed. "For the second time, the armed forces have had to come in to take over the reins of government to save the country from maladministration and corruption of politicians, and to save the nation from total economic collapse."[32]

In the month before the second coup, the price of cocoa had reached a five-year low. The fall in cocoa prices occurred simultaneously with a 44 percent devaluation of the Ghanaian currency in the same month. The devaluation was a part of Busia's austerity program, necessitated by the continued dependence on export earnings and the consequent need to curb imports and limit private consumption. Furthermore, cocoa prices and the import-export sector had coalesced to produce political instability in Ghana, but in both cases, one can argue that it was instability born of continued colonial economic relations rather than instability derived from the birth of a new order. Once again, the political structure of Ghana was dismantled.

A BRIEF EXAMINATION OF THE ECONOMY OF GHANA UNDER THE NATIONAL REDEMPTION COUNCIL (N.R.C.)

The National Redemption Council (N.R.C.), which was formed to head the government, immediately suspended the constitution, banned political parties, abolished the Supreme Court, and dissolved the National Assembly. Busia had devalued the currency with the primary objective that it would increase the export trade and also help the country withher balance of payment difficulties. Neither of these happened. The National Redemption Council proclaimed that "the whole question of the devaluation will be looked into along with the entire Busia program for urgent development of the rural areas where the crops are grown at the expense of the city dwellers."[33]

The message was clear: development programs initiatives taken by Busia administration will be temporarily suspended while the N.R.C. designed its own developmental plan that would set Ghana in motion. Our finding here is that it is this kind of discontinuity of development programs as government changes from one hand to another that hinders the economic development of Ghana.

By the mid 1972, the N.R.C. revalued her currency to about two-thirds of its original value and repudiated the nation's debt. Strict import controls were exercised. For a while the economy looked very promising.   Ghana at the first time of military regime experienced signs of economic recovery.   There was a good harvest in 1972 and again in 1973 which coincided with the N.R.C.'s agricultural program of "Operation Feed Yourself" (O.F.Y.). The O.F.Y. had helped in rice production to increase from 11,000 tons in 1971 to 62,000 tons in 1973; maize from 53,200 to 430,000 in the same period.[34]   Meanwhile, the inflation rate had increased from 18.7 percent in July 1974, to 50.5 percent in July 1976.[35] Under economic pressure from the Multinational Corporation whose loans to Ghana the National Redemption Council had repudiated, the Acheamong regime was forced to honor debts and in some cases plead for their rescheduling with higher interest rate.

Meanwhile, the Operation Feed Yourself program had failed due to the lack of adequate irrigation schemes to transcend the 1974-1977 excessive droughts. Besides, farmers whose farms were located very close to boarder areas, managed to smuggle their crops across and sold for hard currency in either Togo, Ivory Coast and/or Upper Volta. As result, Acheamong and his government the S.M.C. were still facing the problem of food shortages and high prices of commodities as a result of excessive inflation in the economy. During this period, however, everybody started to demand a change in government to civilian rule. Student's anti-government demonstration was strongly suppressed. To make matters worse, S.M.C. wanted a "Union Government For Ghana. This is nothing but to form a coalition government with Army, police and civilian to govern the country by institutional representation. The demand by the S.M.C. was fully rejected by the people through a referendum carried out to determine the mind of the people. Given the fact that the "Union Government" idea was rejected by the people at the referendum, the results were manipulated to reflect the desires of the S.M.C.

In the wake of accusations that governmental activity had become a "One-Man Show."[36] General Acheampong was forced to resign as head of state on July 5, 1978, and was immediately succeeded by his deputy, Lt. General Frederick Akuffo. Akuffo promised a return to civilian rule by mid 1979 through general elections. But the wish of the people at the time was positive action against corruption. His inability to handle the problem resulted in another military coup on June 4, 1979, led by junior military officers. The next day, an Armed Forces Revolutionary Council (A.F.R.C.) was established under the chairmanship of Flight Lt. Jerry John Rawlings. In the process of "cleaning up exercise" prior to elections and handing over, according to Agbango, eight high ranking military and civilian officials were executed on the grounds of corruption despite wide international protest." Among these were the three former heads of state namely: Lt. General Ankrah (who led the coup against Nkrumah), Gen. Acheampong (who led the coup against Dr. K. A. Busia), and Gen. Akuffo (who staged the palace coup against Acheampong).[37] As soon as the A.F.R.C. came into power, it went around ruthlessly attacking corruption. Military and civilian officials who were in government and could not account for their extraordinary wealth, were tried for corruption and sentenced for long terms of imprisonment and their assets were converted to state ownership.[38] The A.F.R.C. did try its best to eliminate if not eradicate corruption in Ghana within a short period of stay in office.

THE THIRD REPUBLIC:
GHANA UNDER HILLA LIMANN ADMINISTRATION

During the general election of that summer (1979) the People's National Party (PNP) won the election. Dr. Hilla Limann was sworn in as the new President of Ghana. The Limann administration inherited the office of government with total economic collapse. The economy of Ghana at this time was at the virgin of its collapse. Debts owned by the previous governments were all ready for repayment. Once again, Limann and the P.N.P. were responsible for the repayment of these debts. Limann and P.N.P. government pursued a positive Non-aligned Foreign Policy (which even annoyed the Eastern Bloc which expected the new government to pursue socialist as its counterpart (C.P.P.) did under Nkrumah. The administration also increased and encouraged freedom of speech, press, and publication.[39]

During this period, agriculture was fully encouraged. Agricultural loans were given to both small peasant and large scale commercial farmers. Imported agricultural equipment were available, and fertilizers were imported mostly from Eastern Germany to improve agricultural productivity. Private investments were encouraged as opposed to state ownership of the means of production introduced by Nkrumah and its government (C.P.P.). A trade liberalization bill was passed by the Parliament which enabled the wealthy people to import goods needed by the society. This had also helped to solve the problem of shortages of certain essential commodities.

Meanwhile, Limann administration was faced with the problem

of increase in the price of crude oil. Furthermore, because Limann government proved unable to halt further deterioration of the nation's economy, the army seized control in a coup on December 31, 1981. A Provisional National Defense Council (P.N.D.C.) was proclaimed with Jerry John Rawlings as the chairman and head of state. Parliament was dissolved, the constitution was suspended, and the President and his Cabinet were all dismissed from office.

One of the first decisions taken by the Provisional National Defense Council was to suspend the 1981-82 budget of the Limann administration. Second was the creation of "National investigations Committee" to evaluate charges of impropriety by the members of the previous administration, as well as a "citizen's voting committee" (CVC) to review individual assets whose lifestyle appeared inconsistent with the declared income.[40] The outcome of this measure was that the savings rate in the banks dropped seriously as people rushed to withdraw their savings and more especially it discouraged individuals from keeping their money in the savings account deposit. The immediate effect was shortage of liquid cash in various banks.

Since the 1981 coup, the Rawlings regime has come under increasing pressure on several fronts: economically, a steady decline in the world price of cocoa and population expansion resulting from the expulsion of Ghanaians from Nigeria have led to serious food shortages and profiteering: politically, three attempted counter-coups and a number of clashes between pro- and anti-government forces have resulted in radical state policy changes, which include reorganization of the judicial and administrative structures. Rawlings has been in office for nearly twelve years now. But the economic situation of the country has completely deteriorated beyond expectation. There are chronic shortages of petrol all over the country. Since 1982, the killing and destruction of human personnel in Ghana is very deplorable. The creation of an interim People's Tribunal Council in 1983 with the authority not subject to appeal, to try individuals in absentia and to hand down death sentences, has given the P.N.D.C. very strong dictatorial power over its subjects. Regardless of Rawlings dictatorship, he has failed to mobilize the people. Agriculture which was the priority program of the Limann government has not been given adequate attention. Consequently, food prices have sky-rocketed. Ghana which has been the producer of agricultural food has now turned to become the buyer of agricultural foods. To sum up, Ghana has failed to build agricultural base as a result of political instability. We strongly believe in this writing that political stability is a positive step toward achieving economic development.

TENTATIVE ASSESSMENT, EVALUATION AND PREDICTION OF THE FUTURE ECONOMY OF GHANA

In the overall analysis, an attempt has been made to show the socio-politico-economic development of Ghana before and after independence. A brief account of each of the regimes that have ruled Ghana from 1957 to the present has been given. Some of the possible socio-economic factors that led to the military takeovers of the government have been analyzed. The economic development has been examined. First, we observed that Nkrumah had been unable to lead Ghana out of the trap of dependency and underdevelopment which was bequeathed the country by its colonial rulers. Even though he was ideologically committed to socialism, he did not have a sufficient political base to take either the initial steps, such as nationalizing the foreign owned sectors of the economy or turning decisively to the communist bloc for new trade arrangements. Either of these could have a positive impact in the economy of Ghana. Any success in eliminating foreign domination of the major sectors of the economy could have only been achieved under Nkrumah's strategy if and only if sufficient foreign exchange had been available to obtain essential imports needed for the operation of the state enterprises.

All the same, after thirty-three years of political independence, Ghana's economy is still in shamble.

Her economic development has remained stagnant. Strictly speaking, there can be no marked progressive economic development of any country that is politically unstable. Therefore, political stability should be a positive step toward achieving economic development of Ghana.

The major solution to the instability in underdeveloped countries in general and Ghana in particular is good honest, and dedicated government. As stated by Anthony Ochefu in *Daily Star of Anambra,* "Only those with transparent honesty and dedication would come near to the corridor of power."[41] Secondly, any meaningful economic development must depend upon good planning, organization and feasibility study of the economy as a whole. Good development programs should not be abandoned simply because they were initiated by the previous government in power.

African continent in general is blessed with natural resources. And Ghana in particular has large reserves minerals such as diamond, bauxite, iron and many others in abundant. What it entails is stable government to establish good investment climate which will attract foreign investors. Again, the problem of corruption must be dealt with if progress is to be found in Ghana.

After political independence, the Nkrumah's regime made a serious endeavor to accelerate economic growth and development; but during those first few years of its independence, the government conservatively followed the economic development plans designed by Arthur Lewis. This western economist advocated a pragmatic approach based on continued reliance on external capital and trade with Western Europe and North America. Ghana's macroeconomic measures henceforth reinforced the nation's external economic dependency. From 1957 to 1961, the policy measure was as Card indicates:

No direct efforts were made to eliminate foreign influence. During this period of "competitive coexistence," only the Ghana Commercial Bank, founded in 1953, provided any serious competition to foreign business enterprises. During this time, CPP-affiliated and state ventures were launched in insurance, shipping, lumber, construction, and cocoa-purchasing, but there was no government restriction of foreign competition with these enterprises.[42]

It was argued that, with indigenous private firm generally restricted to small scale operation, direct government action would be necessary in almost every area of operation. The main emphasis was upon state investment as the major source of capital in the absence of large accumulation in the hands of Ghanaian citizens.

In conclusion, therefore, despite these measures, the internal structure of the Ghanaian economy did not change sufficiently to offset continuing losses in export revenues and generate sufficient development and working capital necessary for economic growth and stability. Changes in the internal structural arrangement of the economy as well as revised foreign trade are equally important to freeing a dependent economy. Since the nation's external trade continued to resemble the colonial pattern, not surprisingly, the Ghana's internal economy did not change its composition and structure enough also.

Confronted with the necessity for economic growth and development, the Ghanaian government realized that its failure to structurally transform the colonial past seriously limited economic alternatives available for Ghana's economic development. However, in the absence of total transformation of the economy, Nkrumah's strategy became that of decolonization or post independence, anti-colonial nationalism rather than socialist revolutionary change. Meanwhile, the Nkrumah government endeavored to reorganize the internal economic, political, and social order of Ghana while at the same time maintaining the nation's major trading patterns. However, on the surface it seemed that greater control of the internal economy by the government was being made, internal economic measures continued to be dominated by external hegemonic influences. The economic choices made during the dyarchy and Ghana's continuing position as an exporter of primary products combined to circumscribe severely Ghana's ability to free itself from continuing external economic dependency through building an integrated economy.[43]

NOTES

1. Richard Harris, *The Political Economy of Africa*, Schenkman Publisher Inc., Massachusetts, 1975, p. 2. Roe Alan, *Instruments of Economic Policy in Africa* (London: James Currey, 1992) for further African Subordination to Foreign Interest See Richard OLaniyan, *African History and Culture* (New York: Longman, 1992). Fredoline O. Anunobi: *The Implications of Conditionality: The International Monetary Fund and Africa* (Maryland: UPA, 1992). Also see the work by Anne O. Krueger, *Economic Policy Reform In Developing Countries* (Cambridge: Blackwell 1992). Michael C. Desch, *When the Third World Matters: Latin America and United States Grand Strategy* (Baltimore The Johns Hopkins University Press, 1993).

2. George Abango, Political Economy of Instability in Ghana (*unpublished Research* Paper, Clark-Atlanta University, 1988). See also the work by Nii Kwaku Sowa, "Ghana", ed. in. Aderanti Adepoju, *The Impact of Structural Adjustment on the Population of Africa* (London: James Currey, 1993).

3. Speech made by Nkrumah on March 6, 1957 at Ghana's Independence.

4. George Abango, Political Economy of Instability in Ghana.

5. Kamarack Skalyn, The Economic of African Development, pp. 204.

6. Kwame Nkrumah, *Dark Age in Ghana* (Panaf Books, Ltd., 1965), p. 126.

7 .Clark Leith, *Foreign Regimes and Economic Development: Ghana* (Columbia University Press, New York, 1974), p. 6. Michael C. Desch, *When the Third World Matters.*, John Adijimah, Ghana and Nigeria Economic Development: A Comparative Studies (Ibadan: Ibadan University Press) 1983 Ralph Austen, *African Economic History* (London: James Currey, 1987). A deranti Adepoju, *The Impact of Structural Adjustment on The Population of Africa.*

8. Nkrumah, "Education Program", p. 130.

9. Ibid., p. 188.

10. George Abango, The Political Economy of Instability in Ghana.

11. Ukandi Damachi, *Nigeria Modernization, The Colonial Legacy*, 1972, p. 74.

12. A Highlife song quoted in Dennis Austin *Politics in Ghana* (London: Oxford University Press, 1964), p. 275.

13. Nkrumah, "Analysis of Major Export Crops in Ghana", p. 61.

14. Ibid., p. 72.

15. Emily Card, *Political Economy of Africa, ed in The Political Economy of Africa* by Richard Harris. See also the work by Anne Krueger, *Economic Policy Reform in Developing Countries* (Cambridge: Blackwell, 1992) And the work by Simon Commander, *Structural Adjustment and Agriculture: Theory and Practice in Africa and Latin America*. Maseem Abmad, Deficit Financing, Inflation and Capital Formation: A Case Study of Ghana (Washington, D.C.: *World Bank, 1970*). Jean M. Due, Development Without Growth: The Case of Ghana in the 1960s, *Economic Bulletin of Ghana* 3(1), (1973).

16. Ibid., p. 52.

17. Ibid., p. 53.

18. Ibid., p. 54.

19. Franz Fanon, *The Wretched of the Earth* (New York: Grove Press, 1963).

20. Card, *The Political Economy of Africa*, p. 55.

21. Ibid., p. 56.

22 Fanon, *Wretched of The Earth*, p. 124.

23. Ibid.

24. Ibid., p. 103.

25. Ibid., p. 116.

26. Ibid., p. 120.

27. West Africa, 22 April, 1967. Anthony G. Hopkins, *An Economic History of West Africa* (London: Longman, 1975). Institute For African Development: A Report of the Special Programming Mission to Ghana, Report No. 0105 GH, 1988. *World Bank*, Ghana Living Standard Surveys: Preliminary Studies and Social Dimensions of Adjustment (Washington, D.C.: *World Bank*, 1988). World Bank, Africa's Adjustmeent and Growth in the 1980's (Washington, D.C.: *World Bank*, 1983). World Bank, Ghana Structural Adjustment for Growth (Washington, D.C.: *World Bank*, 1989).

28. Richard Harris, "External Economic Relation", p. 203.

29. West Africa, 20 June 1969.

30. Samuel Decalo, *Coups and Army Rule in Africa* (Yale University, 1976), p. 25.

31. Harris, "Economic in the Political Kingdom", p. 147.

32. Ibid., p. 153.

33. Issaka Naba, "Economic Disorder in Ghana" (an article in *Africa Youth*, Vol. I No 9. State University of New York, Binghamton, New York, August 1978).

34. Naba, "Economic Disorder" p. 170.

35. Ibid. p. 153.

36. George Agbango, *Unpublished Paper* on The Political Economy of Ghana's Instability, p. 14.

37. Ibid.

38. The A.F.D.C. was in office for only four months but within this period, inflation was highly reduced even though figures are not available to support this.

39. Agbango *Unpublished Research Paper*.

40. *Political Handbook of World*.

41. Anthony Ochefu, A Speech on the Mismanagement Fund in Anambra State, Daily Star, 1976.

42. Card, *The Political Economy of Africa*, p. 78.

43. Card, p. 81.

CHAPTER 8

Political Dynamism and The Rise of Military in Sudan

The major responsibilities that must be achieved by the government of Sudan, as in most new African nations, consist of an extra ordinarily heavy task. At the same token, a new political arrangement and national identity must be created. Expectations for essential improvement in living conditions must be accomplished, and the mechanisms of external regulation must be minimized. Sudan does not have the opportunity of achieving these challenges one after the other, as was the case in most industrialized capitalist states. Majority of these objectives are of equal importance and need urgent consideration. Their answers are in reality interdependent and really the endeavors to resolve these problems and/or crises would accelerate balanced prosperity. Furthermore, the method will result to disequilibrium and emphasize stability instead of development per se. The general features of the challenges facing the Sudanese government and the manner in which those problems are being solved create a useful focus for this analysis.

THE HISTORICAL FOUNDATION
OF SUDANESE NATIONAL IDENTITY

The emergence of the Sudanese Republic could not fail to show many Sudanese of the foundation, over seventy five years before, of the Mahdist state. Still, there was little true similarity between and among the two identities. The ideology of the Mahdia was mainly religious; and compromise between it and the Medieval government in the Sudan was out of point. The Mahdist state was created out of the crisis of a revolutionary war, in which the created administrative and/or functionary system had been subverted, and the precarious economic self reliance of the Turco-Egyptian era affirmed. Meanwhile, the Sudanese nationalist who had created the Republic were seriously affected by Western political culture, political socialization, and political philosophies. These nationalists sought not to destroy, but to control or regulate the regime which had been built up under the foundation. The nationalists also professed with differences of sincerity and understanding attachment to parliamentary democracy. Thus, the Republic was most importantly not the supplanter but the successor of the condominium and/or foundation government. January 1, 1956 establishes simply in a conventional perspective, a new direction in Sudanese political history.

Also, at the time of political independence, January 1, 1956, Sudan comprised a number of ethnically and culturally distinct entities who were not tied together by a common national respect. Even within Africa, Africans were divided by different cultural heritages, languages, religions, historical traditions, and ways of life. Therefore, in Sudan the struggle for political independence was the first important endeavor to consolidate these disparate entities and the significance of the recent slogan, "One Sudan, One Nation", reflects the continued desire to create a strong and viable national identity and/or political autonomy.

THE NATURE OF POLITICAL PROCESS IN SUDAN

The fact that the legacy of colonialism is the main reason for the absence of national integration in Sudan, the struggle for political independence has had the implication of disrupting previous political processes and demanding for the creation of new rules of the game. The nationalist struggle was basically a demand for the political independence of Sudan. Therefore, the main targets of the struggle were the organizations and the patterns of the colonial administration.

> The leaders of the struggle for independence attacked the legitimacy of the way in which individuals were recruited to positions of authority, the manner in which policies were formulated and administered, and the fundamental goal of white domination over the indigenous population that pervaded the whole colonial political system. In that the nationalist movement was successful in destroying the structure and dynamics of the existing political order, it made necessary the establishment and acceptance of new institutions and procedures.[1]

The consequence of a colonial economy is that an alien, culturally unique minority has created and imposed itself in a position of political, economic and social hegemony. As Dresang states, "the resources of political power, economic wealth and social prestige are all the property of this ruling minority". Regulation and/or control over and access to these instruments are jealously guarded by the people in political authority for fear that the ownership of one instrument may lead to its use in securing the others and hence challenge the existing political arrangement. The capability of political institution to allocate public revenues, for example, can be exercised in a direction to redistribute national wealth in a way to benefit the group with a predominant political authority. The cotton control board was a classic example in which Europeans utilized their political power to preserve their economic hegemony. During the colonial administration, Sudanese were denied high levels of education, earning high wages, exercising important political authority, and becoming accepted into European society.[2]

The true line of demarcation must be indicated earlier either on the appointed day of January 9, 1954, when the significant transfer of power from British to Sudanese hands occurred; or on November 17, 1958, when the military coup d'etat marked the end of the first parliamentary democracy in Sudan. As soon as political independence was achieved, Azhari was able to retain his position as prime minister. January 18, 1956 saw a dramatic change in Sudanese political process. It was a period in history that marked the down fall of Azhari administration in the lower house on a budget vote. Meanwhile, he was able to maintain his office because he won a confidence motion the following day. Also, the resignation of three ministers forced Azhari to form a coalition government. On February 2, the new cabinet was sworn, which included Muhammad Nural-Din, Mirghani Hamza, Ibrahim Ahmad and Abdallah Khalil. The formation of the People's Democratic Party by members of Azhari's parliamentary party clearly marked the total collapse of his administration. On July 5, Abdallah Khalil, was elected Prime Minister against Azhari by a total vote of sixty to thirty-two.

The new political arrangement, by bringing together the proponents of the rival religious leaderships, seemed generally to welcome the preference of national over sectarian loyalties. The general history of the first parliamentary democracy was to be characterized by what P.M. Holt, and M. W. Daly called "unpromising start by petty rivalries and the crippling mutual suspicions of coalition partners." These two scholars proceeded:

> The paper alliance of the rival sects' supporters was reminiscent of the efforts, some thirty years before, of the two sayyids to crush the nascent secular nationalism of 'Ali'Abd al-Latif. The alliance of 1956 was if anything more artificial and tactical: the coalition partners had divergent views on even the most fundamental questions of policy, and united only for the purpose of defeating Azhari. The Western-oriented Umma was seen to be maneuvering for the appointment of Sayyid 'Abd al-Rahman as life-president of

the Sudan under a constitution as yet unwritten; the PDP one wing of which looked to revolutionary Egypt for inspiration, was vigilant of the interests of Sayyid 'Ali'. The depressing resiliency of this sectarian rivalry robbed the new republic of even a brief period of political vitality.[3]

With the advent of political independence during 1956-1958 parliamentary era, the features of sovereignty were maintained. At this point however, the Republic of Sudan was officially and diplomatically recognized by foreign governments. Between January and February 1956, Sudan became a member of the Arab League and United Nations respectively. Sudan further joined other international organizations such as the International Monetary Fund and the International Bank for Reconstruction and Development popularly known as World Bank. At the same token, a diplomatic corp was created and presided over by Mohammed Ahmed Mahgoub, the Umma Foreign Minister, who represented the Sudan on the International arena.

GENERAL EXPECTATION OF ECONOMIC CONDITIONS

The Sudanese citizens expect their standard of living conditions to be better now that political independence has been achieved. In reality, this expectation is the product of promises engendered by those leaders who mobilized support for the nationalist movement. In fact, a less realistic thinking process is added. Sudanese nationalists who perceived the life styles of Europeans and then believed that Europeans were no longer in authority or power could clearly expect that there would be a redistribution of Sudan's wealth to provide for the social welfare of Sudan. Regardless of the circumstances, Sudanese leaders are aware of the need to satisfy existing expectation and future demands for enhancing the quality of living condition.

Beside, Sudan has enough potential for becoming a very rich

and wealthy state given the availability of natural resources. The present economic strength of Sudan is received from cotton. Meanwhile, more than 92 percent of Sudan's export earnings and 65 percent of government revenues come from cotton production. Evidence indicated that Sudan has enough mining activities which are not well developed. There are for instance, enough deposits of tin, copper, coal, tungsten and many other minerals. Enough industries have been created to use these mineral wealth. Hydroelectric power can be erected to enhance the development of these industries and to supply private consumer goods and services. The construction of Roseires Dan 1961 was a classical example of this effort. Also, a substantial amount of investment in communication in 1965-1970 was a positive step toward self-sufficiency in the production of electric power.

Again, Sudan has enough resources for the growth and development of a richly productive agricultural industrial base. As I indicated to the editor of the Montgomery Advertizer in my interview of January 8, 1993, no single country in Africa prior to 1960 had suffered from hunger and starvation. In the first decade of political independence, self sufficiency was achieved in the production of cotton, sugar, maize, poultry and diary products. Majority of Sudanese foodstuffs could be produced within the nation. Furthermore, export products such as cotton, tobacco, groundnut, beans and many other are grown and represent activities that could be enlarged.

The main salient issue in Sudanese political-economy is government's performance in promoting accelerated economic growth and development. The primary objectives are to raise the general levels of welfare and education, to accomplish regional and sectorial balance in the economy, and to avoid the growth of wide-gap in levels of income distribution. The achievement of these objectives would create a heavy burden on any government.

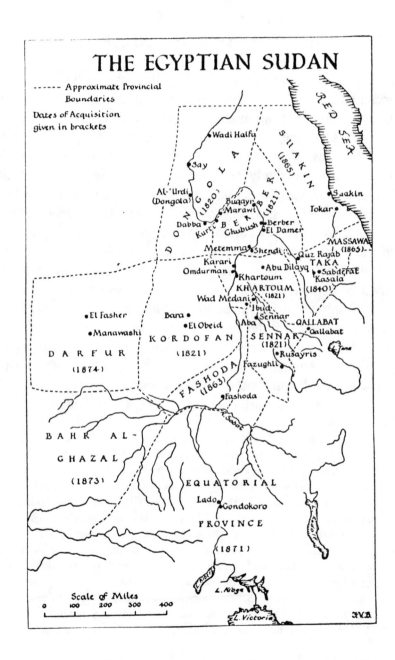

THE EGYPTIAN SUDAN

- - - - - Approximate Provincial Boundaries

Dates of Acquisition given in brackets

THE FIRST NATIONAL
DEVELOPMENT PLAN IN SUDAN 1957-1962

The macroeconomic measure during the first parliamentary era concentrated on expanding the Sudan's agricultural capability and enhancing communication and transport system. Meanwhile, the Managil Extension to the Gezira Program, to put additional 800,000 acres of irrigated land and increase the region under cotton to approximately 500,000 acres, was in place in 1956. This new five year Economic Development Plan starting in 1957 was estimated to cost $138 million. However, the concentration of capital resources in cotton growing zones, according to Holt and Daly was to prove disastrous in the late 1950s. During 1957 and 1958, cotton crops were poor, and a declining international market combined with the government insistence on maintaining a fixed minimum price for cotton resulted in a serious shock and a serious depletion in the nation's currency reserves.[4]

Closely associated with the economic crisis as a cause of the coalition government's failure was the conduct of Sudan's international relations. Two issues were of primary concern in the 1956-1958 era of parliamentary democracy in Sudan.

> As before independence, the Sudan's dealings with the outside world were dominated by the bilateral relationship with Egypt. The Suez crisis in 1956 strained relations with Britain and produced strong Sudanese support for Egypt. But serious tension nonetheless arose over the question of the allocation of Nile waters. The Sudan had ignored provisions of the 1929 Nile Waters Agreement when implementing its new irrigation projects. Egyptian plans to construct the High Dam at Aswan made a settlement of the issue more urgent. The Sudan government demanded that a revision of the 1929 Agreement must precede a dam construction which would have serious economic and demographic repercussions in the Sudan. The groundwork for agreement was laid by the government of 'Abdallah Khalil, but its conclusion fell to the successor regime.[5]

Another major concern of international affairs was the Sudan's acceptance of American foreign economic assistance.

Interactions between the Sudanese and American governments started in mid-1957. The declining economic position and over ambitious economic development plans of the Sudan gave rise to the government's willingness to accept American foreign aid.

> But a political backdrop of growing Arab hostility to the West, and the United States' moves to counter this with the Eisenhower Doctrine, created serious tension between the coalition partners. The increasingly pro-Egyptian PDP, despite assurance from the Umma leadership, saw the proposed aid agreement as necessarily strengthening US (and anti-Egyptian) influence in the Sudan. Resolution of this internal rift awaited the convening of a new parliament after 1958 elections.[6]

Meanwhile, the relationship between Umman and People's Democratic Party (PDP) persisted until the 1958 election campaign, since the coalition groups agreed not to oppose each other in the constituencies. However, the distribution of seats as indicated above and the naturalization of great number of pro-Umma Fallata, led to the victory at the polls for the coalition. Thus, the new parliament comprised sixty-three Umma, twenty-six PDP, forty Southern Liberal and forty-four NUP. When the NUP won the highest number of votes, a new coalition governmental arrangements was agreed by the Umman and the PDP.[7]

THE SECOND DEVELOPMENT PLAN

In October 1962 a Ten-year Development Plan for social and economic growth and development was announced. Investment over the period of time covered by the development plan was totaled to be 512 million pound of which 285 million pound was to be realized from special development budgets for major activities. However, the activity of the plan centered around agricultural and irrigation schemes; improving communication, transport and electric; and reducing the nation's dependence on the agricultural area particularly cotton. The Ten-Year Development Plan was blamed and proved to be over ambitious, as the government, like its predecessors, failed to take into consideration the important dependence of the Sudan, for surplus income on the dominant agricultural sector, which remained submissive to international market conditions. Therefore, as budget surpluses failed to reach the level required to finance the special development budgets, programs were trimmed and confidence disappeared, while Sudan's indebtedness increased significantly.

Before this plan, the Sudanese government in February 1960 created the central bank. Also an agricultural bank was established in 1959 to provide credit facilities and assistance for agricultural farmers, and in August 1962 the Industrial Bank of the Sudan started its financial activities of providing credit for the promotion and expansion of private industrial activities. Furthermore, in June 1960, the International Bank for Reconstruction and Development (IBRD) provided a loan of $15 million to finance completion of the Managil extension, and provisions were made in 1961 with the West Germany and World Bank for financing construction by an Italian group of the Roseires Dan. Again, in March 1962, a railway line was extended from Southern Kordofan to Wau in the Bahr al-Ghazal. At the same time, trade agreements and/or arrangements were reached with the United States, Britain, Soviet Union and other Eastern European nations. While bilateral economic relations and/or interactions with West Germany and Yugoslavia were common place. Colonialism involves more than political domination. The main dimension of colonial rule is economic exploitation. Therefore, the pattern of economic development that occurred during the colonial era was designed to extract indigenous wealth from the submissive colony. Hence, any improvement in the welfare of the colonized people that may result is at best described as a by product.

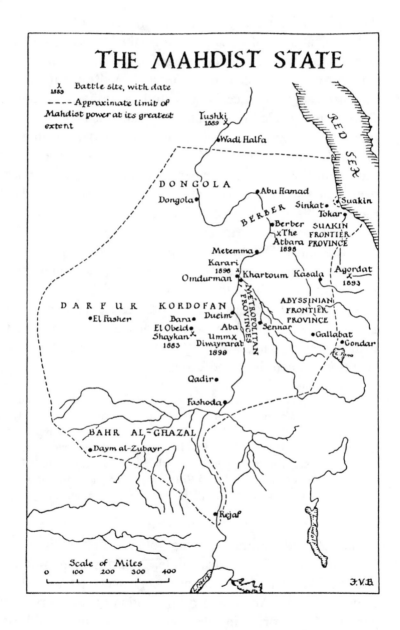

THE MAHDIST STATE

THE RISE OF MILITARY IN SUDAN

The mid-1950s were years of significant change for the newly independent state of Sudan. Neither the British authority, which surrounded power, nor the indigenous leaders who accepted the power from the British in 1956 anticipated the structural and/or dimensional crisis that would follow political independence. During independence, Sudan was hailed as an illustration of multi-ethnic coexistence, of citizens joined together in a common political establishment. It became a classic example of the federal institution of government and democracy in Africa. The events and circumstances of the late 1950s and early 1960s, therefore, threw the example into doubt and challenged the claim of the newly formed national entity.

In the mid-1958, the condition of the civilian government was soon becoming unacceptable. Declining economic conditions were perceived by the obvious inability of the present administration to cope with these problems. Some major national issues were perceived to be subordinated to increasingly rapid maneuvers engendered by the uncompromisable Umma-PDP coalition to quote Holt and Daly:

> Political machinations reached a final in the late summer when the Umma leadership began actively to explore the possibility of coalition with Azhari's NUP. This was complicated by reports of a possible NUP-PDP alliance which, if consummated, would remove the Umma from power in yet another bizarre manoeuvre. Before any of these plans could be fulfilled, however, the army had stepped in and swept away parties, politicians and the parliamentary regime itself.[8]

There is no accurate account of the first military coup in November 17, 1958. Meanwhile, it seems there was an early attempt by some key military personnel, particularly Major General Ibrahim Abboud to rid the nation of the corrupt political parties. Therefore, in the state of national address, the commander in chief, Major General Ibrahim Abboud announced the necessity of military takeover as the only viable alternative to save the nation from the chaotic administration of the civilian politicians. At the same time the state of emergency was declared. The five-man supreme commission which since political independence had replaced the governor general was dismissed. The former constitutional arrangement was suspended, government officials and ministers were arrested, political parties were dissolved and trade unions were abolished. Holt and Daly summarized the military activities in Sudan in the following way:

> The Sudan was proclaimed a 'democratic republic' with popular sovereignty. Power was invested in a thirteen-member Supreme Council of the Armed Forces which in turn delegated 'full legislative, executive and judicial powers' to Abboud. A council of ministries was named, seven of whom also sat on the Supreme Council, while five were civilians. Two ministers of the last coalition government were also included. Abboud himself was named prime minister and minister of defence. A statement by the civilian minister of foreign affairs, Ahmed Kheir, promised that the government would honor the international commitments made by its predecessors, pledged to strengthen ties with African and Arab states, placed special emphasis on improving relations with Egypt and Ethiopia, and gave diplomatic recognition to the People's Republic of China.[9]

The coup was bloodless in nature. To use the word of Holt and Daly, the "coup triggered feelings neither of euphoria nor of great regret at the passing of parliamentary government.[10]" On the global perspective, the coup was viewed as the latest event within the history of Muslim dynamism, starting with Egypt in 1952 and continuing in Iraq and Pakistan in 1958. In the context of Sudanese history, there was a general feeling of relief in the country that the corrupt civilian administration had been removed from office. Also, the belief that the military coup was primarily organized as a temporary strategy received further attention because of the events and circumstances of the military governments behaviorfirst year in power. While the coup itself ended with happiness among many, internal conflicts and struggles within the military raised doubtful issues, as factions and/or personalities competed for dominance and power.

> Abboud himself was a benevolent figure, seemingly removed from and indifferent to these internal disputes, and to this may be laid the fact that he survived them. On 2 March 1959 Brigadier Muhyi al-Din Ahmad ' Abdallah, the commander of the Eastern Area who had not been included in the Supreme Council, and Brigadier 'Abd aL-Rahim Shannan, Commander of the Northern area moved troops into the capital. General 'Abd aL-Wahhab and two other members of the Supreme Council were arrested. The intervention of 'Abdallah Khalil and the two sayyids resulted in the freeing of 'Abd al-Wahhab and the withdrawal of the troops. But two days later they reappeared in Khartoum in greater strength. The disgruntled commanders demanded and got the resignation of the Supreme Council. Abboud appointed a new Supreme Council of ten members, including Muhyi al-Din and Shannan. On 9 March General 'Abd al-Whhab was removed from all his posts and retired with a grant of three thousand acres of government land.[11]

Hence, by November 1956, the stage had been established for a revolutionary change in Sudan. The political and economic turmoil resulting from the civilian politicians had reached a critical level. Therefore, on November 17, 1958 major General Ibrahim Abboud and other military officials overthrew the civilian government. Abboud was quoted as proving that they wanted to get rid of corrupt political parties, ministers, politicians, trade unions and the major ugly apparatus of the federal institution, which according to them were responsible for lack of development in Sudan.[12] For this reason, the aim of November 1958 military coup supposedly was to remove Abudallan Khalil from political power and end the corrupt practices into which the nation had sunk under the leadership of civilian politicians. The second successful military coup of 1969 reflected the destructive impact of ethnic differences on the whole structuralarrangement of Sudanese life. As a result, Sudanese started to wonder about the genuineness of nationalist ideology that was supposed to be shown by the army.

THE HISTORY OF THE SECOND
PARLIAMENTARY DEMOCRACY IN SUDAN 1964-1969

As a result of 1964 elections, Umma's Mohammed Ahmed Mahgoub was sworn in as the new Head of State of Sudan. He was able to achieve a coalition government between his party and the NUP. This was superficially a national government in that the coalition groups between the two commanded a vast majority in parliament. They would have maintained political stability through strong leadership and a unity of purpose.

> But personal ambitions, especially of the vainglorious Mahgoub and the cynical Azhari, the NUP's veteran leader, were too strong to be subordinated, and party differences made nonsense of the coalition. Tinkering with the still-provisional constitution was by now habitual, and an amendment allowed Council of State, thereby politicizing that institution. Each coalition partner took six seats in the cabinet, while the traditional reservation of three ministerial appointments for southern was initially maintained.[13]

Majority of these political parties were ephemeral avenues for individual candidatures. The basic structures and positions of the main political parties were little different from those engendered in 1956. Meanwhile the Umma still depended largely on massive support from zones where the Ansar were predominant, while the NUP retained its position in the towns, cities and regions along the Nile. Also the results of polling, which took place in April and May, gave the Umma seventy-six seats, Islamic Charter Front five, NUP fifty-four, PDP three and communists eight.

The evolution of second parliamentary government is faced with two major internal and/or domestic problems: the persistent disturbances in the South, which in reality would have resulted in civil war if not prevented; and unprecedented internal disputes between and among political parties. These problems combined with the resulting lack of direction and/or confidence in economic activities to destroy the second, as they did the first, parliamentary democracy in Sudan. In its address of Southern issues, the administrative government of Mahgoub seemed to have learned very little from the downfalls of its military predecessor. A month after the new government was sworn in office, two major events of serious violence in the South raised the Southern crisis to an unprecedented scale.

> On 8 July 1965 northern troops at Juba went on a rampage that left hundreds of southern residents dead and whole sections of the town in ashes. On 11 July at Wau a further mass killing of southerners occurred. While the government reacted by restating its policy that lawlessness must be crushed and order restored before constitutional reforms could be discussed, SANU in exile demanded the intervention of the United Nations to bring a halt to atrocities. The Juba and Wau incidents sparked a new exodus of southerners into neighboring states, where tens of thousands were settled in refugee camps. The Anya Nya, with arms acquired through the Congo and from other foreign sources, responded to the new government offensive with atrocities of their own. A pattern developed, sickeningly familiar, in which the civilian population was caught up in the heightening spiral of violence. Villages spared the torch by one side were burnt by the other. Government control was soon limited to the major towns and heavily fortified posts; elsewhere it ceased to exist, and in some areas was replaced by a rudimentary Anya Nya administration.[14]

Furthermore, the accelerated decline in the South was shown in a confusing history of political organizations both within and outside the Sudan. In the capital city, the Southern Front, which had been in existence since the overthrow of Abboud, became in 1965 an official political party under the leadership of Clement Mboro. For all practical purposes, the Front encouraged and supported the Southern division as a separate independent political entity to govern itself.

In the economic front, economic growth and development are

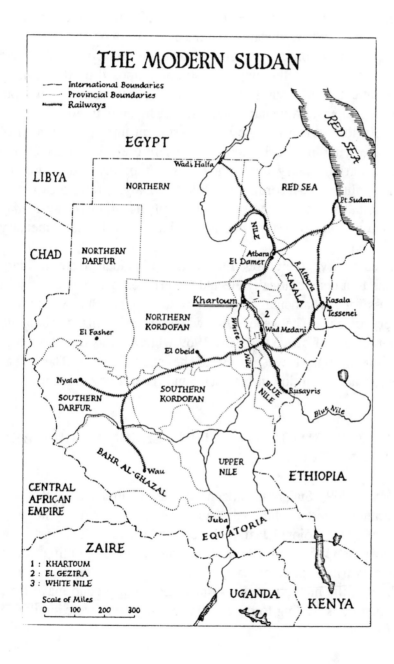

THE MODERN SUDAN

- International Boundaries
- Provincial Boundaries
- Railways

1 : KHARTOUM
2 : EL GEZIRA
3 : WHITE NILE

Scale of Miles
0   100   200   300

stagnated because of the instability of successive coalition government and the dynamic nature of trade unionism. After the October revolution a rapid growth of trade union movement had taken place. Also, the major constraints imposed by the military government were removed, only to be replaced by indepth fashion of its parliamentary successor. The civilian government's inability to regulate labor crisis and student unrest was a sign of an underlying political jealousy. Therefore, the crisis of the second parliamentary democracy was not purely economic, but rather political. According to Holt and Daly, strong measure in the capital city was necessary not simply to address day to day operations, but to restore public confidence in the parliamentary institution.

In summary, therefore, the return of Sudan from military regime to a democratically elected government was perceived as a success for parliamentary democracy in Sudan. But the political history of sudan between 1964 when Prime Minister Mahgoub took the oath of office and May 1969 when he was overthrown in a military coup leaves much to be appreciated. There was widespread corruption in both state and federal governments.

THE EVOLUTION OF THE SECOND MILITARY GOVERNMENT

In May 1969, Sudanese citizens awoke to understand that the government under Mahgoub had been overthrown. The new head of state, Colonel Jaafar Nimeiri, who had on two instances in the past (1957 and 1966), been suspected of plotting coups against various governments, succeeded in a bloodless coup. Although, the method used for the 1969 military coup maydiffer, the conditions leading to the second military coup were similar to the first one.

As in 1958, so in 1969, the prestige of the politicians and of parliamentary institutions had reached a lowebb, as they drifted from one crisis to another. The economy had suffered from mismanagement and neglect. The situation in the south showed no sign of improvement and was damaging the Sudan's foreign relations. Broad agreement between the Umma and al-Azhari on the establishment of a presidential system seemed destined, as had their agreement to form a coalition in 1958, only to prepare the way for another showdown. The 1969 coup was thus, in its origins, not simply a bid for power by disgruntled officers determined to undermine the system inherited from the co-domini, but a reaction to the collapse of that system under the weight of its own failures.[15]

Throughout the nation, there was a general consensus of the coup, citizens felt that the Mahgoub administration had failed the country and a change was necessary if not inevitable. For one thing, Mahgoub administration was charged for three major reasons: the administration's inability to meet the aspirations of the citizens despite the resources available to the nation; Mahgoub's inaccessibility to the people; and the indecision and indifference of his government.

When Colonel Jaafar Nimeiri came to power, he unilaterally suspended the national constitution, dissolved the consitutent assembly, the five-man Supreme Council of State, the public service commission and the electoral commission, banned all public meetings, closed down newspapers, outlawed all political parties and seized their property, retired twenty-two senior military personnels, placed under arrest some leading politicians such as Azhari and Mahgoub and finally promoted himself to the rank of Major General. He also renamed the country as the Democratic Republic of the Sudan.

One of the major significancd of the coup was the relative strengths of Major General Nimeiri and Awadallah who brought together the officers of the civilians, military, communists and more moderate members of the government. It is important to note that the new military administration considered itself the successor not of the old military regime of Abboud, but to the combined forces of young officers and the professionals' Front which had toppled Abboud's regime in 1964. The reality that the communist party was, despite its strong representation in the government, not exempted from the order to disband all political parties was an evidence of Nimeiri's importantly centrist position. This period marked the elimination of challenges from the right and the left and ended in the consolidation on Nimeiri's power.[16]

With this in built structural and power arrangements, the new military government had little to fear. As the leaders of former government were under house arrest or in jail, and their major weapons, an appeal for the defense of the parliamentary institution, blunted by their own transparent self interest, the institution and/or parties were generally powerless to amount organized attack. Inspite of this self confidence, there was still unexpected coup of July 19 organized by Major Hashim which temporarily toppled Major General Nimeiri regime and placed him in detention. Although, with the help of Libyan leader, Colonel Gaddafi and Egyptian troops stationed South of Khartoum to resist the coup, Nimeiri was able to escape and survived the coup.

However, the July 1971 coup had significant long-run consequences on the Nimeiri's administration. These consequences and effects of the coup were summarized by some writers as follow: First, the subordination of the Ansar and communist undoubtedly increased Nimeiri's personal popularity, but left the administration without the strong support of any major political and/or sectarian entity. Major General Nimeiri however, responded promptly, through changes in domestic and foreign policies, to improve and/or strengthen the ground of his political support and to shore up his personal position by means of a referendum on the Presidency. This, however, started on September 15 and led to 98.7 percent supportive vote for Nimeiri, who was duly sworn into office for a six year period as President.

Another serious implication of the coup was according to Holt and Daly, the realization by the Nimeiri that foreign policy should be more closely associated with, and in fact contingent upon, domestic political considerations. Hence, these scholars itemized and/or summarized president Nimeire's foreign policy posture in this form:

> Upon assuming power in 1969 the regime had asserted the Sudan's support for national liberation movements in Africa, closer ties with Eastern Europe and a total commitment to the Arab cause in the struggle with Israel. One of the regime's first acts was to recognize the government of East Germany, and Nimeiri embarked on tours of Eastern Europe, China, and North Korea in 1970. Trade with the Eastern Bloc increased greatly, and the Sudan looked to Moscow for the supply of arms and for economic assistance. The Sudan took a greater interest in Arab affairs, spurred by Nimeiri's attachment to views of Arab Socialism identified with those of President Nasser and Colonel Gaddafi. In December 1969 Libya, Egypt and the Sudan agreed in the Tripoli Charter to co-ordinate their foreign policies, a scheme that developed into a Federation of Arab Republics which, despite domestic opposition and his own misgivings, Nimeiri publicly supported. Relations with the West deteriorated in 1969-71 period, owing to continued American support for Israel, Israeli support for southern secessionists, and the government's nationalization, under unacceptable terms of compensation, of foreign, mainly British, banks and companies.[17]

With regard to economic performance, Sudanese economy seemed to complement after the 1969 revolution between periods of great optimism characterized by the launching of over ambitious national economic development policies, and periods of total collapse, when international credit was the only source of finance. Sudan is seriously in a dangerous economic crisis, whose real severity, dimension, and social and political consequences are not fully welcomed by Sudanese citizens. The main factors of this worsening economic crisis include a widerange of internal weakness, and a hostile external economic relations.

Furthermore, the ambitious development projects the nation embarked in 1969-1971 necessitated increase resort to external borrowing thereby largely increasing external indebtedness. The current economic crisis has led Sudan to experience payment imbalances so serious that it has been unable to pursue the development plan and/or strategies initiated.

The economic crisis reported in Sudan since 1970s and 1980s originated from both internal and external dimensions. The economic growth of Sudan depends largely on external resources in the form of both export revenues, whose level further depends on international market terms and borrowed capital. The external relations of Sudanese economy, again makes this nation sensitive to external shocks and vulnerable in global market exchange rates.

In addition, negative influence in Sudan included the combined implications of inflation and slackening economic operation (stagnation) in the industrialized capitalist nations. Therefore, the increase in oil prices resulted in a slow down in the productive activities of developed countries at a time when inflation was high. In the case of Sudan, these circumstances led to the collapse of its export product prices and to higher prices for its imports, leading to the deterioration of her terms of trade and widening current account disequilibrium.

Generally, they restrained the possibilities for national development. As Sudan came to know that her socio economic success was not a matter of internal economic operation and measure only. The pursuit of unbalanced growth emphasizing first agricultural development for export, led Sudan into an economic environment influenced largely by conditions beyond her control. For this reason, however, Olanjiwola concludes that Sudan became dependent upon global supply and demand conditions that determined her export revenues, limited her capacity to attract international investment in areas other than her growth areas, established the terms of foreign exchange, and as a result determined her direction and terms of trade.[18]   This condition was further explained by Holt and Daly:

> Problems were caused also by unbalanced investment policies, mismanagement, investors' uncertainties, and the difficulties of long-rang planning when investment capital was closely tied to export performance.   In the later years of the Nimeiri regime corruption was an increasing problem which, becoming rampant, had deleterious effects on the economy, while the announced implementation of the Shari'a in 1983 disrupted an already confused situation.   By the mid-1980s an enormous foreign debt, inflation, shortages, devaluation and ultimately, famine, combined to bring the Sudan to a crisis of unprecedented proportions which, in part, led to the downfall of Nimeiri.[19]

Furthermore, the unsuccessful coup of July 1971 was the foundation in economic measure as it was in domestic political and international relations.   Before that, the administration had put in place, a sweeping nationalization measure, involving both international based and Sudanese enterprises and insurance and banking businesses.   Majority of these expropriations were reversed in 1973.   Also, bilateral trading agreements with socialist nations, particularly Eastern European countries, expanded dramatically, and foreign aid came generally from the same sources.

In addition, a Five Year National Development Plan was implemented in 1970, and was later extended to seven years operation.   At the end of the coup in 1971 and Addis Ababa agreement of 1972, the Sudanese government turned largely for economic assistance and close relations to the Western World and to Arab neighbors.   As a result, emphasis shifted from state intervention to a more balanced relationship between and among the government and its specialized agencies on the one hand, and international firms, governments and global agencies on the other. Again, while attempts were made to raise the Sudanese manufacturing   capability,   particularly   in   textiles   and other agricultural based enterprises, the administration realized that progress would largely depend, as before, on the success of agriculture.

Evidence indicates that ambitious programs for accelerated economic and national development came at a period of global recession and trade stagnation.   While these conditions were beyond the government's control, its measures for approaching them were not.   Two basic errors according to Holt and Daly analysis, proved clearly expensive: concentration on new programs at the expense of those already in force, and the financing of large, long-run programs without the financial resources to meet their short-run costs.   However, these errors were exacerbated by the large increases in the price of petroleum in the 1970s, leaving the Sudanese economy seriously vulnerable to external shock.

> Cotton production may serve as an example of the general problem. As always, the country continued to depend on cotton as its major cash crop. A boom in world prices in 1973 was mismanaged by the government's marketing agencies, with disastrous results for its revenues and foreign reserves. After 1974, a new emphasis on diversifying agricultural exports led to a reduction in cotton production, which had halved by the early 1980s. The Gezira Scheme itself was threatened by falling yields, rising costs and mismanagement, and in 1980 a renovation program was undertaken with the assistance of the World Bank.[20]

The implication of these external disequilibrium was compounded by inadequate domestic economic and financial policies pursued by the Sudanese government. However, the convergence of these factors therefore led to high growing external and internal disequilibrium, high rate of inflation and unemployment, and slackening economic growth in Sudan.   Furthermore, the situation was aggravated by structural weakness created by colonialism and later neocolonialism the highest stage of imperialism.

NOTES

1. Dennis Dresang, *The Political Economy of Africa*, p. 196.

2. Leo Kuper and M.G. Smith, Eds. *Pluralism in Africa*, (Berkeley: University of California Press, 1969). Holt T. Rod, *An Assessment of The Political Economy of Sudan* (New Haven: Half John Publishers Inc., 1967) Kelly Maryln, *Africa Before and After Independent: An Overview of African Colonial Historical Experiences* (New York: International Publishers, 1968). See also The Historical and Economic Analyses done by K. N. Jeltry ed in Karl Anderson, *The Political Economy of Africa South of Saharan* (London: James Currey, 1971) Paul Nixon, *The Background Study of Economic Development in Sudan* (Cambridge: Hult Co., 1969).

3. P. M. Holt and M. W. Daly, *A History of the Sudan: From the Coming of Islam to the Present Day*, (New York: Longman, 1988), p. 168.

4. Holt and Daly, *A History of the Sudan*. Adelman Robison, *Income Distribution Policies in Developing Countries* (Standford, Cal.: Standford University Press, 1970. A. A. Ahmed, *Agricultural Price Policies Under Complex Socio-Economic and Natural Restraints* (Washington, D.C.: *The International Monetary Fund*, 1978). Peter Colber, *Labor and Poverty in Sudan* (Oxford: Oxford University Press, 1969). Dennis Radwan, *Land Policies and Farm Productivity in Sudan* (London: Hult Co, 1980).

5. Ibid., p. 169.

6. Ibid., p. 170.

7. *Africa Today*, (Summer 1980) and Holt and Daly, *A History of the Sudan*. See also the work done by Ralph Austen, *African Economic History*. (London: James Currey, 1987). Jean F. Bayart, *The State in Africa: The Politics of The Belly*. (New York: Longman, 1993). Roe Allan, *Instruments of Economic Policy in Africa* (London: James Currey, 1992). Richard O. Laniyan, *African History and Culture* (New York: Longman, 1992). Richard Harris, The Political Economy of Africa (New York: John Wiley and Sons, 1975).

8. Ibid., p. 171.

9. For details analysis, see the work done by Holt and Daly on *A History of the Sudan,* (New York: Longman, 1988), p. 171 see G. N. Sanderson, "Sudanese Nationalism and the Independence of the Sudan", in Michuel Brett (ed) *North Africa: Islam and Modernization*, (1977), Peter Bechold, *Politics in the Sudan* (New York: 1978).

10. Ibid., p. 172.

11. Ibid.

12. *African Development*, Vol. 10, No. 3 (March 1976).

13. Holt and Daly, p. 187.

14. Ibid.

15. Ibid., p. 195.

16. Holt and Daly, *A History of the Sudan.* Jannet Alice, *Africa in the World Economy* (New York: International Publishers, 1966). Ahamed Alakomo, *Sudan in Economic Crisis* (London: James Currey, 1975). See also Alakomo, *Imperialism, Neocolonialism or Independence: Africa and the Problem of Self Government* (Cambridge: Cambridge University Press, 1971).

17. Ibid., pp. 199-200.

18. Peter Olanyiwola, *Petroleum and Structural Changes in a Developing Country: The Case of Nigeria* (New York: Praeger Publishers, 1987).

19. Holt and Daly, *A History of the Sundan,* p. 210.

20. Holt and Daly, p. 211.

CHAPTER 9

The Political Economy of Neo-Colonialism and the Role of State in Nigerian Reality

This chapter examines and analyzes the structure and nature of Nigerian external economic dependency and underdevelopment for a particular reason; to provide a description of the economic situation in Nigeria so as to show that the development of underdevelopment is a useful theoretical and conceptual framework to understand economic nationalism. Also, examined are the economic implications of the colonial ties on the post independent Nigeria. The degree to which the citizens were allowed to engage in economic operations determines the nature and control over economic activities that continue to be modified to suit the changing circumstances.

One of the major linkages between foreign interest and host government interest is trade. Hence, those who control trade, which was the activity with which foreign capital was involved in Africa, determined the structure of economy which promote their interests. During the colonial administration in Africa, the Royal Niger Company (RNC) controlled and/or regulated a major portion of the trade and commerce by Royal Charter until 1900, and continued to dominate African trade.[1] Smith in *The Journal of Development Studies* summarizes the challenges and difficulties faced by Africans who wanted to carry on trade in Nigeria in this form:

> In territories controlled by the RNC, every foreigner wishing to engage in barter or retail selling had to obtain a retail license costing $100: the licensing system was created with the deliberate intention of excluding the African traders who wanted to engage in foreign trade and/or trade. This almost always caused Goldie to lose his sense of proportion. Difficulties were thus created for African trying to conduct small scale trade; however, African traders operating on a scale significant enough to effectively challenge British monopoly power were destroyed by military means. Restrictions were also imposed on entry into other economic activities; for example, after 1909, licenses for prospecting were granted only to existing license holders, and all license-holders applying for renewal had to prove that they had a capital of at least $500. Furthermore, Africans were effectively excluded from shipping and the import trade by the operation of a shipping ring.[2]

Therefore, one of the major features of the economic change of West Africa was the monopolization of some economic operations by the British--shipping mining and the import-export trade--and the destruction of African economic power in these areas if African were able to effectively challenge British capital. Other aspects of changes in terms of economic were operation indirectly related to the ways in which African manufactures were replaced in African consumption by British imports, and in which 'encouragement' was given to the production by Africans of primary products for export.

Despite the above strategies adopted in Africa generally, other economic institutions were created by the various administrations elsewhere. Before World War II, the British penetration of Nigeria was completed. Therefore, the colonial administration began a second phase of their development--that is, the process of institutionalization of export commodities control. For the same reasons therefore Callaway has this to say:

> Following World War II the British effort to better organize the export trade centered upon the establishment of the first marketing boards. Monopolistic boards were created for Nigeria's main export crops in 1947. The primary objective of these boards was to buy the local crop through purchasing agents who were usually employees of commercial firms which had dominated trade prior to the establishment of the boards. The boards monopolized the sale of these products on the world market and attempted to stabilize the price paid to indigenous farmers when the world price of commodity products was high. The difference between the world price and the price paid to the farmer was banked by the boards in London banks where it was held as sterling balances credited to Nigeria's account.[3]

However, this form of control continued even after Nigeria had attained political independence in 1960 because the British created monopolistic marketing boards and passed incentive policies which enable the foreign investors to expand and dominate the Nigerian export trade and manufacturing sector.

As indicated in our previous chapter, because of the need and demand of foodstuffs and raw materials for the emerging industrialization of Western European nations and later North America, Nigeria's and productive structures were targeted from the beginning at the export market. During and after the colonial era, the economic specialization was imposed by the liberal orthodox school to emphasize comparative advantage between and among nation states in international economic relations. At this point, however, colonial production in Nigeria was not directed according to the needs of the nation. The directions of production were structured and executed to compromise with an order determined by the imperial powers. As Falola and Ihonvbere put it:

The country's trade relations continued to be completely tied to developments in the Western World. Given the dependence on oil wealth, the United States remained the single largest market for this mono-export. The efforts to raise huge loans from Western financial markets, the petty capitalist disposition of the members of the ruling political party, the internal conditions, particularly food imports, and dependence on the West not only served to mortgage the future of Nigeria but also watered down whatever status or influence the country was able to win among the community of nations.[4]

They further argue that:

The failure of Nigeria to emerge as a Newly influential Country (NIC) and the evident decline in its influence and status in Africa and the world-at-large, coupled with the crisis in the world oil market, which completely devastated the economy while generating contradictions of dangerous proportions, meant that the leadership had to initiate accommodating policies if it were to persist. The acceptance of International Monetary Fund conditions for assistance, the devaluation of the naira, and the decisions to sell off some state parastatals and to involve international finance institutions in the agricultural sector at greater financial and social costs are just a few cases in point.[5]

In addition to the foregoing dilemma of newly independent nations, some writers think that, during the initial years of post-independence, the structural relationships between the former colonial power and the new state are best described as neo-colonialism.[6] According to O'Connor,

In the pure case of neo-colonialism, the allocation of economic resources, investment effort, legal and ideological structures, and other features of the old society remain unchanged--with the single exception of the substitution of 'internal colonialism' for formal colonialism, that is by the transfer of power to the domestic ruling classes by their former colonial masters.[7]

In the Nigerian case, Callaway defines and illustrates the phenomenon in this way: Neo-colonialism is the situation by which colonial structures of dependency are sustained after the granting of formal political independence. The primary goal of neo-colonialism is to maintain the former colony as a controlled source of raw materials as well as a market for investment and the sale of goods manufactured abroad by local subsidiaries of international monopolies. The realization of a large market and the promotion of certain types of consumption habits are essential to the foreign investors. Hence, the major private institutions and industrial businesses of the Western, developed nations invested heavily after Nigerian independence in national market and feasibility studies. Nigeria, according to Callaway is a neo-colonial society in that political independence did not significantly reduce the nation's economic dependency before the post-1970 development of the oil industry. During the first ten years of its existence as a country, Nigeria followed a conservative monetary policy, avoiding foreign exchange controls and remaining open to international investment and international companies. Therefore, at the beginning of the 1970s, foreign interests controlled savings, investments, the money supply and the prices of most consumer goods. All large trading and manufacturing enterprises were foreign controlled or owned. Nigerian firms were small and there was little Nigerian investment.[8]

Apart from these conditions imposed on the Nigerians during the pre-independence years, some were fairly successful in the areas of "bread and cake making, garment manufacturing, tire retreading, saw milling, furniture making and foresting." In particular, many inroads were made in joint venture activities with foreign technical partners. The nature of joint venture in the Nigerian economy has been described by Callaway:

> Firms with a prior interest in the market turned to supporting import-replacing industrialization in order to meet the rising competition. Most of the manufacturing enterprises in this form of industrialization consisted of the old merchant firms lowering the cost of imported commodities through processing, assembling or

TABLE 9:1
PRIVATE FOREIGN INVESTMENT IN THE
OIL INDUSTRY 1960-1968

YEAR	Million	% INVESTED IN OIL
1960	24.0	
1961	27.3	25.0
1962	17.7	42.0
1963	37.9	33.0
1964	63.0	57.0
1965	37.0	47.0
1966	34.0	83.0
1967	49.4	92.0
1968	60.8	71.0

SOURCE: Edwin Dean, Plan Implementation in Nigeria, 1962-1968 (Ibadan: Oxford University Press, 1972).

packaging them in Nigeria.   The government granted tariffs to protect such finished products ('made in Nigeria') from "outside" competition, while leaving imported materials as well as capital and equipment for construction of the plant duty free, and provided 'tax holidays' and permitted repatriations of profit.   UAC, for instance, built sewing machine assembly plants, cigarette, and beer factories and bicycle assembly lines in order to maintain its dominant share of the consumer market.   It is thus very profitable for foreign firms to engage in this type of import substitution.[9]

Unfortunately, instead of increasing the role of indigenous business and women, government incentives encouraged further domination by foreign investors in Nigeria; *Lagos*, in 1983 shows that foreign domination was still prevalent.   Foreign investment accounted for about 70 percent or more of the total industrial investment.   In addition, foreign investment amounted to at least 90 percent of the total investment in many basic industries. In the manufacturing sector, foreign investment was at least 80 percent of the total investment.[10]

As we see it, during the nineteenth century, exports were strongly carried out by the politically dominant classes. However, the independence movement did not endeavor to change internal productive and structural arrangements. In support of this view, Fallola and Inhonvbere also summarize the behavior of Nigerian dominant class and the role of multinational corporation in this way:

> The conspicuous and extravagant lifestyle of the dominant class, and its corruption, subservient mentality, and largely unproductive nature make it predisposed to accepting junior positions as agents, shareholders, managers, legal advisors and so on in transnational interests. The oil industry on which the bourgeoisie and state became dependent is dominated by Western companies--Shell, Gulf, Mobile, Exxon, Elf, Pan Ocean, etc. The Shagari administration as the governing arm of the bourgeoisie, conveniently over looked how substructural (internal) contradictions and relations of production and accumulation had combined to influence policies toward the outside world. On the contrary, the government focused attention at the United Nations, the New International Economic Order, problems of technology transfer, and terms of trade with developed countries. Even in these broad super structural aspects the rhetoric was louder than concrete achievements. The nature of the bourgeoisie and of the dependent and distorted economy continued to expose the fragile base on which the loud proclamations and boasts were made. Thus the great powers did not take Nigeria very seriously.[11]

THE POLITICAL ECONOMY OF AGRICULTURE, MANUFACTURING AND PETROLEUM IN NIGERIA

There are three major areas in the Nigerian economy. These are agriculture, manufacturing and petroleum. The agricultural sector is the oldest among the three. Agriculture ranked highest in export products before the commercialization of petroleum. As far as the manufacturing area is concerned, Nigeria has had a very little success in reducing its dependence on imported commodities. However, the oil production, is a recent operation, in comparison it has produced more revenues than both manufactured and agricultural combined. Also, Nigeria's membership in the Organization of Petroleum Exporting Countries (OPEC) has improved her political and economic status in the Third World in particular. At this point, we are concerned in the share of Nigerians and foreigners in each area, and the extent to which foreign penetration and control might have existed between 1960s and 1980s. To advance the discussion that follows, we are making two possible assumptions. First, that to understand the scope and the dynamic nature of external economic dependence in Nigeria, one must examine closely its economic activities and linkages with the advanced industrial societies.   Second, we think that Nigeria's economic relations with the industrialized capitalist countries in essence involve dominance and dependence.

The Political Economy of Agriculture in Nigeria

However, it is important to mention that agriculture led Nigeria's economic activities between 1960 and 1973.[12]   During this period, agriculture recorded its peak by accounting for 59 percent of the gross domestic product (GDP) in 1960. The lowest record of 42 percent of the GDP was in 1973.[13]   Hence, Nigeria's agricultural economy during this period was characterized by export of primary products and an import of manufactured goods. Control of the agricultural sector was in the hands of the British during the colonial period.[14]   This was through the creation of marketing boards in 1947.[15]   Nigeria's agricultural products for export were mainly cottonseed, palm oil and kernels, cocoa, groundnut, benniseed, and timber.   Other commodities were produced for domestic consumption.

Table 9:2 presents the GDP by sectoral origin for 1950-1960 and 1960-1970, and the average annual sectoral growth rate for 1960-1970. A critical examination of the table indicates that from 1960 to 1970, no growth actually took place in the agricultural sector. In reality, it decreased at an average annual rate of 0.4 percent. For instance, in 1950-1960, agriculture as a share of GDP was 64.3 percent, but during 1960-1970, its share of GDP dropped to 56.7 percent. After 1967, the area was generally affected by the civil war. The table also indicates that while agriculture experienced stagnation during the 1960s, the manufacturing area expanded dramatically, at an average annual growth rate of 9.1 percent. Thus, increased demands generated by this rapid growth of industrial production, as well as export agriculture, led to very substantial growth in the public utilities and construction sectors. In the 1960s, the mining area began to play the role of the potential leading growth sector in the economy. It increased at an average annual growth rate of 20 percent. The mining sector especially petroleum, thus became the dominant development area between 1960 and 1970, as oil production in Nigeria began on a significant scale. Our assessment is that Nigeria's economic development was, and remained in the first decade of independence, highly dependent upon conditions in world markets. This dependence quickly created problems for post colonial Nigeria. Table 9:3 shows Nigeria's exports and imports between 1950 and 1970. The table below shows that between 1950 and 1955, Nigeria enjoyed favorable terms of trade. After 1955, however, the favorable terms of trade disappeared; prices of Nigeria's exports began to decline while import prices continued to increase.[16] Imports expanded rapidly, from 219.3 million in 1950 to 934.7 million in 1970. Also, import-substitution industries in processed food, beverages and textiles, and restrictive imports policies during the civil war prevented further expansion of import. Still, food and raw materials imports as a percentage of all imports increased from 19.9 percent in 1960 to 21.5 percent in 1970.[17]

In addition, the unprecedented growth of the industrial area caused imports of machinery and equipment to rise from 24 percent in 1960 to 37.4 percent in 1970.[18] These changes in the trade structure produced considerable fluctuations in Nigeria's balance of payments.   Trade deficits continued annually until 1966, when import substitution and expanding petroleum export brought a surplus.   Again, most of the import-substitution industries were financed to a large extent by international capital. Added to this was the fact that petroleum production in Nigeria was controlled by international monopolies and, like many Nigerian exports in general, the return to Nigerians was very low.

The Political Economy of Manufacturing in Nigeria

For any Third World nation like Nigeria to reduce its dependence on imported goods, it must be able to manufacture enough goods for the domestic markets. The degree of manufacturing activities may indicate to some extend the progress being made in the area of technological advancement. The manufacturing sector contributes directly to gross domestic product and employment. The Nigerian manufacturing sector has expanded its size and value of output. Evidence just shows that by 1950 manufacturing activities accounted for only $26 million; in 1971, it rose to $672 million.[19] Furthermore, manufacturing generated 0.6 percent to the gross domestic product in 1950 and by 1972 it had increased to 7.8.[20] The manufacturing sector consists of a wide range of processes, technology and organization. Therefore, it is difficult to describe it in a precise manner. Peter Kilby has demonstrated this issue in this fashion:

> European or government-owned enterprises, medium-scale processing and assembly of a more labour intensive character but still employing advanced technical processes, small-scale yet capital-

intensive producers, skilled artisanal industries utilizing mainly hand tools, marginally employed semi-skilled producers making crude consumer good, and lastly commercial processing in the household. Industrial Production in Nigeria thus exhibits wide diversity in terms of the degree of specialization and division of labor, technology, factor proportions, the quality of raw material input and product finish, the character of markets being served, and entrepreneurial organization.[21]

Due to import-substitution efforts, most Nigerian manufacturing industries emphasize low-technology. The areas where industries mainly focus are textiles, cement, beer brewing, tobacco production, soap, and cosmetics.[22] High technology industries are now developing in the areas of industrial chemicals, pharmaceutical, machinery and electronic equipment. There is a Volkswagen assembly plant in the Lagos vicinity built in 1976. Investment capital in manufacturing has increased from 66 percent to more than 80 percent between 1970 and 1980. High technology and agro-industries are receiving great attention in recent years. It has been estimated that 33 percent of all investments in manufacturing are located in Lagos-Ikeja areas. Other areas of great concentration are Port Harcourt and Aba in the East and Kaduna and Kano in the North--both regions account for about 37 percent.[23] Furthermore, in his study, Biersteker indicates that:

of the paid-up share capital of limited companies covered in the industrial survey of that year (1972), 50 percent was supplied by foreign private capital. Approximately 16 percent was supplied by Nigerian entrepreneurs. Other sources including international institutions, holding companies, and shares held on trust or for distribution accounted for the remaining 14 percent. Those subsectors in which Nigerian firms predominated in 1972 included meat products, vegetable oil milling, bakery products, tanning, footwear, wooden furniture, printing, drugs and medicines, tire manufacture, and cement. In all other subsectors the share of paid-up capital owned by foreign firms exceeded 50 percent in 1972.[24]

The study shows also that since the 1960s, ownership of the industrial sector in Nigeria has not changed significantly from the colonial era.   Between 1972 and 1989 no substantive changes have occurred in foreign ownership of industries in Nigeria. Another phenomenon in the manufacturing sector in the Nigerian

TABLE 9:2
AVERAGE ANNUAL GROWTH RATE OF GDP,
1960-1970 (PERCENT)

GDP By
Sectoral Orgin

SECTOR	1950-1960	1960-1970	AVERAGE GROWTH
Agriuclture	64.3	56.7	-0.4
Mining Including Petroleum	1.2	3.5	20.0
Manfacturing	3.5	6.5	9.1
Construction	3.8	5.0	6.0
Electricity Gas, Water	0.7	0.7	10.3
Trade, Finance	14.3	12.7	-
Transport and Communication	5.5	4.8	-0.3
Public Administration and Defense	3.3	3.9	13.6
Others	3.5	6.3	-
TOTAL	100.0	100.0	3.1

SOURCE: World Bank Statistical Abstract 1983 b:1, 134-135; Federal Office of Statistics Second national Development Plan: A Review of The First National Development Plan (Lagos 1975).

TABLE 9:3
EXPORTS AND IMPORTS
1950-1970
(MILLION OF NAIRA)

YEAR	EXPORTS	IMPORTS
1950	266.7	219.3
1955	273.2	368.1
1960	278.5	481.0
1961	341.4	487.0
1962	366.8	456.4
1963	379.0	455.0
1963	379.0	445.7
1964	423.3	547.0
1965	567.4	590.0
1966	585.5	575.2
1967	571.7	556.8
1968	462.4	517.9
1969	599.5	629.2
1970	890.5	934.7

SOURCE: World Bank World Table 1976: 179; Central Bank of Nigeria Annual Report, Lagos, 1971, 1972, and 1974.

economy is that in 1990 foreign investment originating from Britain, United States and Germany accounted for 66 percent of the total foreign investment.[25]

The Political Economy of Petroleum in Nigeria

As, we indicated previously that the British were not keen in the acquisition of land or in the establishment of foreign operated plantation system, at least in West Africa. Nevertheless, the British attitude toward the exploration of mineral wealth was remarkably different. Biersteker was able to observe this:

Africans had engaged in mining operations centuries before the arrival of the first Europeans, but the colonial government did not permit African ownership of any mining operations until 1927 and thereafter made ownership difficult with the establishment of exorbitant lease fees. Africans with experience in mining operations were employed solely as laborers in the expatriate-owned and managed mines.   In the petroleum industries incentives were established to lure expartirate investors, including territorial unlimited exploration rights for thirty years that were automatically renewable.[26]

The forgoing shows that mineral wealth in Nigeria (as in most African states) was not available to the Nigerians until very recently.   The monopolization of wealth was a widespread practice during the colonial era.   The French and the Germans in Africa were all engaged in similar exploration exercises in their respective colonies.[27]

Again, the first significant oil production activities began in 1955 when the government granted licenses to some oil companies-Shell-BP, Mobile Exploration Nigeria Incorporated, AMOSEAS, Texaco Mineral Company, and the Nigerian Gulf Oil.[28] Each company was required to pay over $1 million.   The first discovery of commercial quality occurred at Oliobirim, Rivers State. Other locations include Afam and Bornu.   By April 1967 Shell-BP production had reached about 350,000 barrels a day.   In the present Bendel (then Mid-Western State), oil production began also in 1967 with 145,000 barrels per day. Before the Nigerian civil war, oil production reached 580,000 barrels per day.   By 1971 the government under General Gowon established the Nigerian Oil Corporation (NOC).   This corporation was to undertake activities similar to those of the private oil corporations.

Hence, as of 1985, Nigeria needed foreign exchange to finance its development.   Its major source of such foreign exchange has been mainly dollars earned from oil exports to the United States (about 50 percent of the total oil export) and other countries.

Roughly from 1973 to 1980, oil revenues increased and Nigeria expanded development activities based on expectations of continuing huge oil sales and rising prices. Unfortunately, there was a drop in foreign exchange earning resulting from a decrease in oil demand and prices. Thus development activities in Nigeria have been allowed in some areas, while other have been abandoned completely. Nigeria now is dependent on oil trade to earn hard-currency foreign exchange. By being dependent, she is thus vulnerable to events affecting the world oil market, and the U.S. economy. In fact, the recession of 1981-83 in the U.S. economy hurt the Nigerian oil export trade seriously.

A BRIEF OVERVIEW OF THE NATIONAL DEVELOPMENT PLANS

Like other African states, the development strategies drawn up in Nigeria before independence were not really development strategies. The British, anxious that the economic viability of Nigeria be considerably improved, were aware of the fact that certain infra-structures had to be supplied; hand in hand with these came certain social services which could provide for the most basic welfare needs of the Nigerian population who would provide the labor for the exploitation of the nation's resources. Hence, the colonial officials, at the request of the home government, drew up budgets for anticipated expenditures which in turn allowed the home government some criteria for the allocation of revenues to the colony. These so-called plan strategies, had no coherent development plan, and there was simply no coordination of the various segments of the economy. Karmarck, writing on the beginning of the planning process in colonial Africa, offers us a useful descriptive account of planning at this early stage:

Africa is the continent of economic plans. Every country in Africa (except South Africa has had at least one since World War II, and most have had several. The preparation of economic plans began under the colonial regimes and under the stimulus of the colonial powers. Both the British and the French decided that aid to their colonial territories after the war had to be provided within the context of development plans, worked out for each colony by the territorial governments themselves with help from London in the case of the British colonies and by Paris for the French colonies. Perhaps the one point upon which everybody now agrees is that these development plans were defective; they were prepared by administrators with little or no economic background; coordination of the investments in various sectors was largely non-existent; there was no consistent development strategy. In short, the plans were 'no more than lists of projects.'[29]

The Nation's first plan, "The Ten Year Plan of Development and Welfare for Nigeria 1946" evolved as a result of a request from the colonial office in Britain that all colonies draw up development plans to help in the disbursements of colonial development and welfare funds. Dean, Lamenting on the plan states:

> The plan was oriented toward the allocation of these funds; it emphasized education, health, water supplies and transport and communications; it was based on programs drawn up in individual government departments and was in part a set of schemes for the expansion of services and facilities based on departmental policies.[30]

The plan strategy was hardly half way through when "A Revised Plan of Development and Welfare" for Nigeria 1951-1956 superseded it. This was fundamentally the same in approach as the earlier plan as Adedeji perceives:

> However neither the Ten Year Plan nor its successor, the revised Five Year Plan was comprehensive. Both were essentially series of

development schemes devoted largely to the provision of basic social and economic services. Neither covered all of the intended development activities of the Nigerian governments. The limited scope of the plan became increasingly obvious as from 1949 when, the establishment of regional authorities, quasi government development institutions such as the Regional Production Development Boards were set up. As there were no overall economic goals, no serious effort was made to relate the project to one another or to any overall objective. And no attempt was made to coordinate governmental activities with development in the private sector. Thus during this phase, planning was far from being comprehensive and integrated.[31]

In the fiscal year of 1953, the Nigerian and British governments requested the International Bank for Reconstruction and Development to undertake a study of the Nigerian economy. The Bank was asked "to appraise the economic development prospects of Nigeria and recommend practical measures for their realization." The product of the mission was a report entitled, The Economic Development of Nigeria, and apart from being a truly integrated approach to the development prospects of the Nigerian economy, the report is a reliable economic document on the economic state of Nigeria at this period.[32]

In this section, we define "development planning" as practiced in many less developed countries with a particular reference to Nigeria. The practice has more to do with the economic activities as envisaged by the various administration in Nigeria. This section will also show the role assigned to external economic resources in the achievement of each development plan. Here also the scope of external reliance for the accomplishment of development plans will be brought to focus. Thirdly, we discuss the implications of external dependence in development planning. This section is not intended as an evaluation of the success or failure of Nigeria's development plan which we consider relevant to this section:

Development planning involves deliberate, reasoned, and orderly use of measures to achieve stated economic goals in determined sequence. The terms 'reasoned' and 'orderly' merit particular emphasis. Reasonable use of government power presupposes knowledge of the probable effects of alternative actions-information about the structures and operating characteristics of the economic system and about the responses of individuals to changes. Reliable statistics, economic analyses, sustained research activity-these are all a part of reasoned government economic policy.[33]

The idea of development plans has been a part of Nigeria's economic process for a long time. Perhaps what seemed to have encouraged planning all along is the fact that available resources are limited while the economic needs of the people are not. Therefore, planning has always involved how to use limited resources now or in the future in order to produce enough scare goods and services to satisfy human wants. It also involved what to encourage or discourage within the economic processes. But, as we discuss below, Nigeria, like many ex-colonies, inherited institutional structure and resource allocation patterns that have made the country externally dependent. Seidman in his book, *Planning for Development*, comments that:

Given slowly expanding world demand and the domination of the world markets by oligopolistic multinational corporations, the African nation that remains dependent on overseas sales of crude materials is likely, over time, to be condemned in economic growth rates that barely keep pace with population expansion. This underscores the necessity for state action to formulate and implement national plans designed to change the institutional structure and resource allocation patterns to attain a balanced, nationally integrated economy capable of achieving increase productivity and higher levels of living for all inhabitants. Examination of the conflicting classes that had emerged at independence further emphasizes the added requirement that the institutional changes made must include channels enabling those who may expect to benefit from this kind of development to exercise a sufficient degree of influence over the machinery of the state.[34]

Moreover, within the West African economic region, either during the colonial time or the post-independence administrations, there were some general objectives of development plans. Oyebola Adeoye in his book, *Modern Economics of West Africa* states that:

(a) Acceleration of the rate of economic growth. If the rate of economic growth is faster than the rate of population growth, the level of living of the population can be raised. The plans therefore seek to achieve a rise in the national output every year.

(b) The development of infrastructures. These include roads, railways, waterways and electricity, which will promote economic development in general.

(c) Effective utilization of resources. All resources are to be harness for economic growth. This means that governments, governments agencies, private foreign and private indigenous businessmen will co-operate in the execution of capital projects. Private entrepreneurs are encouraged by the governments through the provision of loans, tax holidays, industrial estates and expert advice.

(d) Increase in the facilities for education, housing, health and other components of social development.

(e) Diversification of the economy. It is hoped that the plans will reduce the present precarious dependence of West African countries on a few export crops. Diversification of farm products will result in variety in exported products and make the countries self-sufficient in domestic food requirements. Factories that will process the increased farm output are to be established. Industrialization will also lead to the avoidance of the past heavy reliance on economically advanced countries for capital and consumer goods. This will save foreign exchange.

(f)   Creation of employment opportunities. With the implementation of the various projects in the plans, more people will be employed. New skills will be acquired by West Africans so that fewer of the highly skilled workers from foreign countries will be required.

(g)   Raising the level of economic and social well-being through and expansion of per capital income.[35]

Meanwhile, these general aims reflect the direction of all the development plans which Nigeria pursued between 1960 and 1980. To discuss the post-independence national development plans, we first review the British pre-independence development planning in general. The manner in which the British colonial government operated economic planning can be summarized as follows:

> The governments of the British colonies, particularly after World War II, drew up a variety of plans for development. These were, however, particularly limited. For the most part they consisted essentially of "departmental shopping lists," indicating the kinds of projects and the funds needed to implement proposals strung together by the various governmental departments. Wedded to the idea that for the most part only private enterprise should invest in productive activities, the plans provided the social and economic infrastructure needed to encourage private firms-of necessity mainly foreign-to make those investments. The net result was that the colonial plans, if anything, served primarily to further the expansion of the export enclave and the increased external dependence, of the colonies.[36]

With the above observations in mind, we now discuss the nature of British development plans in Nigeria. The First National Development Plan by the British government was introduced in 1946--the 10-year-Plan for development and welfare. It was criticized by various Nigerian elite groups for lack of inputs from the people of Nigeria leading to a series of evisions within the plan. By 1954, a revised version was put into operation.[37] Nevertheless, the plans faced other crises.

> Shortage of capital funds as well as highly qualified and experienced professionals, technical and administrative staff hindered the implementation of the 1946-1954 and the 1955-1960 Development Plans. Their general feature was a lack of comprehensiveness. They were primarily a collection of development schemes designed mainly to provide basic economic and social services. Furthermore, there was no clearly set out integration plan whereby economic development in the public-private sectors of the economy could be harmonized.[38]

However, from the surface one might have the impression that the colonial government was concerned with the economic activities of the colonies, it is evident that their plans were more or less self-serving. For example, when the Balewa government took office on October 1, 1960, Nigeria inherited a long-term adverse balance of trade which was fifteen times greater than the year 1955.[39] In short, imports generally grew faster than income.

The Post-Independence National Development Plans:

Also the discussion of Nigeria's post-independence national development plans, as pursued by the different governments, only highlights those aspects of the plans that relate to external economic resources. The reason for this focus is that this study is directed to the examination of those areas of Nigeria's economic activities which relied heavily on external resources. Also, we examine the potential influences that they might have had on foreign investment policy outputs during the period 1960s through 1980s. In a study of newly independent states, Seidman summarizes the general characteristics of National Development Plans in African which we consider to have influenced the nation fundamentally.

After the achievement of political independence, the first stage of African plans publicly proclaimed the goal of augmenting the per capita incomes of the African population.   In reality, however, they continued to prescribe measures not unlike those implemented by the colonial government planners.   True, a greater emphasis was placed on social as well as economic infrastructure: many more schools and hospitals, as well as roads and ports, were to be built.   But private enterprise was still expected to provide the main engine for development in the productive areas.   The fundamental assumption apparently continued to be that government's expanded efforts to construct infrastructure and create an 'hospitable investment climate' would attract the necessary private investment to achieve proposed production objectives.[40]   According to Seidman, at the end of the Development period, it became increasingly self-evident that the first round of national plans had achieved little notable success in spreading productivity and raising the levels of living of the broad masses of the population in any African country. What effort had been made to expand production--much of it still concentrated on exports appeared to have been vitiated by falling global prices.   Balance of payments crises had spread as governments sought to increased the import of capital goods and equipment to meet plan objectives International finance anticipated in the plans for development did not appear to be forthcoming in the amounts expected.   Some nations, notably Ghana and Nigeria, began to use high-cost suppliers' credits in an effort to build promised social and economic infrastructures.   The required repayment of interest and principal increased the burden on the future balance of payments.[41]

Given the realities of the circumstances facing the newly independent African states, it should have surprised no one that their initial plans turned out to be little more than paper documents.   One observer suggested, in addition, that 'men and organization can easily become captives of rite and ritual, thus reducing planning activities to little more than formal, symbolic

TABLE 9:4
FIRST NATIONAL DEVELOPMENT PLAN
1962-1968:
SECTORAL DISTRIBUTION OF PUBLIC
SECTOR CAPITAL INVESTMENT

SECTOR	%OF TOTAL
Agriculture	13.6
Transport	21.3
Electricity	15.1
Communication	4.4
Trade Industry (including mining)	13.4
Education	10.3
Health	2.5
Water	3.6
Town and Country Planning	6.2
Labor, Social Welfare, Sports	0.7
Cooperative and Community Development	0.6
Judicial	0.1
Information	0.5
General Administration Defense	7.1
Financial Obligations	0.6

SOURCE: Federation of Nigeria 1961:41, Federal Ministry of Economic Development, First National Plan 1962-1968: Sectoral Distribution, Lagos, 1965.

exercises.' Sometimes this was justified by the experts: after all, it was said that the purpose of planning was merely to providesome sort of propaganda tool to arouse African populations to necessary development efforts. Others concluded that there was really no point in planning anyway. The best that could be hoped for under the circumstances, they held, was a kind of year-to-year effort to evaluate progress and suggest next steps.[42]

However, the period following Nigeria's independence was characterized by a combination of economic and political challenges. A choice had to be made. Simultaneously with independence Nigeria accepted planning as an instruction of policy to carry out her transition. In this respect, economic planning is seen as giving a concrete expression to the aspiration that led to independence, and investment policy is intended to create the framework which facilitates the realization of the development plan.[43] Accordingly, independence, planning, and investment policies have followed each other in close chronological sequence. For example, Nigeria attained independence on October 1, 1960. By 1962, the First National Development Plan was introduced. From 1960 to 1980 Nigeria pursued three national development plans.

The First National Development Plan 1962-1968

The first Nigerian National Development Plan, which was introduced in 1962, covered a six-year period--1962-1968. The general aims were:

I.   To surpass the past growth rate of the economy of 3.9 percent and to achieve a rate of 4 percent per year and if possible to increase this rate.

2.   To achieve this aim by investing 15 percent of the Gross Domestic Product, and at the same time to endeavor to raise the per capita consumption by about one percent per year.

3.   To achieve self-sustaining growth not later than by the end of the Third or Fourth National plan. This involves raising the domestic savings ratio from about 9.5 percent of GDP in 1960-61 to about 15 percent or higher by 1975 in order to sustain the bulk of domestic investment.

4. To develop as rapidly as possible opportunities in education, health and employment; and to improve access of all citizens to these opportunities. This includes the training of a great increased number of doctors, the provision of a greatly increased number of places for university students, the provision of primary education for a rapidly increasing proportion of children of school age, the expansion of hospital services commensurate with the ability of the economy to sustain them.

5. To achieve a modernized economy consistent with democratic, political, and social aspirations of the people. This includes the achievement of a more equitable distribution of income both among people and among regions.[44]

The estimated capital expenditure under the First-Plan was N2.2 billion or $3.63 billion.[45] The 1962-1968 Plan called for a total of $1.1 billion private investment. It was hoped that $460 million or slightly more than half of the private investment total would be invested by foreign private business.[46] Unfortunately, by 1964 the amount received and the foreign investments made were short of the projected target. One problem in particular was that foreign aid donors imposed too many unacceptable conditions. For instance,

> each donor country had its own requirements, and as a result project documentation had to meet the idiosyncrasies of particular lenders. This called for greater versatility on part of planning officials, and thus accentuated the problems of shortage of skilled manpower. Secondly, the terms on which the aid was given also discouraged its utilization. Many donor countries tied their aid to the financing of particular projects in the development plan. These projects were not necessarily those to which the government attached a high priority from the point of view of development strategy. Thus, the government was not prepared to release its limited resources for implementing such low priorities in the early years of the plans. This in effect meant that the foreign exchange made available could not be utilized even though there were highly priority projects which had been properly appraised and documented and were therefore ready for execution.[47]

However, many variable factors were probably responsible for the failure to implement and therefore complete the first Nigerian National Development Plan. Among these were the Nigerian Biafra War, shortage of foreign exchange, technical know-how and manpower combined. For the purpose of this study, it is necessary to note that Nigeria's over dependence on the external resources caused the initial frustration by 1964, at least before the war. for instance, the federal government even went to the extent of guaranteeing foreign investors that nationalization would not take place at least during the period covered by the 1962-1968 Development Plan.   To be perceived as a serious partner, the government included in the Plan a clause which states that:

> It is the intention of the Government to enable Nigerian businessmen to control increasing proportion of the Nigerian economy, not through nationalization but by the accelerated training of businessmen, the provision of advisory and training services, and the improved flow of capital and technical and market information.[48]

The government also promised the foreign investors "access to all the incentive policies and facilities available to the Nigerian investor" in the Plan. However, all these efforts did not seem to amount to any substantial inflow of foreign capital during the Plan period. Perhaps it is logical to think that foreign investors and their governments had a more accurate assessment of the events in Nigeria than the Nigerian planners themselves.

In the overall analysis, the first plan shows that even though Nigeria was politically independent, its national planning efforts continued to be colonial in nature. Like the pre-independence plans, it was drawn up by foreigners who were from capitalist societies, and who lacked the knowledge of the historical backgrounds and indigenous customs of Nigerian people. The First Plan was, however, a direct transfer of a Western model and value. Again, by emphasizing programs that were specifically complementary to rather than competitive with the private foreign investment, the plan was designed to encourage foreign investment, particularly in manufacturing. Thus the emphasis on building infrastructure such as roads, bridges, electricity, transport, railways and the like. Agriculture which employed more than 75 percent labor force in Nigeria was virtually neglected.

The Second National Development Plan 1970-1974

Officially, the 1962 National Development Plan expired in 1968. But because of the Civil War, a second plan was not implemented until 1970. The Second National Development Plan of 1970-1974 has its objectives as follows:

> (1)promote even development and fair distribution of industries in all parts of the country; (2) ensure rapid expansion and diversification of the industrial sector of the economy; (3) increase the incomes realized from manufacturing activity; (4) create more employment opportunities; (5) promote the establishment of industries which cater for overseas markets in order to earn foreign exchange; (6) continue the program of import-substitution as well as raise the level of intermediate and capital goods and production; (7) initiate schemes designed to promote indigenous manpower development in the industrial sector; and (8) raise the proportion of indigenous ownership of industrial investment[49]

The above plan called for a capital expenditure of N3.192 billion or $5.266 billion.[50] According to the government document, the total capital expenditure actually spent was N5.3 billion. The public capital expenditure was N2.37 billion while the private sector contribution amounted to N3.1 billion or $5.115 billion. The public and private sectors have contributed shares of 41.6 percent and 58.4 percent, respectively.[51]

One major characteristic of the planning process of the Second Plan (as well as the Third Plan) from the First Plan is the greater degree of centralization of planning under the Federal Government; this was opposed to the lack of coordination which characterized the pre-coup planning period. In this area the biggest single sector of the plan was transportation where 23.7 percent of the total public sector investments were to be found. This shows the preferential arrangement given by the military government to the reconstruction of roads and bridges destroyed in the war and ultimately necessary for the reactivation of normal economic activities. Also, as compared with the 1962-1968 plan in which 66.9 percent of planned investments were to go into the economic sector (the sector actually absorbed 71.4 percent of investment funds), the Second National Plan earmarked only 56.7 percent of total investments for the economic sector.

Another characteristic of the Second National Development Plan 1970-1974 is the "Indigenization Policy." According to the federal government source, in order to give effect to the indigenization policy contained in the Second National Plan, the Nigerian Enterprises Promotion Decree was promulgated in February 1972.[52] The Decree set out in its first schedule 25 industries and commercial ventures which were reserved exclusively for Nigerian citizens and associations. For instance, Schedule 2 of the Decree requires 40 percent Nigerian participation.

Also, the First National Development Plan emphasized an accommodationist theme toward foreign investments, the Second National Development Plan of 1970-1974 reflected a change in federal government policy. The federal government was more ambitious and aggressive than ever before in its approach toward foreign economic influence and dominance in the country. According to the Plan provision, beginning with the present Plan the Government will create an Agency whose sole function will be to ensure that all employers (private and public) conform to the Nigerianization policy to which the nation has been long committed. The Agency will work closely with the Expatriate

Quota Committee, which is responsible for processing applications for allowing expatriates into the country. Also, Government will create a strict time-table for Nigerianization of various sectors of the economy, taking into consideration the peculiar manpower requirements of individual industries. It will be naive, indeed dangerous, to believe that in the process of industrial development, a set of national goals will automatically be accomplished by their mere declaration. A truly independent nation cannot allow its objectives and priorities to be distorted by the manipulations of powerful foreign investors. To this end, the government will seek to acquire, by law if necessary, equity participation in a number of strategic industries that will be specified from time to time.[53]

The Third National Development Plan 1975-1980

The Third National Development Plan 1975-1980 laid emphasis on the need to give Nigerian Investors some assistance to continue with the indigenization measures.[54] Again, an examination of the provisions of the Third Plan shows that it is different from the past two plans in many aspects.

> Firstly, it is the biggest and most ambitious Plan ever prepared in Nigeria. While the 1962-1968 and 1970-1974 Plans involved capital expenditures of N2.2 billion and N3 billion respectively, the present Plan envisages a capital programme of N30 billion. Again, while the two last Plans postulated growth rate of 4 percent and 6.6 percent in real terms the present Plan postulates a growth rate of over 9 percent. The size of the Plan is meant to ensure a radical transformation of the economy during the Plan period.[55]

Under the third plan, the government continued to pursue those broad goals as outlined in the first and second plans. However, there were specific short-term objectives which the third plan was to focus on. These objectives are: (1) More even distribution of income, (2) Increases in the supply of high level manpower,

(3) Reduction in the level of unemployment, (4) Increase in per capita income, (5) Indigenization of economic activities, (7) Balanced development, (8) Diversification of the economy.[56]
Within the realms of "general policy measures" the Third Plan emphasized economic integration of the West Africa sub-region. Perhaps the efforts under this Plan led to the formation of the Economic Community of West African States (ECOWAS) in 1975.[57]

Of the N30 billion or $49.5 billion estimated for capital expenditure in the third plan, the private sector was to contribute N10 billion. Again, as indicated elsewhere, the private sector in the Nigerian economy usually depended heavily on foreign investment. Thus, based on past records, the government expected over N5 billion or $8.25 billion from the foreign investors. Initially, the federal and state governments were expected to generate a total of N20 billion or $33 billion toward the Third Plan. Later this figure was "revised upward up to a new figure of N43.3 billion or $71.445 billion." The assumption probably was based on the revenue projected from Petroleum sales. But, by the end of the fourth year of the Plan the actual amount contributed by the public sector was only N22.68 billion out of the revised figure of N43.3 billion. Apparently there was some problem with the projected revenue expected during the Plan period. President Shehu Shagari put the problem this way in an address to a joint session of the Nigerian National Assembly:

> The Third National Development Plan was launched against a background of rapidly rising price and production of crude oil. Our production was projected to rise from 2.3M barrels per day at the beginning of the plan to about 3.0M barrels per day by the end of the plan period. This projection under the circumstances then prevailing justified optimism in the potentiality of public sector investment. This was what was responsible for the upward revision of the public sector side of the Third Plan. As it turned out the dream did not come true. It was probably a case of over-optimistic

optimism. The reason was simple. Soon after launching the plan, the oil market situation changed, not for the better. Added to this, on account of developments in the world economy generally, our level of oil production fell sharply from 2.3M barrels a day to 1.3M barrels a day during the plan period. It was not until 1979 that we were able to regain our 1974 level of production.[58]

The above explanation has at least two major implications related to this study. First, it shows that Nigerian exports relied heavily on crude oil. Second, as a corollary of the first point, the public sector was solely dependent on export revenue in financing its programs. In conclusion, therefore, the National Development Plans seriously relied heavily on foreign financial sources, such as foreign private banks, International banks, foreign governments, and multinational corporations for implementation. Under the First National Development Plan 1962-1968, the main domestic source was agriculture. However, the Second and Third National Development Plans relied heavily on revenues from petroleum sales in foreign markets. Since Nigeria's political independence in 1960, the country has depended on foreign private funds, and foreign direct private investment for the implementation of its development plans.

THE STRUCTURE AND NATURE OF NIGERIAN STATE

Clearly, the increasing gap between the progressively impoverished masses and the privileged few is creating an explosive social crisis in Nigerian political economy, and it is in this circumstance that both the present character of the governments and the function of state in Nigerian reality can be best comprehended. The present ruling class inherited a state apparatus, created by her former colonial masters, which it has retained obviously even now. As Nkrumah puts it:

At the end of the colonial period there was in most African state a highly developed state machine and veneer of parliamentary democracy concealing a coercive state run by an elite of bureaucrats with practically unlimited power...a professionally army and a police force with an officer sorts largely retained in Western military academies and chieftaincy used to administering at the local level on behalf of the colonial government.[59]

In the case of Nigeria, this state apparatus has served as the main organ by which the Nigerian bourgeoisie have imposed their hegemony on the subordinate classes and secured the privileged power in the present neo-colonial political arrangement.

In reality, no single scholar has done a better work of accurately describing the character of the present governments in Nigeria than Nwaoha. His work is all the more remarkable because his observations were made in the late fifties before the present state of Nigeria had yet gained her political independence. Nwaoha indicated in *Economist* that the African nationalists, including Nigerians who led the nationalist and independence movements, would increasingly turn their backs on the masses and ally themselves with foreign interests. These nationalists are forced to collaborate with international capital and build an authoritarian government around a popular leader because they lack the economic power to secure their hegemony in any other fashion.[60] Fanon also shared the same view with Nwaoha. According to Fanon:

The bourgeoisie turns its back more and more on the interior and on the real facts of its underdeveloped country and tends to look toward the former mother country and the foreign capitalist who count on its obligating compliance. As it does not share its profits with the people, and in no way allows them to enjoy any of the dues that are paid to it by the big foreign companies, it will discover the need for a popular leader to whom will fall the dual role of stabilizing the regime and the perpetuating the domination of the bourgeoisie.[61]

Again, to use Harris's phrase "without an economic power base of its own the Nigerian ruling class has no choice but to become the willing accomplice of neocolonialism and to depend on an

TABLE 9:5
OIL EXPORTS AS PERCENTAGE OF TOTAL EXPORTS
1960-1983 (MILLION NAIRA)

YEAR	TOTAL EXPORTS	PETROLEUM	% OF TOTAL
1960	339	9	2.65
1961	529	131	24.75
1970	886	510	57.56
1971	1,304	964	73.93
1972	1,433	1,175	82.00
1973	2,319	1,935	83.44
1974	6,104	5,592	92.97
1975	4,791	4,592	95.85
1976	6,322	5,895	95.85
1977	7,594	7,046	92.78
1978	6,707	6,033	90.00
1979	10,676	10,035	94.00
1980	14,640	13,999	95.62
1981	11,892	11,250	94.60
1982	11,145	10,503	94.24
1983	8,427	7,786	92.39

SOURCE: International Monetary Fund. International Financial Statistics Yearbook, 1984, pp. 454-455. Central Bank of Nigeria Annual Reports and Economic and Financial Review, various issues posted prices (of API 34 crude) from UN Monthly Bulletin of Statistics, November 1976.

authoritarian dictatorship to maintain its domination and privileges."

If economic nationalism is to be anything but an empty token gesture, the programs and strategies of the Nigerian state must involve jeopardizing the interest of foreign capital in the nation and eventually disengaging the economy from the exploitative global division of labor. In other words, the State must be organized to doing real battle against global capitalism.

Meanwhile, the Nigerian state presently is not in a position to fight against imperialism. This is true because:

> The ruling class lacks a strong material base, a weakness arising from the colonial legacy. Colonialism ensured the underdevelopment of authentic capitalist among the nascent bourgeoisie by discouraging local entrepreneurship. Foreigners controlled mining, industrial enterprises, banks, wholesale trade and large-scale farming. The nascent bourgeoisie was therefore, in fact, a comprador bourgeoisie whose class position stemmed not from the ownership of the means of production but from being class agents or allies of foreign capital.[62]

After consolidating themselves as a ruling class, they specifically enriched themselves at the public expense through bribery and corruption as well as deals with international capital. Fanon prosaically explains this condition in the following manner:

> By dint of yearly loans concessions are snatched up by foreigners; scandals are numerous, ministers grow rich, their wives doll themselves up, the member of parliament either their nests and there is not a soul down to the simple policeman or the customs officer who does not join in the great process of corruption.[63]

Furthermore, factional antagonism within the ruling class according to Nwoke, prohibits it from presenting a serious national resistance to imperialism. This factional enmity is compounded by petroleum production, which gives rise to large state funds. These large funds give impetus to factional struggles to dominate the instrument and thereby to control the spending of the petronaira. There are two main antagonistic groups of Nigeria's ruling class today: bureaucrats and business elites. The former includes top civil servants, technocrats and military officers. While the latter included a small group of local "capitalist" and a larger group of middle men, general merchant and importers and exporters. To survive in their struggles, each faction has specific relations with sections of international monopoly capital.

For this reason according to Nwoke:

> Nigeria's class faces the potential threat of a generally disgruntled proletariat, whose grievance arises from its alienation in the distribution of the national product. The problem for the ruling class is that the wretchedness and poverty of the masses exist alongside a relatively well-developed political consciousness to demand material betterment and egalitarianism from the state. The ruling class has thus far effectively used coercion to deal with the revolutionary potential of the under-classes, but the latent threat persists.[64]

For this reason, the Nigerian bourgeoisie have become largely obligated to foreign interests who are only very happy to give grants, loans, and credits which will place them in debt with foreign nations, organizations, institutions, and/or banks. Hence, for them to finance their conspicuous consumption, the ruling classes have mortgaged both the local economy and the nation at large to international monopoly capital. To date, the operating revenues of Nigerian state are largely dependent upon loans and grants from one or more of the major industrialized countries, while the local enterprises and businessmen are dependent upon loans and credits from foreign banks and firms to finance their activities. The final result is a neocolonial state tied in a varieties of ways to international capital.

Furthermore, much have been commented about tribalism in Nigeria and the role of ethnic loyalties in particular. Meanwhile, it is essential to note that tribalism or tribal politics is a new invention in Nigeria which owe its origin to colonialism and colonial policy of "divide and rule". During colonialism, selected groups were given more favorable treatment than others and different ethnic groups were played off against one another. Therefore, the economic growth of each region was more often than not geographically uneven, and as a result the people in certain geographical areas have gained more than those in other areas from this arrangement.

However, this according to Harris has given way to regional and/or ethnic animosity over differential access to education and public employment in Nigeria. In the post-colonial era these differences and ethnic identity in common ground have been exploited by bourgeois politicians anxious to obscure the class differences in Nigerian society and direct the discontent of the masses away from themselves as a privileged and exploiting class.[65]   The degree to which tribalism is a result of class exploitation and neo-colonial control in Africa is observed by Nkrumah in his book, on, *The Class Struggle in Africa*. He explains:

> In the era of neo-colonialism, tribalism is exploited by the bourgeois ruling classes as an instrument of power politics, and as a useful outlet for the discontent of the masses. Many of the so-called tribal conflicts in modern Africa are in reality class forces brought into conflict by the transition from colonialism to neo-colonialism. Tribalism is the result, not the cause of underdevelopment. In the majority of "tribal" conflicts, the source is the exploiting bourgeois or feudal minority in cooperation with imperialists and neo-colonialist seeking to promote their joint class interests.[66]

Nkrumah in the final analysis shows that, it is the ruling classes who incite feeling of ethnicity to further their own objectives. In the case of Nigeria, this behavior has been adopted to the extreme and has led to violent and ethnic conflict. Hence, it is important to mention that this conflict is the result of the structural pattern of neocolonial state. Such conflict does not occur spontaneously or as a result of popular initiative. In reality, it is initiated and manipulated by ruling class anxious to promote their own interest through tribalism and ethnicity.

In conclusion therefore, the Nigerian state is henceforth not really a "national" state according to Beckman, because it is not a carrier of national resistance to foreign monopoly. Neither is it really a "comprador" state, because it is not mainly a provider of social forces external to the economy. The Nigerian state, more accurately illustrated, is an instrument of capital in general, that is, both domestic and foreign.[67] Therefore, the Nigerian state is , in the words of Beckman, an instrument of the domestic bourgeoisie, "not (so much) because of the sectional rivalries between national and foreign (which do exist), but because of the strategic role of this class in bringing about the subordination of its territory to the rules of international accumulation."[68] In reality, the Nigerian state is furthermore an instrument of foreign capital, "not so must because state institutions are directly controlled by foreign businesses and their local agents (which is done, but because of the way in which international, world-market-oriented accumulation has been internalized into the Nigerian political economy."[69] In the final analysis, there is no way to assume that economic nationalism will become an effective policy that will lead to the revolutionary overthrow of imperialism in Nigeria. On the other hand, the state will tend to accomodate foreign capital while at the same time expressing the "revolutionary" impulses, that arose from the experiences of exploitation within the existing division of labor.

NOTES

1. Shella Smith, "Colonialism in Economic Theory: The Experience of Nigeria, *"The Journal of Development Studies"* Vol. 15, No. 39 (April 1979) p. 45. See Goulet Denis, *Cruel Choice: A New Concept in The Theory of Development. Center for the Study of Development and Social Change* (Cambridge: Alheneum, 1977). Jason Finkle and Richard Gable, eds *Political Development and Social Change* (New York: John Wiley, 1971). See further the work by Barbara Callaway ed in Richard Harris book, *The Political Economy of Africa* (New York: John Wiley, is the Third World: The Social Dilemmas of Underdevelopment (N.J.: Littlefield, Adams, 1982). J. Adams, "The Economic Development of African Pastoral Societies: A Model." *Kyklos* 28 (1975)

2. Smith, *Colonialism in Economic Theory*: p.45.

3. Barbara Callaway, "The Political Economy of Nigeria," *The Political Economy of Africa* ed by Harris, (New York: John Wiley and Sons, 1975) p. 100.

4. Toyin Falola and Julius Ihonvbere, *Nigeria and the International Capitalist System* (Boulder, Colorado: Lynne Rienner Publishers, 1988), p. 118.

5. Ibid.

6. J. O'Connor, "The Uncanning of Economic Imperialism," *Imperialism and Underdevelopment:* A Reader, ed by R. I. Rhodes, (New York: Monthly Review Press, 1970), p. 118. *See also *Yearbook of National Account statistics* Vol. III (1974). Richard Harris, *The Political Economy of Africa*, (New York: John Wiley and Sons, 1975), pp. 96-106 and Kame Nkrumah, *Neo-Colonialism: The Last State of Imperialism* (New York: NY Publishers, 1966).

7. J. O'Connor quoted in *Imperialism and Underdevelopment*: A Reader, p. 118.

8. Callaway quoted in *The Political Economy of Africa*, pp. 104-105. See also the work by Ann Seidman, *Planning For Development in Sub-Saharan Africa, Praeger Special Studies in International Economics and Development* (New York: Praeger, 1974). Adrew M. Kamarck, *The Economics of African Development* (New York: Praeger, 1971). P. Robson and D. Lury, The Economies of Africa (Evanston, III: Northwestern University Press, 1968). Shankar Acharya, "Perspectives and Problems of Development in Sub-Saharan Africa", *World Development*, 9, (1981).

9. Ibid., p 105.

10. Central Bank of Nigeria Survey of Industrial Development, Nigerian Daily Time (April 1990).

11. Falola and Ihonvbere, p. 116.

12. Yearbook of National Accounts Statistics, Vol. III, (1974) p. 83.

13. Ibid.

14. Daily Time (March 11, 1974), p.8.

15. Ibid., p. 9.

16. World Bank. World Tables (Washington, D.C.: World Bank, 1976), p. 178.

17. Ibid., p. 458.

18. Ibid., p. 459.

19. Thomas Biersteker, *Distortion or Development: Contending Perspective on the Multinational Corporation*, (Massachusetts: Massachusetts Institute of Technology Press, 1982), p. 79.

20. Ibid. See also Kumar A. Bagchi, *The Political Economy of Underdevelopment* (London: Cambridge University Press, 1982). V.V. Bhatt, "Economic Development: An Analytic Historical Approach" *World Development* 4 (July). L. Currie, "Sources of Growth", *World Development*, 14 (April 1986). Inn Adelman, "Beyond Export Led Growth." *World Development*, No. 9, (September 1975). Claude Ake, *A Political Economy of Africa* (Nigeria: Longman, 1981). Adeoye Akinsanya, *Economic Interdependence and Indigenization of Private Foreign Investment: The Experience of Nigeria and Ghana* (New York: Praeger, 1983).

21. Peter Kilby, *Industrialization in an Open Economy: Nigeria 1945-1966* (Cambridge: Cambridge University Press, 1969), p. 17.

22. Biersteker, Distortion or Development, p. 79

23. Ibid., p. 80.

24. Ibid., pp. 80-81.

25. African Economic *Digest, London*, 10 June 1985.

26. Ibid., p. 70.

27. Mars, "Estra-territorial Enterprise," Mining, Commerce and Finance, p. 13. Further comment see An Analysis by A. A. Ayida and H. M. A. Oniri, ed *Reconstruction and Development in Nigeria* (Ibadan: Oxford University Press, 1986). Henry Bienen and V. P. Diejomaoh (eds) *The Political Economy of Income Distribution in Nigeria* (New York: Holmes and Merer, 1981). V.I. Bello, "The Intentions, Implementation Process and Problems of the Nigerian Enterprises Promotion Decree No. 4, 1972. In Nigeria's Indigenization Policy, Proceeding of the 1974 Symposium Organized by the Nigerian Economic Society (Ibadan: The Caxton Press, 1975). Ukandi Damanchi *Nigerian Modernization: The Colonial Legacy* (New York: The Third Press, 1972). Edwin Dean, *Plan Implementation in Nigeria 1962-1968* (Ibadan: Oxford University Press, 1972). Carl Eicher, *Growth and Development of the Nigerian Economy* (East Lansing: Michigan State University Press, 1970).

28. Ukandi Damachi, "Nigeria Development Paths," *Development Paths in Africa and China,* ed. by Ukandi Damachi, Boulder: Westview Press, 1976), pp. 156-157.

29. Andrew Karmarck, *The Economics of African Development*, (New York: Praeger, 1972), pp. 264-265.

30. Dean, *Plan Impementation in Nigeria* 1962-1966, p. 11.

31. Adebayo Adedeji, "Federalism and Development Planning in Nigeria" in A. A. Ayida and H. M. A. Onitiri (eds.) *Reconstruction and Development in Nigeria* (Ibadan: Oxford University Press, 1971), pp. 98-99.

32. International Bank for Reconstruction and Development, The Economic Development of Nigeria (Baltimore: The John Hopkins University Press, 1955), pp. 120-121.

33. Robert Clower, *Growth Without Development*, (Illinois: Northwestern University Press, 1966), p. 77.

34. Wilcox Seidman, *Planning for Development in Sub-Saharan Africa*, (New York: Preger Publishers, 1974), p. 81.

35. Oyebola Adeoye, *Modern Economics of West Africa*, (Ibandan: Board Publication Limited, 1970), p. 257.

36. Seidman, *Planning for Development, In Sub-Saharan Africa*, p. 82.

37. Adeoye, *Modern Economics of West Africa*, p. 258.

38. Ibid., p. 259.

39. Damachi, Development *Paths in Africa and China*, p. 159.

40. Seidman, *Planning and Development in Sub-Saharan Africa*. See also *The History of Nigeria* by S. A. Burns (London: University of London Press, 1969). Robert Broune, *The Lagos Plan of Action VS The Berg Report* (Washington, D.C.: Howard University Press, 1984). Billy Dudley, *Instability and Political Order: Politics and Crisis in Nigeria* (Ibadan: Ibadan University Press, 1973). Pita Ejofor, "Multinational Corporations as Agents of Imperialism" in B. O. Oribonoje and A. O. Lawal (eds.), *The Indigenes for National Development* (Ibadan: Oribonoje Publishers, 1978). Edward George, "Nigeria's Economy, faces New Burden" *New York Time 27* 272(January 1986). Norman Girman, Corporate Imperialism: Conflict and Expropriation (New York: Monthly Review Press, 1980).

41. Ibid.

42. Seidman, *Planning and Development in Sub-Africa*, pp. 82-83.

43. Abboja Krishna, "Development Legislation in Africa," *The Journal of Development Studies*, (April 1966), p. 298.

44. First National Development Plan 1962-1968, Lagos: Federal Ministry of Economic Development, (1962), p. 9.

45. Federal Republic of Nigeria, Third National Development Plan 1975-1980, Lagos The General Planning Office, Federal Ministry of Economic Development, 1975, pp. 29-30.

46. Ibid., p. 33.

47. Damachi, *Development Paths in Africa and China,* p. 162.

48. The First National Development Plan 1962-1968, p. 24.

49. The Second National Development Plan 1970-1974, Lagos, Federal Ministry of Economic Development 1970, p. 113.

50. Federal Republic of Nigeria, Third National Development Plan, 1975-1980, Lagos, The General Planning Office, Federal Ministry of Economic Development, 1975, p. 30.

51. Ibid., p. 12.

52. The Second National Development Plan 1970-1974, Lagos, Federal Ministry of Economic Development, p. 113.

53. Ibid., pp. 288-289.

54. Third National Development 1975-1980, p. 10.

55. Ibid.

56. Ibid., p. 29.

57. Richard Vengroff, "Neo-Colonialism and Policy Outputs in Africa," *Comparative Political Studies*, (July, 1975), pp. 234-245.

58. Tijjani and Williams, *Shehu Shagari: My Vision of Nigeria*, (London: Frank Cass and Company, 1981), pp. 138-139.

59. Kwame Nkrumah, *Class Stuggle in Africa*, (New York: International Publishers, 1970), pp. 55-56.

60. Stephen Nwaoha, "The Structure of Nigerian State", *Economist*, 10 July 1970, p. 21.

61. Frantz Fanon, *The Wretched of the Earth*, (New York: Grove Press 1963), pp. 165-166.

62. Nwoke, *Africa Today* 4th Quarter, 1986, pp. 60-61.

63. Ibid., p. 172.

64. Ibid.

65. Harris, *The Political Economy of Africa*.

66. Nkrumah, *Class Struggle in Africa*, p. 59-60.

67. See Bjorn Beckman, "Whose State? State and Capitalist Development in Nigeria," *Review of African Political Economy*, No. 23, January - April 1982, pp. 37-51.

68. Ibid., p. 49.

69. Ibid., p. 50.

CHAPTER 10

South Africa and the Political Economy of Apartheid: The Dominant-Submissive Configuration

THE HISTORY OF APARTHEID SYSTEM

The seed of the present situation in South Africa was sowed over hundred years ago. A land rich in minerals and other natural resources, South Africa had attracted foreign settlers starting with Dutch immigration into the African subcontinent in the 1700s. The native African population who welcomed them with open hands was eventually subjugated and the Dutch ruled the area from 1625 to 1795. The British, who immigrated to the area, soon gained enough strength and with the cooperation of the British government took over the control of South Africa. The country became officially a British protectorate in 1796, until 1910 when it became independent. After independence South Africa was still politically dominated by the more moderate English settlers until 1948 when the Afrikaner National Party, A Dutch Settler Party, won the general election and officially made South Africa an Apartheid State. Employing methods used by the Nazis, they entrenched themselves firmly enough, ensuring that they can not be voted out of office. After acquiring a firm grip on the government, the Nationalist Party proceeded to pass a number of Laws and Statutes that embodied their belief in inequality.

The South African Whites consist of about 5 million out of the total population of 32 million. At the present time, minority has succeeded in occupying unto power, making South Africa the anomaly in contemporary African Affairs. Meanwhile, the crisis of the mid-1980s, is placing the system of minority government to great internal strain and to unprecedented external investigation. The South African condition has become a serious international concern, not only for its African States, but for other countries as well. In America, for instance, the issue of foreign policy toward the South African government and its controversy has assumed major significance. For these reasons and other similar reasons, we devote this chapter to the issues and problems of South Africa.

The nature and scale of European settlement and its deep historical foundations set South Africa separate. Observers have noted a larger fortress, mentality in white South African society. The administration is however, under siege as the majority population, cantoned in ghettos and so called homelands, seek to achieve the fundamental human rights. Violence is the product of this divided economy institutionalized in white dominance and a police state, on one hand; always spontaneous in the protests, and riots of the disfranchised, on the other. Meanwhile, armed struggle is consistently being organized by black nationalist against the formidable power of the South African society. The two nations in one society, in other words, has become a battleground for the past and present time history.

In this chapter, we examine and analyze South African Society by utilizing the concept of state as we have already done to other African nations. In addressing societal structures, we focus on the nature of state in social life into minority and majority entities. Our study of the state seriously emphasized the concentration of the instruments of coercion in white dominated hands along side the creative proliferation of associational forms, religious youth and cultural groups in black nation. The political process in this dual political system is energized by the conflicting ideologies of apartheid and liberation. Therefore the clash between the minority regime and the majority is over the rule of the game.

HISTORICAL DEVELOPMENT AND THE THEORETICAL JUSTIFICATION OF APARTHEID

The contemporary order was established in 1910 when the colonies of the cape, the Transvaal, Natal and Orange Free State were united to form the Union of South Africa. Britain allowed the white internal colonists, but the newly created parliamentary system excluded virtually the entire black population. In the mid 1931, South Africa became a sovereign member of the British Commonwealth of Nations. In handing over power to the minority regime, Britain sanctioned the government of white supremacy that deprived Africans of political and economic rights in their own nation and treated the black citizens sincerely as a pool of forced and/or cheap labor. During this racially exclusive parliamentary system, political parties representing different political, social, economic, ideological, linguistic and cultural segments of the white population competed for political power through popular election. In 1948, a coalition representing the most militantly racist element of Afrikaner nationalism narrowly won a parliamentary majority. Afrkaners have been in power for the past four decades, adopting their ideology of apartheid. We shall see that control of state apparatus has been a source of economic advantage for the Afrikaners, who hence hold a strong vested interest in retaining and maintaining power in South Africa.

The theories of apartheid drew on the legacy of cultural

nationalists who believed in a God given mission of the Afrikaner people.   Historically, the Calvinism of the Dutch Reformed Religion, the Afrikaan Language, and the Tales of the Great Trek bestowed a settlement of unique identity whose destiny apartheid was meant to protect.   The theory called for the separate development in accordance with their respective inherent and implied features of South Africa diverse citizens.[1]   In the language of its apologists, separateness allowed the desire of the Afrikaner people discover a lasting and ethically working solution to the Union's color issue in general, and the native question in particular.   In reality according to these apologists, separate development rationalized a project of racial hegemony and material right.

Even in recent time, the whites who rule South Africa in 1987 constitute about one-sixth of the total population.   Their racial law divides the rest of the people into three different groups: 3 million coloreds or people of mixed racial descent, who comprise only 9 percent; Asians, or people generally of Indian origin, who constitute about 1 million, or 3 percent of the entire population; and Africans, or indigenous peoples, whose 23 million represent 73 percent of the whole population.   The National Party government elaborated a complex system of laws and principles that created varying rights for these different racially designated entities.   Central to the establishment of this policy was the concept and the idea of "Bantu-Homelands", specifically ethnic reserves set aside for the Black Africans.   According to the theory of separate development, blacks were to be considered citizens of these ethnic enclaves whether they lived there or not, thus removing or preventing any obligation to provide them with political and economic rights outside the homeland.[2]   In accordance with the above statement, Mortimer and Chazan added that:

> About 13 percent of the national territory (generally the poorest land) was thus set aside as home for 73 percent of the population.

The government carved out ten such "bantustans" and eventually purported to grant independence to four of them (Transkei, Ciskei, Bophuthatswana, and Venda, although no other country has ever accorded these entities recognition. What the bantustans actually represent, of course, is a claim by the white minority to decentralize responsibility for these overcrowded and poverty-stricken areas while excluding blacks from political participation at the center. In 1985, President Botha proposed to restore South African citizenship to blacks who permanently reside in the urban areas outside the homelands. Although abolishing the fiction of homeland citizenship for urban Africans, this reform still leaves black political rights very narrowly circumscribed. In effect, it merely acknowledges the necessity of a black urban labor force.[3]

South Africa stays alone from the rest of Africa according to McWilliams and Piotrowski, not only as the most economically and politically developed country on the continent, but as the only country ruled by a white minority. Within the nation, the rulers of South Africa have maintained political power by means of a racist policy known as apartheid. Apartheid determines the fundamental laws of the Republic of South Africa. Contrarily, it means apartness, in fact it is a political and legal system that demands the most rigid form of discrimination and segregation anywhere. The Laws forbid the most common interaction between the four racial entities in South Africa: The black (otherwise known as Bantus), the whites (generally of English and Dutch descent), the colored (of mixed black-white parentage), and the Asians (mainly Indians).[4]

The whites of Dutch descent are today the primary factor in South African political and economic affairs. Since 1948, they have replaced another group of European settlers, the English, as the dominant political force in shaping the destiny of a country they considered to be theirs. The Dutch, having settled on the South African coast as early as 1652, consider it their native land. In fact, they call themselves Afrikaner, Dutch for Africans. (They also call themselves boers, or farmers, and are often referred to by that name.) They claim that they had arrived in South Africa no later than the Bantu speaking blacks whom they conquered in the 1830s.

They argue that their claim to the land rests on discovery, conquest, economic development, and ultimately on the will of God.[5]

Also, apartheid is based on the old law of racial superiority. The blacks, the Afrikaners believed have contributed nothing to civilization. Their existence has been one of savagery. The two cornerstones of apartheid-racial superiority and religious determinism are the foundation of the Afrikaner's long struggle against Western liberalism, heresy and the black, native population of South Africa.

Again, apartheid is embodied in the teachings and preaching of the Dutch Reformed Church, which perceives Afrikaner as God's chosen men, destined to dominate the area as well as the peoples they found in there. Apartheid, the Afrikaners have believed is the word of God and is particularly sanctioned in the Dutch Bible. Therefore, by the end of the eighteenth century, the Dutch had established a strong root in the South African soil. In 1795, the British conquered the South African Cape. The result was a struggle for religious and political power between the Dutch and the British who had lived long enough around the Cape of Good Hope. As McWilliams and Piotrowski argue:

> It was a contest the Afrikaner could not win and brough about their decision to move into the hinterland to escape the discriminatory English laws. Moreover, the Afrikaner opposed the English ban of slavery; which in 1833 became the law of the empire. In 1835, the boers set out on the Great Trek northward into the high plains of Natal and Transvaal. It was a journey filled with bitterness and determination, coupled with a religious fervor seldom matched. The trek became a triumphant religious procession by which God's elect, a people with a most narrow view of salvation, set out to build a new Jerusalem.[6]

In addition to the above mentioned conflict between the Dutch and the British, the British once more encroached on boer region. The boers stood and fought two wars, meanwhile it was the British who emerged victorious by 1912. As McWilliams and

Piotrowski perceived this as a bloody and brutal struggle in which the Afrikaners were defeated in what they believed to be their own state. Since that time however, they prepared for the day of liberation to redress their defeat and to restate the religious and social laws of the Great Trek. Really, that golden opportunity just came in the year 1948, when their nationalist party under the leadership of D. F. Malan won the political victory. However, it was at this time that British endeavor to maintain racial harmony in South Africa were put to an end and the South African segregation and discriminatory laws emerged. Between 1937 and 1948, the British authorities had tried to establish a form of representative government for South Africa only to see that little harmony existed between and among different racial groups.

Furthermore, in 1948, the Afrikaners, driven by an unusual sense of cultural self preservation, self identity and religion, refused to accept any previous proposals for social and racial integration. They argue that the races must be kept apart by law and that no one had the right to cross the color boundary. The first of the segregation laws, enacted in 1949 forbade miscegenation the marriage or cohabitation of individuals of a different race. Another law passed in 1953, barred interracial sexual activity and other discriminatory or segregation laws followed in rapid succession. Jobs, schools, pay scales were determined by the segregation laws and principles. Furthermore:

> The Population Registration Act listed individuals on the basis of race; another law demanded residential segregation and limited the rights of blacks to remain in designated cities. Political organizations and strikes by non-whites were outlawed. All public facilities - from hospitals to park benches to beaches became segregated. Whites and non-white were not permitted to stay under the same roof for the night. Every aspect of sexual, social, religious, and economic intercourse between the races was regulated, both among the living and the dead, for even the cemeteries were segregated. The number of apartheid laws, now runs well over three hundred.[7]

Any system so powerful constructed upon racism usually requires also powerful instruments of enforcement. According to Mortimer and Chazan, after a century of incessant warfare, the first three prime ministers of the South African nation (Louis Botha, Jan Smuts, and J. B. M. Hertzong) were all high rank military officials, no less than generals. The Prime Minister (now President) since 1978, P. W. Botha was a minister of defense for twelve years before inheriting power under institutional transformations in the early 1980s, the title of the head of the government became President.[8] A powerful police force and powerful military have been used to maintain this type of scheme. As Philip Frankel explains:

> In general the police have been in the forefront in combatting political unrest since the establishment of the Union, black political unrest in particular. Nevertheless there are numerous instances in twentieth-century South African history where the Defense Force has been used, either alone or in conjunction with the police in quelling domestic insurrection on the part of either blacks or white. There is in fact an entire tradition of the police and military being used on an interchangeable inter-external basis to defend the interests of the South African state.[9]

What has been clear since the early 1960s is that the police force has increased more than three time in order to carry out its necessary roles of riot control and enforcement of the pass laws which have controlled the movement of blacks in one way or another. An institutionalized security police agency exists with authority and "ordersity" to arrest, detain, interrogate political opponents of the administration. In addition, there is according to Chazan, a separate National Intelligence Service, successor to the Bureau of State of Security, whose objective was to infiltrate and disable black political institutions and/or organizations that will resist or challenge the minority regime in South Africa. with President botha administration, the military as professional institution has replaced the police as the most powerful organization within the country. This condition has necessitated an increase in the military budget up to 75 percent from 1970 to 1985. The rapid expenditure has resulted in the growing military participation in both social and political activities.

It is important to note that in June 1991, South African President F. W. DeKlerk led the South African parliament to repeal the Population Registration Act of 1948, which grouped South Africans by race and color. However, majority of people believe that this may mark the total collapse of apartheid policy in South Africa; not minding that the repeal of the act is a minor event that will do little or nothing for long oppressed black majority of South Africa.

In summary, the systematic process of oppression practiced by South African government in their practice of apartheid is the process of denationalizing their nonwhite majority population. A process designed to rob African of their ancestral rights to South African citizenship. The first stage of this process was the creation of homelands for the nonwhites as articulated by the Stallard Doctrine of 1922, which made urban areas, white area, to which blacks were permitted entry only in so far as they catered to the needs of the whites.

> This is part of what the government euphemistically calls "separate development", or "plural democracy," words that sound more appealing than apartheid, which has acquired a stigma throughout the world. The Bantustans are the sole legal residences for the nation's black population. The significance of their creation lies in the argument that the black population, the nation's essential work force, consists of strangers who have no right to be in, let us say the city of Johannesburg. It also means that although black fathers may find work in an area set aside for whites, their families must remain behind. Thus not only blacks and whites, are divided but black families as well, frequently for eleven months at a stretch. They are but visitors at the pleasure of the host, the whites of that city. The blacks of South Africa have thus become aliens in their native land.[10]

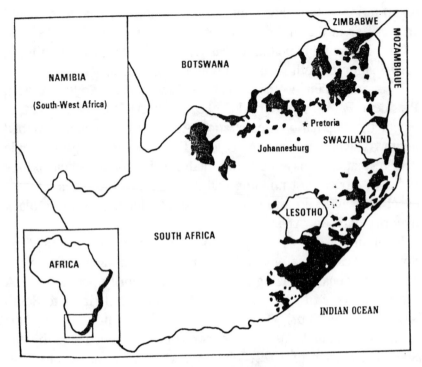

South Africa's "Homelands"

The next stage of denationalization is to declare these homelands independent. Their independence washes the South African government of any form of responsibility to the nonwhites. It also enables the central government to escape its social, economic and political responsibilities to urban blacks. Blacks in the so called urban White areas have no claim whatsoever to any property or public resources. This is in accordance with the government's stated policy that there will one day be no black people who are South African citizens. In furtherance of this objective, the Bantu Citizenship Amendment Bill of 1978 bars all urban blacks from ever acquiring South African status once their respective homelands become independent.[11]

The so called homelands are nothing other than concentrated settlement camps. Already up to 10 million Africans have been set in these homelands, Verda (1970), Transkei (1976) and Bophuthatswana(1977). These areas consist of 14% of the land, while it hosts 74% of the population, leaving an unbelievable 86% of the land to 36% of the population.[12] By removing Africans from the urban centers where most of the economic and commercial activities are carried out, the Apartheid System proves to prevent the economic growth and development of blacks.

In fact, economic subjugation of the nonwhite population is seen as essential for the survival of the Apartheid System. Even when some blacks hold the same job and qualification as their white counterparts, their salaries are significantly lower than the whites. This practice is widely accepted and indoctrinated into the system. As McWilliams and Pitorowski put it:

> The segregation laws are also the linchpin of economic exploitation. The laws exclude nonwhites from the better paying jobs and positions of authority. In the construction industry, for instance, whites earn twice the salary of Asians, three times that of coloreds, and five times that of blacks. A white miner earns $16,000 a year; a black miner, $2,500. And this pattern of exploitation and discrimination exists throughout the entire economy. The combination of rich natural resources, industrial planning, and cheap labor provided by the black work force has turned the nation into the African continents's only modern, industrialized state, but only for the white population. The defenders of apartheid have pointed out that the wealth of the nation has also trickled down to the black population, whose standard of living is the highest of any blacks in Africa. The blacks regard this argument as irrelevant.[13]

The message of the above statement is not only accepted by the majority of the South African whites but also implemented, with the result that 16.7 percent of the population of South Africa (whites) receive 65 percent of the disposable income (nearly two thirds), while 71.2 percent of the population (nonwhites) receives just 25 percent of the disposable income.[14]

EDUCATIONAL PHILOSOPHY

The academic system is equally permeated with the same oppression and control. The government recognizes the impact intellectuals could have among the populace if allowed to express their views. As a result, strong measures are taken to pressure the few black intellectuals into conformity with South Africa's authoritarian principles. Academic dissidents are treated like criminals, even those opinions voiced in school, which appear or are critical of the government are taken as treason.

The South African government seeks to keep its black population uninformed by deempahsizing education. In the few schools available for blacks, education is utilized to condition blacks into accepting their subordinate position in society. The government fears that an educational system that enlightens the natives is very threatening to the survival of the minority regime. H. F. Verwoerd, South African Prime Minister in the 1950s espoused these positions in one of his speeches to the Senate, he argued that blacks are subjected to a school system which draws them away from their community and mislead them by exposing them to the green pastures of European Society in which they are not allowed to graze... because there are no place for blacks in an European community above the level of certain forms of labor.[15] In the South African design for education, schools were not to be spread out widely nor was it intended that many students would spend more than a few years at such schools, resulting in the graduation of half-educated students who are not equipped with sufficient skills to compete effectively with their well-educated white counterparts.

POLITICAL STRATEGY

The Apartheid government in its scheme of things recognizes that firm control over the political machinery of the country is necessary for the survival of Apartheid System. The first step towards the realization of this belief was the disfranchisement of the majority of nonwhite South Africans. Prior to 1948, some urban nonwhites were permitted to participate in the political process. The nonurban South African blacks were totally excluded on the grounds that they were not familiar with the governmental system of South Africa. The election victory of the Afrikaner Nationalist party extended the policy to include urban blacks. Henceforth, nonwhites in general were not allowed to participate in South African politics.

Political views inimical to the apartheid state are ruthlessly suppressed. The South African government achieved this leeway in exercising control through the promulgation of a number of Laws. One such law, the South African Internal Security Act, contains some laws that allow for the arrest and punishment of any person or groups suspected of anti-government activities.[16] In 1980, this Act was responsible for 132 hangings, punishment by Secret Police of 966 people, and the issuance of banning order to 16 people.[17] People issued with banning orders are not allowed to attend a gathering of more than two people, whether of political or social in nature. Banning orders deny the victim access to more than one member of his family in the same room. Breaking a banning order carries a penalty of up to five years imprisonment. According to the wife of Reverend Theo Kotze, a methodist Minister arrested and issued with a banning order:

> He (Kotze) is prohibited from attending any gatherings of himself and more than one person... This includes the family, so that Theo and I cannot meet together with one of our children. He may not give any educational instruction...(and) he may not appear, collate, publish, distribute or dispatch any document.[18]

THE DOCTRINE OF PRECEDENT AND WHY IT FAILS

In spite of the oppressive characteristics of apartheid, world opinion has not rallied strongly against the system as with other similar situations. In this century alone, the world has acted together to dispose of numerous oppressive governments. In Italy, Mussolini and members of this fascist movement were strongly condemned. Hitler's position in Germany witnessed the strongest condemnation, which culminated in a world war. The war put a stop to Mussolini's fascist policies in Italy and Hitler's Nazist policies in Germany. More recently, Idi Amin's reign of terror in Uganda was unanimously condemned by the world community leading to the fall of Amin. The government of South Africa, judged by the extent of her repressiveness can be compared with Nazism in Germany. In some cases, the government has developed the repressive techniques utilized by Hitler to a more sophisticated level.

Furthermore, non-whites are subjected to a level of control by the state unparalleled in all but the most totalitarian phases of Nazi Germany or Stalinist Russia. Not only are they rigidly restricted to inferior facilities in all public amenities down to toilets and benches, not only are they denied all the fundamental human rights such as, speech, social interaction, religion, publication, movement accompanied with contemporary capitalist economies, but they are subject in their day to day operations. For many years, to the extent that non whites and even some whites have contested the policies and nature of the South African administration, the system has been maintained by ruthless repression, based on a vast military techniques, more powerful secret police, and the use of the most refined and brutal forms of physical and mental torture of suspected of opponents of the white dominated regime.[19]

At this point, however, South Africa has retained largely impervious to the cries of the leaders of the newly independent nations on the African states who have requested to the international community, the great power nations and the United Nations for a united effort against the white dominated and supremacist government in Pretoria. African states have requested economic sanctions and the diplomatic isolation of

South African state.   However, these efforts have had very limited success. This is because the dominant powers of the west have been more than very slow in giving their support for a complete boycott, simply because their professed outrage against apartheid is over weighted by vested economic interests and/or objectives in doing business with South Africa.   It seems that effort from inside rather than outside is what South African whites need to fear.

ALTERNATIVE THEORETICAL CONSIDERATION AND EXPLANATION

Many theories can be used in explaining both the internal relations in South Africa and the lack of response from the West, with special emphasis on United States, whose foreign policy in recent times has embraced the South African government more than any other big power.   Galtung's theory of imperialism and the dependency theory give an insight to it.   Galtung's theory of imperialism takes root in the tremendous inequalities within and between nations and the resistance of these inequalities to change. This will help to explain the bottom line of the problem existing in South Africa.   But to get a better insight as well as applicability, the dependency theory serves as a better illustrative measure.

Thomas Vasconi's concept of dependency fits in best with the South Africa's situation. He emphasizes the distinction between underdevelopment and development on one hand, and between the Center and the periphery, on the other. Dependency theory argues that the world is divided into center and periphery nations, with each nation divided into its own center and periphery. In this case we can see the developed nations such as the United States as the center in the center and South Africa's apartheid government as the center in the periphery, the nonwhite people of South Africa make up the periphery in the periphery.

Vasconi will argue that the policies of the center in the periphery cannot be carried out effectively and successfully without the backing of the center in the center. In other words, South African government cannot carry out discriminatory policies against the poor rural people in South Africa successfully without the backing of the United States or other Western governments. Also, the dependency relations that exist between the periphery (South Africa) and the center nations serve as a justification to the Center in the periphery when carrying out their policies.

Pablo Gonzalez Cassanova's analysis of internal colonialism provides a better explanation with South African issue. He argues that with the elimination of direct foreign domination, the notion of natives domination over natives appear to replace it. In such situations, one faction, the South African whites in this case, tries to monopolize all things and keep others nonwhites dependent on their good will. The metropolis dominates, the isolated areas in all aspects; production, distribution, social control, and land. In fact, the Center discriminates in every aspect of life to enable her to keep others down. Albert Memmi, sums it up better while distinguishing the relationship between the Center and the periphery in the periphery. The difference is that:

> One is disfigured into an oppressor, a partial unpatriotic and treacherous being worrying only about privilege and their defenses; and the other into an oppressed creature, whose development is broken and who compromises by his defeat.[20]

Radical theorists provided some interesting arguments from their premises. First, they argue that the relationship between the Center and the periphery in the periphery cannot be explained by the image of a dual society. In other words, their response to international influence cannot be disregarded or neglected. Second the urban commercial bourgeoisie often align with the manufacturing bourgeoisie in South Africa's case, the apartheid government represents the commercial bourgeois while the

United States and/or other western countries represent the manufacturing bourgeois. Third, the radical political economy theorists argue that the dominant class interests are dependent on the international economy for manufactured goods of some sort, foreign currency and capital. Even if South Africa's government wants to change their policies, they cannot do it easily, because the ruling class (whites) depend on the Western World for a considerable part of their welfare. They have more to lose from the relationship if it breaks off. So, as long as the Western World's foreign policy favors the South African government, there will be no hope for change.

AMERICA AND THE WORLD OPINION: THE FOREIGN POLICY AGENDA

With occasional exceptions, U. S. Policy makers do not place primary emphasis on national and regional politics in and around South Africa. Because U. S. policies on South Africa are taken against changing racial perception in the U. S. and world wide. There are no doubts that policy makers can be influenced by cultural or racial stereotyping to affect them in the South African case. Did they support the South African government because they were white, while down playing the importance of the various opposition movements because they were blacks? However, South Africa seems remote to majority of American citizens, what happens in that nations seriously affects the United States. Past United States regimes have accepted this, analyzed U.S. national and strategic interests and attempted to implement them. American governments at different times, have sought to protect strategic interests, including the Cape Sea route and access to essential minerals. They have also avoided soviet influence in this region. Political instability and armed struggle in South Africa have been recognized as the greatest direct threats

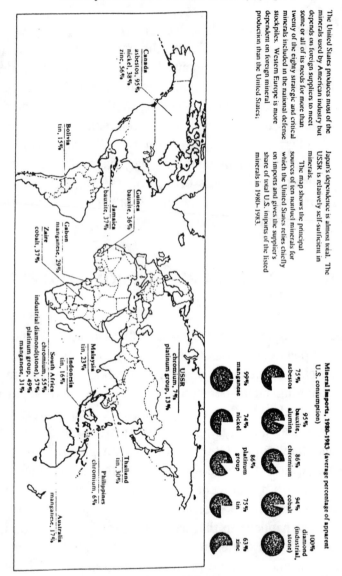

The United States produces most of the minerals used by American industry but depends on foreign suppliers to meet some or all of its needs for more than twenty of the eighty strategic and critical minerals included in the national defense stockpiles. Western Europe is more dependent on foreign mineral production than the United States;

Japan's dependence is almost total. The USSR is relatively self-sufficient in minerals.

The map shows the principal sources of ten nonfuel minerals for which the United States relies chiefly on imports and gives the supplier's share of total U.S. imports of the listed minerals in 1980-1983.

Canada
asbestos, 95%
nickel, 38%
zinc, 56%

Bolivia
tin, 15%

Guinea
bauxite, 36%

Jamaica
bauxite, 37%

Gabon
manganese, 29%

Zaire
cobalt, 37%

USSR
chromium, 7%
platinum group, 13%

Malaysia
tin, 23%

South Africa
chromium, 55%
industrial diamond (stone), 57%
platinum group, 49%
manganese, 31%

Indonesia
tin, 16%

Thailand
tin, 30%

Philippines
chromium, 6%

Australia
manganese, 17%

Mineral Imports, 1980-1983 (average percentage of apparent U.S. consumption)

75% asbestos

95% bauxite, alumina

86% chromium

100% diamond (industrial, stone)

99% manganese

74% nickel

86% platinum group

94% cobalt

75% tin

63% zinc

Figure 10.1
Sources of U. S. nonfuel mineral imports, 1980-1983

SOURCE: Harry F. Young, *Atlas of United States Foreign Relations* (Washington, D.C.: Department of State Publication 9350, December 1985), p. 61.

to American interests, and therefore, United States foreign policy has aimed at reducing those dangers.

Unrestricted use of the Cape Sea route, along which much of the Western oil passes, is of great strategic significance to the U.S. as well as to other Western Nations. Therefore, reducing Soviet influence and/or presence in the Southern African area became the first step toward American Foreign Policy. The issue at hand is how best to address these interests. One group of experts perceives the Cape Sea Route as a potential "fuel pumpum". They suggest that the Soviet Union could pose a potential threat to the route if it controlled, or had friendly access to South Africa. Thus, a close relationship with the South African government, it is argued, is unavoidable to prevent the Soviet threat.

Also, a major source of danger to American interests is the growth of Soviet influence promoted by political instability and armed struggle in this area, the other group of analysts argues. According to this group, United States access to minerals, freedom to trade, and political influence could all be adversely affected by the transformation of South Africa into a close ally and/or periphery of Soviet Union. Political instability and armed struggle in the region open the door to Soviet involvement and penalize the United States. Maintaining sufficient supplies of important minerals exported by South Africa is another American strategic interest. The South African government describes almost all of its mineral exports as strategically essential to the western capitalist economies. These minerals include: Chromium, ferrochrome, managenses, ferromanganese, vanadium and platinum. The threat of stoppage of any of these minerals will affect the Western world.

As far back as the Kennedy regime is concerned, the U. S. Policy makers showed neglect for what was happening internally in South Africa. They viewed South Africa as the elites as South Africa viewed themselves. The South African elites sawthemselves, as a western enclave at the tip of Africa, who governed themselves according to a Westminster model of parliament.[21] U. S. policy makers basically saw South Africa as separate from sub-Saharan Africa and a part of the European community. These perceptions ran through all the successive regimes until Nixon got into office. Even then, the policy makers believed that the minority government in South Africa is prone to strong or devastating opposition from the blacks in the region. But the events of June 1975, that put in a Marxist government in Mozambique and broke Angola into a three sided civil war, made it clear that neglecting the majority of the people could lead to radicalization, major revolutionary violence, and possibly deepen Soviet involvement in the area. So the U.S. first major involvement with the black South African people, came as support for a guerilla group, (FNLA) National Front for the Liberation of Angola. Though this was done to prevent Soviet and Cuban involvement in the area.

The Carter administration presented a new policy line for South Africa. President Carter in an interview put it in this way: "we have made it clear that we oppose apartheid. We think that because South African system is unjust, it may well lead to increasing violence over the years.[22] For the first time, the policy makers viewed the problem in South Africa as a result of the apartheid system itself. The solution was not dealing with just the South African government but openly identifying with the aspirations of the black Africans. But inspite of the rhetoric of Carter's administration, it obviously did not do much to change the situation. The same Carter administration insisted on maintaining an open trading system in South Africa. They saw U.S. investment as a positive force in South Africa. They hoped that U.S. business, by following the Sullivan principles would moderate things in the system.[23] To put it differently, what the policy makers were arguing is, that an economically strong South Africa will be in a better position to improve the conditions of her nonwhite citizens. This line of argument completely misses the issue at hand - that of equality. An economically stronger

South Africa agreeably will be in a better position to provide better conditions to her oppressed citizen, but this does not change the basic philosophy of apartheid - that the nonwhites are essentially inferior. Also, there are no indications that money earned from trading is being invested in improving the economy at home. What is certain is that most of this revenue is pumped into security budget for the increase and maintenance of security agencies, as this is viewed essential for the survival of the apartheid state.

For the Reagan and part of Bush administration the basic value in South Africa is not the race relationship, it is not a question of who is oppressed or for what reason. Rather, it is a power struggle between the United States and the Soviet Union.[24] They consider South Africa, economically, politically and strategically important to the United States. Chester Crocker, who is currently the Assistant Secretary for African Affairs, expressed the Reagan's administration line of thinking better. He viewed United States "real choice" in South Africa in the 1980s, as their readiness to compete with other powers (USSR) in a changing region, whose future depends on those who participate in shaping it.[25] However, the west, particularly the U. S. cannot deny the fact that without their very favorable policies, South Africa will not be operating as it is right now. A South African minority regime without the political and economic backing of countries like the U.S. will be like a millionaire without money. A change of policy by the U.S. will not stop the oppression instantly, but it will weaken it considerably now the Soviet Union is no long posing a military threat to the western world. At this point; if the western world fails to adopt dramatic measures that will put to an end apartheid policy in South Africa at this time, it will be appropriate then to conclude that American and Western interests in South are more of economic motive than strategic and/or political consideration.

APARTHEID IN THE GLOBAL ECONOMY

Minorities have always constituted a source of cheap labor for industrial capitalism.   But the way in which minorities are incorporated into the paid labor force differs for minorities of different cultures, classes and stages of capitalist development. However, international labor migration did not evolve as a significant labor supply system until the phase of consolidation of the international capitalist economy.[26]   The earlier stages of capitalist penetration and incorporation into a single global economy under the hegemony of Europe had generated different kinds of systems for the supply of labor.   Meanwhile, the most essential ones depended on a) forced movement of people from one area of the periphery to another, and b) the subjugation of indigenous and hitherto autonomous population and their forced transformation into laborers through such avenues as slavery, peonage, mita, encomienda and tribal contract labor.[27]

Colonization of migrations was the first step of Western imperialism in the 18th century.   They are to be differentiated from forced labor supply systems as well as from the global labor migrations that evolved at a later period.   In contrary to these, colonizing migrations originated in the center nations where colonists were perceived as a valuable asset.   Therefore, the incorporation of most regions of the global community into the capitalist system resulted in the disintegration or subordination of noncapitalist forms of subsistence.[28]   This disintegration was more common and widespread in Europe than in the less developed nations.   However, it was enough to move large number of people in Africa and other LDCs into the labor market, thus creating a supply of potential migrant workers. Capitalism has the capacity to transform land into a commodity. Land being the basis for noncapitalist modes of subsistence, its commodification left a mass of landless peasants with little or no alternative to becoming part of a rural or urban labor reserve. This was particularly common in periphery regions where the disintegration of non capitalist modes of subsistence did not emerge out of the expanded reproduction of capital. As a result, the exchange of labor into means of production that occurred on such a large scale in Western Europe and North America occurred only minimally in the less developed countries of Africa, Asia and Latin America. Further more, the consolidation of the global economy through the peripeheralization of large regions of the world brought about a significant shift in the flow of labor.

An effective labor supply is very important to achieve the surplus generating possibilities of an area. In reality, the development of labor supply systems has been an integral portion of the broader process of incorporation into the international capitalist economic system. Characteristics of the labor supply system in a given region for instance, slavery, wage, peonage labor-can be accounted for by that region's function in the global economy. These labor supply systems have historically incorporated a variety of methods through which workers from foreign areas, both capitalist and non capitalist, were forced into capitalist global economy.

However, majority of the writing on South Africa has tended to situate its contemporary social transformation into a mechanism established with reference to the experience of modernization and/or westernization. Industrialization, scholars argue is inevitably associated with progressive urbanization, progressive assessment of individuals on criteria of accomplishment (merit) rather than ascription (birth), with equality of justice and opportunity, free social mobility and with gradual levelling of political, economic, ideological and social inequalities.[29] Also, in South Africa, it is argued that some change of this method must permit for the existence of a "dual society", of a pre-existing African "subsistence economy" which according to Legiassick, is only gradually being absorbed into the white created market economy". This perpetual of the subsistence economy, traditional and providing no income opportunities is used to explain the abundance of nonwhites on the labor market and the low degree of nonwhites wages and salaries.[30]

In light of this situation, Legassick provided the following explanation:

> Within the "market economy," and as the subsistence economy gradually disappears, it is maintained that the social consequences of industrialization should follow. If progressive "cooperation," "integration," and "interdependence" of black and white in the economic sphere is not followed by similar effects in the social and political spheres, then the cause is white racial attitudes. And such attitudes, the argument continues, are an archaic inheritance from earlier periods of South African history: from slavery, Calvinism, the competition of the frontier, and the group-consciousness of Afrikaners against both non-whites and the British.[31]

Many lines in recent social theory cast doubts on this exercise. According to Barrington Moore, there is no one method of social relationships impact on industrialization, and the different mechanisms of modernization are produced by different class relations in pre-capitalist economy.[32] However, neither in South Africa nor in the overall analysis does a dual society exist. In reality, the so-called less developed economies are strongly influenced by the interaction and existence of the international capitalist economy. At this point, Barrington Moore's indepth analysis needs to be complemented and observed. For different economies have evolved autonomously with different models of class relations. The fact still remain that since the fifteenth century European growth, the social systems and relations of classes in the periphery of the world have been dramatically altered by their incorporation in the international capitalist economic system. These mechanisms have resulted in dependence, unequal and combined development, imperialism and development of underdevelopment.

To start with, this is not to say that the white racial behavior and attitudes which emerge from the ideology of white racism are not essential to understand the dynamic nature of South African economy.   Our argument is that neither such attitudes in themselves nor the "dual society dichotomy" explains either the recent unfolding dynamics or the structure of South African political economy.   In support of our argument, Legassick contemplated that:

> If South Africa is unique it is not because growing economic cooperation and integration have been impeded by competitive and racialist forces. It is because the forms of that "integration," of the incorporation of non-whites into the world capitalist economy, have been consistently shaped by white political power and manifested in a system of racial differentiation.[33]

However, South Africa economy is inextricably bound up with the politics of apartheid.   Indeed, for quite a number of years, economic requirements have been subordinated to the overriding political initiative of racial separation and racial discrimination, particularly in the area of labor.   South African economy, like many other aspects of South Africa, is a study in contrasts and inequality.   South Africa has modern cities like Johannesburg and Cape Town, but many areas outside the cities are characterized by the rural poverty of an underdeveloped nation. The society is in reality, a dual society, divided not only between an urban industrial sector and a rural subsistence area but also, as the enormous differences between income levels and living standards, indicate between white and black.

Even in today's history, South Africa has its roots in the discovery and exploitation of gold and diamonds in the last third of the nineteenth century.   Meanwhile, the years that followed the initial mineral discoveries saw the economy diversify largely, minerals are still the main stem of South African economic prosperity.   The mining industry now attracts over forty different minerals in mines all over the economy, but diamonds and gold remain synonymous with South Africa.   South Africa, as a nation is the world's major producer of mineral quality diamonds, and the third large producer of industrial diamonds, after Zaire and the Soviet Union.   South Africa further produces some 65 percent of the world's gold, and gold sales are by far the country's single most essential source of foreign exchange. With the price of an ounce of gold averaging $614 for 1980, the value of gold exports in 1980 superceed the value of all exports combined, and South Africa thus experienced an impressive 8 percent growth rate for the year. In 1980, minerals amounted to 76 percent of South Africa's total foreign exchange reserves of $26 billion, up from 66 percent of $19 billion the previous year.[34] Despite of large gold production, the major export earners are coal, diamonds, platinum, uranium, iron ore, and copper, as well as the strategically significant ferroalloys, ferrochrome and ferromanganes.

Protesting South African worker, Johannesburg, South Africa, Aug. 13, 1986.   *(AP/Wide World Photos)*

Also, as many Third World nations, South Africa has seen its agricultural area fall as the manufacturing and mining areas have increased. Given the fact that one-third of the labor force is in agriculture, the sector contributed only about 7.5 percent of the GDP in 1978. By way of contrast, in 1912, two years after the creation of the Union of South Africa, agriculture's share of goods and services was 24 percent and its share of employment rate was 66 percent.

The economic inequality between white and black South Africa is most recognized in the area of agriculture. The commercial farming area is dominated by whites, while the subsistence area comprises African family and traditional communal establishments. However, each area employs almost the same number of employees, the large white farms of the commercial area cover approximately seven time the land sector of the subsistence area, and the productivity per commercial employees is roughly twenty times the productivity of a subsistence farmer.

Within this century, commercial farming has increased drastically, transforming South Africa from a food importer in the 1920s into an important food exporter. The main export products have been mainly maize, sugar, fruit, tobacco and wool. Between 1928 and 1975, the value of agricultural exports increased at an annual rate of 6.6 percent, and in 1976 agricultural products accounted for 30 percent of South Africa's foreign exchange earnings.[35]

Subsistence farming is mainly completely confined to the homelands. The output of the subsistence area has remained at a very low rate for the past thirty six years, and the output per capita has seriously declined during this period. Also, since agricultural production in the African rural areas cannot support the inhabitant population, many are forced to seek for job in white sectors as migrant employees. Therefore, between 1916 and 1950 nearly one million Africans left the homelands to settle permanently in urbans and/or on commercial sectors.

Thus, notwithstanding these outflows of people, the population of the African rural sectors tripled between 1937 and 1970. With subsistence farming, productivity growing much more slowly than the number of people dependent on it, and with clearly no commercial industry in the homelands, per capita income in the various rural sectors has remained unchanged and in some instances has declined.

Furthermore, industrialization has been the dominant economic and social force of the twentieth century in South African gross domestic product. Between 1912 and 1920, industrial production accounted for about 4 percent in South Africa's economy. In 1940, the manufacturing area was contributing 12 percent of the nation's goods and services. From 1950 to 1980, manufacturing product has increased at an annual rate of 7 percent, and today the area accounts for 35 percent of South Africa's Gross Domestic Product. Meanwhile, urbanization has followed industrialization and modernization. In 1912, only 25 percent of the population lived in urban centers; now including migrant employees, about half of South Africa's population lives in urban centers.

South African whites have enjoyed all rights and privileges. They are wealthier, better educated, have better jobs and live longer than any other racial group in South Africa. In descending order of economic well-being come Asians, coloreds, urban African men, urban African women and rural Africans. Although economic growth has helped to break down some ethnic barriers in the urban industrial economy, whether growth alone will result in black political emancipation is a matter of uncertainty. Harry Oppenheimer, Chairman of the Anglo-American Corporation of South Africa and a leading exponent of the "growth theory" has constantly argued that the growth of a contemporary, free enterprise economy will change South Africa's political and social system in a basic way that would undermine apartheid. Other professional candidates Argue that black living conditions have not improved significantly in the first century of capitalist development in South Africa, and that the stark economic and political inbalances between whites and blacks have not been reduced by economic growth and may well be enhanced by it. The future progress of economic growth raises other questions. Some intellectual Afrikaners worry-that Oppenheimer's "growth hypothesis" is correct. They are concerned that growth will not only undermine traditional racial obstacles in the job area, but will further weaken Afrikaner political and social control. While blacks perceive growth within the context of separate development as an avenues by which the white establishment hopes to divide the black community, thereby making it weak to act as a group.

THE DOMINANT - SUBMISSIVE RELATIONS

The historical background of South Africa since the mid - seventeenth century has been significantly expansionist, a portion of the absorption of most of the world into international capitalist economic system. The wide spread network of economic relations has been repeatedly buttressed by exertion of political power and the rationale of racialist philosophy. State power and ideology according to Legassick, have been the avenues by which white groups within the colonial economy have wrested a share of economic surplus from the metropolis, and arrested it by further exploitation of the indigenous population. This can be seen in the development of commercial farming, the cattle trade and the entrenchment of the position of white employees in mining industries and manufacturing.[36] With regard to the importation of labor and the export of capital, this economic expansionism began to increase beyond the domestic boundaries of South Africa from the beginning of the twentieth century, and with it an impetus towards political expansion.

The implications of South African economic expansionism can be seen in the light of the history of South Africa. Economic growth and development brought about a concentration of industrial activity around limited geographical zone: Durban, Capetown, Port Elizabeth - East London and the Witwaterstrand. Within and outside the geographical limits of South Africa, African regions became peripheral satellites of these growth zones, providing to them labor and/or primary products. The dynamics of this simultaneous dominant and submissive relations have created a condition where South Africa needs outlets for capital and manufactures, while the submissive groups are dependent on exporting labor and raw materials.

Nelson Mandela, leader of the African National Congress, imprisoned on Robben Island, South Africa

THE EXPLOITATION OF THE
INDIGENOUS CITIZENS OF SOUTH AFRICA

In concluding this chapter, it is important to highlight the following points. The most basic fact which we demonstrated in this chapter is that fundamental and critical inequalities based on race and ethnicity continue to operate in South African Society. This remains true inspite the substantial elimination of overt discrimination; in spite hundreds of civil rights laws, ordinances, and court decisions at the federal, state and local levels; and inspite of the fact that conditions have substantially improved for some colored and urban black groups. In spite of all this, the aggregate pattern remains one of racial and ethnic inequality. This is true whether we talk about employment, income, education, wealth, political representation, or any other measure of status in South African society. Furthermore, for many blacks, conditions have not improved, and for some they have really gotten worse.

These fundamental realities carry serious implications for all South Africans. For some blacks, they mean that life is a day to day struggle for survival. For all non whites, they mean facing socially imposed disadvantages that they would not face if they were white. For white South Africans, it means facing the real certainty of turmoil and social upheaval at some time in the future. As long as the basic inequalities that led to past upheavals remain, the potential-indeed the strong likelihood of future turmoil remain. All that is required is the correct set of participating social conditions to set off the spark. The conclusion is inescapable. The issue or racial and ethnic relations will somehow affect the life of almost every South African in the years ahead.

This chapter has been written before the election took place in South Africa. However, we are more than happy to see one of our predictions take place before the publication of this text. That is, the achievement of political independence with Nelson Mandela as the new President. Now the political independence is over, many Western experts and scholars began to wonder whether the new President will reverse apartheid policy, eliminate income, social, and economic inequalities. Also whether South Africa, will still remain a developed capitalist first World Country while being governed by a Black Man will be the primary aim of revising this text in the future.

NOTES

1. *Politics and Society in Contemporary Africa.* Richard Olaniyan, *African History and Culture* (New York: Longman Publishing Group, 1992). Ralph Austen, *African Economic History* (London: Currey, 1987). Charles Reed, *The Political Economy of South Afri*ca (London: Austin Publishers, 1980). John D. Hargreaves, *Decolonization in Africa* (New York: Longman, 1990). Richard Harris, *The Political Economy Africa* (New York: John Wiley and Son, 1975). Peter Lawrence, *World Recession and The Food Crisis in Africa* (London: Currey, 1986). Jean F. Bayart, *The State in Africa: The Politics of The Belly* (New York: Longman, 1993).

2. *Politics and Society in Contemporary Africa.*

3. Ibid., p. 394.

4. Wayne McWilliams and harry Piotrowski; *The World Since 1945.*

5. Ibid., p. 256.

6. Ibid., p. 257.

7. Ibid.

8. Ibid.

9. Philip Freankel, *Pretorial's Pretorians*, (Cambridge: Cambridge University Press, 1984), pp. 101-102.

10. McWilliams and Piotrowski, *The World Since 1945*, p. 259.

11. "Alone with Apartheid Regime", *Africa* (October 1981), p. 26.

12. *Africa Today* (May-June, 1986). Percy Selyn (ed) "Southern Africa: The Political Economy of Inequality" *IDS Bulletin II*, (1985). Paul Streeten, *South Africa and The Political Economy of Development* (New York: Longman, 1979). David Godfrey *The Impact of Racism and Inequality in South Africa* (London: James Currey, 1980).

13. McWilliams and Piotrowski; *The World Since 1945*, p. 260.

14. Martin Legassick and Duncan Innes, "Capital Restructuring and Apartheid: A Critique of Constructive Engagement." *African Affairs*, 76 October 1977, p. 438.

15. "Rebusoajoang' Education and Social Control in South Africa," *African Affairs* 78 (April 1979), 229.

16. *The Journal of Africa History*, (1982), p. 412.

17. Ibid.

18. Grant McClellan, *South Africa* (New York: H. W. Wilson Company, 1979), p. 45.

19. Legassick, *The Political Economy of Africa*.

20. Ingolf Voegler and Anthony De Souza, *Dialects of the Third World Development*, (Montclair: Allanheld, Osmun 1982), p. 303.

21. Andrew Nagorski, "U.S. Options Vis-a-vis South Africa", in *Africa and the United States Vital Interest*, Jennifer Seymour Whitaker (New York: New York University Press, 1978), p. 188.

22. Ibid.

23. Ibid.

24. Chester A. Crocker, "South Africa: Strategy for Change", *Foreign Affairs* Vol. 59 (Winter 1980-1981), p. 345.

25. Ibid.

26. June Nash and Maria P. F. Kelly, *Women, Men and the International Division of Labor* (New York: State University of New York Press, 1983).

27. Alejandro Portes, "Illegal Mexican Immigrates to the U.S.", *International Mitigation Review*, 12, 1978, Winter Special Issue; Saskia K. Sassen, "The International Circulation of Resources and Development: The Case of Migrant Labor" *Development and Change,* Vol. 9. (Fall, 1978), pp. 509-546; Saskia K. Sassen, "Towards Conceptualization of Immigrant Labor" Social Problems, 29 (October 1981), pp. 65-81; Francis Wilson, "international Migration to South Africa", *International Migration Review*, 10 (1976 Winter), pp. 451-488; Harold Wolpe," Theory of Internal Colonialism: The South African Case" in Oxaal Barnett and Booth (eds), *Beyond the Sociology of Development* (London: Routledge and Kegan Paul, 1975), pp. 208-228; Aristide R. Zolberg, "International Migration Policies in a Changing World System: in William H. McNeil and Ruth Adams (eds) *Human Migration Patterns and Policies* (Bloomington: Indiana University Press, 1979), pp. 241-286.

28. Samir Amin, Modern Migrations in West Africa (New York: Oxford University Press, 1974: Immanuel Wallerstein, *The Modern World system, Capitalist Agriculture and The Origin of the European World Economy in the Sixteenth Century*, (New York: Academic Press, 1974); Richard Walker, "Two Sources of Uneven Development Under Advances Capitalism: Spatial Differentiation and Capital Mobility" *the Review of Radical Political Economy* Vol. 10, 1978.

29. *Political Economy of Africa*.

30. See, for example, H. Hobart Houghton, *The South African Economy* (Oxford: 1964), pp. 19, 45, 67-71, 150, 159-160; Oxford History of South Africa, ed.s, L. M. Thompson and M. Wilson (Oxford: 1971), vol. 2, 1-48 passim; R. Horwitz, *The Political Economy of South Africa* (London: 1967), pp. 215-220, 238-9; van den Berghe, South Africa: A Study in Conflict (Berkely: 1967), pp. 91-2, 95-6, 183-190. A key theoretical underpinning here is W. A. Lewis, "Economic Development with Unlimited Supplies of

Labor, "Manchester School 22 (1954), 26 (2958); for a critique of which see the important article by G. Arrighi, "Labor Supplies in Historical Perspective: A study of the Proletarianization of the African Peasantry in Rhodesia," *Journal of Development Studies* (1970): 197-234.

31. Legassick, *The Political Economy of Africa*, p.230.

32. Barrington Moore, *The Social Origins of Dictatorship and Montgomery, Workers' Control* (Cambridge: Cambridge University Press, 1979); Also see An Analysis and Examination done by T. C. McGee *Rural-Urban Mobility in South Southwest Asia: Different Formation Formulation, Different Answer* in William H. McNeil and ruth Adams, op cit.

33. *Political Economy of Africa.*

34. *Africa Research Bulletin* (April 1984).

35. *African Today* (Fall 1984) Africa Economic Digest May 16, 1985 West Africa, October 1985.

36. Legassick, *The Political Economy of Africa.*

CHAPTER 11

The International Economic System and African Development Experience

HISTORICAL BACKGROUND OF THE AFRICAN ECONOMIC CRISIS

In 1960s when most African states received their political independence, proud leaders, policy makers, and citizens heralded the dawn of a new age for their peoples. As soon as they were freed from the shackles of European Colonial rule, they looked confidently to a new social, political and economic order that promised an end to the Africa's economic underdevelopment, backwardness and dependence on the capitalist nations. However, the problems of the mid-1960s soon gave room to a more somber reality, for as years went by their shared objectives of economic development, of national self-reliance and respect, and of African unity and cooperation remained unattainable. In reality, after twenty-seven years of political independence, those dreams were in danger as most African states became increasingly impoverished and more dependent on international aid than in the past. During that time, African states experienced poverty, declining economies, hunger and starvation, wide spread of diseases, deteriorating terms of trade, over crowded and declining cities, high rate of inflation, massive unemployment and underemployment, and growing rates of desperate refugees. See tables 11:1 and 11:2. Majority of those hopeful Africa's new states did not live to observe the dashing of their dreams, for they would become victims of military coups, which become rampant throughout African states. In all practical realities, political, social and economic changes in different African states faced strong internal and external obstacles after the 1960s of their independence.

INTERNAL VARIABLES

The economies of newly independent states of Africa were fragmented and weak showing centuries of colonial subjugation, subordination and exploitation. Very little or no foundations had been established for accelerated development. A majority of African states had suffered from a colonial strategic policy that knowingly inhibited industrial development and accelerated heavy reliance on the export of primary commodities. In Africa, primary product commodities have throughout been subject to serious fluctuation in global prices, and in the post-war period the direction in the terms of trade has generally been adverse to the primary producers. Transport and communication were inadequate apart from those areas connecting plantation and mining centers.

Furthermore, the avenue for developing human resources of the citizens through education and training was generally ineffective. The standard levels of literacy education and skills were primarily poor. The social and economic deficiencies were compounded by rapidly increasing population and by fast-

TABLE 11:1
Characteristics of African States

Country	Population (million)	Population Growth Rate (%)	Infant Mortality Rate (%) (per 100 live births)	Population Under 15 Years of Age (%)	Life Expectancy (Years)	Urban Population (%)	Literacy Rate (%)	Arable Land (%)	Per Capita GNP (1983 $$$)
NORTHERN:									
Algeria	22.2	3.3	109	46	60	52	46	13	2,400
Egypt	48.3	2.7	80	40	57	44	40	4	700
Libya	4.0	3.5	92	46	58	64	40	1.4	7,500
Morocco	24.3	2.9	99	45	58	42	24	2	750
Sudan	21.8	2.9	118	45	48	21	20	12	400
Tunisia	7.2	2.3	85	40	61	52	62	30	1,290
WESTERN:									
Benin	4.0	2.8	149	49	43	39	20	11	290
Burkina Faso	6.9	2.6	149	44	44	8	7	10	180
Gambia	.8	2.0	193	43	35	21	12	50	290
Ghana	14.3	3.2	107	46	52	40	30	70	320
Guinea	6.1	2.4	147	43	40	22	48	30	300
Guinea-Bissau	.9	1.9	143	44	43	27	9	8	180
Ivory Coast	10.1	2.8	122	45	47	42	24	12	720
Liberia	2.2	3.1	112	47	49	39	24	20	470

TABLE 11:1 CONTINUED

Country	Population (millions)	Population Growth Rate (%)	Infant Mortality Rate (%) (per 100 live births)	Population Under 15 Years of Age (%)	Life Expectancy (Years)	Urban Population (%)	Literacy Rate (%)	Arable Land (%)	Per Capita GNP (1983 $$$)
WESTERN CONTINUED:									
Mali	7.7	2.8	137	46	42	18	10	2	150
Mauritania	1.9	2.9	137	46	44	35	17	2.3	440
Niger	6.5	2.8	140	47	43	16	5	3	240
Nigeria	91.2	3.1	105	48	50	28	25	25	750
Sengal	6.7	3.1	141	45	43	42	10	15	440
Sierra Leone	3.6	1.7	200	41	34	28	15	8	380
Togo	3.0	2.8	113	44	49	20	10	15	280
EASTERN:									
Burundi	4.6	2.7	137	44	44	7	25	61	240
Djibouti	.3	2.6	122	45	47	74	20	1	400
Ethiopia	36.0	2.1	142	45	43	15	8	12	140
Kenya	20.2	4.1	82	52	53	16	40	20	340
Madagascar	10.0	2.8	67	44	50	22	53	5	290
Malawi	7.1	3.2	165	48	45	12	25	34	210
Mauritius	1.0	1.5	27	33	56	43	61	55	1,150

TABLE 11:1 CONTINUED

Country	Population (millions)	Population Growth Rate (%)	Infant Mortality Rate (%) (per 100 live births)	Population Under 15 Years of Age (%)	Life Expectancy (Years)	Urban Population (%)	Literacy Rate (%)	Arable Land (%)	Per Capita GNP (1983 $$$$)
EASTERN CONTINUED:									
Mozambique	13.9	2.8	110	46	49	13	14	30	220
Rwanda	6.3	3.6	110	46	49	5	37	48	270
Seychelles	.1	1.9	15	37	70	37	60	18	2,400
Somalia	6.5	2.6	143	44	43	34	5	2	250
Tanzania	21.7	3.5	98	45	50	14	66	15	240
Uganda	14.7	3.5	94	48	52	14	25	25	220
Zambia	6.8	3.3	101	47	51	43	54	10	580
Zimbabwe	8.6	3.5	70	48	56	24	45	40	740
MIDDLE:									
Angola	7.9	2.5	149	45	42	24	20	2	500
Cameroon	9.7	2.6	117	43	48	42	34	4	800
Central African Republic	2.7	2.4	143	43	43	41	20	15	280
Chad	5.2	2.1	143	42	43	22	15	7	120
Congo	1.7	2.5	124	44	47	48	80	2	1,230
Equatorial Guinea	.3	2.2	137	41	44	60	20	12	175

TABLE 11:1 CONTINUED

Country	Population (millions)	Population Growth Rate (%)	Infant Mortality Rate ($) per 100 live births	Population Under 15 Years of Age (%)	Life Expectancy (Years)	Urban Population (%)	Literacy Rate (%)	Arable Land (%)	Per Capita GNP (1983 $$$$)
MIDDLE CONTINUED:									
Gabon	1.0	1.7	112	36	49	41	65	1	4,250
Sao Tome and Principle	.1	2.9	69	38	65	32	50	45	310
Aaire	33.1	2.9	106	45	50	34	30	50	160
SOUTHERN:									
Botswana	1.1	3.7	79	50	54	16	30	1	920
Lesotho	1.5	2.6	110	42	49	6	55	13	470
Namibia	1.1	2.8	115	44	48	51	99 white 38 black	1	1,760
South Africa	32.5	2.1	70	38	54	56	98 white 50 black	10	2,450
Swaziland	.6	3.1	129	46	47	26	65	19	890
COMPARISON STATES:									
United Kingdom	56.4	.1	10	20	73	76	99	30	9,050
France	55.0	.4	9	22	75	73	99	34	10,390
East Germany	16.7	.1	11	19	72	77	99	58	7,180

SOURCE: "1985 World Population Data Sheet," Population Reference Bureau, Washington, D.C.; United Nations Demographic Yearbook; United Nation Statistical Yearbook; and the World Bank.

TABLE 11:2
Inflation Rate 1973-82
(Percent)

	1973	1975	1977	1979	1981	1982
African	9.3	15.4	18.1	17.8	20.4	15.9
(non Oil)						
All Africa	7.6	19.2	17.1	14.3	18.6	12.2

Source: International Monetary Fund, International Financial Statistics Yearbook, 1984.

spreading urbanization, as people crowded to the urban centers in the hope of a better life. As Kegley and Wittkopf put it:

> High population growth was identified as the single most important factor underlying the widening gap between rich nations and poor. Among the other things, higher birthrates mean that developing nations generally have a far larger proportion of young people in their societies than do developed nations. "This means that the poor countries have to devote much more of their resources to the tasks of raising a new generation of producers, besides providing services of a given standard to an enlarged and rapidly urbanizing population".[1]

This added additional pressure to the government as the demand for public utilities and welfare services increased. African governments possessed neither the effective productive mechanism nor the finance to support these demands. African states also lack the administrative ability or financial institutions to extract such resources as did exist and channel them to meet public demands.

Also, low income levels are the major feature that distinguishes African states from other developing countries. In Africa, low levels of income create poor and inefficient economic and social conditions, and they further prohibit poorer nations from generating sufficient economic surplus to make sizable investments in their future economic development. At this point, however, Singer and Ansari have this to comment:

New sectors of modern economic growth thus remain very small, especially in terms of employment, and they are often foreign-controlled. The national economy at large remains deprived of new capital infusion. In the poor countries agricultural production accounts for about 40-50 percent of GNP, while in the rich countries the ratio is 5-10 percent. Moreover, about three-quarters of the total population of a poor country is engage in agriculture.[2]

The differential implication of the investment increase can be seen for the period 1975-1980 with rate among nations between 19-28 percent. However, GDP growth rates according to Table 11:3, have decreased seriously from around 4 percent of the whole of Africa in each of the two decades up to 1980, to virtually zero sum at 1980. Hence, falls in consumption and per capita incomes are generally, the primary effect. As can be seen from this table the rate of gross domestic investment in the (1960-1970 decade) was fairly the same across the various units of Sub-Saharan African states at close to 17 percent of GDP. It went up to 18 percent in the first half of the 1970s, again without large variation among nations.

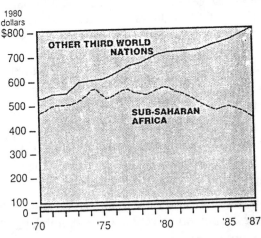

Gross National income per capita in Sub-Saharan Africa and other third world countries, 1970-1987   Source: World Bank

Again, inherited social structures further prevented the conduct of the publicly declared war on unity and peace. For example, in Africa, the fragile political organizations of most of the newly independent nations faced the formidable responsibility of forging national unity. This is very true because their borders had been created when European countries drew possibility lines on Africa's map at the Berlin Conference in 1844-1845, without respect to natural geographical boundaries as well as cultural and ethnic demarcations. In Africa Today, social tension were further exacerbated by linguistic, ethnic and cultural claims and counter claims. As a result, unclear or arbitrary borders imposed for the convenience of colonial administrations left a mark of potential disagreement between and among many new African states.

EXTERNAL DIMENSION OF THE CRISIS

In the external dimension of the African economic problems, we claim that African states are poor because international imperialism has exploited their natural and human resources and economies beyond dependency. Attempts to enrich themselves, European and American capitalists have been extracting the Africa's natural resources and treating their employees as slaves laborers. In reality, the less developed countries of Africa is not only underdeveloped but also over exploited. The gap between rich and poor countries is not due to the neglect of the latter by the former as has been assumed. For more than forty-five years we have heard how the countries of the North must help close the poverty gap between themselves and the less developed countries of the South, transferring some part of their technology and capital to the task. However, this gap between the rich and the poor only widens because of investments in the LDCs are not designed to develop the capital resources of the poor countries but to enrich the international investor and multinational

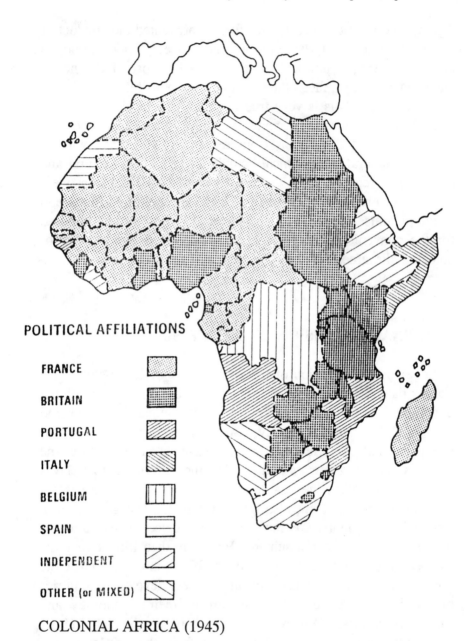

POLITICAL AFFILIATIONS

FRANCE

BRITAIN

PORTUGAL

ITALY

BELGIUM

SPAIN

INDEPENDENT

OTHER (or MIXED)

COLONIAL AFRICA (1945)

TABLE 11:3
GROSS DOMESTIC INVESTMENT IN AFRICA, 1960-83
(annual average, as percentage of GDP)

	1967-70	1970-75	1975-80	1981	1982	1983 Estimate
Low-income countries	14.1	16.9	17.8	17.7	9.3	10.6
Low-income semiarid	14.5	17.8	20.5	17.9	19.0	19.2
Low-income others	14.2	16.8	17.4	17.7	8.7	10.2
Middle-income oil importers	16.0	20.8	23.0	22.8	22.2	17.9
Middle income oil exporters	16.5	20.2	26.6	27.2	26.1	18.0
All Africa	15.7	19.4	23.7	24.0	19.8	14.8
All except oil exporters	15.1	18.8	20.2	20.0	14.0	12.5

SOURCE: World Bank Data Files

corporations. Between 1970 to 1980, the flow of investment capital from the Americans to the LDCs resulted to about $8 billion. Meanwhile, the return flow from the LDCs to the United States in the form of interest, management fees, royalties, dividends and/or branch profits was $163.8 billion. Also multinational corporations and their financial institutions take as much as $210 billion annually from the LDCs.

It is important to note that Africa has been one of the areas most often misrepresented as primitive and/or underdeveloped by Western imperialists. The truth according to Parenti is:

> As early as the 1400s, Nigeria, Mali, and the Guinea Coast were making some of the world's finest fabrics and leathers. Katanga, Zambia, and Sierra Leone produced copper and iron, while Benin had a brass and bronze industry. As early as the thirteenth century, finely illuminated books and manuscripts were part of the Amharic culture of Ethiopia, and impressive stone palaces stood in Zimbabwe. Yet Africa under colonial rule soon was exporting raw materials and importing manufactured goods from Europe, like

other colonized places. The advantages Europeans possessed in seafaring and warfare proved decisive. "West Africans had developed metal casting to a fine artistic perfection in many parts of Nigeria, but when it came to meeting with Europe, beautiful bronzes were far less relevant than the crudest cannon." Arms superiority also allowed the Europeans to impose a slave trade that decimated certain parts of Africa, set African leaders against each other in the procurement of slaves, and further retarded that continent's economic development.[3]

Efforts by African rulers at development including the area of arms and technologies were frustrated by British, French and other European colonizers. Between seventeenth and twentieth centuries, Europe impose imperialist trade relations, pressing Africa to sell its raw materials and buy manufactured goods, on increasingly disadvantageous prices. To quote Walter Rodney:

"There was no objective economic law which determined that primary produce should be worth so little. Indeed, the [Western capitalist] countries sold certain raw material like timber and wheat at much higher prices than a colony could command. The explanation is that the unequal exchange was forced upon Africa by the political and military supremacy of the colonizers.[4]

The unequal development of the global economy goes back to the sixteenth century with the formation of international capitalist economy in which majority nations in the industrial societies were able to specialize in industrial production of manufactured commodities because the less developed regions of the global economy which they colonized provided the necessary primary products, agriculture and minerals, for consumption in the center states. In Africa as elsewhere in developing nations, the international division labor profound by orthodox economic theory did not lead to paralleled development through comparative advantage. The advanced industrial societies gained at the expense of the peripheral nations.

As mentioned early, because of the need for raw materials and foodstuffs for the emerging industrialization of Germany,

England, France and later United States, African productive structures were geared from the beginning at the export market. Throughout the colonial era, the economic specialization was imposed by the European trading partners. As we have seen in this study, colonial production was not structured or directed by the needs of national consumers. The trends of production were directed, structured and transformed to compile with an order determined by the imperial powers. The African economy was eventually shaped and reshaped by its complementary character. Those products that did not compete with those produced in England, France, or Portugal in the metropolitan international market were only encouraged to be produced by Africans.

After most African states gained independence during the 1960s, their economies are still shaped in part by their past experience as European colonies. Under colonialism the nation which possessed the colony exported its raw materials to Europe where the raw materials were converted into finished manufactured goods. Some of these goods were sent back to the colonies for sale. This same pattern occurs in almost every country in Africa. African states have weak domestic economies which are kept afloat by exports. for this reason, Mai Palmberg names this type of relationship neocolonialism and explains how it continues the exploitation that colonialism began.

Added to this is the problem of technological dependence. African states have not proved themselves capable to evolve an indigenous technology appropriate to their own resource endowments and are therefore dependent on the industrialized countries to meet their technological needs. This is particularly true of the poorest of the poor, but it is also true of the relatively well-off African states, whose backwardness and socio-economic infrastructures impede economic growth and development. Singer and Ansari described the problem of technological development of the LDCs in this way:

> Almost all world expenditures on science and technology take place inside the richer countries, and research and development are

therefore quite naturally directed towards solving their problems by methods suited to their circumstances and resource endowments. The problems of the poorer countries, however, are not the same; for instance, they need research to design simple products, to develop production for smaller markets, to improve the quality of and develop new uses for tropical products and above all to develop production processes which utilize their abundant labor. Instead, emphasis is placed on sophisticated weaponry, space research, sophisticated products, production for large high-income markets, and specifically a constant search for process which save labor by substituting capital or high-order skills.[5]

The major concern to Africa's condition is "development", the term that has different meaning to different people. For example, in the western sense of the term Africa's development started some five hundred years ago with the internationalization of trade, capital and production. As European nations gained control of the global water-ways, they saw the "dark continent" as a source of raw materials and the gold to underpin their growing money economy. From 1500 to 1870 European nations had exploited the hearts of Africa, taking some 22.9 million able-bodied farmers out as slaves. At the end of 1800s, Africa was divided into spheres of European influence based not on the equitable development of the African economy, but on European's economic self interest.

However, in the 20th century, African states started to demand for control over their political futures. State by state, they fought for and won political independence from European colonial masters, but economic independence proved elusive to achieve. The nature and structure of African states, which had been developed not to feed African citizens, but to meet the demands and needs of European colonial masters, undoubtedly remain unchange. Smith illustrated this situation very well by using Sudan as a case in point:

Sudan, Africa's largest country, is a good example of the kind of development that has made Africa the "Third World's Third World," a site of recurring famines and unpayable debt. Although never wealthy, the Sudanese had maintained the ability to feed themselves for centuries. When Britain governed the country, it decided that Sudanese farmers should grow cotton, to supply burgeoning British mills. Using the latest in agricultural technology, the British developed huge cotton-growing schemes on Sudan's most fertile land. When Sudan became independent in 1956, the new government, encouraged by "development" banks and foreign donors, continue to emphasize cotton production. Two things happened: over time, the world market price of cotton fell, and Sudan's supply of foreign currency plummeted. Since agricultural resources were tied up in cotton, food production kept steadily declining. With no foreign currency, the country had to take out loans to import food. The mills of Northern England, however, still had a constant supply of cheap Sudanese cotton.[6]

Smith further comments that not all of Africa's problems, however, started or ended with colonialism, local struggles for political power, unjust and corrupt administrations, and inter-African rivalries have played significant roles in African economic deterioration. But the international capitalism has had its own agenda for developing Africa-one that sees the African economies as the supply of raw materials for its production and a market for its goods.

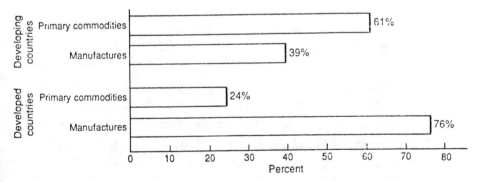

Composition of World Exports, 1985 (Percentages of Primary and Manufactured Products.)

SOURCE: World Bank, World Development Report 1987, Table 11.

To many of these must be added the losses incurred by African countries from deteriorated terms of trade. This means that most raw materials which as we have seen make up the major share of the exports in underdeveloped countries of Africa, have declining prices on the international market whereas the prices of manufactured goods which the less developed countries of Africa import generally increase. Palmberg also states that:

> The main aim of colonialism was to facilitate the expansion of European capitalism. Africa became a cheap source of raw materials and a market for excess industrial output. Apologists for colonialism often point to the development and education that came with European influence. But these advances were the result of the exploitative relationship between Europe and its African colonies.[7]

As we mentioned before, majority of African States are small and open (with external trade sectors clearly representing 30-50 percent of Gross National Product and thus particularly exacerbate to external shocks. However, vulnerability is compounded by structural variable factors such as infant industrial sector and a narrow export base. The degree of the shocks (explained the movement in the terms of trade and the slowdown of international demand for the African's export). The external causes of shocks in all African countries can be attributed to the decrease in terms of trade, external indebtedness, protectionism, exchange rate volatility, and high interest rates.

Furthermore, on a general ground, and in certain circumstances, almost all developing African states have suffered from adverse external developments in the mid 1970s and early 1980s. However, the effect of external disequilibria on the African continent has been more serious because of the weak base of African economies, the degrees of natural disasters, and the serious weight of primary goods in their export receipts.

Therefore, external economic shocks are a general manifestation of the dependence relations of the less developed countries on advanced capitalist nations and their susceptibility to external disequilibria. African exports mainly depend on the production of primary commodities, of which the supply of these commodities is price inelastic in the short run and susceptible to a capricious global economy. The less developed African countries are price takers instead of price makers with regard to their export products. Mainly, imports into the less developed African economies consist primarily of intermediate and capital goods whose prices they are unable to influence. Although African terms of trade fell by 4 percent in 1970-1976 and declined by additional 6 percent in 1977-1981, current account deficits increased rapidly from $437 million in 1970 to over $20 billion in 1981.[8]

As economic transaction reducing mainly because of deflationary policies in the west countries, the prices for African states' export products have declined dramatically in real terms. Also, misalignment and volatility in the foreign exchange rates of the Key currencies, specifically the appreciation of the United States dollar, have destabilized the trade position of the African states and hence, exacerbated their external payments difficulties.

Also, the serious, rapid and prolonged debt servicing problems between African states are the financial representation of disappointments and difficulties experienced in many areas of the African economy. Statistical data on the external debts and debt service ratio of less developed countries of Africa and Asia indicate that African countries have a relatively high share of both debt to private financial institutions and average share of public external debt in real term. See Table 11:4 and 11:5 respectively. Furthermore, the ratio of external debt to gross domestic product and of external debt to exports of goods and services had been increasing more rapidly in Sub-Saharan African states. Table 11:4 reflects this reality generally because of a slow increase in export receipts by Sub-Saharan African countries. While large increase in arrears on commercial payments as well as on debt-service payments, are generally often as explain in Table 11:6.

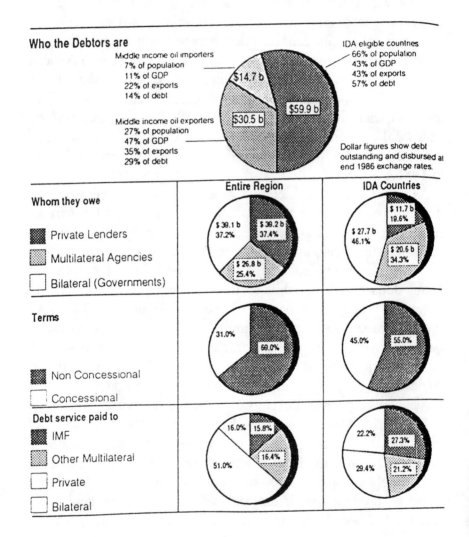

Who the Debtors are

Middle income oil importers
7% of population
11% of GDP
22% of exports
14% of debt

IDA eligible countries
66% of population
43% of GDP
43% of exports
57% of debt

$14.7 b

$59.9 b

$30.5 b

Middle income oil exporters
27% of population
47% of GDP
35% of exports
29% of debt

Dollar figures show debt outstanding and disbursed at end 1986 exchange rates.

	Entire Region	IDA Countries
Whom they owe		

Private Lenders

Multilateral Agencies

Bilateral (Governments)

Entire Region: $39.1 b 37.2%; $39.2 b 37.4%; $26.8 b 25.4%

IDA Countries: $11.7 b 19.6%; $27.7 b 46.1%; $20.6 b 34.3%

Terms

Non Concessional

Concessional

Entire Region: 31.0%; 69.0%

IDA Countries: 45.0%; 55.0%

Debt service paid to

IMF

Other Multilateral

Private

Bilateral

Entire Region: 16.0%; 15.8%; 16.4%; 51.0%

IDA Countries: 22.2%; 27.3%; 21.2%; 29.4%

Profile of Sub-Saharan Africa's debt (1986 data).

TABLE 11:4
AFRICA'S EXTERNAL DEBT, 1975-84
(billions of dollars)

	1975	1980	1981	1982	1983	1984
Africa	**22.7**	**77.2**	**83.9**	**94.5**	**101.3**	**104.3**
Medium & long term	22.6	73.2	80.0	83.9	92.6	96.8
of which (percent share):						
Multilateral	14	14	15	16	17	18
Bilateral	41	35	36	40	40	41
Financial Institutions	21	35	34	33	32	30
Others	24	16	15	12	11	10
Short-Term		4.0	3.9	5.2	8.7	7.5
North Africa	**7.3**	**29.9**	**30.0**	**30.7**	**30.5**	**30.7**
Medium & long term	7.3	27.8	28.2	28.0	27.9	28.0
of which (percent share):						
Multilateral	7	5	6	7	9	9
Bilateral	35	26	28	31	32	33
Financial Institutions	33	50	47	45	44	44
Other	25	19	18	16	15	15
Short Term		2.1	1.7	2.7	2.7	2.7
Sub-Saharan Africa	**15.4**	**47.3**	**53.9**	**63.9**	**70.8**	**73.6**
Medium & long term	15.3	45.4	51.7	61.4	64.8	68.8
Of which (percent spent)						
Multilateral	17	20	20	19	21	22
Bilateral	44	40	41	43	44	45
Financial Institutions	16	26	27	28	27	25
Others	23	14	13	9	9	8
Short Term	0.1	1.9	2.2	2.5	6.1	4.8

SOURCE: International Monetary Fund, World Economic Outlook, April 1985.

For African state as a group, the ratio of debt service payments to exports of goods and services had increase up to 32 percent in 1984 from about 15 percent in 1980. However, for Sub-Saharan African states, the ratio had climbed to over 28 percent in 1985-1986. See Table 11:7 for details.

TABLE 11:5
AVERAGE TERMS OF PUBLIC EXTERNAL BORROWING, AFRICA AND LOW - INCOME ASIA, 1975-84

	1975	1980	1981	1982	1983	1984
Africa						
Interest (percent)	6.5	8.3	7.6	9.2	8.1	8.5
Maturity (years)	15.8	13.9	16.0	13.9	16.7	13.8
Grace period (years)	4.4	4.4	4.5	4.0	4.4	3.4
Grant Element (percent)	21.6	12.0	17.8	8.3	15.9	13.0
Low income Asia						
Interest (percent)	4.2	5.2	4.5	4.8	4.2	3.0
Maturity (years)	23.7	20.7	22.6	25.1	28.1	30.9
Grace period (years)	6.1	5.5	5.8	6.1	6.6	7.2
Grant Element (percent)	41.8	34.1	40.0	40.8	45.8	55.1
Low income Asia						
Interest (percent)	2.5	2.8	4.0	4.4	5.4	3.7
Maturity (years)	31.9	32.4	30.2	32.1	30.1	34.5
Grace period (years)	8.2	7.9	7.3	7.5	7.3	7.9
Grant Element (percent)	59.5	58.3	49.5	48.8	39.5	53.5

SOURCE: World Bank, World Debt Tables; and Fund Staff estimates.

TABLE 11:6
DEVELOPING COUNTRIES: EXTERNAL DEBT RELATIVE TO EXPORTS AND TO GDP, 1977-86
(percent)

	1977	1982	1983	1984	1985	1986
Ratio of external debt to exports of goods and services						
Indebted developing countries	126.7	148.0	157.9	151.3	148.5	141.5
Small low income countries	207.7	315.5	330.8	341.5	349.1	346.4
Sub-Sharana Africa	120.0	199.8	216.6	223.2	230.7	230.9
By region						
Africa	112.2	145.6	160.4	161.7	162.8	154.6
Asia	87.5	85.7	90.4	85.5	86.3	84.7
Europe	117.8	121.5	129.1	127.0	121.4	110.9
Non-oil Middle East	165.7	151.4	173.6	175.6	183.6	181.9
Western Hemisphere	191.8	270.7	294.1	280.0	269.6	257.6
Ratio of external debt to GDP						
Indebted developing countries	24.9	32.9	35.6	36.3	36.7	32.5
Small low income countries	32.2	44.4	45.8	47.7	49.9	46.9
Sub-Saharan Africa	33.8	49.7	54.2	62.6	68.9	68.0
By region						
Africa	31.4	37.2	38.8	39.8	39.9	35.8
Asia	17.2	21.3	22.6	23.7	25.4	24.9
Europe	21.6	29.2	34.4	38.4	35.7	33.5
Non-oil Middle East	53.0	60.0	57.7	58.3	57.9	43.4
Western Hemisphere	29.0	42.0	47.6	46.0	45.6	36.9

Source: International Monetary Fund: World Economic Outlook (April 1985).

TABLE 11:7
ESTIMATED AFRICAN EXTERNAL PAYMENTS ARREARS, 1980-84
(billion of dollars)

	1980	1981	1982	1983	1984
Africa					
Amount	4.2	4.6	9.7	9.3	9.4
Number of countries	20	21	19	18	16
North Africa					
Amount	0	0	0	0	0
Number of Countries	0	0	0	0	0
Sub-Saharan Africa					
Amount	4.2	4.6	9.7	9.3	9.4
Number of countries	20	21	19	18	16

Source: International Monetary Fund: World Economic Outlook (April 1985).

The contemporary debt-servicing obligations of African economies are generally widespread and indicate deep-seared financial and economic difficulties. While it is not the objective

of this chapter to trace the macroeconomic or historical causes that have led to the past and present debt-servicing difficulties, a general agreement seems to be developing among recent observers that inappropriate macroeconomic policies on relative prices, resource allocation and demand management-exacerbated by negative external economic influences are the major causes of the predicament.

Since realization and achievement of the development aspiration of African states will continue to depend largely on access to foreign savings, it becomes imperative that African governments deal with their respective debt-servicing obligations in   a fashion acceptable or at least considerable to the international financial establishment, irrespective of their domestic problems. This includes payment on debt servicing when it is not possible to do so.

TABLE 11:8
EXTERNAL DEBT SERVICE, 1980-86
(billion of dollars)

	1980	1983	Actual 1984	1985	Scheduled 1986
Africa	10.9	14.1	17.4	19.2	18.9
Interest	4.7	5.5	6.5	6.8	6.6
Amortization	6.2	8.6	10.9	12.4	12.3
As percent of exports of goods and services	13.9	25.5	30.3	32.4	30.0
North Africa	5.5	5.7	7.4	8.3	8.2
Interest	2.1	2.0	2.2	2.1	2.1
Amortization	3.4	4.7	5.2	6.2	6.1
As percent of exports of good and services	26.2	35.0	38.4	40.6	37.8
Sub-Saharan Africa	5.5	5.8	10.0	11.0	10.8
Interest	2.6	3.5	4.3	4.8	4.6
Amortization	2.9	3.9	5.7	6.2	6.2
As percent of exports of goods and services	9.5	20.6	26.2	28.1	26.0

SOURCE: International Monetary Fund, World Economic Outlook, April 1985.

Again, economic measures in the advanced capitalist industrial societies have led to higher nominal and real interest rates. Higher interest rates have in turn increased the cost of servicing external debts for the less developed countries of Africa. Total debt service payments by African states increased rapidly from $1.8 billion in 1974 to $8.9 billion in 1986. Thus, high rate of increase in debt service payments result to the rapid decrease in net resource inflows, which reached a height of $10.2 billion in 1978.

Furthermore, foreign investment has a great implication on all the countries of Africa, even if the quantity that enters into each nation may represent only a little percentage in real term of the total foreign investment of any given foreign business. However, the implication of this investment has not resulted to the industrialization or development of African economies but to perpetuate structural imbalance and external economic dependence of African society.

Moreover, the main aim of foreign investors in African states has been to invest primarily in the high profit areas of the African societies. The large profits which they realize from these areas are quickly sent back to western financial institutions. This type of practice prohibit domestic capital establishment and results in a net outflow of funds from the African states to the industrialized capitalist states in the form of royalties, interest and/or repatriated profits. For this reason and other similar reasons, Green and Seidman explain that:

> On the whole, the post-war level of interest and profit remittance had been extremely high in relation to capital invested, to the value of production by foreign firms, and to taxes paid. To profits, moreover, must be added the interest on loans for the infrastructure in support of foreign investment and the cost of government services provided to the import-export, plantation, extractive, and consumer goods manufacturing sectors...It has been estimated that profits, interests, and personal remittances exported from Africa total as much as one quarter of the continent's gross annual income.[9]

Despite the fact that foreign investment prohibit domestic capital establishment in most of the African economies, it further results in a drain on their valuable foreign exchange reserves. The transfer of profits and remittances to the metropolitan nations according to Harris, require that the African economies give up for this reason the foreign exchange earned from the sale of their exports and needed for the purchase of their important inputs for development strategies.

Also, Arrighi has realized that a new method of foreign investment in African continent has been growing in recent years as a by product of changes in the structure of the advanced industrialized states. However, this new method is characterized by: 1) a relative decrease of foreign investment in African states and 2) the growing relative significance of direct foreign investment by large oligopolistic corporations. This method shows the decrease of competitive capitalism in the developed countries and the emerging predominance of MNC. As Arrighi put it:

> "The upshot of these changes has been the emergence of a new pattern of foreign investment in which financial and merchanting interests and small-scale capital (mainly in agriculture but also in secondary and tertiary industries) have decline in importance relative to large scale manufacturing and vertically integrated mining concerns. The typical expatriate firm operation in Tropical Africa is more and more what has been called the multinational corporation or the "great territorial unit," i.e., an organized ensemble of means of production subject to a small policy-making center which controls establishments situated in several different national territories.[10]

Arrighi proceeded, the investment strategies of these multinational corporations are biased against the growth and development of capital - goods industries in African states, and biased in favor of the use of capital - intensive strategies in their extractive and export - oriented policies in these African economies. Hence, both of these biases prevent the balanced growth and development of the African societies. Since African economies are dependence upon a few foreign markets for the sale of their exports and the predominance of foreign investment and businesses in their economies, the economic programs and development strategies of African economies tend to be influenced and further determined by international capitalist interests.

In Africa as elsewhere in underdeveloped countries, the main share of investment in these nations tend to be direct foreign investment, and this investment is concentrated in the extractive and export - oriented area rather than in the production of capital goods or heavy manufacturing. For this reason, the investment strategy is primarily in the controls of foreign private interests and the development of African economies continues to be imbalanced.

Moreover, a majority of African states are by nature handicapped since they are located in a desert area that imposes physical and emotional restrictions or development endeavors. Despite of physical structural limitations, a majority of these nations are further prone of floods, drought, desertification, earthquakes, crop and animal diseases, and deforestation. The scale and severity of these devastating natural variable factors in Africa are greater than in the other parts of the world. The most serious devastating plaque on developing African states is the drought, which has been continuous and severe. Right now it is spreading to include before unaffected regions. Also, desertification is seen to be spreading at a pace that spells disaster for the entire African states if left unchecked. Evidence indicated that more than 44 percent of the land in Africa has been affected by drought and desertification, which combined together have reduced agricultural and food production by more than a half.[11]

To these issues were added in the post-war era global arrangements for the international economy designed fundamentally to serve the interests of the industrialized capitalist states. The aim of the Bretton Woods Conference of 1944 was to stabilize the economy of member states. The international organizations that emerged - The IMF and IBRD, were therefore intended to promote stable exchange rates, facilitate global movements of capital and foster the growth of international trade. However, the major participants - the developed economies were guided by the desire to prevent what they thought of as the disastrous shortcomings of their pre-war system of external economic relations. Prominent among them were beggar-thy-neighbor trading and exchange rates strategies, involving protectionism and competitive devaluation.[12] Again, there was generally a lack of concern for the interests of African states and other less developed countries because at that time, a majority of them were still colonies and therefore not represented at the Bretton Wood system. Hence, the development strategies and policy alternatives of African states were neglected and their interests received little or not consideration.

NOTES

1. Charles Kegley and Eugene Wittkopf, *World Politics: Trends and Transformation* (New York: St. Martin's Press, 1984), p. 95.

2. Singer, Hans and Javed Ansari, *Rich and Poor Countries* (London: Allen & Unwin, 1982), p. 49.

3. Michael Parenti, "Imperialism: Third World Poverty", *The Third World* (San Diego, CA, Greenhaven Press, 1989), p. 22.

4. Walter Rodney: *How Europe Underdeveloped Africa.*

5. Singer and Ansari, p. 50.

6. Gayle Smith, "International Aid Worsens Famine: *Africa* (San Diego, CA: Greenhaven Press, 1992), p. 111.

7. *Africa: Opposing View Points* (San Diego: Greenhaven Press, Inc., 1992), p. 21.

8. *Economist*, 14 May 1982. Leipziger Danny, The International Monetary System and The Developing Countries (Washington, D.C.: Agency for IDA. 1976). See also the work by Kenneth Dan, *The Rules of the Game: Reform and Evolution in the International Monetary System* (Chicago: Chicago University Press, 1982). Richard Cooper, *International Monetary System: Eassays in World Economics* (Cambridge, Massachusetts: Mit Press. 1982)/ For the Information and Analysis of Debt Service ratio, in Africa see the writings of Jones Walker. Mary Johnson, Peterson William, Paul Edwin, and Paul Clark (ed) *Third World Debt Crisis: Who is responsible* (London: Currey, 1980). Fredolin Anunobi, *The Implications of Conditionality: The International Monetary Fund and Africa* (Maryland: University Press of America, 1992). Also see International Monetary Fund Annual Reports 1986, 1988, 1990 and 1993. International Monetary Fund, *World Economic Outlook*, April 1985.

9. Reginald Green and Ann Seidman., *Unity or Poverty Economic of Pan Africanism* (Baltimore: Penguin, 1969), p. 128-129.

10. Giovanni, Arrighi, "International Corporations, Labor Aristocracies, and Economic Development in Africa", in Robert T. Review Press, 1970), p. 225.

11. International Monetary Fund, *World Economic Outlook*, April 1986.

12. *The Challenge to the South* (New York: Oxford University Press, 1990), p. 27. For Further Analysis see Willy Brandt, *Independent Commission on International Issues North Sourth: A Program For Survival* (Cambridge, Massachusetts: MIT Press, 1980). Michael Boddie, "Africa, the IMF and the World Bank, *New Nigeria* (March-April 1983). David Blake and Robert S. Walters, *The Politics of Global Economic Relations* (New Jersey: Prentice Halls, Inc., 1987). E. Spero, *The Politics of International Economic Relations* (New York: St. Martins Press, 1990). Richard Cooper, *The International Monetary Sustem Under Flexible Exchange Races* (Cambridge, Massachusetts, MIT Press, 1982). Oji F. Dike, *The Political Economy of the International Monetary Fund* (IFE; University of IFE Press, 1987). Chandras Hardy, "Africa Debt Structural Adjustment with Stability, *New Nigeria* April 1985. Gerald Helleiner, *The IMF and Africa in the 1980'S* (Princeton, New Jersey: Princeton University Press, 1983).

CHAPTER 12

Africa,
the Debt Crisis, and the International
Monetary Fund Austerity

This chapter examines the role played by the International Monetary Fund in Africa's debt crisis. For this reason, we are concerned with the validity and\or reliability of the macroeconomic stabilization measures prescribed by the International Monetary Fund. The critical concern is that of conditionality, the idea of insisting on the adoption of a specific set of policy conditionalities before giving balance of payments support. However, at this point, we are not concerned with the ethics of conditionality, but instead with its rationale and with the likely effectiveness of the policies prescribed. Meanwhile, before providing detailed analysis of the IMF and Africa, it is important to trace briefly the evolution and\or origin of the Bretton Woods System. This will enable us to address two basic questions: What rules have guided the Fund since its inception? Have these rules changed to accommodate the less developed countries including Africa?

AFRICA AND THE EVOLUTION OF BRETTON WOODS SYSTEM

The International Monetary Fund was created at Bretton Woods Conference, New Hampshire, in 1944, near the end of World War II. The establishment of The IMF was not a simple act, it was followed by five years of extensive planning within the governments of the United Kingdom and the United States. The experience of the 1920s and 1930s influenced this effort.[1] During that period, American Management officials saw the practices of the 1920s and 1930s that affected trade arrangements such as competitive currency devaluations, the use of multiple currency practices whereby a currency would be exchange at one rate for one purpose and at a different rate for another, bilateral trade establishments, and the wide use of exchange controls and import licensing as causes of the world-wide depression, unemployment in export industries, and even World War II. One of the major "concerns" of the postwar period as perceived by the U.S. was "to prevent the disruption of foreign exchange and the collapse of monetary and credit institutional establishment."[2]

As we mentioned earlier, the overriding concern of the U.S. was the recreation of a genuinely multilateral system of international trade. This believed that nations would agree to cooperate to reduce barriers to trade and barriers to payments. Barriers would be minimized to moderate levels of and nondiscriminatory in application. Currencies would become convertible. In specific, exporters receiving a foreign currency in exchange for goods and\or services would be able to convert that currency and use its proceeds in other nations.[3]

At this point, however, the British conception of the postwar monetary institutions was set forth by the Chancellor of the Exchequer on the floor of the House of Commons in early 1943:

We want an orderly and agreed method of determining the value of national currency units, to eliminate unilateral action and the danger which it involves that each nation will seek to restore its competitive position by exchange depreciation. Above all, we want to free the international monetary system from those arbitrary, unpredictable and undesirable influences which have operated in the past as a result of large-scale speculative movements of capital. We want to secure an economic policy agreed between the nations and an international monetary system which will be the instrument of that policy. This means that if any one Government were tempted to move too far either in an inflationary direction, it would be subject to the check of consultations with the other Governments, and it would be part of the agreed policy to take measures for correcting tendencies to dis-equilibrium in the balance of payments of each separate country. Our long-term policy must ensure that countries which conduct their affairs with prudence need not be afraid that they will be prevented from meeting their international liabilities by causes outside their own control.[4]

The Bretton Woods establishment was essentially an American-British plan in which the interests of the other industrialized capitalist nations were rarely put into consideration. Also, the Bretton Woods Conference was mainly a conference of about financial and monetary crises of the developed capitalist economies. Despite of the fact that these nations were in a numerical minority, their interests and views-specifically those of The United Kingdom and above all, the United States-were predominant. The British economy was dependent upon trade, and London had been the center of global trade and finance. The United States emerged from the postwar period with both political influence, military hegemony and economic strength. However, the Soviet Union was represented at the Bretton Woods Conference but chose not to become a part of the International Monetary Fund (IMF) and\or the International Bank for Reconstruction and Development (IBRD). Some few Eastern European states which did enter the International Monetary Fund and\or Bank eventually under the Soviet pressure later with drew. Meanwhile, Africa and Asia were represented by only seven nations. A part from China, all of these nations in one way or another were under the British or American hegemonic influence.

The remainder of Africa, Asia and the Caribbean was represented by proxy; that is, by colonial masters.[5] The only major Less Developed countries presence at Bretton Woods negotiations was that of the Latin American states. Therefore, the Third World representatives at Bretton Woods, despite some efforts to bring development strategies and initiatives on the high table were overwhelmed by the influence and weight of the big nations. In addition to these facts, Abdalla has commented that the national Liberation movements struggling to achieve political independence were not fully conscious of the need for Third World solidarity, nor of the tough demands of development. Therefore, it is by no reasons an overstatement to belief that the spirit of the group of 77, born some three decades later, was completely absent from the Bretton Woods arrangements.[6]

The International Monetary System had been in trouble since World War I. British hegemony in International Trade and the gold standard functioned well from 1870-1914. The first World War caused a total disintegration of that system. During the 1920s, the efforts to return to a gold standard failed. The 1930s saw an era of fluctuating exchange rates and the use of dollar, pound and francs to back gold, but these attempts also failed. Thus, the major developed nations met at Bretton Woods, New Hampshire to work out an international agreement that would deal with balance of trade deficit, exchange control, economic growth, and monetary and fiscal policy.

It is important to mention that the Bretton Woods negotiations created two major international financial institutions, the International Monetary Fund and the World Bank, to assume the responsibility of central banking roles for the management of international monetary activity. The General Agreement on Tariffs and Trade (GATT) was not in reality a part of the Bretton Woods negotiations; instead, GATT evolved from the wreckage of the International Trade Organization (ITO), an institution proposed by the United States to negotiate tariffs reductions in an attempt to establish a free trade zone. General Agreement on Tariffs and Trade unlike IMF and IBRD, was developed as a temporary mechanism until the International Trade Organization began to function. By accident, GATT became as permanent as the World Bank and the International monetary Fund.

The Bretton Woods System provided for a global financial structure based on fixed exchange rates. Majority of the representatives in the conference were convinced that the system of floating exchange rates that existed between 1920s and 1930s contributed significantly to the collapse of the global economic system and the emergence of economic nationalism that, eventually led to World War II. Hence, at Bretton Woods conference, economic stability became the principal concern for the framers. Within the Bretton Woods institution of fixed exchange rates, every nation agreed to establish the value of its currency in terms of gold and to maintain that exchange rate within a plus or minus 1-percent. Member nations agreed to the convertibility of their currencies into gold and\or other currencies and accepted in concept free trade.[7] The International Monetary Fund was to assume the responsibility of managing the International Monetary System. As the world's strongest financial and economic strength, the United States received the preponderance of power within the International Monetary Fund. Consequently, the U.S. Dollar became the dominant monetary force because of the weakened economies of Europe and Japan. As the United States began to rebuild and lend monies, to these depressed economies, the United States dollar, henceforth, became the major international currency. It had become so powerful that the United States was able to insist that the dollar backed by gold at thirty-five dollars per ounce.

Furthermore, the membership of the International Monetary Fund was changing; its initial forty four members grew to one hundred and fifty-one by 1986. The majority of new members were small, dependent economies that were depending on the generosity of European and North American developed nations.   The International Monetary Fund objectives and principles were not directed at these nations and any adjustments to help them have been minuscule.[8]   The problem was exacerbated by those small nations demanding true independence and an end to their dependence on the North.

In addition, the major objectives of the Bretton Woods Conference were the avoidance of competitive rate manipulation and the maintenance of stable exchange rates between and among trading currencies, so as to promote international trade and payments. Currency devaluation was envisaged as a last resort to be approved by the Fund only in cases of fundamental disequilibrium and to be avoided if possible by the automatic use of International Monetary Fund credits.   In dealing with the monetary and debt crises of the less developed countries including African states one has to question its fundamental strategy of emphasing devaluation of national currency in favor of other available alternative solutions to African economic crises.

Having established this brief overview of the evolution of Bretton Woods system and the position of African states in that system, we now turn our attention to the role of the International Monetary Fund in dealing with African economic crises; bearing in mind that the causes of African economic crises have been provided in chapter 11. It has been our intention to examine the International Monetary Fund's role in Africa so as to evaluate and   assess   the   usefulness   and\or   effectiveness   of   its macroeconomic stabilization policies in the continent.

AFRICAN DEBT CRISIS: COMPETING PARADIGMS

In this section, we focus our attention on long-run or "structural features" of African relations with the international capitalist economic system, and on the political and economic hegemony of domestic and international capitalist monopolies. We strongly believed that both the easy access of borrowing of the 1970s and the African debt crisis of the 1980s were the product of structural characteristics inherent to the world capitalist system. It is important to note that since the debt crisis, the Fund has been an advocate of local financial discipline in Africa on behalf of international monopolies. In our perspective, while the International Monetary Fund policy conditionalities may be in the best interests of African capitalists and international monopolies, these measures have deteriorated African growth and development.

To begin with, International Monetary Fund generally considers a less developed country to be facing a debt crisis when its debt service ratio exceeds more than 20 percent of its foreign exchange or export earnings.[9] Since 1970s and 1980s, the primary and most active function of the IMF has become lending to African countries experiencing balance of payments disequilibrium, and, as part of this effort, prescribing economic austerity measures that open the door to debt rescheduling and correcting balance of payments disequilibrium. Because of this general development, African states have become increasingly significant borrowers so that by the beginning of the early 1980s, African economy had become of the Fund's major concerns. Between 1973 and 1979, the rise in African nations' borrowing took place generally under special credit lines designed to finance balance of payments deficits due largely to accelerated increase in oil prices, temporary shortfalls in export earnings or provide soft credit from the proceeds of the International Monetary Fund's sales of gold. However, since 1979, African states have become major and\or common borrowers under the stand by agreement and\or extended fund facility which are tied to the Fund conditions.

For this reason, Africa has henceforth, come to the forefront controversy over the role of the Fund in various African economies. Its public attack has ranged from riots in Nigeria and Zambia over policies emerging from the Fund Loans (1985) and (1987) to open confrontation between Sudanese government and the IMF policy recommendations. As we indicated earlier in chapter 11, Africa is experiencing one of the major profound economic crises in her post-independence historical record. Recently, it has been seen that about 210 million able-bodied Africans are unemployed; the prices of most significant commodities have increased beyond reasonable doubt; some of the goods and services are even difficult to find. The balance of payments is in a chronic condition and in some countries, various anti-democratic laws, rules, regulations and measures have been passed to impose some order on the lifestyles of citizens.

The crisis encountered by Africa in refinancing her debt and development has become increasingly very critical with the twin crises of decreasing terms of trade with the advanced industrialized states and the rise in oil prices. Africa has a definite development strategy. The International Monetary Fund has its own set of strategies and in order to receive the International Monetary Fund assistance, African states have to agree with the International Monetary Fund conditionalities.

Another version of the history that was increasingly but often reluctantly used by nations facing balance of payments imbalance and private international debt crises was to renegotiate loans with private foreign banks in an attempt either to stretch out the payment period for principal and interest or receive further finance on more favorable grounds. Again, whatever the case may be, such debtor nations had to deal with the International Monetary Fund before a consortium of foreign banks would agree to refinance or defer existing loan reschedules.

It is important to mention that the International Monetary Fund's role is in reality unique, as its granting of an upper-credit tranche financing (upon which indebted nations eventually must call, because their real "quotas" have been used up) is conditional on the implementation of the Fund economic stabilization program by the debtor nation (conditionality). The implementation of the Fund stabilization and\or adjustment measure has become a "Sine qua non" for the consideration of a Paris Club rescheduling since 1966. However, for commercial banks rescheduling, this has been the case only since 1977.[10] Depending on the International Monetary Fund to impose its unique conditionality or as Todaro called it "medicine of tough stabilization policies" before it finally agreed to lend Africa funds in excess of their legal International Monetary Fund quotas. The creditors insist on the Fund economic stabilization and\or adjustment program, believing this to be the most corrective way for a nation to implement policies leading to more financial and economic stablilty. The Fund economic stabilization measures have a significant psychological implication on commercial banks, whose confidence in nations adopting such measures is enhanced.

The word "adjustment" is defined by the IMF as a timely implementation of appropriate polices over a broad range financial and economic programs to ensure that the current account deficit is manageable, given the availability and the terms and international financing.[11] Meanwhile, the measures proposed by the IMF envisage to create sound demand management coupled with policies to improve supply conditions and to strengthen the productive base of the economy. The major macroeconomic measures prescribed by the IMF to Africa and other less developed countries include a combination of reduction of fiscal deficits, curbs on the expansion of domestic credit (reduction of inflation), a substantial devaluation to return to a more exchange rate and other measures to increase export promotion. The IMF stabilization programs further include abolition or liberalization of exchange and import controls. A stringent, domestic anti-inflationary measure comprising (1) control of bank credit to increase interest rates and reserve requirements; (2)control of wage increases, in specific assuring that such increases are at rates less than the inflation rate;

(3) control of the government deficit through reductions on spending, particularly in the area of social services for the poor; and (4) dismantling of major forms of price controls. The last but not the least, liberalization of international trade and investment policies.

A CRITICAL ANALYSIS OF THE IMPLICATIONS OF CONDITIONALITY IN SUB-SAHARAN AFRICA

Since 1980s majority of indebted African states with largely depleted foreign reserves such as Nigeria, Zambia, Tanzania and Sudan, had to turn to the Fund for financial assistance and to secure additional foreign exchange. To receive this, they were required to implement some and\or all of the above mentioned IMF Macro-Austerity measures. At this point, however, we will provide a critical evaluation and assessment of these policies so as to point out their implications on the economy of Africa, particularly on the life of the poor. As we mentioned earlier, the conditions attached to International Monetary Fund financial assistance that require deflationary domestic economic measures, reduction of public expenditures (often designed to minimize income inequalities within economy), and liberalization of global trade and investment policies expose the International Monetary Fund to harsh criticism from decision makers in Africa and other less developed countries.[12]

The acceptance of IMF stabilization programs immediately limits the options of the less developed countries including Africa. In many instances, they may be required to leave socialist policies designed to reduce, if not eliminate, domestic income inequalities, or to protect local production from displacement by foreign investment, or even to sever existing relations with the international capitalist nations. Also, Harry Magdoff charges that "the very conditions which produce the necessity to borrow money in the first place are continuously reimposed by the pressure to pay back the loan and to pay the interest on these loans."[13] One radical critic of the International Monetary Fund writes that "International Monetary Fund missions descend like vultures in the wake of right-wing coups in countries such as Ghana, Indonesia, and Brazil."[14] In addition, "the financial discipline imposed by the International Monetary Fund has often eliminated the need for direct military intervention in order to preserve a climate friendly towards foreign investment."[15]

Radicals argue that it is no coincidence that President Buhari was unable to find any loans after the International Monetary Fund rejected his request for funds because of his unwillingness to accept and implement International Monetary Fund policy conditionalities. Also, they point out that in the wake of the military coup in August 1985, the International Bank for Reconstruction and Development indeed provide fund with the advice of the International Monetary Fund. What is more, this was followed by loans from other sources, both private and public.[16]

The Brandt Commission of 1983 has clearly maintained that the conditions imposed by the IMF on deficit countries had forced unnecessary and unacceptable political burdens on the poorest, on occasions leading the IMF riots and even the downfall of governments as was in the case of Jamaica.[17] It has been charged that the IMF programs are not solving the structural balance of payment problems that most debtor countries confront; rather, the exorbitant costs of the IMF restructuring fall on the weak shoulders of the poorest segment of the population as was the case in Chile, Nigeria, Zambia, Egypt, Sudan, Peru, and Jamaica to name a few. The draconian measures ignite social unrest in these countries. This is the focus of our study in examining the role of the Fund in Africa.

As noted, nation after nation assessments point to the fact that the IMF policies do not work in many of the cases. The prescriptions preferred by the IMF for solving the balance of payment problem of African states, particularly those committed to reform rather than radical change, end in disaster. Instead, the IMF medicine exacerbates the illness of the patient not only socially but economically as well.[18] Further, it has been charged that the IMF is politically biased in its overall thrust of its policies when it encounters reform-oriented regimes. The bottom line in this case is to realign these Third World government's policies in accordance with a defined package of economic and political priorities suited to the needs of center nations.[19]

In the case of Nigeria, Onyema Ugochukwu, another prolific writer on Nigeria-IMF relations reviews the complaints against the IMF. After reviewing Article I of the IMF Agreement, its goals and objectives, he pointed out that the IMF policies are not designed to achieve these objectives under current economic circumstances. The Fund's policies, with the austerity they entail, do in fact tend to produce the opposite result in Nigeria. To quote Ugochukwu:

> Instead of promoting high levels of employment and real income, cuts in government expenditures produce retrenchments, and often a counteraction in the utilization of productive resource. The drive to achieve adjustment over a rather shorter period, has in most Third World countries involved import restrictions, rather than expansion of trade and consumer prices have often gone up rather than down following the inception of the IMF policies.[20]

He also argued that the IMF policies are ineffective in addressing the problems of the Africa. Ugochukwu also rejected the IMF interpretation of its policy based on the banking principles. That is, ability to repay the principal plus interest on the loan as a precondition for borrowing from the Fund. While this approach may once have been adequate for the Fund's customers he said, "it seems entirely inappropriate for the current customers, who happen to be predominantly African states."[21] Also, in Nigeria, the former federal minister of finance, Dr. Onaolapo Soleye, while giving details of the budget on October 1, 1984 clearly stated the effort the developed countries are making to make refinancing on Nigeria's debts almost impossible by making an agreement with the IMF policy a precondition for refinancing. Even if Nigeria can survive without the IMF loan, he said, "an agreement with the IMF is essential because western export credit agencies have made it a precondition for refinancing Nigeria' trade debts of about 3,000 million."[22]   Even the IMF itself maintained the same.

In the situation of improved credit worthiness, we also find out that in terms of the long-term development prospects, this gain is an illusion.   The Africa's success at rescheduling much of the external debt service obligations which accrued in 1983 and 1985 may give temporary relief, but it has also led to an increase in the continent's outstanding stock of external debt.   According to the World Bank Annual Report 1988 figures, external debt has increased from about $190 billion in February 1984 to about $201 billion and $218.5 billion in 1985 and 1986 respectively.[23] Observers have noted that, by its debt rescheduling and quest for more borrowing, the African governments are accumulating an unbearable debt burden for future governments, a situation that could form the basis for future economic and political crisis.

With regard to measures aimed at reducing the current account deficit are concerned, the Fund's conditions put excessive emphasis on regular debt-service payments which at present absorb an excessive share of external means of payments of African economy. This emphasis has led, in some cases, to a substantial reduction in the import of goods required for recovery and adjustment and has created further overall economic decline. Again, very problematic is the economic policy of currency devaluation typically imposed by the International Monetary Fund upon almost every African states as a precondition for access to substantial International Monetary Fund Loan package. Devaluation of national currency as we see it in the case of Sudan has led to further increased in inflation and worsened Sudan's balance of payments as it is to reduce its payments deficits.   A large proportion of its imports, such as immediate and heavy industrial goods are vital to the effective functioning of the domestic economy, so the volume of Sudan's imports cannot be reduced without undermining her economy. Devaluation, rather than reducing imports, merely increases the size of Sudan's import bill by raising the cost of all foreign goods. Again, most primary products (the chief exports of Sudan) exhibit a price inelasticity of demand - that is, lower prices made available to foreign consumers by devaluation did not lead to a proportionate increase in the volume of purchases. The demand for cocoa or coffee, for example, did not increase much when the price dropped in 1986. The dilemma is that currency devaluation in Sudan neither increases export revenues nor reduces import expenditures in the manner expected by the International Monetary Fund and liberal economic theory.

In the case of Zambia, Zambians had paid a painful price for reform. Average per capita income for the country's 10 million people is 40 percent less now than in 1976. From 1984 to 1986, per capita income of Zambia had dropped in more than half from $740 to $300.[24] In formal recognition of this new poverty, the World Bank plans to reclassify Zambia from a "middle-income" country to a "low income" country. Another case of the IMF Policy that we examined in Zambia context is the demand for internal suspension of all subsidies including fertilizer and petroleum. Insistence in IMF programs that the government cut subsidized credits to farmers has led to severe shortages of pesticides, fertilizers, and other essential agricultural inputs for small scale farmers. In Zambia, for example, a 1986 IMF-advised cutback in rural credits led to a precipitous drop in rice, maize and garri production and an increase in malnutrition. Today, in Zambia, such measures have combined with the worst drought in the last few years to dispossess thousands of agricultural producers. The IMF officials are often quick to point out that one of their favored policy recommendations can benefit the rural sector, namely lifting government controls that have kept urban prices of agricultural products quite low. While partially true, the Fund ignores the fact that such resulting price increases are seldom passed on to agricultural workers on fixed salaries, and are devastating to the urban poor.

However, urban poor in our definition, which include unemployed and marginally employed populations, are especially vulnerable to such pricing policy changes. Many have incomes that are unstable or fixed at very low levels. Overnight doubling or tripling of prices of essential commodities following the IMF austerity measures have resulted in food riots in Zambia.

With these austerity measures and cutback of government expenditures in other areas, including employment, social and public services life becomes extremely difficult for poor people. At this point, however, women make up the majority of African rural (and particularly rural poor) population. They produce the bulk of food in Africa and, for example, make up 50-60 percent of the agricultural work force in the society.[25] Hence labor-displacing that shifts from food to export crops hit women the hardest. Furthermore, sex discrimination has left women with few economic resources to weather still austerity plans. Fewer opportunities for wage employment are open to women, who also suffer lower wage level and more layoffs.[26] Likewise, women usually have less access to basic education, health care, clean water and agricultural services, and are therefore especially hard hit by austerity measures that cut government spending in these areas in Africa.

Apart from the weight of the crisis that is shouldered by rural and urban poor in Africa, they play only a minimal role in decision-making in the institutions that advocate and administer austerity both nationally and internationally. Urban workers are affected by most of the same factors that erode the economic sustenance of the urban poor. In addition, the IMF stabilization programs generally involve a freeze in workers' real wages. However, wage controls without price controls erode the already marginal living standard of the working poor. An average middle income African family cannot afford two square meal a day.

Furthermore, affected by current policies of the Fund implemented by the majority of Africa governments is domestic entrepreneurs. Many entrepreneurs producing for domestic markets have gone bankrupt as policy incentives are shifted to favor exporters. The elimination of protective tariffs and the difficulty in obtaining foreign exchange for vital raw materials and machinery imports have accelerated the liquidation of small and medium-sized enterprises. In the process, tens of thousands are thrown out of work.[27] Small scale local industries are further being killed by import liberalization because foreign manufacturers are deliberately selling at uneconomic prices, with imported goods costing less than the price local manufacturers pay for their raw materials.

Moveover, the liberalization of prices is one of the Fund-supported adjustment program in Tanzania. These measures aim at transmitting exchange rate movements throughout the economy, improving incentives, and encouraging a more efficient resource allocation. Administered prices benefitted both traders in illicit markets and bureaucrats who administer the controls at the expense of low-income producers. Also, the IMF-induced stabilization and austerity programs generally seek to limit aggregate credit expansion. Within this overall constraint, they limit the access of the public sector to credit from the banking system in order to ensure that an adequate share of total credit is available to the private sector. In a repressed financial system like Africa, according to Helleiner credit controls and the associated credit rationing have strengthened the position of larger firms and farms relative to their smaller counterparts, with the latter being forced to turn to curb markets in which higher interest rates are charged. This process prevented the poor engaged in either small-scale enterprises in the informal sector or small farms in the rural sector from expanding their productive capacity, thus limiting their participation in the process of economic development and structural adjustment program.

AFRICA AND THE INTERNATIONAL MONETARY FUND: TOWARDS A THEORETICAL PERSPECTIVE

The International Monetary Fund, according to radical political economic theorists, impose capitalist domestic and foreign economic measures on borrowing nations, thus ensuring the dominance of the advanced and free market economies over the less developed nations. The IMF's reliance upon conventional liberal economic advice, its rejection of non-capitalist measures, and its efforts to bind indebted economies to the current political-economic system (through their vulnerability and indebtedness) are all seen as evidence that the Fund serves the interests and views of the dominant capitalist societies. In support of the above argument Michael Todaro has this to say:

> Alternatively, they have often been viewed by Third World leaders as representing a double standard-harsh adjustment policies for LDC debtors and no adjustment of the huge budget and\or trade deficits for the world's greatest debtor-the United States. Finally, because IMF policies are being imposed by an international agency that is perceived by many, especially those of the dependency school, to be merely an arm of the rich capitalist nations, stabilization policies are often viewed as measures primarily designed to maintain the poverty and dependency of Third World nations while preserving the global market structure for the industrialized nations.[28]

In addition, the International Monetary Fund is perceived by many to be the Linchpin of the whole international monetary and economic order, which is designed to perpetuate capitalism, and dependency of developing countries to the advanced capitalist economies. Cheryl Payer argues in this manner: The [global loan] system can be compared case by case with peonage on individual scale. In the peonage, or debt slavery system, the worker is unable to use his nominal freedom to leave the service of his employer, because the latter supplies him with credit (for overpriced goods in the company store) necessary to supplement his meager wages. The aim of the employer-creditor-merchant is neither to collect the debt once and for all, nor to starve the employee to death, but rather to keep the laborer permanently indentured through his debt to the employer. The worker cannot run away, for other employers and the state recognize the legality of his debt; nor has he any hope of earning his freedom with his low wage. Clearly the same system operates on the global level. Nominally independent countries find their debts, and their continuing inability to finance current needs out of imports [sic], keep them tied by a tight leash to their creditors. The IMF [and IBRD] orders them, in effect, to continue laboring on the plantations, while it refuses to finance their efforts to set up in business for themselves.   For these reasons the term "international debt slavery" is a perfectly accurate one to describe the reality of their conditions.[29]

Cheryl Payer indicates the negative or adverse implications of such a prescription in this fashion:

> The programmes result, typically, in the takeover of domestically owned businesses by their foreign competitors. The stabilization program puts a squeeze on domestic capitalists in several ways. The depreciation which it causes cuts deeply into their sales. Devaluation raises the costs, in local currency, of all imports needed for their business, and of all the unpaid debts resulting from past imports. This, a severe blow in itself, is compounded by the fact that the contraction of bank credit makes it more difficult than before to get the loans they need to carry on operations.[30]

Payer further argues that: The liberation of imports robs these countries of the protected markets they had enjoyed before, thereby making them vulnerable.   The author asserts that liberalization of imports tends to benefit the international firms, which are dependent on foreign inputs--raw materials, machinery, and spare parts--imported from another branch of the

same multi-national enterprise.[31] As Payer pointed above, these
policies bring about untold hardships and misery to millions of
people in these developing countries. Severe reductions in such
programs as government spending on social services and
subsidies always inevitably raise havoc with domestic markets.
Robert Pollin and Eduardo Zepeda pointed out in the *Monthly
Review* that, "the IMF was never ambiguous in its intention to cut
back sharply on public enterprise, government subsidies, price
controls, and deficit spending."[32] They stressed the fact that the
Fund did not realize that such public sector activities provide the
primary basis for effective demand in all economies of most
Third World nations.[33] The authors assert that, the IMF on its
way:

> Argues that domestic firms should shift to an export orientation after
> the public sector contracts.   But this ignores what almost all
> economists recognize, that capturing export markets requires the
> time and sustained promotional effect, even after a country's
> products have become more competitive through devaluation.[34]

Moreover, Kenneth W. Grundy, in *The Atlanta Journal and
Constitution,* argues that "to many in the West, the International
Monetary Fund (IMF) is the financial white knight sent to save
sick Third World economies from collapse. But to Third World
leaders, the cure may be worse than the disease.[35] Pollin and
Zepeda, writing in the *Monthly Review*, hit at the heart of the
IMF politics.   They convincingly believed that, the IMF has
always represented the interests of the international banks and the
developed countries' governments, particularly those of the
United States, and has taken the initiative in organizing this
group into what is in effect a coherent creditors cartel.   The
objective of the Fund's austerity program is therefore in full
accord with the primary goal of the creditors cartel.[36] It was as
a result of this factor among others that led to the Arusha
Initiative of 1980, which called for the Fund's replacement by a
new world monetary order.   To quote the Arusha Initiative:

Money is power.   This simple truth is valid for national and international relations. Those who wield power control money. An international monetary system is both a function and an instrument of prevailing power structures.[37]

Furthermore, African States are now suffering from another form of colonialism known as recolonization as Isebill V. Gruhn indicates in *Africa Today*, this could be seen for the fact that majority of African countries are now trying to reach an agreement with the International Monetary Fund.   At this point, Gruhn has this to comment:

> Symbolically, the extent of this recolonization is seen in the fact that Nigeria is about to succumb to the dictates of the International Monetary Fund (IMF). Nigeria, Africa's most potent state with a population of 80-100 million or one-fourth to one-fifth of the continent's population, is in sufficient economic difficulties that it must submit to externally-dictated discipline.   Nigeria's indebtedness is relatively small compared to that of Latin America, but this does not reduce the dramatic symbol for poorer African states that even oil-rich Nigeria is in serious distress.[38]

Gruhn further states:

> The most capital flows to low income African states made up mainly of concessional aid, much of it from the network of international donor agencies themselves.   These flows, their targets and their management, are directly and intentionally held in the hand of international bureaucrats.   In this second context, the IMF, by design, and in the previous context, by default and design, can influence the quantity and type of international capital flows to the Africa LDCs. But perhaps as serious as this power over funds is the increasing control over African policies -- economic, political, social - which can be demanded as preconditions for a favorable consideration for assistance. Not only can the IMF tell a country what policy reforms it must institute but in quite a few African states the IMF and other international agency personnel can and do insist that African ministries be supervised by international officials on the ground.   It is not surprising that the term recolonization

comes to mind as one views such a degree and extent of external, albeit international, bureaucratic control.[39]

In support of the above view, President Nyerere in the North-South Conference of July 1980 on the International Monetary System and the New International Economic Order indicated that: There was a time when a large number of people were urging that all aid to the Third World countries should be channeled through international organizations. They honestly argued that such organizations would be political and ideologically neutral.[40] The Fund has an ideology of economic and social development which it is trying to impose on the poor countries irrespective of their own clearly stated policies. And when we reject IMF conditions, we hear the threatening whisper: "without accepting our conditions you will not get our money, and you will get no other money."[41]

Following a similar argument, Teresa Hayter has documented the purpose and objective of foreign aid to the Third World countries. In her book, *Aid As Imperialism,* she demonstrates how the global institutions such as, the IMF, the World Bank and the United States Agency for International Development have colluded by acting only in their interests, under the guise of aid for the developing countries. It is an open secret that aid serves the purpose of the advanced capitalist nations.

> Aid is, in general, available to countries whose internal political arrangements, foreign policy alignments, treatment of foreign private investment, debt serving record, export policies, and so on, are considered desirable, potentially desirable, or at least acceptable, by the countries or institutions providing aid, and which do not appear to threaten their interest.[42]

On the first sight, this would appear to be the necessary conditions to solicit another's help, but one has to consider the history of exploitation and the terms of trade that developed countries have had over developing ones. Hayter also elaborated on her observation by examining the operations of these agencies in four Latin American countries: Columbia, Chile, Brazil, and Peru. Although the circumstances were not quite similar, the underlying results were. In working with those nations that have had populist governments intent on making mild reforms, such as expansion and redistribution of land, the IMF will call for devaluation of their currency and cuts in government expenditures which also conflict with the national policy, therefore hindering further negotiations with the IMF. The World Bank and AID have tried to influence the political process, but because their aid was on a long term basis, it was not easy to sever relationships. The question that needs to be asked is who benefits from aid given by those international agencies?

> The critical issue is whether the present systems of economic and social organization in Latin America, based on private enterprise, a respect for property, however unequally distributed, and economic and political dependence on the United States, are capable of providing real improvements in the conditions of life of the masses of people. The policies of the international agencies imply that they are, or that such improvement is unnecessary secondary to other considerations or simply that the United States, supported by the major financial agencies, is determined to preserve the existing situation for as long as possible. . . .[43]

As we indicated in *The Implications of Conditionality*, the increased significance of African countries as recipients of the IMF's upper tranche and extended Fund facility credit, and the expectation that this trend will continue in the 1980s, makes the less developed countries of Africa critical for the IMF and the IMF critical for the Less Developed Countries of Africa. This is true because the IMF was not formed with Africa in mind. Also, it was not the Fund's intention to finance large and persistent deficits. Much comment on the IMF is directed toward proposing reforms in its lending practices, but here we have two major theoretical concerns that will guide our study: (1) what rules govern IMF actions when confronted with a set of development objectives somewhat at variance from its own? In other words, can the IMF be used for development and economic prosperity of LDCs? (2) what scope does the typical less developed country of Africa (say Sudan) have for charting its own course while at the same time operating within an international capitalist framework?

The IMF is a global institution designed to manage global monetary problems. It operates under the aegis of the western capitalist system and is dominated by the Group of Ten. In a broad generalization, there are three worlds in the capitalist mold. The first consists of those nations that can attract international commercial loans mainly because of the structure and strength of their economies. The second world comprises those nations that cannot attract these loans because they are relatively underdeveloped. They have limited infrastructure and their economies are weak. Then there are those grey area nations that lie in-between the two axises.[44]

The present IMF policy is to treat all member countries alike:

> The Fund has always avoided dividing its members into categories and has sought to preserve the principle of uniform treatment of all members. This is attractive if it can be done without jeopardizing the interest of either group. But can it?[45]

Nowzad had summarized the philosophy of the Fund towards LDCs as follows:

> The Fund (as is evident from the Articles) has a market-oriented, pro-free enterprises, pro-capitalist, anti-socialist philosophy, with a pronounced bias in favor of free trade, private investment, and the price mechanism. This reflects a 'vision of the world' inspired and imposed by industrial countries, in particular the United States, on debtor (implicitly developing) countries. Many economists and politicians genuinely believe that the policies implied by this philosophy are in the best interests of developing countries. It must be recalled, however, that these officials are western-trained and believe in the efficiency of the market. The imposition of this philosophy is facilitated by the dominant voting power of the industrial countries; in this way, the Fund serves the interests of creditor countries and helps to preserve their resources from claims

by developing countries to larger resource transfers. In brief (as one head-of-state has put it), the Fund is a 'device by which the rich countries increase their power over the poor.[46]

For all practical purpose, the IMF has two fundamental philosophies that express the above view in its "low conditionality" and "high conditionality." The former applies to the developed countries which are characterized by relatively full employment, high industrialization and strong economies that might suffer periodic "balance of payment problems." What these nations need from the Fund are small adjustments of their currency and small loans relative to their economies to make these adjustments. "High conditionality" loans are large loans relative to the economy of the debtor nations.[47] These loans address major financial problems characterized by repayment of former loans and the building up of some basic infrastructure.

As we indicated in *The Implications of Conditionality,* the main difference between low conditionality and high conditionality is the level of IMF influence. Low conditionality nations have access to commercial banks, so the percentage of the money needed to correct their balance of payments deficit from the IMF only allows for nominal IMF advice to correct the problem. "High conditionality" nations with a greater dependency on the IMF have to undergo more stringent IMF dictates.

> The Fund clientele has shrunk to this second group of countries, in which the commercial banks seek to avoid exposure, . . . low income countries, which currently receive two-thirds of the Fund's total commitments, account for a mere 7 percent of the banks' exposure in non-oil developing countries.[48]

The Fund specifically has the role of managing the LDCs' financial problems. Fund insistence on "high conditionality" causes severe shocks to the economies of the LDCs. However, the organization would become an aid donor if there was no conditionality. The LDCs not only want loans at lower rates, but they also advocate a restructure of the IMF to reflect the present realities of its functions. It was funded to adjust world monetary policies, but today's main influence is on the economies of LDCs. The Fund has a major role of constructing and maintaining a global economic system based upon capitalist forms of production and exchange. Constructing an environment in which market forces operate without state restraints, and profit is accumulated by private capital is, therefore, central to this role. The growth of the international economy on this basis was seen as the priority of the Fund, with the development of national economies as secondary. The Fund was originally formed to facilitate the expansion and balanced growth of the international trade, and to contribute thereby to individual states' growth and development. Although the founders' orientation at the time was toward the fractured economic relations of the advanced capitalist states, the same priority toward the global system and the construction of a global market system characterizes the IMF's role in contemporary time.

The building and\or construction of such a global economic system according to Harris, requires the IMF to have leverage over the national economies within it, for the rules of the global economic system rest upon the policies and rules of national states. The IMF's ability to operate on these also rests on its role regarding member states' balance of payments. In this system, countries' external payments represent a real constraint on policy, and the IMF's role in providing balance of payments finance enables it to operate on these constraints so that they exert pressure towards the adoption of national policies which contribute to a market-based global system rather than to prevent it.[49] The IMF's theoretical framework and policy prescriptions ignore the structural and inevitable nature of payments disequilibria that result from the development process over which leaders of LDCs do not have control. These considerations bear upon all the IMF's operations and, particularly the conditionality it implies on loans to African and similar states. But how these policies bear upon the question of power, class interest and imperialism, remains an open debate among the LDCs.

WHY BLAME?: THE IMF RESPONSES

The advocates of the IMF first attack the concept that the IMF has a market oriented, free-enterprise ideology, which it imposes on the poor countries. It is a misunderstanding that the IMF has specific socio-political views that determine the way it operates. Leaving aside the practical issue of whether an institution that is owned by 151 countries could apply a homogeneous view, the fact is that as a matter of explicit policy, the Fund does not take positions on social and political issues, but works within the existing socio-political system of its member countries. In formulating its policies, the Fund is concern with the broad economic aggregates that promote a viable balance of payments and economic growth. In so doing, it will seek to adapt the instrument of macroeconomic management available in the country   to its economic system.[50]   The advocates further rejected the acquisition that the IMF and the World Bank collude in dealing with developing countries problems. According to them, such suspicion is based on a misunderstanding of the purposes of the two organizations and the manner in which they operate.

Also, IMF and the World Bank have been entrusted, under their respective statutes, with separate mandates but with a broad common interest, namely to work for the economic prosperity, and greater welfare of their members.[51] However,, the IMF's mandate extends to both developing and developed countries. It works to promote monetary cooperation and exchange stability, facilitate the expansion and balanced growth of trade, and provide financial support to assist members facing balance of payments disequilibrium.[52]

Again IMF policy prescriptions were also under attack at a recent London conference which was organized by the Institute for African Alternatives, to discuss among other things the "impact of the IMF's stabilization policies on Africa." The IMF representative at the conference defended its policies in this way: they not only consider their policies correct and effective, but also deem their programs to be having the desired long-term result.[53] As a reality, the IMF contends that the programs are not designed with intent to cause poverty and hardship in Africa, or to undermine the sovereignty of African governments, these are rather the by-products of necessary corrective measures.[54]

> The participants were outraged by the Fund's statement, and consequently charged that, "the assiduous supervision of a world financial and economic order conducive to the continuing safe and profitable operation of multinational corporations, in the actually existing African context, necessarily leads to the dire social and economic consequences of the people of Africa.[55]

Pollin and Zepeda took their argument a step ahead by agreeing with the IMF popular defense, that is, Third World government's mismanagement. They argued that much of the loans received by these countries were not spent on productive development projects, but were used to finance military hardware purchases, wasteful construction projects, and capital flight.[56] There is a substantial fact in the above contention because a large body of materials we come across supports this premise. For example, Kuczynski, who wrote in *Foreign Affairs*, shares the same view in this way:

> The largest reservoir of funds that is in theory available to the debtor countries is the capital which left these countries during the period of high external borrowing. Much of the money borrowed from commercial banks fled because overhauled exchange rates, themselves made possible by the borrowing, made such flight attractive.[57]

Cheryl Payer indicates the basic foundation of the IMF operations in her book, *The Debt Trap: The IMF and the Third World*. It is essential to have an institution like the IMF because of growing interdependency and trading among nations. When nations trade, they have different balances because of the division of labor and capital around the world. The developed countries trade among themselves predominantly in finished goods and trade with the LDCs for raw materials. Historically, the developed countries have had the advantage in trading, because raw materials are inelastic depending on the whim and fancy of the developed countries. As importantly, the developed countries have control of the markets, and often use the market forces to depress or accelerate the usage of developing countries' raw materials. As it turns out, the developed countries have had the privilege and advantage over the less developed countries in trading resulting in unequal exchange rates. The fluctuation in demand for raw materials and the pricing of them by the developed countries have exacerbated the unequal exchange problem. The Fund as an international institution should be addressing the problem of equity in trading and unequal exchange rate, but its record is one of failure to address those issues, while it blames the victim, the Third World countries, for inefficiency.

The IMF Payer perceives serves as a forerunner to all major sources of credit in the developed capitalist world whether private lenders, governments or multilateral institutions such as the World Bank. If not approved by the IMF, the particular country will find it difficult to refinance its trade deficit from its creditor nations and their agencies. She, therefore, concludes that, in fact what occurs is:

> The IMF is not the real villain of the piece, though it is the agent of the villains. They are in multinational corporations and capitalist governments which are the natural enemies of Third World independence and can usually mobilize the resources to crush it.[58]

This corresponds to Hayter's ideas, that aid was a secondary source of influence. I believe, now, that the existence of aid can be explained only in terms of an attempt to preserve the capitalist system in the Third World. Aid is not a particularly effective instrument for achievement; hence, its current decline. But, insofar as it is effective, its contribution to well-being of the people of the Third World is negative, since it is not in their best interest that exploitation should continue.[59]

In defense of the above mentioned implications of the Fund's conditionalities, the IMF has maintained that its policies are working fine, except the fact that most developing nations have no clear sense of direction and purpose. The Fund believes that most of the alleged criticisms are misconceptions. For instance, on the issue that the Fund-supported programs impose austerity on member countries, the IMF defended itself. First, nations fall into balance of payments difficulties because of inappropriate domestic policies, unfavorable external developments or a combination of both. It is this initial disequilibrium and lack of financing prospects that force a country to adopt austerity measures.[60] In these circumstances, a country can draw down its reserves of foreign exchange or can borrow abroad to subsidize its deficits, but only to a point. Eventually, its reserves, as well as the willingness of foreign creditors to continue to lend, will be exhausted. Sooner or later, with or without the Fund, the country will have to adjust. At this point, however, the Fund does agree that every adjustment carries austerity. In reality, while it cannot be denied that adjustment programs may involve some costs, Fund-supported programs are designed to achieve the necessary adjustment in a manner that maximizes the potential for growth while attempting to minimize the unavoidable austerities attendant on all adjustment.[61]

CONCLUDING REMARKS

The complaints of the Third World nations about the International Monetary Fund extend beyond the limits upon and terms attached to their borrowing condition.   They seek a more potent role of the International Monetary Fund's decision-making process.   The Fund relies upon a weighted voting arrangement reflective of countries' quotas.   Although less developed countries comprise three-fourths of the IMF membership, they hold only about one-third of the votes.[62]   The United States alone has 19.8 percent of the votes in the International Monetary Fund, and the five largest industrial countries of the West together account for 40 percent of the votes in the Fund.   Until well into the 1960s, moreover, the most important international monetary deliberations and decisions took place in the Group of Ten - a body meeting under the auspices of the Organization for Economic Cooperation and Development in Paris that performed a kind of executive function for the entire international monetary order, including the IMF. The Group of Ten comprises only the most important advanced industrial states, and the less developed countries were seldom even consulted about deliberations conducted.

Also, beyond these policy prescriptions of the International Monetary Fund, less developed countries have sought to increase their access to Fund resources through enlargement of their quotas and implementation of a proposal to link new SDR allocations to increase development assistance for the less developed countries. However, between the 1970s and mid-1980s, IMF quotas were doubled. This has expanded the resources of the IMF to SDR 90 billion. Third World nations will be able to borrow more as their quotas, like everyone else's are increased proportionately.   As it turns out, less developed countries as a group still account for only about 30 percent of total Fund quotas.   For many years, the less developed countries have fought to enhance their voting power in the International Monetary Fund and to more international monetary decision making into forums; including International Monetary Fund, where their power could be felt. Thus, in response to these pressures, in combination with other events, the International Monetary Fund has become a more central forum for key international monetary deliberations.[63]

In conclusion, therefore, foreign capital did secure substantial advantage: the dollar value of major African currencies slashed four fold, import restrictions were lifted, import licenses abolished, privatization initiated, subsidies removed, wages frozen, price controls lifted, jobs cut, the minimum wage was eliminated and profitability of foreign investment (especially in oil) enhanced. In return for this structural adjustment program, African governments received a new debt repayment timetable along with new loans from the World Bank and commercial sources. Currently, economists from Washington, D.C. virtually run various African states' Central Bank and finance. In short, IMF conditions were imposed through the back door and under different names. The majority of African states are being bolstered by outside advisors in order to impose the IMF package. While private foreign capital gains, African citizens are pushed further into more or less desperate strategies to avoid destitution and death.

NOTES

1. Fredoline Anunobi, *The Implications of Conditionality: The International Monetary Fund and Africa* (Maryland; University Press of America, 1992). Also see Ragnar Nurkse, *International Currency Experience: Lessons of Inter-War Period* (Geneva: League of Nations; Princeton: Princeton University Press, 1944); Kenneth Dan, *The Rules of The Game: Reform and Evolution in The International Monetary System* (Chicago: Chicago University Press, 1982), pp. 42-70. See further Charles W. Kegley and Eugene R. Wittkopf, *World Politics: Trend and Transformation,* Second ed. (New York: St. Martin's Press, 1985), pp. 174-175. J.E. Spero, *The Politics of International Economic Relations* (New York: St. Martin's Press, 1985) pp. 35-46.

2. Statement of H.D. White in the introduction to his Preliminary Draft Proposal for a United Nations Stabilization Fund, and a Bank for Reconstruction and Development of The United and Associated Nations (April 1942), in Margaret Garrisen de Vries and Keith Horsefield, *The IMF, 1945-1965: Twenty years of International Monetary Cooperation* 3 Vol. (Washington D.C.: IMF, 1969) p. 37.

3. Richard Gardner, *Sterling-Dollar Diplomacy* rev., ed. (New York: McGraw-Hill Book Co., 1969), chapter I.

4. House of Commons,Parliamentary Debates (Hansard), 5th Series Vol. 386, February 2, 1943, quoted in Gardner, p. 78.

5. For detailed analysis, see Ismail-Sabril Abdalla, "The Inadequacy and Loss of Legitimacy of the IMF," *Development Dialogue* (Sweden: Dag Hammarshkjold Foundations, 1980-1982), p. 37. See Fredoline Anunobi, *The Implications of Conditionality: The International Monetary Fund and Africa* (Maryland: University Press of America, 1992), chapter 6. Joan E. Spero, *The Politics of International Economic Relations,* 4th ed. (New York: St. Martin's Press, 1990), chapter 2. Charles W. Kegley and Eugene R. Wittkopf, *World Politics: Trend and Transformation* (New York: St. Martin's Press, 1985).

6. Abdalla, Development Dialogue.

7. Papp, *Contemporary International Relations.*

8. Anunobi, *The Implications of Conditionality.* See also Michael C. Desch, *When the Third World Matters: Latin America and United States Grand Strategy* (Baltimore: The Johns Hopkins University Press, 1993). South Commission, The Challenge to the South: The Report of the Commission (New York: Oxford University Press, 1991). Aderanti Adepoju, *The Impact of Structural Adjustment on the Population of Africa* (London: James Currey, 1993). Anne O. Krueger, *Economic Policy Reform in Developing Countries* (Cambridge Massachuetts: Blackwell Publishers, 1992). Allan R. Roe, *Instruments of Economic Policy in Africa* (London: James Currey, 1992). Jeff Haynes, "Debt in Sub-Saharan Africa: The Local Politics of Stabilization," *African Affairs* No. 86 (July 1987).

9. Latin American Bureau, *The Poverty Brokers: The IMF and Latin America* (London: Latin America Bureau Research and Action LTD., 1983).

10. Anunobi, *The Implications of Conditionality.*

11. Manzsche Verlage, *External Debt Rescheduling* (Wlen, Austria: Vienna Inc. 1985). For detailed ecamination of the word adjustment, see Gerald Helleiner's work on T*he IMF and Africa in the 1980S* (Princeton, N.J.: Princeton University Press, 1983). Robert Aliber, *Monetary Reform and the World Inflation* (California: Sage Publication, 1973). Stanley Black, *Exchange Rate Policies for Less Developed Countries* (Princeton, New Jersey: Princeton University Press, 1976). Fred Block, *The Origins of International Economic Disorder* (Los Angeles: University of California Press, 1977).

Kennedy Grundy, "To Some Poor Nations, IMF Cure is worse than the Disease", *The Atlanta Journal and Constitution* (4 October 1987). Dennis Goulet, *Economic Development in The Third World* (New York: Longman Inc., 1981).

12. Anunobi, *The Implications of Conditionality: The International Monetary Fund and Africa*.

13. Harry Magdoff, *The Age of Imperialism*, (New York: Monthly Review Press, 1966), p. 98.

14. Cheryl Payer, "The Perpetuation of Dependence: The IMF and the Third World", *Monthly Review Press*, Vol. 23, No. 4, September 1971, p. 37.

15. Ibid., p. 38.

16. The same incident happen in the case of Jamaica under leftist Prime Minister Michael Manley. His refusal to accept International Monetary Fund conditions of reduced public employment, budget cuts, and higher prices for desperately needed loans during 1980 led commercial banks to refuse extension of further credits until Jamaica resumed negotiations with the International Monetary Fund. Manley's electoral defeat by Edward Seaga, a strong advocate of private enterprise, resulted in a prompt renegotiation of the Fund Loan package and the resumption of private bank credits. The same is true with President Allende of Chile who refused to accept the Fund policies because of its socio-economic and political effects. Also see *New Nigerian*, October 8, 1986, p. 5.

17. As indicated in the *Poverty Brokers*, pp. 30-31.

18. "The Bank, the Fund and the People of Africa," *West Africa* (September 1987): p. 1839.

19. President Nyerere, *Development Dialogue*.

20. Onaolapo Soleye, "Nigeria/IMF: The Prudence and the Fear," *West Africa,* (1 October 1984), p. 1976.

21. Onyema Ugochukwu, "The Trouble with the IMF," p. 5.

22. Soleye, Nigeria\IMF, p. 1976. See African Market, Nigeria's Shh Devaluation *"New Africa"* (September 1986). *African Development* Vol 13. No. 6 (Summer 1986). Adebayo Adedeji, Economic Commission for Africa and Africa's Development 1983-2008: A Preliminary Perspective Study (Addis Ababa, ECA. 1983) *African Review* (January 1988). *African Research Bulletin, Economic Series*, (June-July 1981).

23. *World Bank Annual Report*, 1988.

24. *African Review* (December, 1988)

25. Anunobi, *The Implications of Conditionality*, chapter 11.

26. Ibid.

27. *Africa Today* (May 1987).

28. Todaro, *Economic Development in The Third World*, pp. 420-421.

29. Cheryl Payer, "Perpetuation of Dependence: The IMF and the Third World", p. 40.

30. Cheryl Payer, *The Debt Trap: The International Monetary Fund and the Third World* (New York: Monthly Review Press, 1974), p. 41.

31. Ibid.

32. *Monthly Review* (February 1987).

33. Ibid.

34. Ibid., p. 4.

35. Kenneth W. Grundy, "To Some Poor Nations, IMF Cure is Worse Than the Disease," *The Atlanta Journal and Constitution,* (4 October 1987), p. 6D.

36. Monthly Review 38 (February 1987): p. 3.

37. The Arusha Initiative 1980, as quoted in *The Poverty Brokers*, p. 30.

38. Isebill V. Gruhn, "The Recolonialization of Africa: International Organization on the March", *Africa Today*, Vol. 30, No 4, (1983) p. 37.

39. Ibid., p. 38.

40. Ibid., p. 1843.

41. President Nyerere, *Development Dialogue*, (Hammarskjold Foundation, July 1980-1982), p. 8.

42. Teresa Hayter, *Aid as Imperialism* (England: Penguin Books, Ltd., 1972), p. 15.

43. Ibid., p. 163.

44. Anunobi, *The Implications of Conditionality*.

45. John Williamson, *The Lending Policies of the International Monetary Fund* (Washington, D.C.: Institute for International Economic, August 1982), p. 13.

46. Bahran Nowzad, *The IMF and Its Critics* (Princeton: Princeton University Press, 1981), p. 7.

47. Anunobi, *The Implications of Conditionality*.

48. Nowzad, *The IMF and its Critics*, p. 7.

49. Harris, "Conceptions of the IMF's Role in Africa" ed in Peter Lawrence, *World Recession and The Food Crisis in Africa* (London: James Currey, 1986).

50. Margaret DeVries, *The IMF 1966-1971: The System in Stress*, (Washington, D.C.: International Monetary Fund, 1976), p. 213.

51. The IMF, "Ten Common Misconceptions about the IMF" (Washington D.C.: External Relations Department, 1987), p. 18.

52. Ibid., p. 22.

53. *West Africa*, "The Bank, The Fund and the People of Africa," (September 1987), p. 1839.

54. The IMF, p. 30.

55. Ibid.

56. Pollin and Zepeda *Monthly Review*, Vol. 38, (February 1987) p. 2.

57. Pedro-Pablo Kuczynski, "The Outlook for Latin American Debt" *Foreign Affairs*, (Fall 1987), p. 143.

58. Payer, T*he Debt Trap: The International Monetary Fund and the Third World*, pp. xii-xiii.

59. Hayter, *Aid As Imperialism*, p. 9.

60. The IMF, p. 15.

61. Ibid.

62. *International Monetary Fund, Annual Report* (Washington, D.C., IMF, 1984), p. 73.

63. In reality, this has not eliminated regular consultation among the advanced industrial states under the auspices of the Organization for Economic Cooperation and Development, *The New York Times,* September 9, 1980, p. 48.

Regional Per Capita GNP

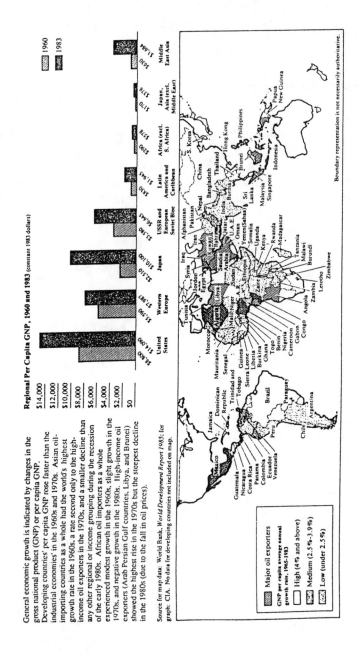

General economic growth is indicated by changes in the gross national product (GNP) or per capita GNP. Developing countries' per capita GNP rose faster than the industrial economies' in the 1960s and 1970s. Asian oil-importing countries as a whole had the world's highest growth rate in the 1960s, a rate second only to the high-income oil exporters in the 1970s, and a smaller decline than any other regional or income grouping during the recession of the early 1980s. African oil importers as a whole experienced modest growth in the 1960s, slight growth in the 1970s, and negative growth in the 1980s. High-income oil exporters (Arab Persian Gulf countries, Libya, and Brunei) showed the highest rise in the 1970s but the steepest decline in the 1980s (due to the fall in oil prices).

Source for map data: World Bank, *World Development Report 1985*; for graph: CIA. No data for developing countries not included on map.

CHAPTER 13

Africa and the North-South Cooperations: Rhetoric or Reality

After the end of World War II, the United States was the only major capitalist nation not affected by the war. While the cold war proceeded, the international communist bloc nations and the international capitalist bloc nations became economically, socially, ideologically and politically insulated from each other. In this situation the United States and the other industrialized capitalist powers established a series of measures that constituted an international economic order. However, the postwar economic order according to Spero, centered on three political frameworks "the concentration of power in a small number of states, the existence of a cluster of important interests shared by those states, and the presence of a dominant power willing and able to assume a leadership role."[1] The centralization of both economic and political power in the advanced industrial economies of North America and Western Europe according to Spero enabled them to dominate the Bretton Woods system. They faced no challenge from the communist countries of Eastern Europe and Asia, including the Soviet Union, which were isolated from the rest of the global economy in a separate international economic system. Although the Third World countries were fully integrated into the international economy, they had no voice in management because of their political and economic weakness. Finally, Japan, weakened by the war and lacking the level of development and the political power of North America and Western Europe, remained subordinate and outside the management group for much of the Bretton Woods period. The concentration of power accelerated the economic system's management by confining the number of actors whose agreement was necessary to establish rules, institutions, and procedures and to carry out management within the agreed-upon system.[2]

Thus the concentration of power prevented the number of states whose participation was necessary in order to make the international economic system operate effectively and democratically. The foundation of that agreement was a shared belief in international capitalism and liberal economic theory. The system's operation was accelerated by the shared beliefs and interests of these nations including their preferential arrangement of an open international economic system, combined with a commitment to minimize government intervention. Given the fact that the Western industrialized societies saw themselves as having a common external enemy, economic cooperation came to be seen as a necessary and sufficient condition, not only for progress, but also for national security. The emerging economic order was based on the principles of free trade (although there were some variation); on the free flow of capital to wherever rewarding investments could be made; and on an international division of labor designed to allow each nation to take advantage of its resources. The advanced capitalist states relied generally on market mechanisms and private ownership of the means of production.

Accordingly, the advanced capitalist states favored a liberal economic system, one that depended on a free market with the historical experience of 1930s, when large number of exchange minimum of barriers to the flow of private capital and trade. The controls and trade barriers resulted to economic warfare, remained fresh in the minds of planners. However, they disagreed on the particular implementation of this liberal economic system, all agreed that an open international economic system would lead not only to economic progress and economic harmony but also to world peace and solidarity. As Cordell Hull, a prominent American Security Analyst argued:

> unhampered trade dovetailed with peace; high tariffs, trade barriers, and unfair economic competition, with war...if we could get a freer flow of trade-freer in the sense of fewer discriminations and obstructions-so that one country would not be deadly jealous of another and the living standards of all countries might rise, thereby eliminating the economic dissatisfaction that breeds war, we might have a reasonable chance of lasting peace.[3]

DESIRABILITY AND RESPONSIBILITY OF U. S. MANAGEMENT OF INTERNATIONAL MONETARY SYSTEM

To achieve economic stability, economic growth and development and political harmony, industrialized countries agreed to cooperate to regulate the world economic system. The common interest in economic cooperation, according to Spero was enhanced by the outbreak of the Cold War at the end of the 1940s. The economic weakness of the capitalist economies, they were perceived would make them vulnerable to internal communist threats and external pressure from USSR - hence economic compromise and cooperation became necessary not only to reconstruct capitalist economies and to enhance their continuing vitality but also provide for their political strength and military security. Spero summaries the whole situation in this way:

The developed market economies also agreed on the nature of international economic management, which was to be designed to create and maintain a liberal system. it would require the establishment of an effective international monetary system and the reduction of barriers to trade and capital flows. With these barriers removed and a stable monetary system in place, states would have a favorable environment for ensuring national stability and growth. The state, not the international system, bore the main responsibility for national stability and growth. Thus, the members of the system shared a very limited conception of international economic management: regulation of the liberal system by removing barriers to trade and capital flows and creating a stable monetary system.[4]

Global management depended on the dominant power to lead the system. According to Spero, as the world's foremost economic and political power, the United States was generally in a position to assume that responsibility of leadership. The U. S. economy, undamaged by war and with its large market, great productive capability, financial facilities, and strong currency, was the dominant international economy. The capability to support a large military force plus the possession of an atomic weapon made the United States the world's strongest military power and the leader of the Western bloc. The European states, with their economies in shamble owing to the war, their production and markets divided by national boundaries, and their armies dismantled or weakened by the war, were not in a position to assume the responsibility and leadership function. Japan defeated and destroyed, was not then even considered part of the management system.[5]

The west was greatly influenced by the lesson drawn from the experiences of the interwar period, specifically, the Great Depression of the 1930s. The major concern was that the United States could not remain isolated from international affairs, as it did after World War I. For this reason and other similar reasons, the United States was very active in building the various regulations, rules, and institutions that were to govern international political economy in the post-World War II era.

However, in the international economic area, these regulations, rules, and institutions came to be known as the Bretton Woods system. As indicated at the Bretton Woods Conference of 1944 in New Hampshire, these regulations and institutions would result to postwar international monetary system characterized by stability, predictability and orderly growth. As Charles Kegley and Eugene Wittkopf put it:

> Governments would have the primary responsibility for enforcing the rules and otherwise making the regime work effectively. They would be assisted by the International Monetary Fund (IMF), created at Bretton Woods as a formal mechanism to assist states in dealing with such matters as maintaining equilibrium in their balance of payments and stability in their exchange rates with one another. The International Bank for Reconstruction and Development (IBRD), now known popularly as the World Bank, was also designed as a vehicle to facilitate recovery from the war, although its role has since expanded to include promoting economic development in the Third World.[6]

The Western European and Japanese economies that were exhausted by the war further demanded American leadership. These nations needed United States financial and economic aid to reconstruct their domestic production and to finance their international trade. The political and economic effects of American unilateral management of international economic system, were perceived as positive, because it was seen that the American economic aid would improved domestic economic and political problems and facilitate international stability. To quote Spero:

> What the Europeans feared was not U.S. domination but U.S. isolation: the history of the late entry into the two world wars by the United States was fresh in their minds. Throughout the Bretton Woods period, the United States mobilized the other developed countries for management and, in some cases, managed the system alone. The United States acted as the world's central banker, provided the major initiatives in international trade negotiations, and dominated international production.[7]

THE EMERGENCE OF U.S. DOLLAR
AS INTERNATIONAL LIQUIDITY ASSET

Also, the International Monetary Fund and the World Bank have become essential instruments for the efficient management of the international economic system during the postwar era, they proved ineffective for managing the postwar economic recovery because the two institutions were given limited authority and too few financial support by international community to cope with large economic disequilibrium suffered by Western Europe and Japan during the war period. Thus, United States had to come in as a savior. The American dollar became the cornerstone to United States managerial function. Supported by enormous and healthy economy, a fixed exchange rate relations between gold and the U. S. dollar (that is $35 per ounce of gold), and an agreement by the government to exchange gold for dollars came into operation known as dollar convertibility. At this point, also, dollar became as good as gold. In reality, it was preferable to and better than gold as the liquid assets for many different countries having balance of payments surpluses and savings.

As one international economist indicated at that time, dollars received interest rate while gold did not. The U.S. dollars do not incur storage and insurance costs and they were needed to purchase raw material imports necessary for postwar reconstruction, development and survival. To put it differently, Kegley and Wittkopf have this to say:

> The postwar economic system was not simply a modified gold standard system; it was a dollar-based system. Dollars became a major component of the international reserves used by national monetary authorities in other countries and of the "working balances" used by private banks, corporations, and individuals for international trade and capital transactions. Moreover, the dollar became a "paralled currency" that is, it was universally accepted as the currency against which every other country sold or redeemed its own national currency in the exchange markets. In order to

maintain the value of their currencies, central banks in other countries either bought or sold their own currencies, using the dollar to raise or depress the currencies value.[8]

One major concern of the immediate postwar period was how to accumulate the U.S. dollars into the hands of those people who needed it seriously. One way was the Marshall Plan, which provided Western Europe and Japan $17 billion to purchase the U.S. commodities needed for reconstruction and development of their war torn economies.

Between 1947 and 1958, the United States supported and encouraged an outflow of dollars, which provided liquidity for the international community. International liquidity was also provided by the deliberate U. S. encouragement of deficits in its own balance of payments, through excessive outflow of foreign aid and through military expenditures to maintain the bourgeoing U. S. overseas military stability and commitments. To support long term adjustment process, the U. S. encouraged Japanese and European trade competiveness and swallowed certain forms of protectionism such as Japanese restrictions against goods imported from America and discriminations against the dollar. For instance, the European payments union - a multilateral European entity that supported and encouraged intra-European trade against the U. S. Financial assistance to Europe and Japan was designed to reconstruct productive and export capability. At the same token, it was envisioned that the recovery of Europe and Japan would benefit the American economy by increasing markets for American made goods.

In reality, the international economic system worked well as planned. Europe and Japan recovered and then prospered. The American economy expanded simply because of the dollar outflow, which resulted in the purchase of American goods and services. However, by 1960, the American managed international economic system was in shamble.

As we mentioned earlier that the world monetary and multilateral lending institutions that emerged during the postwar decade did so generally under the control of industrialized capitalist powers whose interests and objectives they served. The Third World countries on the periphery of the advanced capitalist states were not inside the privileged zone; however, the perpetuation of colonial economic ties into the period of political independence entangle the less developed countries in international capitalist economic system over which they had little or no control. Since the end of World War II, the less developed countries have implemented different strategies in an endeavor to alter their underdevelopment and dependence. In trade, investment, finance and commodities, they have sought greater benefits from the greater participation in the international economic system. For many years those strategies have alternated between seeking to transform the global system and seeking to accommodate to it.[9] In the early 1960s, the LDCs generally began to operate together to demand for changes in the international economic system. This section will review the present status of North-South cooperations. It will then address the major issues, concerns, and questions raise during the debate.

THE NEW INTERNATIONAL ECONOMIC ORDER: WHAT IS AT STAKE?

The debate concerning what the New International Economic Order is needed and desired creates a very wide range of economic issues. There is a need to consider what norms, rules, institutions or principles that should govern economic interaction between and among nation-states, as well as what should be the overall goals. For instances, should the new international economic order desire to: 1) make recent performance in market the main determinant of price, 2) assist the poorest of the poor within the less developed countries? 3) Narrow the economic gap between the rich and poor countries of the world? 4) Establish mutually beneficial regulations modifying the operations of the market structure and, at the same time provide assistance for those countries who could not compete effectively in the existing market? Among the issues addressed are:

Raw materials: should the price of copper, oil, bauxite and other raw materials be set by the consumers, by the producers, by market mechanism of demand and supply and/or by political authority?

Foreign Aid: should aid be viewed as a charitable behavior and hence closely managed and controlled by the donor, or a right of less developed countries and hence an automatic transfer payment? At what level should financial assistance be given?

Commodities: should commodities price be linked to the price of industrial manufactured goods, should commodities reserves be created to stabilize the fluctuation of prices within accepted standards?

International Trade: should trade among nations be free, restricted to protect infant industries and domestic businesses, or depended on particular negotiated agreements and compromise among nations?

Foreign investment: under what circumstances should the multinational corporations or nations invest in other nations? Who should control and regulate their operation, trade and taxation? Under what circumstances is nationalization of foreign businesses necessary? And who should determine the compensation?

Foreign debt: should the existing debts from the LDCs be forgiven, rescheduled or refinanced?

Exchange rate: should trade imbalances be paid by currencies valued at floating exchange rates, or at rates pegged to major currencies? Or should the former fixed exchange by gold standard re-established? Should the International Monetary Fund be a credit-establishing international organization and, if so, should the Third World nations receive credits from it according to financial need or as reward for past exploitation?

Transfer of technology: should patent restrictions be removed or modified, thereby making it simpler to transfer or copy new technological discoveries?   Should advanced capitalist states create research facilities in LDCs which are designed to the production of technological discoveries appropriate to the need of the host nation?

Decision: should decisions concern all such issues be carried out in forums, conferences, and organizations based on the sovereign equality of states, or should important discretion be allotted to those countries with the largest stakes in the decision?

These are the main issues of concern between and among nations particularly the African countries. However, general and specific answers to these questions, as well as others, have been agreed on by some 125 less developed countries. The answers to these questions are what is known as the proposed New International Economic Order.

THE HISTORICAL EVOLUTION OF THE NEW INTERNATIONAL ECONOMIC ORDER

In reality, the less developed countries see their origin of underdevelopment, poverty and dependence as the result of previous colonial exploitation and recent economic inequalities in international trade, pricing system, and exchange operations. For this reason, the South demands both expanded assistance from the North and a restructuring of the existing international economic system.

New International Economic Order's roots may be traced to the first United Nations Conference on Trade and Development (UNCTAD) held in Geneva in 1964. At the first UNCTAD, the less developed countries formed the group of 77 to articulate and unify their rejections to aid, trade, multinational operation, technological transfer, and development practices of the 1960s. Since 1970s, the Third world countries' proposals for international economic transformations first made known by UNCTAD emerged to compromise a chain of formal demand for a New International Economic Order. In 1974, the New International Economic Order has provided the agenda for North-South establishment in a wide variety of institutional arrangements.

In general, the NIEO comprises the aggregated demands for economic transformations of interest to the third World countries in the numerous issue concerns. These demands or proposals would assure increased resource transfers from North to South on improved terms and with little or no accountability on the part of Third World nations. Puchala summaries the less developed countries' proposals for international economic reforms as follows:

1. Implementation of UNCTAD's Integrated program for commodities along with the establishment of the common Fund as its centerpiece.

2. Liberalization and extension of the Generalized System of Preferences for less developed countries' exports of manufactured and semi manufactured goods to advanced industrial states.

3. An increase in the less developed countries' share of the world's industrial output to 25 percent by the year 2000. (In 1979 less developed countries accounted for only 9 percent).

4. Establishment of a link between the creation of new special drawing rights in the IMF and development assistance.

5. Increased stabilization of the value of international reserves and exchange rates by movement away from the dollar as the linchpin of the international monetary system.

6. Increased access to IMF and commercial loans with lower interest rates, longer repayment periods, and less conditionality.

7. A comprehensive international approach to the management of debt rescheduling or cancellation confronting less developed countries.

8. Conformity of all advanced industrial states with the target of 0.7 percent of GNP in official development assistance to less developed countries.

9. Development of an enhanced research and development capacity within less developed countries.

10. Enhancement of science and technology transfers more appropriate to the particular needs of less developed countries, at reduced cost.

11. International regulation of multinational firms to prevent their most pernicious impacts on the social, cultural, economic, and political development of poor states.[10]

As Table 13:1 indicates, among the industrialized capitalist western states, only France, Denmark, Netherlands, Norway, and

Sweden reached this target in 1988. The United Kingdom and above all, the United States refused to meet up this requirement. The Soviet Union and other Eastern European nations supported the New International Economic Order proposed by the South but refused not to contribute for it. This is because the Soviet Union and its Eastern European allies believed the problems that the LDCs face were products of past western colonialism and recent capitalist imperialism and neocolonialism.

Figure 13:1

Current Account Deficits of Non Oil Exporting LDCs, 1973-1985 ($Billion).

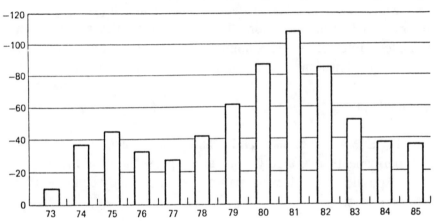

SOURCE: IMF, *Finance and Development*, 17, no.3 (September 1980), p.7: *IMF World Economic Outlook*, April 1985, p. 239.

The less developed countries of the group of 77 have further utilized their numerical advantage in the United Nations General Assembly to demand for a New International Economic Order. Algeria, as the spokesman for the nonaligned nations, led the call for what today became the Sixth Special Session of the United Nations General Assembly, held in 1974. Specific proposals that the group of 77 dominated General Assembly passed were the Charter of Economic Rights and Duties of States, The

Declaration of the Establishment of a New International Economic Order, and its Action Program.

It is important to note that Third World Countries make these and other demands with the believe that the existing liberal global economic system dominated by industrialized countries has caused inequality of income, wealth, power, and influence at the expense of developing countries. The transfer of resources proposed in the New International Economic Order would, in their opinion eradicate or at least minimize the global sources of their economic and political vulnerability.

Furthermore, New International Economic Order also aim at the need for general recognition of new principles and practices the Third World Nations would appreciate to see guiding international economic interaction. The principles advanced in the New International Economic Order include the rights the Third World nations claim for themselves and the duties they would place on advanced capitalist societies. As UN monthly chronicle put it:

1. "Every state has and shall freely exercise full permanent sovereignty, including possession, use and disposal,over its wealth, natural resources and economic activities."

2. "Each state has the right to nationalize, expropriate or transfer ownership of foreign property in which case appropriate compensation should be paid by the state adopting such measures taking into account its relevant laws and regulations and all circumstances the state considers pertinent. In any case where the question of compensation gives rise to controversy, it shall be settled under the domestic law of the nationalizing state and by its tribunals..."

3. "It is the duty of states to contribute to the development of international trade of goods particularly by means of arrangements and by the conclusion of long term multilateral commodity agreements, where appropriate, and taking into account the interests of producers and consumers."

4. "All states have the right to associate in organizations of primary commodity producers [such as OPEC] in order to develop their national economies to achieve stable financing for their development, and in pursuance of their aims assisting in the promotion of sustained growth of the world economy, in particular accelerating the development of developing countries. Correspondingly all states have the duty to respect the right by refraining from applying economic and political measures that would limit it."[11]

Figure 13:2

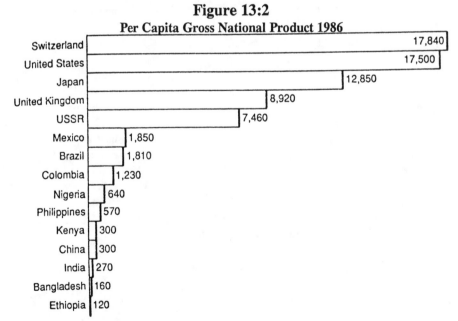

Per Capita Gross National Product 1986

Switzerland	17,840
United States	17,500
Japan	12,850
United Kingdom	8,920
USSR	7,460
Mexico	1,850
Brazil	1,810
Colombia	1,230
Nigeria	640
Philippines	570
Kenya	300
China	300
India	270
Bangladesh	160
Ethiopia	120

SOURCE: Population Referernce Bureau, 1988 World Population Data Sheet (Washington, D.C.: 1988)

TABLE 13:1
Official Development Assistance from
"Northwest States" (Organization for Economic Cooperation
and Development Members), 1988, and the Impact that NIEO
Proposals Would Have on Development Assistance

Country	Actual Development Assistance, 1988, in Billions of Dollars	Actual Development Assistance, 1988, as Percentage of GNP	Proposed Billions of Development Assistance, 1988, at NIEO .7 Percent GNP Level	Billions of Dollars Incr in 1988 Developme Assistance i .7 Percent Adopted
Australia	1.1	.46	1.7	.6
Austria	.3	.24	.9	.6
Belgium	.6	.39	1.1	.5
Canada	2.3	.50	3.2	.9
Denmark	.9	.89	now above .7	
Finland	.6	.59	.7	.1
France	7.0	.73	now above .7	
Ireland	.1	.20	.4	.3
Italy	2.7	.36	5.3	2.6
Japan	12.3	.36	23.9	10.6
Netherlands	2.2	.98	now above .7	
New Zealand	.1	.27	.3	.2
Norway	1.0	1.12	now above .7	
Sweden	1.5	.87	now above .7	
Switzerland	.6	.32	1.3	.7
United Kingdom	2.6	.32	5.7	3.1
United States	12.2	.25	34.2	22.0
West Germany	4.7	.39	8.4	3.7

SOURCE: World Bank data, obtained January 1990.

Other elements of the proposed New International Economic Order is tariff reduction and quota increases on all end products produced in the less developed countries. If this is granted, it will increase the demand for less developed countries' products, hence reducing unemployment in that area.

Another dimension of the Third World proposals for NIEO includes institutional changes that would improve their authority and power in global economic decision making. Majority of Less Developed Countries were under The European colonial rule at the time the major international economic organizations were created after World War II. For this reason, they were able to exercise little or no influence over the formulation of international law or the management of international economic institutions affecting most directly their conduct of global economic interaction.[12] To improve their voting power and position in multilateral economic decision making, Third World nations have pressed for the following:

(1) expanding the membership of existing organs of the U.N. family of institutions (such as tripling the size of the U.N. Economic and Social Council with increase less developed countries' participation), (2) bringing negotiations of economic importance from forums excluding less developed countries into institutions where they are represented (such as moving key deliberations on international monetary relations from the Organization for Economic Cooperation and Development to the International Monetary Fund's Group of Twenty), and (3) creating entirely new international economic institutions to champion particular less developed countries interests (such as UNCTAD, the United Nations Industrial Development Organization, (UNIDO), and the U.N. commission on Transnational Corporations). Overall, the developing states are trying to subordinate multilateral decision making on economic matters in the IMF, IBRD, GATT, and elsewhere to the authority and supervision of organs in the United Nations, where less developed countries enjoy an overwhelming voting majority. This was at the core of their dispute with the United States and other advanced industrial states in the North-South negotiations at Cancun, Mexico in 1981.[13]

Further issues of great concern were brought up at subsequent regular meetings and Special Session of the General Assembly and at the United Nations Conference on Trade and Development. Prominent among them were commodity price stabilization, debt relief for Third World Countries through debt cancellation or rescheduling, compensatory financing methods to stabilize export earnings and price indexation which would link the prices that the less developed countries receive for the commodities they export to the manufactured goods they import from the industrialized states.[14] Table 13:2 summarizes and illustrates the major issues, background and evolution of these demands and concerns in the six UNCTAD Conferences held during the past three decades as shown on the following pages.

As a result, the United Nations Conference on Trade and Development has undoubtedly become a spokesman for the less developed countries. It has become a central pivot on which the North-South competition, conflict, cooperation and/or compromise has been played. Moreover, the less developed countries have further pressed the issues indicated above in many recognized international bodies such as, the International Monetary Fund, the Conference on International Economic Cooperation, the World Bank, and the United Nation Conference on the law of the Sea.

Meanwhile, the advanced capitalist states did not agree willingly to the LDCs' demands. The North has seriously resisted those major concerns regarded as most expensive.

MAJOR CONCERNS OF THE NORTH-SOUTH CONFRONTATION

Major concerns may be derived from the persistent of present levels of unequal distribution of wealth between North and South. Before going further to explain these concerns, it is first important to indicate the fundamental fact that the gap between

TABLE 13:2

Stages of UNCTAD

UNCTAD I, Geneva 1946

The creation of a forum to attract attention to issues supporting the developing countries, not covered by existing institutions.

The formalization of the Group of 77 and beginning of discussion on a few issues such as terms of trade, resource gap, and Generalized System of Preferences (GSP).

UNCTAD II, New Delhi 1968

Between 1964 and 1968 the UNCTAD secretariat focused more seriously but still sporadically on GSP, the needs of developing countries for assistance, terms of trade, technology transfer, and selected development policies.

The conference led the OECD to initiate work on a scheme of preferences.

Dr. Raul Prebisch retired in 1969 as the Secretary-General of the UNCTAD.

UNCTAD III, Santiago 1972

Unlike the Geneva and New Delhi meetings, where these issues were considered separately, UNCTAD III saw discussion on interrelationships between trade, money, finance, and development at a technical level.

Initiation of an effort by Mr. Robert McNamara, President of the World Bank, to mobilize global support for the poor, suggesting ways to integrate the bottom 40 percent of the population in the development process.

TABLE 13:2 CONTINUED
UNCTAD IV, Nairobi 1976

Stocktaking of progress in various forums (CIEC, GATT) on decisions taken at the Sixth and Seventh Special Sessions of the UN General Assembly in 1974 and 1975, respectively, particularly in the light of the oil price increase, monetary instability, recession, inflation, increased balance of payments gap of the non-oil developing countries, decline in commodity prices, and the uncertainty that the minimum development needs in many developing countries would be met.

Main emphasis on commodities (Integrated Programma for commodities - Common Fund) and to a lesser degree on external debt.

Resolution on a Common fund symbolized G-77 unity.

UNCTAD V, Manila 1979

Emphasis on trade and financial flows aspects of the relationships between developed and developing countries.

Emphasis on growing in interdependence between different parts of the world economy.

Efforts to bearing socialist countries into the dialogue on economic issues. Emphasis on trade liberalization and concern about expanding protectionism.

UNCTAD VI, Belgrade 1983

Movement by G-77 toward immediate issues relating to the global economy and Third World development and away from demands for structural reform.

Emphasis on a common analysis of the world economic situation and an agreed strategy for economic recovery and development.

Continued concern for the issue of trade protectionism.

Recognition of the important role of the World Bank and International Monetary Fund as multilateral development institutions.

SOURCE: Charles W. Kegley and Eugene R. Wittkopf, World Politics: Trend and
          Transformation (New York: St. Martin's Press, 1985), pp. 211-212.

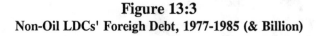

Figure 13:3
Non-Oil LDCs' Foreigh Debt, 1977-1985 (& Billion)

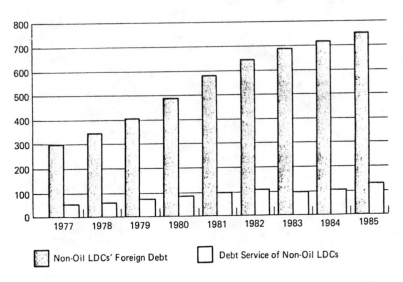

Non-Oil LDCs' Foreign Debt   Debt Service of Non-Oil LDCs

SOURCES: IMF Survey, January 7, 1985, p. 3; *IMF World Economic Outlook,* 1985, p. 265.

the rich countries of the North and the poor countries of the South is, in most instances expanding dramatically. Table 12:3 indicates those nations that have experienced economic growth rates greater than industrialized capitalist countries of the Northern between 1965 and 1987. However, the list of countries in Table 12:3 are the only less developed countries of the South that are narrowing the gap. Strictly speaking, even for most of these countries, no opportunity exists to eradicate the widening gap during the next century. Hence, the North-South gap will seriously continue, and in most instances expand, at least if present measures and recent rates of growth persist.

Also, the continued growth expansion of the rich and poor nations-gap may be generally explained in another dimension. For instances, in 1850, the ratio between developing countries' incomes and those of the rest of global societies was 2:1. By 1950, the ratio was 10:1, and by 1960, it was approximately

Hunger is a problem throughout much of the Third World. It is one measure of the huge disparity in wealth between the South and the North. (UN Photo/John Issac.)

15:1. However, the projection for the year 2000 reach as much as 30:1.[15]

Furthermore, the quality of life, it may be argued, is not necessarily reflective of either per capita income or income ratio between two countries. This observation is a legitimate one in nations where the population has had its fundamental needs for food, shelter, water, clothing, and health care met and where possibilities exist for efficient education and employment opportunity. In majority of the LDCs, however, those fundamental needs are not there for the entire population. As a matter of fact, in many LDCs per capita income and comparative ratios present an overly realistic picture of actual condition.[16] What concerns, then, exist because of real and growing differences in the distribution of wealth between North and South? One major concern is that North and South may find themselves further more deeply entwined in the rhetoric of conflict and enmity.

INSERT TABLE 13:3
Third World States Whose Economic Growth Rates Exceed that of the Combined Western Industrialized OECD States

Country	GNP per Capita 1987, in Dollars	Average Annual Growth Rate 1965-1987	Number of Years until Gap Close if 1965-1987 Growth Rates Continues
OECD Countries	14,670	2.3	
China	290	5.2	over 100
Pakistan	350	2.5	over 100
Lesotho	370	4.7	over 100
Sri Lanka	400	3.0	over 100
Indonesia	450	4.5	over 100
Egypt	680	3.5	over 100
Thailand	850	3.9	over 100
Congo	870	4.2	over 100
Cameroon	970	3.8	over 100
Paraguay	990	3.4	over 100
Ecuador	1,040	3.2	over 100
Botswana	1,050	8.9	43
Tunisia	1,120	3.6	over 100
Turkey	1,210	2.6	over 100
Colombia	1,240	2.7	over 100
Mauritus	1,490	3.2	over 100
Syria	1,640	3.3	over 100
Malaysia	1,810	4.1	over 100
Mexico	1,830	2.5	over 100
Brazil	2,020	4.1	over 100
Panama	2,240	2.4	over 100
Algeria	2,680	3.2	over 100
South Korea	2,690	6.4	36
Oman	5,810	8.0	18
Saudi Arabia	6,200	4.0	65
Singapore	7,940	7.2	14

SOURCE: World Bank, World Development Report, 1989; pp. 164-165.

Apart from its poverty, dependence, and underdevelopment, the less developed countries are without power. Majority of the resources that the advanced industrialized societies need are available mainly in the LDCs. Understanding this, the less developed countries of the South could turn to a policy of resources deprivation and price increases in natural resources and primary goods. As Daniel Papp indicates:

> So far only the OPEC states have employed this strategy successfully, but their impact on the industrialized world has been immense. Although other raw material cartels would not have the same advantages that OPEC enjoyed during the 1970s, a policy of cartelization could appear a useful strategy to Third World governments. Obviously, the virtual collapse of OPEC that occurred in 1986, bringing with it sizable reductions in oil prices, pointed out that cartelization is not a guaranteed answer to the Third World's problems. Nevertheless, even with the difficulties inherent in cartelization, it could prove attractive.[17]

AFRICA AND THE NORTH-SOUTH CONFLICT

The Organization of Petroleum Exporting Country's relative success in drastically increasing the price of oil in 1973-1974 enabled the less developed countries to raise North-South economic problems to the top of the global agenda. According to Naomi Chazan and Robert Mortimer, although the group of 77 had been in existence since the creation of United Nations Conference on Trade and Development (UNCTAD) in 1964, it had previously been unable to force advance capitalist societies to give major consideration to the demands for international reform. As Chazan and Mortimer put it:

> New concerns in industrialized countries regarding the future security of supply of raw materials changed this situation-at least temporarily. With the proclamation of the Charter of Economic Rights and Duties of States, and the Declaration on the Establishment of New International Economic Order in the mid-

1970s, African governments believed that their joint action with other developing countries in the United Nations had established the basis for a radical restructuring of their external economic relations.[18]

However, according to Chazan and Mortimer, African Countries acting individually have little or no power in the overall global economic relations. For example, Nigeria which is the largest African economy accounts for less than one percent of the world's exports-imports-a lower volume than of Hong Kong or such small developed capitalist countries as Switzerland and Netherlands. The trade of the next largest black African economy, Cote d' Ivoire, is only one tenth that of Nigeria. African countries, individually do not have a dominant position as producers of any primary commodity. for example, Nigeria accounts for only two percent of the global's total oil production, Zaire and Zambia for roughly six percent each of the global's copper output, Guinea for 15 percent of international bauxite production. A similar circumstance prevails in the production of agricultural products. The largest single country market share is Cote d" Ivoire's 22 percent of total global cocoa production. However, it is the case that African societies' shares of international trade in primary products are higher, these shares are not enough to enable them to unilaterally exercise power over global market transactions.

Given their economic and political weakness, a viable strategy or policy for African governments to adopt is to act in group with other Third World countries. African leaders and policy makers have perceived joint action in such forums as the United Nations as the best avenues through which they may compensate for the structure inequalities that characterize their external economic interactions. These mechanisms provide opportunity to attempt to change the rules of the game, which African leaders believe as having been against their interests.[19] Also, the success of OPEC in 1973-1974 was seen as a model that might be emulated by entities of other commodity producing nations. Algeria being one of most active advocates of joint action, hosted the first major conference of the group of 77 in 1967, during which the less developed countries established a common ground for the 1968 Session of the UNCTAD. A year after, Algeria initiated the process and/or method that led to adoption of the New International Economic Order. Consequently, from the perspective of African leaders, policy makers, and experts, none of these strategies have brought positive results.

After sometimes, it became very obvious that OPEC's relative success would not be replicated by other commodity producing nations. For one thing, oil has a number of peculiar attributes that explain the capability of OPEC to accomplish short-run relative success. These attributes include: the importance of oil in the economies of advanced industrial societies; the predominance of a relatively small number of Third World nations as its major exporters, including some whose income was so high that they could afford to limit production in order to force prices up; the high costs of providing alternative sources of supply; and the absence in the short-run of already available close substitutes. However, these features were completely absent for majority of the products of most interest to Africa. For example, copper can be substituted for by other metals, specifically aluminum, or replaced by synthetics, such as fiberoptics, or can be recycled from scrape materials.

Furthermore, some industrialized capitalist economies, particularly Canada and Australia, that refused to be members of the less developed countries-dominated commodity cartels and/or unions are among the leading exporters. Hence, the demand for the majority of Africa's agricultural exports is price inelastic in response to price changes. This is purely true because substitutes are generally available for most commodities and it is very cheap to generate alternative sources of supply. In addition, proposals to stabilize and raise commodity prices through the creation of international commodity agreements financed by common fund would have been of major benefits to nations that exported a variety of products amenable to being stockpiled. Again, this is rarely the case for African states. Apart from relative gains that would have been made from a stabilization of their export prices, majority of African States depend largely on one or two exports. These nations would therefore have to pay more for their imports of other products as well as for their imports of goods manufactured from these products. Majority of African agricultural exports, such as banana and cocoa, are almost impossible to be stored for a long period of time and are, thus, not amenable to buffer-stocking arrangements proposed within the framework of North-South relations.

NORTH-SOUTH RELATIONS: RHETORIC OR REALITY

What do the Less Developed Countries desire? More capital and wealth for development. How can the LDCs achieve it? By implementing more economically national strategies consistent with their need. What should the industrialized states do? To accelerate these strategies. How should the industrialized states approach international negotiations? With serious optimism. what should be the outcome of North-South dialogue under normal situation? More equitable distribution of wealth and resources between the rich nations of the industrialized world and the poor nations of underdeveloped world. Have these being able to occur? Not as of this writing. What prevents this from happening? We believe unequal relations between and among actors within the international economic system.

At this point, also, we will set forth an alternative perspective. We believe that less developed countries, like all nations in the global economic system, are concerned about vulnerability and threat. Also, we realize that national political administrations in almost all less developed countries are generally weak both nationally and internationally. This prescribes a very different

Figure 13:4
Population increase in numbers by decades

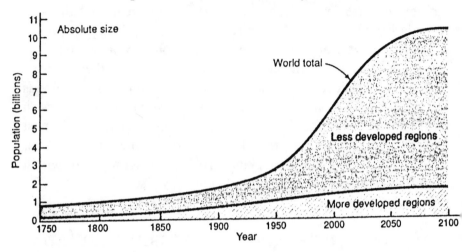

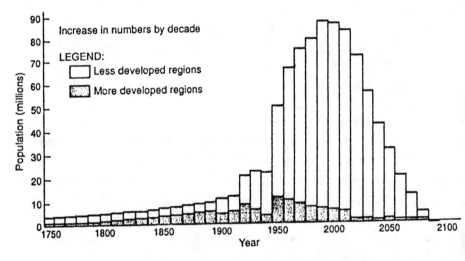

Population Growth, 1750-2100: World, Less Developed Regions, and More Developed Regions. **SOURCE:** Thomas W. Meirick with PRB staff, "World population in transition," *Population Bulletin* 41, no. 2 (April 1986), P. 4. NOTE: Three less developed regions = Africa, Asia (minus Japan), and Latin America. Two more developed regions = Europe, U.S.S.R., Japan, and Oceania (Including Australia and New Zealand) combined and North America (Canada and the U.S.).

answer to the questions raised above. Note, therefore, that LDCs want power and control as much as wealth. One way for realizing this objective is to reform the rules and regulations of the game in many global issue areas. Infact, these endeavors will be incompatible with long-run capitalist interests. Therefore, relations between and among capitalist states and LDCs are bound to be conflictual since most less developed countries cannot agree to cope with their global vulnerability except by opposing principles, norms, regulations, institutions and rules preferred by Northern countries.

The less developed countries consists of about four fifths of the global's population. But, it accounts for only one fifth of the world's total gross national product. Also, the inequities between the rich nations of the industrialized world and the poor nations of underdeveloped world have grown faster than expected, and the gulf is projected to increase further in the future. The present inequalities between the North and South is more likely to continue. Meanwhile, the leaders of LDCs perceive these unequal relations as the result of a system structured so as to ensure their perpetuation within the existing international capitalist framework. For this reason, Arthur Lewis explains the relationship as follows:

> first, the division of the world into exporters of primary products and importers of manufactures. Second, the adverse factorial terms of trade for the products of the developing countries. Third, the dependence of the developing countries on the developed for finance. Fourth, the dependence of the developing countries on the developed for their engine of growth.[20]

In support of this view, Roger D. Hansen, a specialist of the political-economy of North-South cooperations further argues that: endeavors at global trade liberalization through the mechanism of the General Agreement on Tariffs and Trade (GATT) had been specifically biased in favor of products of interest to developed country exporters. The amount and value of foreign assistance flowing from North to South have been unjustifiably low whether measured by "absorptive capacity" of funds in Southern development projects or by proclaimed Northern commitments to assist Southern development attempts. The North had systematically rejected-or stalled for lengthy periods of time before accepting in altered form a wide variety of Southern proposals to increase the availability to the South of scarce foreign exchange needed in the development process.[21]

Northern multinational corporations have in general restricted their potential contribution to the Southern development strategy in countless instances. Among the most evidence and widespread have been (a) the limitation on tax liabilities through certain patterns of transfer pricing, (b) the limitations on job creation through the use of capital-intensive production techniques and artificial limitations on exports, (c) the exaction of monopoly rents on the corporations' technology, and other, less generalized, form of corporate behavior. In addition, these multinational corporations have on occasions interfered in internal politics of host countries, with or without the support of their home governments. Finally, they and their home governments have been able to limit international capital flows to host governments in situations involving serious corporation-host government conflict. The terms of trade have moved consistently against the typical developing-country export basket, and they have done so for reasons that are related structurally to the operations of the Bretton Woods arrangement.[22]

However, political weakness and vulnerability are basic sources of less developed countries behavior. The fundamental weakness is as a result of internal and external variables. Externally, the national power abilities of most LDCs are generally limited. The national military and economic resources at the control of their governments are unlikely to change the behavior of industrialized states or the nature of international relations. The less developed countries are extremely subject to external pressures that they cannot alter through unilateral confrontation.

Internally, the global weakness of almost all Third World

countries is exacerbated by the internal structural arrangement of underdevelopment of their political and social systems. In most LDCs, the social structures are rigid, and their central political institutions lack the power to make national adjustments that could prevent external shocks. The gap between the industrialized states and the less developed countries is already so large that even if the nations of the South grew very rapidly and those of the advanced capitalist states remained unchange (an unlikely set of assumptions in any event), only a few countries of the South would significantly narrow the power and wealth gap within the next century.

Figure 13:5
South-South Trade as % of Developing Country Export

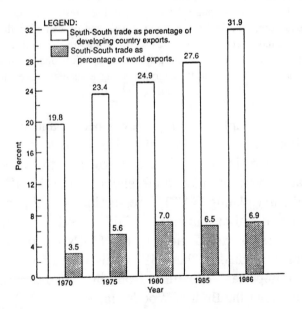

The Expansion in South-South Trade, 1970-1986 (Percentages). **SOURCE:** J.W. Sewell and S. K. Tucker et al. (eds.), *Growth, Exports and Jobs in a Changing World Economy: Agenda 1988* (New Brunswick, N.J.: Transaction Books, 1988), Table A-7.

As we mentioned earlier, a new International Economic Order along the lines proposed by the Third World would constitute a total redistribution of wealth and political economic power in the global economic relations from capitalist societies of the North to the less developed countries of the South. As a result of this, one cannot expect Northern countries to move seriously and voluntarily toward a massive implementation of the new International Economic Order demands. To quote Blake and Walter:

> In addition to considerations of wealth and power losses, however, the leading Western states profoundly disagree with the basic premises of the NIEO demands. As opposed to the NIEO assumption that underdevelopment is primarily a result of past and present inequities in the international economic system, the United States and others are inclined to view domestic policies of less developed countries as the greatest obstacle to their development. Western states are opposed to a massive restructuring of international economic institutions and the norms of behavior that, in their view, have served most states well. They are very reluctant to replace market mechanisms, despite their imperfections, with an elaborate array of formally negotiated agreements governing resource flows as called for in the NIEO.[23]

However, in principle, the less developed countries won a significant concession at Geneva, particularly, extension of the principle of nonreciprocity, hence allowing the advanced industrial states to grant trade preferences to the Third World countries without violating GATT'S regulations pertaining most-favored nations nondiscrimination. This helped the advanced industrial societies to extend more to the LDCs the preferential trade practices embodied in the GSP. This type of preferential practice is an important departure from the nondiscrimination dominant throughout the Bretton Woods era.

In reality, the generalized system of preferences' practical implications on the major issues of LDCs were hence forth insignificant. In fact the Third World countries wanted the GSP extended beyond what the North was willing and able to give. As Charles Kegley Comments in his writing that:

> The latter, led by the United States, adopted a "graduation clause" that brought pressure on the Newly Industrialized Countries to remove themselves from the provisions of the generalized system of preferences. The principle set forth was that "as Southern countries reach higher levels of development, or "graduate," they should be given less special treatment and should trade on a more equal footing with the industrialized nations." The developing countries objected strongly to the graduation principle, seeing it "as a clever device which the North can use to withdraw preferential treatment whenever developing countries begin to threaten Northern economies.[24]

As the total demands of Third World countries for change of the global economic relations are unlikely to be achieved in any comprehensive manner, the continued emphases in the NIEO have achieved a significant agenda-establishment function for the South as a whole. It has given the avenues through which the less developed countries have established their economic-political preferences along side East-West issues and intra Northern economic priorities in contemporary international political economy. This is a serious and comprehensive achievement for a group of countries that for many years were objects of international politics rather than a part of it. At this point, however, it is important to note that the North-South dialogue has been a continuing characteristic of post-World War II international relations. The New International Economic Order may come to be perceived as little more than the rhetoric of debate in our time. It is not until the problems of the poor and related perceptions are solved, the less developed countries will be expected to continue to fight for the overall change of the international economic system they had little or no control in influencing.

NOTES

1. Joan E. Spero, *The Politics of International Economic Relations*, Fourth Edition, (New York: St. Martin's Press, 1990), p. 21.

2. Ibid.

3. Richard N. Garden, *Sterling Dollar Diplomacy in Current Perspective: The origins and Prospects of our International Economic Order*, Expanded ed. (New York: Columbia University Press, 1980), p. 8.

4. Spero, *Politics of International Economic Relations*, p. 23.

5. Ibid. See also the work by M. H. Bouchet, *The Political Economy of International Debt: What, Who, How much and Why?* (Westport, Conn: Greenwood Press, 1987). E. L. Bacha and R. E. Feinberg, "The World Bank and Structural Adjustment in Latin America"' *World Development,* 14 March 1986). W. L. *Austerity Policies in Latin America* (Boulder: Colo: Westview Press, 1988). Anne O. Kreuger, "Orgin of the Developing Countries' Debt Crisis: 1970-1982" *Journal of Development Economics* 27 (October 1988) Manuel Pastor, *The International Monetary Fund and Latin America: Economic Stabilization and Case Conflict* (Boulder, Colo: Westview Press, 1987). Charles W. Kegley and Eugene R. Wittkopf, *World Politics: Trend and Transformation* (New York: St. Martin's Press, 1985). Author W. Lewis, *The Evolution of the International Economic Order* (Princeton, N. J.: Princeton University Press, 1978).

6. Charles W. Kegley and Eugene R. Wittkopf, *World Politics: Trend and Transformation* (New York: St. Martin's Press, 1985), p. 175.

7. Spero, *The Politics of International Economic Relations*, p. 24.

8. Kegley, *World Politics: Trend and Transformation*, p. 176.

9. Spero, p. 154. For further analysis, See Bahram Nowzod, *The IMF and its Critics* (Princeton, N. J.: Princeton University Press, 1981). John Williamson, *IMF Conditionality* (Washington, D.C.: Institute For International Economics, 1983) and his work on The Lending Policies of the International Monetary Fund was held Classical on this endeavor. See also the work by Jagdish N. Bhagwatti, *The New International Economic Order: The North-South Debate* (Cambridge, Mass.: MIT Press, 1977). Ferdinand Van Dan, "North-South Negotiations" *Development and Change* Vol. 12, (1981).

10. For an indepth study and summary of Third World countries demands for a new International Economic Order, see Donald Puchala, ed. *Issues Before the 35th General Assembly of the United Nations 1980-1981* (New York: United Nations Association of the United States, 1980), pp. 73-104.

11. For an indepth study of Economic Rights and Duties of States, see "The Charter of Economic Rights and Duties of states" *United Nations Monthly Chronicle* Vol. 12, No.1, (January 1975), pp. 108-119; Program of Action on

the Establishment of a new International Economic Order *UN Monthly Chronicle* vol. 12, No 5, (May 1974), pp. 69-85; and "The Declaration on Establishment of A new International Economic Order, Ibid., pp. 65-70. For a comprehensive study of the New International Economic Order as an endeavor to replace operations with authoritative form of resource allocation, see Stephens Krasher, *Structural Conflict* (Berkeley: University of California Press, 1985).

12. Blake and Walters, *The Politics of Global Economic Relations*, p. 156.

13. Ibid.

14. Charles Kegley, *World Politics: Trend and Transformation*, p. 210.

15. Lester R. Brown, *World Without Borders* (New York: Vintage Books, 1972), p. 42.

16. Daniel S. Pappa, *Contemporary International Relations: A Framework for Understanding* (New York: MacMillan Publishing Company, 1991). Glenn P. Hastedt and Kay M. Knickrehm, *Dimensions of World Politics* (New York: Harper Collins Publishers, 1991). Michael Tatu, quoted in Spanier, Games National Plan, p. 150. See also Michael Todaro, *Economic Development in The Third World*. David Blake and Robert Walters. *The Politics of Global Economic Relations* (Englewood Cliff, N. J.: Prentice Hall, 1987). Caroline Thomas, In Search of Security: *The Third World in International Relations* (Boulder, Colo.: Lynne R. Publishers, 1987). J. E. Spero, *The Politics of International Economic Relations* (New York: St Martin's Press, 1985). Dennis Pirages, *The New Context for International Relations* (North Scituate, Mass.: Dusbury 1982).

17. Ibid., p. 170.

18. Naomi chazan, Robert Mortimer, John Ravenhill, and Donald Rothchild, *Politics and Society in Contemporary Africa* (Boulder, Colorado: Lynne Rienner, Publishers, 1988), p. 288.

19. Stephen D. Krasner, *Structural Conflict* (Berkeley: University of California Press, 1985).

20. Lewis W. Arthur, *The Evolution of the International Economic Order* (New Jersey: Princeton University Press, 1978), p. 3.

21. Roger D. Hansen, *The North-South Stalemate* (New York McGrawHill, 1979), pp. 48-50.

22. Roger D. Hansen, The North-South Stalemate (New York: McGraw-Hill, 1979), pp. 48-50.

23. Blake and Walters, p. 197.

24. Kegley, World Politics: *Trend and Transformation,* p. 213.

European Colonialization in Africa, 1884

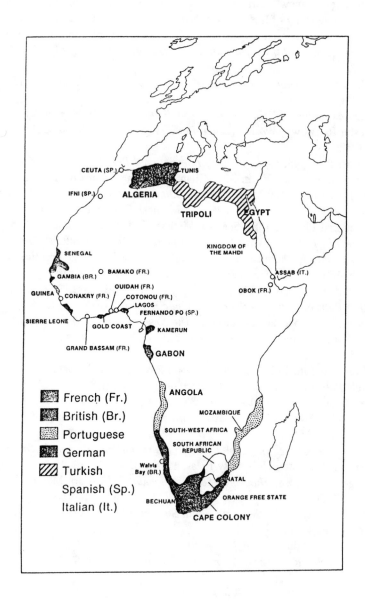

CHAPTER 14

Africa and the International Monetary Relations

GLOBAL MONETARY ARRANGEMENT

The global economic relations include the buying and selling of goods and services, valued in different currency exchange rates. Consequently, some methods have to be created for converting one nation's currency into another. The format that is used is known as the international exchange rate. The exchange rate can be established by global arrangement or by the market forces of demand and supply. For each nation, it comprises the rate at which the nation's central bank will exchange local currency for international currency. However, when currency is determined by market forces of demand and supply, it is said to float. Market forces affect the exchange rate generally through trade transactions. When a nation overtime imports more from a given nation than it exports to that nation, then a trade deficit occurs. For example, if Nigeria is buying more British goods and Britain is buying less of Nigerian goods, then more naira must be exchanged for pound than vice versa. Because there is a greater demand for pound, its value goes up in relation to that of naira.

Also, the exchange rate can further be influenced by speculation. That is, investors purchase currencies when they are relatively cheap and sell them when their values go up. This type of trade interaction affects the market for the currency.

Certainly, debate has been persistent over the question of fixed versus floating exchange rate in international monetary arrangement and trade relations. In a fixed exchange rates system, each nation's currency is valued against particular standard. Exchange rates may be generally fixed and/or periodically adjusted. Fixed exchange rates require a global arrangement and apply only to those nations that join in the agreement. While floating may float freely with or without intervention in the international market system.

For obvious reasons, the prices of goods and services moving across domestic boundaries are influenced by the current exchange rate. When a particular nation's currency is valued highly vis-a-vis another nation's currency, that nation's purchasing power increases. Imports increase, but because that nation's own goods are more expensive to buyers in the other nation, exports fall short.

In theory, when exchange rates are allowed to fluctuate freely, a self correcting method is built into the system. As the value of a nation's currency goes down in relation to its trading partner, its goods become cheaper and exports expand hence, restoring a balance to trade. A nation's balance of payments includes all currency exchanged with other nations, including trade, and other areas such as tourism and foreign assistance. Nations also attempt to build up foreign reserves of generally exchanged currencies, such as the dollars, the pound, the yen, and the mark, in order to meet balance of payments deficits at periods when the balance of trade is not bringing in a surplus of these "hard currencies". Also, countries can draw on reserves established by the IMF (as will be discussed later).

GLOBAL TRADE ARRANGEMENT

Global trade is originated in the unequal distribution of natural resources, capital, technology, and people between and among nation-states. If a commodity or a resource is needed and cannot be produced in a large quantity within a given nation, the nation will either go without it, discover a domestic alternative or trade for it. Going without the needed product or resource may entail that some political or economic objectives must be gone at the detriment of the nation. Close substitutes are sometimes not always available, and even if they are available, the cost to obtain them may be very high. At this point, however, international trade becomes the best alternative arrangement among the three options. The question then becomes what to trade on? And the answer is provided by the Law of Absolute Advantage, which states that a nation should only export products and resources that it produces at least cost per unit factors of production and should only import products and resources that it lacks completely or cannot produce more effectively with combined resources than others.

Furthermore, economic theory believes that a country should specifically follow the principle of comparative advantage in deciding what to trade on. This principle or law holds that, in making trade decisions, the key point of analysis is not the efficiency or effectiveness of the same industry in other countries (the oil industry in Nigeria versus the oil industry in Iraq), but the relative efficiencies of one's own industries(the Nigeria oil industry versus Nigeria shoe industry). Even though a nation can produce everything more efficiently than other nations, trade can still make sense if that country concentrates its resources on producing those products or resources that it does best. A nation enjoys a comparative advantage over another nation if and only if, in producing a particular commodity, it can do so at a relatively lower opportunity cost in terms of the alternative commodities that it must forgo.

However, proponents of comparative advantage argue that where free trade excels, that is, where there are no barriers to the free mobility of goods, labor, services, technology and capital across domestic borders, every nation benefits from global trade. Trade between countries does more than serve as a method for optimizing the use of international resources and producing wealth. Trade further provides policy makers according to Glenn Hastedt with an array of tools that can be utilized to further domestic and foreign policy. For example, from 1944 to 1962, the United States had sought free trade in the guise of access to United States markets as the principal inducement to get other nations to adopt policies it favored, such as promoting the economic recovery of Europe and Japan, strengthening military alliances and establishing markets for American exports.

GLOBAL MONETARY RELATIONS

The Bretton Woods Conference was clearly a British-American strategy in which the interest of the other industrialized states were barely considered. Majority of African states had not yet achieved political independence, and some that were generally independent were in reality, dominated by the major industrial power. As a result, The Bretton Woods Conference at New Hampshire, paid little or no attention to the specific needs of the Third World nations including Africa states. Therefore, African states have come to perceive themselves as being clearly discriminated against by the powerful nations of the North and by the Organizations that these power nations created to manage the post World War II global economic relations in such areas of trade, aid, finance, and debt. To overcome this problem, African states have proposed the formation and establishment of the New

International Economic Order. African States have further sought to acquire more political autonomy in global economic decision making through the formulation of Lagos Plan of Action, through the establishment of common markets and through the implementation of aggressive economic development strategies. This chapter will exclusively examine the reasons why African states are dissatisfied with the global economic arrangement created by the industrialized capitalist states. We will then examine, assess and evaluate some of the efforts by African states to improve their individuals and collective position in the global economic system in the chapters ahead.

THE POLITICAL ECONOMY OF THE INTERNATIONAL MONETARY FUND AND AFRICA FINANCE

Originally, the International Monetary Fund was created to provide short term loans to countries that had balance of payments disequilibrium. Member nations could draw from the IMF while taking economic and policy measures to correct balance of payments disequilibrium. Each nation was allocated a quota, which was divided into trenches.[1] Each nation could draw from the second tranche with the arrangement and/or agreement of the IMF's authorities. After this level, a member state had to enter into agreement with the Fund and agree to adopt those macroeconomic stabilization measures that the Fund considered appropriate to solve the problems that led to the economic imbalance. Provisions were not made for the long-run problems associated with economic development. At the Bretton Woods Conference, India proposed amendments that would have called upon the Fund to help in development with particular attention to the needs and problems of the Third World nations. Meanwhile, the Article of Agreement did not differentiate between developed and less developed countries. At this point, however, we argue that equal treatment of unequal partners is bound to produce unequal results.

Also, majority of African countries have suffered chronic balance-of-payments disequilibrium, and few choose to avoid membership in the Fund. The amount borrowed directly from the IMF is less than the amount from private sources. However, commercial lenders more often than not use the Fund guidelines to determine and decide whether a nation will be given loan. Countries that cannot receive the Fund approval often find their credit opportunities severely restricted; hence, the Fund measures have a severe implications on African economies. For instance, Julius Nyerere of Tanzamia at one point in history broke off negotiations with the Fund, arguing that Tanzamia would not have its economic policy dictated by the International Monetary Fund, he eventually returned to the International Monetary Fund and admitted to it requirements.

The International Monetary Fund is an international institution charged with managing international monetary problems. It functions on the belief that the growth of global trade benefits all member states of the system, and, therefore, its measures are geared at preserving that system. Measures reflect the assumption that a restrictive monetary policy and adherence to financial orthodoxy and the free market mechanism for controlling prices will function toward reestablishing equilibrium condition. The balance of payments deficit according to liberal economic theory, is thought to be caused by excessive demand. Therefore, reductions in government spending, restrictions on credit and lower wages influence aggregate demand by reducing it. Furthermore, removing food subsidies reduces the real income of the citizens. Because larger proportion of income is invested on food, less is available for imports. Devaluation of the national currency further helps by increasing the price of imports and making exports inexpensive for other currencies. Thus, the Fund lending macro-economic policies have come under serious attack from African leaders. Specifically, Fund-imposed cuts on government spending regarding food subsidies, place considerable burdens on an already poor citizens. Reductions of government spending, combined with regulations on wages, are politically sensitive, and there have been many instances of riots and political instability following the application of the IMF macroeconomic stabilization program not only in Africa but other less developed countries. For example, the Venezuelan riots during the Spring of 1989, in which 300 peoples were killed and 1,500 were wounded; the Nigerian riots in 1987 and again in 1989; the Zambian riots in 1986 to mention but a few were classic consequences of the IMF austerity measures imposed after each one of the governments had reached an agreement.

Furthermore, the International Monetary Fund macroeconomic policies are criticized for their failure to address underlying structural realities of African problems. Many scholars have argued that, even if the Fund policy measures restore equilibrium in the short-run, problems will recur without structural transformations, such as the expansion of the industrial base, land reform, and more equitable income distribution. Many African and other Third World Leaders believe that the International Monetary Fund was created to protect the international economic order as it is and that this perpetuation of the status quo is not in their interest at all. In support of this argument, Glenn Hastedt and Kay Knickrehm have this to say:

> Voting in the IMF is based on a system of quotas, which determines not only how much money a state must pay into the Fund but also how many votes it receives. As we noted earlier, five industrialized countries hold 40.9 percent of the votes. Third World states argue that their interests cannot be adequately represented under this arrangement. In an April 1989 statement calling for a comprehensive debt-reduction plan, the Group of 24 (an organization made up of the poorer members of the IMF), asked for an adjustment in the allocation of votes that would allow them more voting power than that to which their quotas entitled them.[2]

As a result, the Fund has responded to some requests for change. Until 1972, the Fund was dominated by the group of ten, all of whom represented industrialized capitalist nations. This was increased to group of twenty-four, including some Third World countries that met the IMF requirements. The compensatory Finance facility (CFF) provides funds to meet balance of payments problems that result from factors beyond the control of the borrowers, and the oil facility of 1974 gives loans to members to assist them with increasing energy costs. However, these loans are subject to high conditionalities. Also, the IMF has extended the grace period within which member nations must show stabilization and has coordinated activities with the World Bank to link macroeconomic stabilization with structural adjustment programs. Meanwhile, many changes have been rejected, specifically those reforms that would basically alter the balance of power in the Fund. As Hastedt and Knickrehm indicate in their book *Dimensions of World Politics*:

> When SDRs were created in 1967, the Third World responded with interest and attempted to use this device to redistribute income. They proposed that, whenever SDRs were issued, more should be given to poorer states and less to wealthy states. This idea was rejected by the developed market economies. The distribution of SDRs heavily favors the wealthier states - 75 percent is distributed to the 25 wealthiest states. However, even without redistribution, SDRs could be of value to the less developed states. They could provide a base in which the exchange rates of Third World currencies with all Western currencies could be established and the value of their reserves could be stabilized. Second, the allocation of SDRs made on a system of quotas could provide a more rational distribution of reserves than would be provided by the distribution of gold that now exists for historic reasons. By 1980, the total value of allocated SDRs was in excess of $18 billion. To this amount, $3.6 billion was reserved for the non-oil-exporting less developed states.[3]

The relations between the International Monetary Fund and Africa is uncertain, but most intellectuals and analysts expect some degree of reform in the system. Some have observed that the Fund may be forced by the debt crisis (as discussed early in the previous chapter) to pay serious attention to Africa's needs.

TRADE: A STRATEGY FOR DEVELOPMENT OR DEPENDENCY

Before and after World War II, African and other less developed countries were encouraged by conventional theory to specialize in the production of primary goods, which were exported in exchange for manufactured goods from the industrialized capitalist nations. Classical economic theory encouraged these countries to engage on those exports that were primarily labor intensive. It was argued that, under a system of free trade, every country is better off concentrating on whatever it can produce most effectively (the Law of Comparative Advantage). Under this condition, it was argued that gradually wages would increase and the price of capital would decrease in these nations, and economic growth, industrialization and development would result. Orthodox economic theory further continued to believe that both developed and less developed countries need to support an open trade policy. Also, the third World nations including Africa should permit competition from abroad for their own industries, bearing in mind that competition results in improved economic efficiency. However, free trade may, in reality, produce the advantages ascribed to it in theory, in practice, this system has not really existed, and inequality among nations has increased.

Moreover, majority of African countries have become poorer in reality during the last few decades (see the chapter on the Economic Crisis in Africa). The African states have come to perceive themselves as disadvantaged by the global economic system, specifically in the area of trade. A serious concern of these countries has to do with the production for export of primary goods, such as raw materials, foods, and minerals. Orthodox or liberal theory holds that the price of primary goods, at least in the long run, declines relative to that of manufactured products. Explanations as to why this happens include among other things: the substitution of synthetics for natural goods, the inelasticity of demand, and improved techniques of production that require lower inputs of primary products. Inelasticity of demand refers to the concept that, as incomes increase, the proportion of wealth spent on primary products decreases. In the case of international trade, as income increases, significantly more of the country's wealth will be spent on manufactured products, so the prices of primary goods tend to decrease relative to that of manufactured products, all things being equal. Also, with improved techniques of production, the manufacturing process often involves a lower level of primary products to produce a finished good. Figure 13:1 shows the fall in real product prices between 1970 and 1987.

African countries continue to specialize in the export of raw materials. More than three-fourths of the total goods that are exported by the least less developed countries of Africa are primary goods. In some areas, specifically sub-Saharan Africa, exports are centered in a relatively few commodities, such as cotton, coffee, groundnut, and cocoa. Standard of living in Africa is relatively the lowest compared with other LDCs. African states have further been affected by their weak positions in the international economy.

The Havana Charter would have given the less developed nations, including Africa access to decision making and would have exempted them from a full commitment to free trade. General Agreement on Tariff and Trade which replaced Havana Charter, however, made no such concessions. GATT contained no provisions for assisting development and industrialization in the less developed countries. GATT provisions did permit each country to use discriminatory import restrictions, with the prior approval of GATT members to assist industrialization, growth and development, but these provisions have been ineffective in fact. The institutional characteristics of GATT place the less developed countries of Africa at a disadvantage for many reasons, but mainly because of the most-favored-nation (MFN) principle and reciprocity. Since the most-favored-nation principle eliminates preferential trading for development, an industrialized country cannot help any African state(s) by reducing tariffs or other barriers without opening itself up to competition from other advanced industrial nations. This restrain is specifically essential when it affects trade relations with former colonies that particularly maintain strong economic ties with their former mother nations.

The poorer of the poor states of Africa are further disadvantaged by their weak bargaining position. This weakness may be as a result of many various factors: (1) these nations import relatively few products for consumption purposes, their imports have comprised heavily of essential inputs for production. These nations are unable to threaten retaliation when a strong nation establishes a tariff because, by placing tariffs on goods that they use in manufacturing, they would raise the price of their own manufactured products, (2) the markets of these nations are small and they cannot offer much in exchange for concessions, (3) they are not among the principal suppliers of essential manufactured products. Therefore, they are left out of negotiations when those topics are considered. They are not strong enough to get the points that most concern them on the agenda, and (4) the last but not the least, African states have lacked the sophistication and full time technical assistance required to be known or recognized. Thus, majority of African states and other LDCs, particularly the poorer of the poor have refrained from belonging to GATT, believing that a system of equal treatment is inherently unfair when all members are not equal in strength in reality.

Furthermore, as a result of their inferior status with regard to GATT negotiations, the least less developed countries of Africa and other third World have gained little than the developed market economies from the GATT reductions that have occurred. Since the Tokyo Round, the average tariffs on those products in which Third World countries specialized in producing remained higher than for those goods produced by the developed capitalist countries. As tariffs on many manufactured products were reduced to less than five percent, tariffs on textiles, processed metals and wood were not reduced and in some cases were really increased. Also, agricultural commodities continue to suffer from a variety of non tariff barriers (NTBs), which are used to protect agricultural products in advanced industrial societies.[4] African countries are further at a disadvantage because tariffs are higher on processed products, so if African nations want to expand their manufacturing area by first processing the raw materials they export, they are going to be faced with higher tariffs, which in some instances may really lower their profits. For instance, the tariff rate on coffee beans is 6.8 percent, but on processed coffee it is 9.6 percent.[5] Currently, international trade continues to work against many African countries. For example, those producing primary products are subject to increase fluctuations in the prices of their products and to falling demand. Those attempt to produce manufactured goods for export are faced by increasing trade barriers from the advanced industrialized economies.

DEPENDENCE AND FOREIGN AID

As an economist, I will define foreign aid from economic stand point. This will enable us to be able to differentiate between aid from commercial activities and to distinguish developmental and humanitarian from miliary aid. The idea as it is generally used in modern time is defined all concessional loans and official grants largely aimed at transferring resources from advanced industrial societies to less developed countries for the primary objectives of growth and economic development. Concessional loans by definition are those for which the interest rate and repayment time period are generally less stringent than for commercial loans. With the above definition in mind, foreign aid excludes loans that are specifically for national security purposes. However, it is very difficult to differentiate aid given for humanitarian and development purposes from aid given to promote the national security of the western world. The amount of foreign aid given by the industrialized states has increased dramatically over time see Table 14:1. This table summarizes the main sources of development assistance. The total value of development aid that was given in 1986 was $37 billion. However, the absolute amount of foreign assistance has increased seriously for the last few decades, aid as a percent of the gross national product of the donor nation has declined. Currently, United States gives less than 0.3 percent of its GNP in aid. In absolute term, U.S. gives more in foreign assistance than other industrialized country.

The Brain Behind Foreign Assistance

Aid, be it a bilateral or multilateral is given for a particular purpose. Political interests have mainly been the most essential of these motives. Aid may also be given to strength an ally or to prevent an ally from switching side ways. The most important post World War II foreign aid package, the Marshall Plan, involved the transfer of resources from the U.S. to Western Europe and Japan to rebuild the war torn economies. The primary aim of the Marshall Plan was to prevent communist expansionism in western Europe and Japan by providingeconomic security. When the Soviet Union started to assist a number of African countries in the early 1960s, United States and other industrialized capitalist countries interest in that region

TABLE 14:1
Major Sources of Development Aid
(In Millions of U.S. Dollars)

Country	Amount 1975	Percent GNP	Amount 1980	Percent GNP	Amount 1985	Percent GNP
Canada	$ 950	0.44	$1,042	0.41	$1,634	0.46
France	2,100	0.66	4,082	0.64	3,807	0.71
Germany	1,706	0.41	3,543	0.43	2,827	0.42
Italy	202	0.09	683	0.16	1,126	0.26
Japan	1,205	0.23	3,529	0.31	3,939	0.29
Netherlands	686	0.84	1,688	0.99	1,150	0.86
United Kingdom	916	0.42	1,745	0.39	1,456	0.31
United States	4,139	0.26	7,179	0.26	9,294	0.23

Source: World Bank, World Development report, 1988, from Table 21 (New York: Oxford University Press, 1988).

industrialized capitalist countries' interest in that region increased. Believing that economic growth and development would increased incomes, lead to political and economic stability, and hence weaken the urge for marxism movement there, the United States extended development assistance to a number of African states. As Larry Minear puts it:

> The success of Castro in Cuba in 1959 and the subsequent establishment of a Communist government there, aided by the Soviet Union, raised the possibility of a Communist threat from the south. In its wake, the United States stepped up economic aid to Latin America (through the Alliance for Progress), with the intent of preserving friendly regimes. National security concerns also prompted the United States to extend its aid to countries in the Middle East and Asia during the 1960s and 1970s. During the Reagan administration, U.S. security assistance to the developing states amounted to $78.1 billion, compared to $51.4 in development aid. In addition to those directly involving national security, political concerns can also include the spread of a particular ideology (demonstrating the advantages of capitalism over socialism) or religion (Islam). The United States is not alone in its ability to be influenced by political interests. Great Britain, France, and the Soviet Union, among others, have also tied aid to their national-security interests.[6]

This adds flavor to Hayler's position, that aid was a secondary source of influence. I believe, now, that the existence of aid can be explained only in terms of an effort to preserve the capitalist system in the less developed countries. Aid is not particularly effective instrument for achievement; hence, its current decline. But, in so far as it is effective, its contribution to the well being of the peoples of the Third World is negative, since it is not in their interest that exploitation should continue.[7]

Furthermore, humanitarian motives affect the granting of foreign aid. Aid that is established to increase incomes and/or food consumption is a classic example of humanitarian aid. Also, famine relief and direct food aid assistance are designed not toward development but rather toward the short-run alleviation of problems. In spite of this, political and economic objectives can play a significant role. A large number of American foreign aid, particularly food aid often is not given to those nations that needed it most. The top recipients of American food aid under the Food for Peace Program in 1986 were India, Egypt, ElSalvador, Ethiopia, and Sudan. These countries were chosen for strategic, rather than for humanitarian objectives.

Nkrumah had demonstrated the economic impact of development and foreign aid in general in his book *Neo-colonialism: The Last Stage of Imperialism.* According to Nkrumah, "unequal exchange" means that for the Third World the loss is often more than what is given in development aid. Nkrumah has this to say:

> In the first place, the rulers of neo-colonial states derive their authority to govern, not from the will of the people, but from the support which they obtain from their neo-colonialist masters. They have therefore little interest in developing education, strengthening the bargaining power of their workers employed by expatriate firms, or indeed for taking any step which would challenge the colonial pattern of commerce and industry, which it is the object of neo-colonialism to preserve. 'Aid', therefore, to a neo-colonial state is merely a revolving of credit, paid by the neo-colonial master, passing through the neo-colonial state and returning to the neo-colonial master in the form of increased profits. Secondly, it is in the field of 'aid' that the rivalry of individual developed states first manifests itself. So long as neo-colonialism persists so long will spheres of interest persist, and this makes multilateral aid - which is in fact the only effective form of aid - impossible.[8]

Again, economic and strategic interest are another major reasons for the granting of foreign assistance in the less developed countries including African states. Economic growth in African states is advantageous to commercial interests in the advanced capitalist countries for the main fact that increasing incomes will help to create new and expanded markets for western commodities. Foreign assistance may further ensure that the industrialized countries can maintain access to natural resources produced in the Third World. Also, the capitalist countries have an economic interest in maintaining a stable political climate in areas where their business interests have investments. Sometimes foreign aid carries obligations that the aid must be spent on products produced by the donor country and shipped by firms head-quartered. Therefore, foreign aid provides a subsidy to domestic businesses, hence providing gains to the donor's economy. As Gayle Smith put it:

> In the context of Africa's food crisis, food aid has become a vital component for the maintenance of stability by governments, not for saving lives. The type of food aid most commonly given to Africa is not that provided in emergency situations, as in Ethiopia in 1983-84, but regular food aid programs of the U.S., the EEC (European Economic community) and the World Food Program. From the supply side, these programs were designed to rid 'donor' countries of surplus and to create markets for commercial sales. From the demand side, food aid offers governments a financially inexpensive way to meet internal demands for select commodities...The official approach in Sierra Leone, and many other African countries, to dealing with the 'food crisis', which becomes defined in terms of urban demand, is to import the food that non-nationals have produced. Local farmers are then by-passed and government is able to postpone dealing with the numerous constraints to production for peasant farmers which would provide them with a reasonable return for their efforts.[9]

In conclusion, therefore, there is a relief aid. If relief foreign aid is what comes in when all other forms of foreign aid have failed, then there is large indication that failure has come to Africa. Since 1980s, African states have received billions in foreign aid most of it from America. During this time, Africa has charted a course of steady decline. African continent today produces less food, has more starving people, and own more money than it did then years ago. At best, the foreign aid programs of the past are not very effective; at worst, they have been part of the main problem.[10] Smith further points another instance that supported his observation in Africa as follows:

Ghana, a cocoa-producing country on Africa's west coast, is often held up by the Bank as an example of successful adjustment. Ghana first adopted an adjustment program in 1983, and by the late 1980s, World Bank statistics showed that the country's cocoa producers were making more money. But statistics can show anything. Upon further scrutiny, it was discovered that 94 percent of the gross income from cocoa had gone to the richest producers. Poor farmers remained poor. At the same time, Ghana's food self=sufficiency declined. The Bank then advocated, and the government agreed to, an emphasis on large-scale commercial fishing. Local fishermen, unable to obtain the credit and equipment made available to commercial enterprises, were squeezed out. Cheap fish, the primary source of protein for Ghana's people, began to disappear from local markets. To obtain the aid needed to solve its economic problems, according to current "development" wisdom, an African country must enter into an adjustment program. But by doing so, it essentially signs on for another round of the export-led-growth approach that has plagued Africa from the beginning.[11]

Future Expectation of Aid

Since 1980s, the commitment of the advanced industrial economies in providing foreign assistance has reduced. Joan E. Spero argues that three crisis-in energy, food, and anti-inflationary measures and recession in the advanced capitalist countries had profound implications on the flow of foreign economic assistance.[12] Spero further believes that at the same time that these crises created a greater need for economic assistance, they undermined political support for aid by the developed nations of the North. In reality, economic recession undermined the advanced capitalist countries' commitment to foreign aid, but political variations further played a significant role. Conservative president of the United States and prime minister of Britain often believed that private investment instead of foreign aid should play a leading role in development. Furthermore, the debt crisis has led to a focus on the more heavily indebted countries of South America and the question of restructuring the debt rather than on providing development aid to

Africa and Asia. Therefore foreign aid programs of the future do not perceive to be much better, if western development authorities succeed in establishing the priorities and preferential arrangements for the nineties. Top on their arrangement are managing the African debt and creating free-market systems in the region.

THE EMERGENCY OF DEBT CRISIS

Since we have provided excellent work on the debt crisis in Africa in our previous chapter, we will briefly mention debt crisis to enable us treat debt management in this section. Between 1970 and 1989, the external indebtedness of the less developed countries increased from $68.4 billion to $1,263 billion, a rise of about 1846 percent.[13] Table 14:2 summarizes this incident in a general perspective. However, debt service ratio increased by more than 1390 percent. Majority of highly indebted nations centered in Latin America countries. Prominent among them are Brazil, Mexico, Argentina, and Venezuela. Meanwhile, among the 17 most indebted nations identified by the International Monetary Fund and the World Bank, only Nigeria is from African continent.

The origin of the 1980s African debt problems was dated back in 1974-1979, when the majority of sub-Saharan Africa experienced OPEC Oil price increased which affected their import receipts. However, in order for African countries to achieve their growth and development objectives, they have to invest more in the importation of capital goods, food and oil. The international economic environment of the late 1970s and early 1980s had a profound effect on the societies of African states. The increase in the price of oil, accompanied by a marked fall in the export prices of commodities generally produced and exported by the African states, led to a decline in the terms of trade in Africa.

Also, a slowdown in industrialized countries' growth and development led to a fall in demand for exports from African states. And a rapid increase in global interest rates accelerated the cost of commercial capital to those nations that were borrowing in private markets.

With this condition in mind, African states had two main policy alternatives. They could either reduce imports and impose discretionary or tight fiscal and monetary policies, hence affecting growth and development objectives. Secondly, they could finance their widening current account deficits through borrowing from external sources.[14] Michael Todaro further comments:

> Unable, and sometimes unwilling, to adopt the first option as a means of solving the balance of payments crisis, many countries were forced in the early 1980s to rely on the second option, borrowing even more heavily. As a result, massive debts and debt-service obligations accumulated, so that by the middle 1980s countries like Brazil, Mexico, Argentina, the Philippines, and Chile faced severe difficulties in paying even the interest on their debts out of export earnings. Now, however, they could no longer borrow funds in the world's private capital markets. In fact, not only did private lending dry up, but by 1986 the developing countries were paying back $11.3 billion more to the commercial banks than they were receiving in new loans. When payback to international lenders such as the IMF and the World Bank are included the net resource flow (new lending minus debt service) for all indebted LDCs went from a positive $35.2 billion in 1981 to a negative $30.7 billion in 1986. Now HICs had no recourse but to seek IMF assistance and face up to the IMF stabilization program, the conditions of which were tantamount to the first policy option.[15]

In conclusion, the main causes of African economic crisis reflect a difficult combination of internal general weakness, unfavorable external economic conditions, and noneconomic factors, such as adverse climatic economic conditions. The crisis requests for a coordinated mechanism, geared generally on development and growth rather than macroeconomic stabilization and adjustment. African leaders, donor nations, and the multilateral lending institutions must seriously engage on agreement concerning development alternatives that will be used to address African economic predicament; otherwise both the donor countries and African states will ultimately bear the entire consequences in the 1990s.

Furthermore, during the whole process of debt accumulation in Africa and other less developed countries, one of the most essential and continuous transformations was the large increase in private capital flight (see table 14:3). During 1976 and 1985, it is proximated that about $200 billion fled from the highly and most debt nations of the LDCs to the other part of the world, particularly the industrialized countries and the institutions they organized and managed. However, this presented the equivalent of 50 percent of the entire borrowing by the Third World nations at that time.[16]

Management Approach of the Debt Crisis

The African debt issue has become clearly a global wide issue with serious economic consequences for both industrialized and non industrialized nations. In reality, the debt problems of the 1980s has called into attention according to Todaro the very existence, viability and stability of the global financial system. Fears were perceived that if one or two of the highly indebted nations (Brazil, Mexico, or Argentina) were to default, the economies of the industrialized capitalist states might be seriously damaged: Hence, urgent meetings between government officials of both industrialized countries and Third World debtor nations and international bankers were called to address this issue to date.

TABLE 14:2
Seventeen Highly Indebted Countries, 1987

COUNTRY	TOTAL (US$ BILLION)	OF WHICH PRIVATE SOURCE (PERCENT)	TOTAL	OF WHICH INTEREST	DOD/GNP 1986	INTEREST/XGS 1987
ARGENTINA	49.4	85.8	23.7	7.9	65.8	33.1
BOLIVIA	4.6	26.7	1.6	0.6	118.8	31.5
BRAZIL	114.5	75.5	61.4	20.0	41.0	30.2
CHILE	20.5	83.2	9.8	4.2	138.8	29.5
COLOMBIA	15.1	49.4	8.5	3.1	46.8	16.6
COSTA RICA	4.5	50.8	2.4	0.7	118.7	18.9
Cote d/Ivoire	9.1	60.5	4.0	1.7	122.7	17.1
ECUADOR	9.0	70.2	4.3	1.8	83.5	24.4
JAMAICA	3.8	17.4	1.6	0.6	197.3	17.4
MEXICO	105.0	86.2	44.9	22.2	83.8	32.7
MOROCCO	17.3	32.0	8.1	2.6	126.7	25.4
NIGERIA	27.0	55.1	12.2	3.8	45.5	11.6
PERU	16.7	53.2	7.9	2.2	62.4	29.0
PHILIPPINES	29.0	60.6	12.0	4.6	93.6	19.0
URUGUAY	3.8	80.1	1.3	0.7	63.4	15.3
VENEZUELA	33.9	99.3	15.9	6.6	70.8	22.5
YUGOSLAVIA	21.8	69.6	10.2	3.7	33.0	7.7
TOTAL	485.0	74.3	229.8	87.0	60.8	23.8

TABLE 14:2 CONTINUED

COUNTRY	1983-87 (ANNUAL AVERAGE VALUE)	BALANCE IN 1982	GDP	EXPORTS	IMPORTS	INVESTMENT	PER CAPITA CONSUMPTION
ARGENTINA	3.1	2.3	0.0	1.4	-11.0	-9.5	-1.2
BOLIVIA	0.0	0.3	-3.5	-0.3	-2.4	-2.6	-5.1
BRAZIL	8.6	-0.9	3.4	3.2	-4.4	-1.1	1.1
CHILE	0.5	-0.4	0.9	4.1	-6.8	-4.6	2.2
COLOMBIA	-0.3	-2.4	2.8	8.0	-3.3	0.9	0.2
COSTA RICA	-0.1	-0.1	1.5	2.1	-2.4	1.3	-1.4
COTE D'IVOIRE	0.8	0.1	-0.6	3.8	-2.8	-15.2	-4.3
ECUADOR	0.6	0.6	1.4	5.9	-2.6	-4.7	-2.2
JAMAICA	-0.5	-0.6	0.2	-5.4	-2.2	1.3	-1.4
MEXICO	9.1	6.2	0.3	6.4	-7.7	-6.7	-2.7
MOROCCO	-1.5	-2.3	3.4	2.9	1.6	-2.2	0.8
NIGERIA	1.5	-3.9	-3.4	-5.9	-19.2	-13.5	-6.5
PERU	0.3	-0.4	0.7	-0.6	-5.7	-12.6	-0.2
PHILIPPINES	-1.4	-3.2	-0.5	-0.5	-4.9	-13.5	-1.0
URUGUAY	0.2	-0.1	-1.4	-0.1	-8.1	-13.8	-2.4
VENEZUELA	3.9	3.6	-0.7	-0.9	-5.7	-3.4	-4.6
YUGOSLAVIA	-1.8	-3.3	1.1	0.5	-0.6	0.4	-0.5
TOTAL	23.0	-4.7	1.0	1.4	-6.2	-4.8	-1.6

NOTES: DOD, "debt outstanding disbursed" - i.e., total debt outstanding; XGS, "exports of goods and services". SOURCE: World Bank, World Debt Tables 1987-88 (Washington, DC: The World Bank, 1988), Table Box 1, p.xiv.

There have been numerous proposals for relieving and/or renegotiating the debt burdens of highly indebted nations. These have ranged from a new allocation of Special Drawing Rights to restructuring of principal payments falling due during an agreed-upon consolidation period, to lower interest rates, to repayments linked to export earnings (the Peruvian model), to the extension of new long-term loans and the maintenance of short-term credit lines. In addition, there has been much discussion of debt-for-equity swaps. These are the sale at a discount (sometimes in excess of 50%) of questionable LDC commercial bank loans to private investors in secondary trading markets. Commercial banks are now more willing to engage in such transaction because new interpretations and regulations for U. S. banks permit them to take a loss on the loan swap while not reducing the book value of other loans to that country. For the LDC part, they are able through debt-for-equity swaps to encourage private investments in local currency assets from both foreign and resident investors as well as to reduce their overall debt obligations. The flip side of these benefits, however, is the fact that foreign investors are buying up the real assets of developing nations at major discounts.[17]

Meanwhile, the IMF has been a principal manager in the management process of the debt crisis in the 1980s. The highly indebted nations have had to turn to the Fund for financial assistance. The Fund first examines, assesses and evaluates the economic condition; finds out a standby arrangement loan, and monitors the country's economic measures to ensure that it is properly used according to loan condition. Private banks clearly perceive Fund approval as an indication that the debtor nation is attempting to implement stable economic measures to solve its economic problems, hence worthy of additional credit. Therefore, in order to renegotiate loans with a private bank, the debtor nation must agree to Fund macroeconomic stabilization measures. These stabilization measures, which specifically call for devaluation of national currency and austerity measures to control inflation, are politically sensitive and place an unwarranted burden on the poorer citizens in the debtor countries.

TABLE 14:3

ESTIMATED NET CAPITAL FLIGHT: CUMULATIVE FLOWS, 1976-85 (IN BILLIONS OF $)

	Total	1976-82	1983-85
Latin America			
Argentina	26	27	(1)
Bolivia	1	1	0
Brazil	10	3	7
Ecuador	2	1	1
Mexico	53	36	17
Uruguay	1	1	0
Venezuela	30	25	6
Other Countries			
India	10	6	4
Indonesia	5	6	(1)
Korea	12	6	6
Malaysia	12	6	4
Nigeria	10	7	3
Philippines	9	7	4
South Africa	17	13	4
Total Capital Flight	198	147	52

SOURCE: Reprinted by permission of the publisher from The ABCs of International finance by John Charles Pool and Steve Stamos (Lexington, Mass.: Lexington Books, D.C. Health & Co., Copyright 1987, D.C. Health & Co).

Baker's Policy Recommendation

The Baker Plan, which is among the proposals advanced in 1985, was designed to encourage renewed lending to support economic growth and development in the debtor nations. The plan actually proposed a three way arrangement between debtors, creditor countries and private banks. The Baker plan encouraged the debtor nations to open their economies to trade and multinational investment and to adopt market oriented strategies. The plan further encouraged the creditor nations to stimulate their own economies and allow them to debtor exports and expand the role of World Bank in leading policy.[18]

The Plan finally called upon the commercial banks to loan an additional $20 billion to the indebted nations to accelerate measure changes and to increase economic growth and development. Baker Plan was seen as important since it marked a recognition of the part of the United States that the debt crisis was long term and because it did not rely wholly on the LDCs endeavors to improve their economic conditions.[19] The Baker Plan failed to succeed because the Western Banks were not willing to provide additional new credits.   Critics argued that, even if it succeeded, it would only create further indebtedness.

Brady's Policy Alternative

Also, the Brady Plan proposed to replace the Baker Plan in 1989, represented a shift toward debt reduction by realizing that majority of the LDC debtor nations could not pay back their loan in full even if payment periods were further extended.[20] In the case of Brady Plan, commercial banks were requested to reduce on a voluntary basis, principal or interest charge on loans to Third World Nations.   This would reduce debt through purchasing backs, conversion of debt into bonds at generally lower interest rate or principal amount, and/or debt equity swaps. Also, in return for an arrangement on the part of creditor nations to reduce principal and/or interest, the International Monetary Fund and World Bank would guarantee part of the remainder on interest and principal.[21]

The problem with some of these proposals for debt alleviation including debt equity swaps is that they require private foreign banks to initiate the measures.   Therefore, some of these countries are not willing to take any major that might affect their short-run balance sheets. Again, to qualify for relief under the Brady Plan, a nation must agree to implement economic measures to encourage and facilitate domestic savings and direct foreign investment. While the plan has been praised for addressing the need to minimize the debt burden of the LDCs; it has been criticized for providing poor financial assistance.

NOTES

1. Fredoline Anunobi, *The Implications of Conditionality,*: *The International Monetary Fund and Africa* (Maryland: University Press of America, 1991).

2. Glenn P. Hastedt and Kay M. Knickrehm, *Dimensions of World Politics* (New York: Harper Collins, publishers, 1991), p. 353.

3. Ibid.

4. Anunobi, *The Implications of Conditionality.*

5. David Blake and Robert Walters, *The Politics of Global Economic Relations* (Englewood Cliffs, NJ: Prentice Hall, 1987), p. 144. For detail examination of tariff of the Gatt. See the work by J. E. Spero, *The Politics of International Economic Relations* (New York: St. Martin's Press, 1985). Charles W. Kegley and Eugene R. Wittkopf, *World Politics: Trend and Transformation* (New York: St. Martin's Press, 1985). Michael Todaro, *Economic Development in the Third World* (New York: Longman, 1989). Chenery Hollin and Nicholas Carter, "Foreign Assistance and Development Performance, 1960-1970", *American Economic Review*, Vol. 64, No. 3 1980. Gyorgy Cukor, *Strategies for Industrialization in Developing Countries* (New York: St. Martin's Press, 1974). Michael Roemer, "Dependence and Industrialization Strategies" *World Development* (1981). Fredoline Anunobi, *The Implications of Conditionality: The International Monetary Fund and Africa* (Maryland: University Press of America, 1992).

6. Larry Minear, "The Forgotten Human Agenda", *Foreign Policy*, 73, Winter 1988-1989, pp.82-83.

7. Hayter, Aid as Imperialism.

8. Kwame Nkrumah, *Neo-Colonialism: The Last State of Imperialism* (New York: International Publishers, 1966), p. xv.

9. Smith, p. 113.

10. Ibid.

11. Ibid., pp., 113-114.

12. Spero, *The Politics of International Economic Relations*, pp. 197-216.

13. Michael P. Todaro, *Economic Development in The Third World* (New York: Longman, 1989), p. 413. See the work by Kathryn Morton and Peter Tulloch, *Trade and Developing Countries* (New York: John Wiley, 1980). M. H. Bouchet, *The Political Economy of International Debt: What, Who, How Much and Why?* (Westport, Conn.: Greenwood Press, 1987). R. Dorrbush and S. Fischer, "The World Debt Problem: Origins and Prospects", (*Journal of Development Planning*, 1985). H. A. Holley, *Developing Country Debt: The Role of the Commercial Banks* (New York: Methuen, 1987). G. K. Helleiner, "Balance of Payments Experience and Growth Prospects of developing countries: A Synthesis" (*World Development Journal* 1986). Aderanti Adepoju, *The Impact of Structural Adjustment on the Population of Africa* (London: James Currey, 1993). Anne O. Krueger, *Economic Policy Reform in Developing Countries* (Cambridge, Mass.: Blackwell, 1992). Simon Commander, *Structural Adjustment and Agriculture: Theory and Practice in Africa and Latin America* (London: James Currey, 1989).

14. Todaro, p. 119.

15. Ibid.

16. J. C. Pool and S. Stamos, *The ABCs of International Finance* (Lexington, Mass: D. C. Health, 1987), pp.52-58.

17. Ibid., p. 422.

18. Hastedt, p. 367.

19. Ibid.

20. For a general discussion of the Brady Plan, see Jeffrey Sach, "Making the Brady Plan Work", *Foreign Affairs*, 68, No. 3, (June 1989), pp. 87-105.

21. Hasledt.

CHAPTER 15

The Myth Of Nonalignment Movement in Africa: Trend And Transformation

The purpose of this chapter is to examine Africa's role in the nonaligned movement. In the first instance, the development of the nonaligned movement will be discussed, with particular emphasis on African states. In as much as most countries believe in nonalignment, or at least profess to do so, this chapter will evaluate and assess the success that the movement has had in reconciling the conflicting competing theoretical concepts and objectives of its members. In addition, Africa's future in the non-aligned movement will be explored. Finally, the experiences of Cameroon and Tanzania two African nations will be used to further illustrate different approaches African states have taken to the general policy of the non-alignment. The success and/or failure of non-alignment movement to achieve its objectives in these two African states will enable us to draw a general conclusion. The term non-alignment is a foreign policy adopted by many newly independent states in the period following World

War II.   The victorious allies had assumed in their planning for the post war era that world peace could only be accomplished through the cooperation of the great powers.   Even before the war ended, tensions between the Soviet Union and American appeared great. This mutual hostility increased and developed into cold war which has been the major feature of international relations.

When the less developed countries have sought to remove the vestiges of dependent relationships implied by the terms neo imperialism, classical imperialism and neocolonialism, most are determined to avoid the East-West confrontation because of fear that one pattern of domination might easily be replaced by another new pattern.   Thus, Third World nations espouse a foreign policy of non-alignment.   The non-alignment movement between and among the less developed, poor nations dated back from 1955 when twenty nine African and Asian countries met in Bangdung, Indonesia, to discuss among other things, the means of eradicating colonialism in their respective regions.   Since 1961 the movement has emerged into a permanent institution, and by then its membership has increased from twenty nine to over one hundred and six, with meetings scheduled every three years.

On the economic front, the Asian-African Conference recognized the urgency of promoting economic cooperation and development between these two continents, hence called for mutual economic cooperation, interest, and respect for national sovereignty.   The participating nations agreed to exchange technical and other similar assistance to one another to the maximum necessary in the form of experts, trainees, pilot projects and equipment for demonstration purposes, exchange of technical know how, regional training, and research institutes for imparting technical knowledge and skills in cooperation with the existing global agencies.

Asian-African conference further emphasized the need to establish regional banks and insurance companies, the development of nuclear energy for peaceful purposes, and the vital need for stabilizing commodity trade in the region. The conference was also convinced that among the most powerful avenues of promoting understanding between nations is the development and expansion of cultural cooperation. Hence, the conference called for the development and expansion of Asian-African culture. However, the culture of Asia and Africa are based on spiritual and universal foundation.

This recognition is based on the fact that some colonial masters have denied their dependent citizens fundamental rights in the area of culture and education, which prevents the development of their personality and further hampers cultural intercourse with other Asian and African populace. This is generally a reality in the case of Algeria, Tunisia and Morocco, where the fundamental right of the citizens to study their own language and culture has been suppressed with no regard. Since similar discrimination has been practiced against Asian and colored peoples in some areas of Africa, the conference argued that these policies amount to a denial of the basic rights of the people, prevent cultural development in this zone and at the same time hamper cultural cooperation on the wider global plane. Thus, the conference rejected such a denial of basic rights in the area of culture and education in some areas of Asia and Africa. In specific, the conference rejected racialism as a means of cultural suppression and exploitation.

At the same time that the Cold War was taking shape, the colonial peoples of Africa and Asia were becoming increasingly determined to gain independence. The Japanese occupation of many Asian countries had already disrupted colonial administration, and it was in Southeast Asia that decolonization achieved its first success. A number of the new nations, including India, Burma, and Indonesia, decided to ally themselves with neither East nor West, but rather to pursue an independent or non-aligned policy. In September 1946,

Jawaharlal Nehru described the foreign policy that India would follow:

> In the sphere of foreign affairs, India will follow an independent policy, keeping away from the power politics of groups aligned one against another. She will uphold the principle of freedom for dependent peoples and will oppose racial discrimination wheresoever it may occur. She will work with other peace loving nations for international cooperation and good will without the exploitation of one nation by another.[1]

The policy of non-alignment was not merely a tactical response of relatively weak nations to a bi-polar great power struggle. The immediate concern of the new nations had little to do with the issues of the Cold War. Basically, they are three major interests which separated the new nations from the great powers and these interests formed the foundation of the non-aligned movement. First, consideration of self preservation strongly indicated that aligning with one bloc could trigger aggressive action against the new nation from the opposing camp. Second, the strong desire for cultural and ideological autonomy led to a fierce desire among the newly independent states to remove all vestiges of colonialism from the world. Finally, almost without exception, the new nations were desperately poor and underdeveloped, partly as a result of colonial exploitation. Therefore, economic and human development became their overriding priorities.[2]

A non-aligned movement can be said to have begun in 1947, when India hosted an Asian Relations Conference in New Delhi. Subsequent conferences of the early non-aligned nations in Colombo (1954) and Bandung Indonesia (1955) were mainly concerned with developing a common approach to the problems of participant nations. In this period, the movement was dominated by Asian and Middle Eastern Arab nations since majority of Africa States were still under colonial rule. A small number of countries were involved and collective action by participant nations was not attempted. Anti-colonialism and suppression of mankind were the primary focus of the movement in this early period.

Indian Prime Minister Jawaharlal Nehru, addressing an audience in the United States, Oct. 11, 1949, two months after independence was granted to India. *(National Archieves)*

Muhammed Ali Jinnah, President of the Moslem League and later the first President of Pakistan, Aug. 9, 1945. *(AP/Wide World Photos)*

An important landmark in the non-aligned movement was the conference of the Heads of States of the non-aligned countries held in Belgrade, Yugoslavia in 1961. The prime key actors behind the conference were Tito of Yugoslavia, Nehru of India, Nasser of Egypt, Sukarno of Indonesia and Kame Nkrumah of Ghana.[3] However, five major criteria were established and they have remained the formal requirements for participation in the non-aligned movement. The criteria were:

I   Belonging to neither the communist nor the West military bloc;

II   Having no bilateral military agreement with any bloc country;

III   Willingly permitting no foreign military base on the nation's territory;

IV   Supporting anti-colonial liberation movements; and

V   Pursuing an independent policy.[4]

However, East-West tensions (over Berlin, the situation in the Belgian Congo, and the Algerian liberation struggle) were very high at the time of the Belgrade Conference, and the participants focused on most of the world peace and peaceful coexistence. At Belgrade for the first time, the non-aligned movement promulgated a joint program, rather than merely stating common principles. The declaration called for, coexistence, mutual support in opposing colonialism, neocolonialism, imperialism, and racism, a reaffirmation of every nation's right to self determination, a meeting of the United Nations to discuss disarmament and increased economic cooperation among all nations. The Non-Aligned nations also made a direct appeal to President kennedy and Premier Kruschev to meet to try and resolve their differences.[5]

Throughout the 1960s, the nonaligned movement added new members, many of them from African. Forty-seven nations were represented when nonaligned heads of state met in Cairo in 1964. These countries include: Afghanistan, Algeria, Angola, Burma, Burundi, Cambodia, Cameroon, Central African Republic, Ceylon, Chad, Congo (Brazzaville), Cuba, Cyprus, Dahomey, Ethiopia, Ghana, Guinea, India, Indonesia, Iraq, Islamic Republic of Mauritania, Jordan, Kenya, Kuwait, Laos, Lebanon, Liberia, Libya, Malawi, Mali, Morocco, Nepal, Nigeria, Saudi Arabia, Senegal, Sierra Leone, Somalia, Sudan, Syria, Togo, Tunisia, Uganda, United Arab Republic, United Republic of

Tanganyika and Zanzibar, Yemen, Yugoslavia and Zambia. Meeting on the African continent for the first time, the non aligned leaders gave strong support to the liberation movements in Southern Africa and pledged to cooperate closely with the newly formed Organization of African Unity.[6] Deeply concerned at the rapidly deteriorating situation in the Congo, the participants:

support all the efforts being made by the Organization of African Unity to bring peace and harmony speedily to that country;

urge the Ad Hoc Commission of the Organization of African Unity to shirk no effort in the attempt to achieve national reconciliation in the Congo, and to eliminate the existing tension between that country and the Republic of Congo (Brazzaville) and the Kingdom of Burundi;

appeal to the Congolese Government and to all combatants to cease hostilities immediately and to seek with the help of the Organization of African Unity, a solution permitting of national reconciliation and the restoration of order and peace;

urgently appeal to all foreign Powers at present interfering in the internal affairs of the Democratic Republic of the Congo, particularly those engaged in military intervention in that country, to cease such interference, which infringes the interest and sovereignty of the Congolese people and constitutes a threat to neighboring countries;

affirm their full support for the efforts being made to this end by the Organization of African Unity's Ad Hoc Commission of good offices in the Congo;

call upon the Government of the Democratic Republic of the Congo to discontinue the recruitment of mercenaries immediately and to expel all mercenaries, of whatever origin, who are already in the Congo, in order to facilitate an African solution.[7]

The newly independent states have, like all other nations, the right of sovereign disposal in regard to their natural resources, and the right to utilize these resources as they deem appropriate in the interest of their peoples without outside interference. The process of liberation is irresistible and irreversible. Colonized citizens may legitimately resort to arms to secure the full exercise of their right to self-determination and independence if the colonial Powers persist in opposing their natural aspiration.[8]

Kwame Nkruman, on a visit to
United States addresses a
New York audience.
(National Archives)
(National Archives)

Kenyan Prime Minister Jomo
Kenyatta, Nov.1964. Ruler of
Kenya from independence in
1963 until death in 1980
(National Archives)

At this point, however, the participants in the conference undertake to work unremittingly to eliminate if not eradicate all forms of colonialism and to combine all their efforts to provide all necessary support and aid, whether material, financial, moral or political, to the peoples struggling against European colonialism, neocolonialism and neo-imperialism.

Beside, the heads of state of Non-Aligned Nations declare that lasting international peace cannot be achieved so long as unjust conditions prevail and peoples under foreign domination continue to be deprived of their basic rights to freedom, self-determination and independence.[9]

Colonialism, neocolonialism and economic imperialism constitute a fundamental source of global tension and conflict because they danger international peace and security. The participants in the conference argue that the Declaration of the United Nations on the granting of political independence to colonial states and their citizens has not been adopted everywhere and call for the unconditional, complete and final abolition of colonialism and/or political domination for economic exploitation.

Furthermore, the exploitation by colonial master, forces of the difficulties and problems of recently liberated Third World states, interference in the internal affairs of these countries, and colonial power efforts to maintain unequal relations, specifically in the economic area, constitute serious and real danger to these newly emerged developing nations. As we all know, imperialism, colonialism, neocolonialism have various forms and manifestations.

For example, imperialism uses numerous devices to impose its will on independent countries. Economic pressure and domination, racial discrimination, intervention, subversion, interference and the threat of force are neocolonialist mechanisms against which the less developed countries of Africa, Asia and Latin America have to defend themselves in the contemporary international economic relations. For these reasons, the less developed countries united themselves to fight against all forms of colonialism, neocolonialism, and neo-imperialism anywhere they exist in their region.

In 1970, the heads of state met in Lusaka, Zambia, with 53 nations in attendance. Economic issues received major attention for the first time. In the similar direction, the heads of government participating in this conference argue that peace can only rest on a sound and solid economic foundation, that the persistence of poverty poses a serious threat to international peace and stability, and that economic emancipation is an important factor in the struggle for the eradication of political domination for economic exploitation. Therefore, the participants insisted that the respect for the right of peoples and countries to control and dispose freely of their national resources and wealth is a necessary if not a sufficient condition for their economic growth and development. The participants in the conference further believe that economic development is an ultimate responsibility of the entire global community. Thus, they argue that it is the obligation of all nations to contribute to the rapid evolution of a new and just economic order under which all countries can live without fear and rise to their full stature in the family of nation-states.

They also believe that the structure of international economy and the existing global institutions of world trade and development have failed either to reduce the inequality in the per capital income of the peoples in less developed and developed states or to promote global action to rectify serious and growing imbalances between the less developed countries of the South and the industrialized capitalist countries of the North. Hence, they call for immediate need to amplify and intensify global cooperation based on equality, and consistent with the needs of accelerated economic growth and development.

The participants moreover, argue that while the Geneva Conference marks the first attempt in the history of a new international economic policy for development and offers a sound basis for prosperity in the future, the results accomplished were neither adequate for, nor commensurate with, the important requirements of the Third World nations. Therefore, they recommend that democratic mechanisms, which afford no preferential position of privilege, are as important in the economic as in the political arena. They believe that a new international division labor is necessary to accelerate industrialization of the Third World nations and the modernization of their agriculture, so as to enable them to expand their local economies and diversify their export activity. They finally conclude that discriminatory measures of any type taken against the less developed countries on the grounds of different socio-economic, political and/or ideological systems are contrary to the spirit of The United Nations Charter and constitute a threat to the free flow of trade and to peace and should be eradicated.[10] While on the political sphere, the participants focused on Africa with strong support being expressed for the liberation movements in Namibia/South-West Africa, Zimbabwe/Rhodesia and Azania/South Africa.

Throughout its history, the non-aligned movement has experienced difficulty in establishing a definition of alignment and in agreeing on common platforms. The non-aligned share basic aims, but have never carried out a coordinated foreign policy. More often than not, members of the non-aligned movement commonly shun the types of names that would place them into the camp of one or other of the two super powers. That makes non-alignment itself reflects more rhetoric than reality. It seems that the movement's claims of unity of purpose and principle have become blurred and less convincing.[11] Also, one writer describes the component of the non-aligned at the period of its seventh summit in 1983 in this way. The majority of its official members have adopted dictatorships in many ways or another; more than a dozen are openly aligned with the soviet bloc nations. However, more than a dozen can be described as more or less pro-America.[12] It has been frequently remarked that there are as many definitions of non-alignment as there are non-aligned countries. This is to a large extent unavoidable because the foreign policy of weak,formerly colonial, underdeveloped immediate environment of the country. For this reason, John K. Galbraith states:

> The will to national independence is the most powerful force of our time. To infringe upon it is to touch the most sensitive of nerves. This has been true for the Soviets; it has been true for Americans. Respecting that independence, one can have friends; impairing it, one can expect only rejection. If the national leadership is strong, effective, and well-regarded, it will not tolerate foreign domination-from anyone. If that leadership is weak, ineffective, unpopular, corrupt, or oppressive, it may accept foreign guidance, support, and a measure of domination. But then it will not be tolerated by its own people.[13]

It should be noted that non-alignment is not the same as traditional neutrality, as practiced by a European nations such as Switzerland. The non-aligned have never felt that non-alignment means not taking sides on international issues. The crux of non-alignment can be said to be the development of whatever foreign and domestic policies that the non-aligned believes to be in its best interests, independent of any outside consideration of allies or bloc leaders.

AFRICAN ROLE IN THE NON-ALIGNED

Africa's role in the nonaligned movement started in the late 1950s and early 1960s when most African Countries gained their political independence. At this time, the Cold War dominated international relations to a greater extent than in earlier years when the first Asian post - colonial governments adopted non - alignment as a policy. It is not surprising that the majority of new African governments also announced policies of non-alignment, in the belief that security and development could best be accomplished outside of either power bloc. Non-alignment in Africa was strongly influenced by the highly developed sense of racial identity which pervaded all the anti-colonial movements on the continent. African nationalism at this time was also marked by strong currents of Pan-Africanism as a result of the universal experience of European rule across the continent.

In the period between the 1961 Belgrade Summit and the next non-alignment Summit in Cairo, the Organization of African Unity (O.A.U.) was established in 1963. The main principles of the OAU are the eradication of colonialism in all its forms, economic development, and defense of the territorial integrity of all member states. The O.A.U. charter also called for the member nations to adopt a common policy of non-alignment. Also, to avoid chaos on the continent, the O.A.U. decided at its 1964 Summit Conference to respect the boundaries established by the colonial powers, regardless of the questionable, rationality, and fairness of many of the borders.

A majority of the independent African nations attended the 1964 Non-alignment summit in Ciaro, but once again, national and regional problems dominated the thinking of most African leaders. Many Africans also believed that the O.A.U. was a more important and appropriate forum for African nations' non aligned policies. Haile Selassie's address at Cairo emphasized Ethiopia's concern over Somalia's claims on her territory and Kenneth Kaunda stressed the difficulties Zambia faced. President Bourgiba of Tunisia stated that problems of national welfare had to be given top priority and the Sudan's President Abboud pointed out that despite all its rhetoric, the non-aligned movement still had not devised any concrete means of advancing the social and economic welfare of participant states.

In the period from 1964 to 1970, internal political strife was endemic among African states and non-alignment continued to have limited practical application on the continent. In certain cases, non-alignment had to be compromised to the higher goal of preserving legally established governments. A case in point of this occurred in Tanganyika in 1964 when Julius Nyerere called in British troops to assist in putting down the East African mutinies and restoring order. Another problem was the belief of some leaders that non-alignment could not be pursued unless development brought a modicum of stability. However, development was impossible without foreign assistance which was often accompanied by demands for concessions from the assisted country which compromised non-alignment.

However, by the time of the 1970 Non-alignment Summit in Lusaka, Zambia civil wars and rebellions in Africa were practically ended, and a period of relative stability had started. African leaders were in the forefront of the trend to concentrate on the economic aspect of non-alignment. President Nyerere of Tanzania urged the conference to consider "the question of how we can help to strengthen non-alignment by economic cooperation." Many African leaders expressed disappointment that rhetoric of non-alignment had yet to lead to practical mechanisms for development. An indication of the sentiment of some African nations can be found in the fact that seven African states: Dahomey, Ivory Coast, Madagascar, Malawi, Niger and Upper Volta--sent no representation to Lusaka.

The three non-aligned summits of the 1970s have given increasingly strong support to the liberation of Southern African. The political declaration adopted in Sri Lanka in 1976 stated in part that:

> The emancipation of Africa, the ending of racial discrimination against people of African origin all over the world, the protection of Africa from the rivalries of the external powers, the denuclearization of Africa should not be merely regional or continental concerns but the priorities of the non-aligned movement and of the United Nation.[14]

Africans noted, though, that repeated calls for economic sanctions against South Africa by the non-aligned movement have been observed in practice by only a fraction of its members. Consequently, the only one way in which the non-aligned movement has avoided divisiveness is by deciding as early as the Belgrade Summit that the internal social and political organization of a nation has no bearing on its participation in the non-aligned movement. No international movement based on voluntary cooperation could very long survive once it began intervening in its members' internal affairs. Non-intervention in the internal concerns of members has also been a cornerstone of O.A.U.'s policy. Of course, the presence in the non-aligned movement of nations with political systems as diverse as those of Cuba and Saudia Arabia has severely hampered the development of consensus on policies and programs. It has been argued that the definition of non-alignment has been stretched almost to the breaking point by the admission of nations with strong ties to one of the great powers such as Cuba. At Colombo in 1976, Rumania (a member of the Warsaw Pact), Portugal (a NATO member) and the Philippines (which permits United States military bases on its territory) were admitted as "guests," participating in discussions but having no procedural role. The desire to develop a broad-based movement including as much of the Third World as possible seems at times to conflict with the expressed philosophy of non-alignment.

An area where non-aligned movement has experienced repeated failures is those situations where the expansionism of one member nation have threatened the sovereignty of another nation or have conflicted with the principles of the movement. The annexation of Go by India, one of the movement's founders, was certainly not in keeping with the principle of self-determination for Colonial peoples that is a primary tenet of the nonaligned movement. Furthermore, the dispute between Algeria and Morocco over the Western Sahara, a former Spanish colony, has been sidestepped repeatedly at non-aligned summits. In Africa, the commitment of the O.A.U. to its members' sovereignty and to the principles of non-alignment has not had any effect on Libya's active encouragement of subversion in Chad and Morocco. The O.A.U. has also taken no stand on Somalia's support of the Eriteran rebels in Ethiopia.

African efforts at coordinated non-aligned action both through the O.A.U. and the world-wide non-aligned movement have been hampered by the presence of three distinct currents of thought on the continent. The Arab nations of Northern Africa, the former French colonies and the former British colonies have often seen their interests as not coinciding with one or both the other groupings.

Another line of cleavage between "moderates" and "radicals", dated to the Congo crisis of the early sixties. The so-called radicals including at times Ghana, Guinea, Algeria, Congo-Brazzaville, Tanzania, and Morocco have been strongly influenced by marxist thought and have attempted to rally support against neo-colonialism. In practice, this had led them to seek closer relations and increase trade with the communist world and in some cases communist arms have been accepted. The moderates or pragmatists, including Senegal, Nigeria and Cameroon, have seen neo-colonialism as more of a slogan than a real threat and therefore continued to trade mostly with Western nations.

Apart from ideological differences over development strategies and political systems, several other factors have worked against unity along non-alignment principles. In several cases, ousted regimes have found refuge in neighboring O.A.U. states from which they have conducted campaigns of rhetoric and sometimes subversion against the new government that replaced them. As has been the case with Libya and Somali, support for liberation movements has been directed towards unseating existing indigenous governments as well as the remaining white minority regimes. Finally, the calls for economic boycotts of South Africa have not been put into practice by certain African states because of the disastrous economic effects a policy of strict adherence would have on their economy.

Africa's future in the non-aligned movement indicates that recent events in Africa have troubling implications for the future of the non-aligned movement on the continent. Over the last three years, the Soviets have been attempting to extend their influence in Africa. The earlier involvement of Cuban troops and Russian military technicians in the struggle for power in Angola was followed in 1978 by similar massive assistance to Ethiopia. With this aid (estimated to involve 20,000 Cuban troops, 3,000

Soviet military technicians and $2 billion in Russian arms), the Ethiopians repulsed a Somalia invitation of Ogaden province and later retook most of the province of Eritrea from rebels who have been fighting there for most of the last 18 years.

Later in 1978, Angola-based insurgents invaded Zaire's Shaba province and the Zaireans were forced to rely on Belgian and French troops, flown in on United States planes and using some American weapons, to put down the invasion. The United States alleged, but other sources failed to positively establish, Cuban involvement in training the invaders. It does seem fairly that certain East German advisors did have a training role.

In both Zaire and Ethiopia, foreign involvement was on the side of establishing governments and hence, in the line with O.A.U. principles on the territorial integrity of African states. However, reliance on big power military force, with its potential for involving Africans in cold war rivalries for influence, is viewed with alarm by most African leaders. The foreign involvement has produced sharp divisions among non-aligned African states. A few have supported the Soviet/Cuban presence while condemning Western involvement. A larger group has taken the opposite position and an influential middle group has condemned all foreign involvement. In Zaire, an African peace-keeping force took over from the European troops, but an effort to establish a permanent pan-African peace-keeping apparatus, with Western backing, was vetoed by African leaders. The lack of any established African mechanism for assisting governments in repelling invasions leaves little choice for African nations which wish to protect their sovereignty other than calling on the major powers.

The continued presence of Cuban troops on the continent must be construed as a threat to the non-aligned movement. Morocco and Somalia have predicted that 30 to 40 members of the movement will join them in a boycott of the Non-aligned Summit conference scheduled for Havana in september of 1979 if any troops are in Africa at that time. According to one report, the

Cubans are intent upon aligning the non-aligned movement with the USSR, claiming that the two are "natural allies." In any case, the question of foreign military presence on the African continent must be faced by the African non-aligned nations.

An apparent shift in the focus of the non-aligned movement presents broad questions about the movement's continued visibility. The success of the OPEC nations in employing control of a natural resource to dramatically change the economic relations between them and the developed countries has led to hope that similar cooperative actions among the non-aligned, third world nations can bring other such changes. It is by no means clear, however, that non-aligned nations with exploitable resources will see their interests as coinciding with the interests of the non-aligned nations that lack such resources. Many black African nations' economies were severely damaged by the quadrupling of the price oil in 1973-1974. To date, the OPEC countries have committed only a small amount of aid to black nations. In 1975, the OPEC group committed $400 million to black African nations, compared to a total of $3.9 billion committed by the Western powers to the continent in the same year.

As of date, the Third World non-aligned nations have seemed to represent an overlapping coalition in attempts to negotiate economic concessions from the developed nations of the East and West. Negotiating proposals presented at sessions of the United Nations Conference on Trade and Development (UNCTAD) and at the North-South Talks in Paris have lumped together the demands of several distinct groups of non-aligned nations. For example, some countries highly dependent on foreign trade are mostly concerned with altering the terms of international commerce, while others are primarily concerned with controlling the exploitation of natural resources. Negotiating stances which merely aggregate the demands of all third world nations make real bargaining difficult, for if the interests of any sub-group are compromised, the entire coalition of non-aligned, less developed countries could collapse. It remains to be seen whether a coalition approach would best suit the needs of individual African nations.

AN EVALUATION OF CAMEROON AND TANZANIA APPROACH TO NON-ALIGNMENT

At this point, approaches to non-alignment in Cameroon and Tanzania which are among the most politically stable countries in Africa will be examined. The countries have had just one head of state since independence. Julius Nyerere has been president of Tanzania since 1962 and President Ahmadou Ahidijo has governed Cameroon since 1960. Both countries were originally German colonies and after World War I were governed by Britain (in the case of Cameroon, France received most of the colony) first under League of Nations mandates and later as United Nations trust territories. These two nations are underdeveloped and heavily dependent on just a few agricultural products for the bulk of their foreign exchange earnings. Coffee, cotton, sisal, cloves, cashew nuts and diamonds account for approximately three-quarters of Tanzania's exports to countries outside of Africa. Major Cameroon's cash crops are coffee, bananas, cotton and rubber and agricultural products account for about 80 percent of the nation's export earnings.

Indeed, these two countries approach to development have been substantially different. There is some degree of centralized government economic planning in Cameroon, but the state does not seek to dominate the economy. Where the government has contributed capital to industrial projects, it has been in joint enterprises with private industry. Nationalization of industries and agricultural production has never been contemplated. Tanzania under Nyerere has committed itself to development via socialism and self reliance--a uniquely African brand of socialism which centered around the Ujamaa Vijijini program. By organizing the populace into cooperative Ujamaa villages,

Tanzania hopes to increase agricultural output and better provide basic services.   Ujamaa is part of conscious decision to move away from massive investment in a few projects to a broad-based program of rural development.   In Tanzania, banks, large importing and exporting firms, milling firms and the largest insurance company have been nationalized.   Nyerere feels that only by government control of the economy can all of the nation's resources be effectively used to solved problems of human and economic development.

In addition, part of the Tanzania approach to non-alignment has involved diversification in trade and aid relationships.   Since 1965, the Tanzanians have received something more than $330 million in aid from the Chinese Communist, but they have also been successful in obtaining substantial aid from Western nations, notably Sweden and Canada.   On the contrary, Cameroon has remained very much in the French economic orbit.   Through out the 1960s, France accounted for approximately 50 percent of Cameroon's foreign aid and 50 percent of its imports.   More than 70 percent of Cameroon's exports go to Western European countries.   Out of Cameroon's seven commercial banks, six are European-owned and the country's largest insurance company is owned by French.   A French owned aluminum company produces aluminum in Cameroon and has a dominant role in the nation's economy.

Cameroon's foreign political relations have concentrated on other Frencophone African countries.   Cameroon has strictly observed the O.A.U. policy of non-intervention and the country has rejected radical Pan-Africanism.   Tanzania has often been identified with the radical faction in Africa.   Tanzania has taken a leading role in the liberation movements in Southern African and has suffered incursions into its territory as a result.   Tanzania has deviated from policies of nonsheltering anti-Amin Ugandan guerrillas.

In conclusion, since Africa nations are not yet ready to unite politically, a vigorous application of nonalignment principles would seem to offer the best chance for African nations to avoid becoming cold war battleground. In other words, once majority rule is accomplished throughout Africa, the non-aligned movement will face a severe test. At that time, anti-colonialism will largely disappear as a unifying force. The nonaligned movement will stand or fall on the basis of its efficiency in promoting development. It is precisely in this area that the non-aligned movement has most often been frustrated, in spite of the rhetoric heard in Sri Lanka.

In effect, the success of development efforts is highly dependent on the attitude of the more developed nations in the Soviet and Western bloc. Neither the self-reliance approach of Tanzania nor the close economic ties that Cameroon has maintained with France and the other Western powers has been successful in protecting either nation from the disastrous effects of wide fluctuations in international commodities prices. Neither approach has resulted in significant changes in terms of trade with developed nations. In light of the fact that 18 of the world's 28 least developed countries are Africa, it must be concluded that no approach to the crucial development goal of the non-aligned movement has yet shown any success.

In summary, the policy of non-alignment has developed from the determination of independent nations to safeguard their national independence and to legitimate rights of their citizens. The expansion and growth of non-alignment into a wide global movement cutting across racial, regional and other barriers, is an integral portion of important transformations in the structure of the whole global community. It is the product of the global anti-colonial revolution and of the growth of a large number of newly liberated states which opting for an independence political orientation and development, have refused to accept the replacement of centuries old patterns of political domination, exploitation or subordination by new forms. At the root of these transformations and/or trends lies the ever more truly expressed aspiration of member-states for freedom, equality, independence, and their determination to resist all forms of exploitation, subordination and oppression. As Singham and Dinh put in:

> The epoch-making scientific and technological revolution has opened up unlimited vistas of progress but at the same time, prosperity has not come to everybody, and as a result, a major section of mankind still lives under conditions unworthy of man. Scientific discoveries and their application to technology have the possibility of welding the world into an integral whole, reducing the distance between countries and continents to a measure making international co-operation increasingly indispensable and ever more possible. Yet the states and nations comprising the present international community are still separate by political, economic and racial barriers, these barriers divide countries into developed and the developing, oppressors and the oppressed, the aggressors and the victims of aggression, into those who act from positions of strength, either military or economic, and those who are forced to live in the shadow of permanent danger of covert and overt assaults on their independence and security. In spite of the great achievements and aspirations of our generation, neither peace, nor prosperity, nor the right to independence and equality, have yet become the integral and indivisible attributes of all mankind.[15]

Global economic and political relations are entering a new phase characterized by increasing interdependence and also by the desire of nations to pursue independent macroeconomic policies. The democratization of global relations is thus a strong necessity of our period. Meanwhile, there is an unfortunate tendency on the part of some of the big powers as Singham and Dinh perceived to monopolized decision making on international issues critical to all nations. At this point, however, Singham and Dinh commented that:

> This has been the substance and meaning of our strivings and actions; this is a confirmation of the validity of the Belgrade and Cairo Declarations. At a time when the polarization of the international community on a bloc basis was believed to be a permanent feature of international relations, and the threat of a nuclear conflict between the big powers and ever-present spectra

hovering over mankind, the non-aligned countries opened up new prospects for the contemporary world and paved the way for relaxation of international tension.[16]

The immediate danger of a conflict between the super powers has ended because of a total collapse of Soviet Union in 1990s. However, the collapse of Soviet Union has not yet contributed to the security of the small, medium-sized and developing nations, or prevented the danger of domestic wars. The practice of interfering in the internal affairs of other countries, and the recourse to political and economic pressure, threats of force and subversion are acquiring alarming proportion and dangerous frequency. Wars of aggression are raging in the Middle East and Africa and are being prolonged in Iraq and have been extended to Palama. The continued presence of foreign forces in Middle East is posing a threat to national independence and to world peace and security.

Also, the persisted suppression and subjugation of the African citizens in Southern Africa by the racist and colonial minority governments, despite of being a blot on the conscience of mankind, poses a serious threat to world peace and stability. This circumstance is becoming dangerously explosive as a result of the collusion between some advanced nations of the North and the racist minority governments in that part of the globe. Furthermore, the abatement of the cold war has not yet resulted in the disintegration of the military blocs established in the context of great power confrontations.

As we can see, the forces of colonialism, neocolonialism, classical imperialism, racism and apartheid continue to prevent international peace. At the same period western colonialism is trying to perpetuate itself in the garb of neocolonialism a little obvious, but in no distance less harmful, means of economic and political domination over the economies of the less developed states. These characteristics of the present day world tend not only to perpetuate the evils of the past but also undermine the future prospect of the less developed countries in all aspects of life.

NOTES

1. Nworah Dike, "Nationalism vs. Coexistence: Neo-African Attitudes to Classical Neutralism" *The Journal of Modern Africa* (June 1977), p. 224.

2. Ibid.

3. Todia Bojana, "Non-Alignment: A Conceptual and Historical Survey," in *Non-Alignment in the World of Today*, (Belgrade: Institute of International Politics and Economics, 1970), p. 121.

4. Ibid., p.122.

5. Ibid.

6. A. W. Singham and T.V. Dinh, *Conference of The Non-Aligned Countries* 1955-1975 (New York: Third Press Review Books, 1976), p. 21.

7. Ibid.

8. Ibid.

9. A. W. Singham and T.V. Dinh, *Conference of the Non-Aligned Countries 1955-1975* (New York: Third Press Review Books 1976).

10. Singham and Dinh, *Conferences of the Non-Aligned*

11. Kegley and Wittkopt, *World Politics: Trend and Transformation* (New York: St. Martins Press, 1985).

12. Ibid., p. 127.

13. John K. Galbraith, "The Second Imperial Requiem" *International Society* (1982-1983 winter), pp. 84-93

14. Shaplen Robert, "Letter from Sri Lanka," *New York Times* (September 13, 1976), p. 9.

15. Singham and Dinh, *The Conference of The Non-Aligned Countries, 1955-1975*, p.49.

16. Ibid.

CHAPTER 16

The Concept of Economic Integration and the Implications of United Europe in 1992 and Beyond on Ecowas

In this chapter, we are concerned with the techniques, methods and/or strategies of nations that integrate and coordinate their diverse resources and activities across national boundaries. We will further examine and analyze the factors which necessitate the formation of regional or international groupings, the advantages of economic and regional integration as well as the problems associated with the formation of regional units. Also questions to be addressed include: (1) why is it that European Economic Community has experienced relative success in their effort of regional integration why ECOWAS has not? Is there any major differences between these two experiments, if so, can ECOWAS learn anything from EEC to enable it creates an economic union between and among its 16 member states? To this end, the role and implications of EEC in 1992 and beyond on ECOWAS will be critically examined, assessed, and evaluated. This chapter is not going to cover the institutional structures and/or operational aspects of EEC or ECOWAS.

The primary purpose of this chapter is to examine in detail and compare the measures, policies and related actions adopted by the picture of their scope and socio-economic implications. We will further analyze the impact of each strategy in terms of intended aims and objectives, as well as unintended effects. This will enable us to evaluate the strengths and weaknesses of the measures pursued and to make a preliminary assessment of the relative utility of each approach for the grander objective of economic integration.

The cross-national integration between and among nation-states activities, however, would not have been possible were it not for the macroeconomic integration within which it occurs. In other words, it presupposes an institutional framework that allows the cross-national dynamics of money, people, technology, goods and services. It is therefore essential to understand the nature of economic integration in general perspective, and the different mechanisms that it may take.

With regard to macroeconomic level, major integration initiatives are now taking place in both North-America and Europe. Many of other initiatives, though generally smaller in scale and scope, can be found in other parts of the world (specifically in East Asia, Eastern Europe, Latin America, and Africa). In all such instances, the brain behind economic integration is to improve economic performance on a regional basis. The same efforts are being made within the General Agreement on Tariffs and Trade (GATT) to improve economic performance on the international level. Macroeconomic integration fundamentally alters the competitive position of countries both within and outside the integrated region. Therefore, it is for this reason particularly that nations need to closely monitor the progress of integration initiatives and to develop strategies to cope with the changing competitive interdependence.

THE MARKET STRATEGIC CONCEPT OF ECONOMIC INTEGRATION

The idea of specialization occurs at the national as well as business level. Hence, United States exports grain and imports oil and other tropical products from Middle East Countries. This specialization otherwise known as division of labor increases overall output and welfare by allowing each nation to specialize in the production of goods and services in which it has the greatest comparative advantage and least comparative cost over others. However, today, economic integration goes far beyond the internationalization of markets for goods and services. This includes the markets for labor and capital, technology and entrepreneurship, and credit and money.[1] The cross- national dynamics of labor, finance, managers and technology have increased dramatically at this time in modern history.

The proliferation of regional trading blocs, in which preferential trade treatment is given to member nations, may serve to the disadvantage of "outside groups". However, the further development of trading blocs in general can be seen as part of a larger process of global economic integration, through which product and factor (input) flows among national economies lead to increased economic interdependence among countries.

Advantages and Disadvantages of Economic Integration or Regional Co-operation

Specialization which results from division of labor at the national level leads to an improved allocation of production factors; human, financial, and material resources are channeled to their most productive uses. Cross-national economic integration creates larger markets (because businesses can now produce for export markets as well as domestic market), and thus provides the opportunity for greater economy of scales. Another important advantage of economic integration is the competitive stimulus which it creates. For example, International competition in the home market forces domestic businesses to become more effective and thereby produce higher quality products at relatively lower cost than would be the case without the competition. Also, movements of financial capital and technology from abroad similarly improve economic efficiency and performance at home.

As we mentioned earlier, free trade improves resource allocation and leads to potential gains in economic welfare. However, under certain circumstances, regional economic integration may have the opposite effect and may lead to a deterioration of economic welfare. Regional economic integration is beneficial if and when it creates trade and improves welfare by letting consumers shift from the consumption of higher-cost domestic made goods in favor of lower-cost goods from the member states. In such situations, the domestic businesses either become more efficient and competitive, or they turn to the production of products in which they are more efficient to start with.

Furthermore, regional economic integration may have non desirable consequences, however, and may reduce economic welfare under certain situations. This is generally the case when discriminatory treatment against nations that are not members of the trading bloc causes consumers to shift their purchases from low-cost non members of the bloc to higher-cost bloc members. At this point, however, one talks of "trade diversion" instead of "trade creation."

The Background and Typoloty of Economic Integration

The concepts, mechanisms, rationale, and objectives of economic integration vary according to the nature of the national economic systems in reality. Hence, one must differentiate among industrialized capitalist market-oriented and others, particularly the less developed countries in the discussion of the economic integration. Therefore, the typology discussed here is based generally on integration in the industrialized capitalist market-oriented perspective.

1. Economic Union: An economic union is a common market in which there is always relatively high degree of unification of fiscal and monetary policies (including the harmonization of taxes and subsidies within the bloc members). This specifically requires the creation of a supernational authority to regulate and control these aspects of the integration. Also, the need for policy harmonization arises naturally from the effects of liberalizing product markets. For instance, after tariff barriers were seriously reduced to minimum within the European Economic Community, enterprises' profit margins and hence competitive positions became more seriously affected by the different systems of taxation between member states. For this reason, therefore, it was thus decided to harmonize tax structures among the members.

2. Customs Union: In a customs union, tariffs and quotas on trade among member states are removed, but in addition to that, the member states agree to apply to a common tariff on products entering the union from outside. Majority of scholars and analysts view the customs union as a compromise and/or cooperation between free traders and protectionists, on the one hand it realizes the important and benefits of free trade, while on the other hand it provides regional protection from outside competition.

3. Common Market: In a common market, the free movement of the factors of production (that is labor, capital, entrepreneurship, and technology) is added to the free mobility of goods within the customs union. Hence, factor as well as product markets are integrated. Therefore, it isunobstructed factor movement that creates an integrated economy out of separate national economic entities.

However, this free factor mobility has far-reaching consequences for national policies.

4. Monetary Union: Monetary integration requires fixed exchange rates and free convertibility of currencies between member states of the union as well as free mobility of capital within the union. Because convertibility of currency is very important for a customs union and capital movement is free in a common market, the distinctive element in monetary union is the maintenance of constant exchange rates. This however requires that member states of the union harmonize their rates of monetary expansion. Hence, entrance into a monetary union requires a country to relinquish its independent monetary policy. Therefore, the primary objective of monetary union is to improve resource allocation by allowing, encouraging, and supporting the free mobility of financial capital.

5. Free Trade Zone: In a free trade zone, members agree to remove all tariffs and nontariffs barrier on trade passing between them (with an exception of agricultural products), but each member is free to determine unilaterally the level of customs duties on imports coming from outside the preferential trade zone. The latter characteristic raises the possibility of outside imports entering the free trade zone through the member state with the lowest external tariff rates, thus it is essential to create "rules of origin" to ensure that preferential treatment is carried out to products originating within the free trade area. However, without such regulations and rules of origin trade deflection would occur, for nonmember state exports would enter "high duty" member countries through "low duty" member countries, with lowest rate for each product becoming the effective rate for the entire zone.

6. Total Economic Integration: In total economic integration, there is complete unification of economic, fiscal, and monetary policies. Theoretically, it would require

further the utilization of all potential opportunities for effective division of labor and the complete interdependence of all economic activities. Also, some theorists would include a final stage of political integration under the taxonomy of integration. At this point, the participating member states assume the identity of a single nation, in which the central authority not only controls or regulates fiscal and monetary instruments but also has a central parliament with the sovereignty of a nation's government.

This typology described above does not preclude alternative approaches. For instance, one may differentiate between and among trade integration, policy measure integration, factor (input) integration, and total integration. Under such topologies of integration, however, one may differentiate between the concepts of positive and negative integration. Negative integration, in which barriers to trade (such as quotas and tariffs) are eliminated, is a basic method among western industrialized capitalist countries. Here one depends largely on market forces of demand and supply to stimulate further integration. Whereas positive integration, which entails the explicit governmental establishment of coordination mechanisms, is a basic approach of integration among planned economies.

Economic Integration: Who Gets What?

Economic integration may be perceived as a process or a state of affairs. Each of the types we mentioned above might well be considered an ultimate goal in its own effort, and to be sure, it seems that the framers of the European Free Trade Association (EFTA) never intended for such arrangement to go beyond thestage of a single free trade zone. However, if one perceives integration as a process, it is easy to assume that the different types of integration represent stages leading to complete economic (and perhaps political) integration.   As of date, no integration framework in reality fully reflects the ideal types discussed above.   Hence, the EEC has been described as a full customs union, a well established common market, a slightly developed economic union, and weakly emerged political entity.

However, this typology is based on increasingly complex integration models, because each model builds on the previous to expand the scope of integration, it is generally believed that an organic process is included.   For instance, the trade-creating and allocational benefits of tariff elimination in a free trade zone or customs union may be greatly minimized if incongruent domestic measures between member states continue.   In such a condition, the benefits of integration can be increased through the harmonization of measures related to such concerns as market and structural balance, income distribution, and monetary and fiscal policies. This is because trade and payments restrictions are generally interchangeable in terms of their implication on trade flows.   A tariff restricts imports by increasing their prices, whereas exchange control lowers imports by limiting the amount of foreign currencies available to finance them.   At the same token, a quota system can discriminate among various products and sources of supply by the manner in which import licenses are issued, but the same implication can occur by use of exchange controls, bilateral clearing arrangements, and multiple exchange rates.   Therefore, it is often of little value to remove one type of restriction without removing the other.

Structural policies which often need union-wide harmonization in order to increase the benefits of integration include the national treatment of cartels, regional measure, factor movement and other variables which prevent the proper functioning of market forces.   Regional measure is particularly essential in this endeavor because unless a coordinated strategy is taken, theadvanced areas will benefit more from integration than the relatively depressed areas most in need of industrial development.

Also, income distribution between the member countries requires explicit attention because integration aimed mainly at allocational and structural efficiency generally favors the most advanced member states of the union at the expense of those who are in greater need of industrial development. Economic inequalities among member states may well widen unless adequate measures are taken to balance the benefits and costs of integration.

Furthermore, monetary institutions and financial policies are also critical areas of concern. Without fiscal harmonization, the diverse patterns of subsidies, and taxes between members may counteract the gains expected from tariff elimination. Without monetary and financial harmonization, it will be difficult to accomplish the allocational objectives of economic integration in reality. For one thing, monetary harmonization derives from the need to promote economic stabilization objectives. Financial policies taken by one nation to control domestic economic activity will inevitably spill over and seriously affect the activity in other members' nations.

It is for these reasons that one can easily believe that the creation of a customs union inevitably sets forces into motion which lead to further integration along the lines of an economic union. It is true that the static economic gains from optimal resource allocation could be increased by integrating factor as well as product markets and by harmonizing domestic measures between the members that affect competition and economic structure. Meanwhile, such economic gains may be of less preference to the national governments than the pursuit of other necessary and valid objectives, such as the promotion of domestic regional balance, full employment, a more balanced income distribution, and etc.

Moreover, the simplest of integration schemes will beprevented by the absence of a monetary system that facilitates foreign payments by securing the convertibility of currencies.

The dilemma here is that a complete monetary policy harmonization will take away from national governments one of the most effective policy instruments of domestic economic control, such as the use of varying interest rates. As a result, the integration agreements of today have induced governments to use earlier available instruments more aggressively and to develop new policy measures.

REEXAMINATION AND REASSESSMENT OF EEC-ECOWAS STRATEGY FOR ECONOMIC INTEGRATION

It is important to note that the United Europe 1992 is according to Carol Lancaster an exercise in deregulation, an exercise in removal of nontariff barriers to trade between and among member states of European Community. It is not an exercise in monetary union, however, that very removal of the nontariff barriers may propel the Europeans further toward monetary union. At this point, it is going to be difficult to evaluate and assess the impact of United Europe on West African states. This is because there are a number of nontariff barriers that are now still available to member states, such as health standard, technical standards, fiscal policies, immigration policies, border controls, and individual bilateral trading agreements among European and non-EEC nations. However, there will be some relative changes if the Europeans succeed in achieving their objectives in 1992. Again, even if they succeed, we will still do not know what they will put in place of the nontariff barriers. As Lancaster puts it:

> Take the case of bananas. There are individual protocols between individual European countries and banana - producing countries of West Africa and Central America. If I am not mistaken theGermans import bananas from Central America at a somewhat lower price than France imports bananas from the Ivory Coast. These

arrangements are going to be changes, but I don't think it is clear yet what is going to be put in their place and which countries will benefit and which countries will not. Will the bananas now come from Central America for the entire EEC? Or, how will the Ivory Coast and other African banana exporters fit into the new regime?[2]

At this point, however, if in America, there has been a major and serious concern about the execution of the European-wide health standard on beef imports, Lancaster will argue then:

My countrymen may be overexercised about this one, but it has been seen there as a sign that will be put in place, in some cases at least, is stricter Community-wide standards on what is imported, and that contributes to this fear of Europe becoming a fortress as nontariff barriers are removed and something is put in its place around the entire Community. Again, it seems that these are not things to become apprehensive about, but I agree that these kind of changes need monitoring for countries that are concerned and are likely to be affected by them.[3]

The implications of the United Europe in 1992, if it progresses, is more likely to stimulate growth and development within the EEC, although there are some variations and several different estimates of how much growth is stimulated. However, the least conservative estimates do perceive growth being stimulated. This in some way might benefit West African nations. This is true because West African nations are generally exporters of raw materials and when there is not surplus production, economic growth will stimulate the demand for raw materials. West Africa may wish to produce and export manufactured products to the European Economic Community. But the question one has asked is : what are going to be the conditions of entrance into the European, and are these conditions going to be more difficult between now and five to ten years later? Evidence indicates that these conditions might be more difficult because the EEC is likely to become more competitive and that will make it necessary for African manufactured product for exports to become more competitive to penetrate into the community.

Another concern is what type of rules and regulations that are going to replace the nontariff barriers that are going to be removed. Will those rules, conditions, and regulations have serious implications on manufactured products exports to the EEC. On this question Lancaster has this to comment:

> The literature I have seen from parts of the developing world where countries are exporting manufactured goods is now reflecting a concern about access to the Community. Again,well based or not, it is a concern for the newly industrializing countries, and so on. On the question of why the Community is more successful in its efforts at achieving economic integration and ECOWAS is really quite disappointing at achieving any progress on economic integration, I have suggested two major differences that I think are important. One is the economic differences between the Community and West African members of ECOWAS. When the Community was set up, there was some prospect of mutual benefit in the expanded trade that was expected to take place mainly between Germany and France- manufactured goods exports for agricultural exports. It seems that in West Africa and other parts of the developing world with economies that are complementary or supplementary, the opportunities for exchange are much more limited. So, removal of tariff barriers can bring costs immediately.[4]

Added to this point is the issue of benefits. When there are benefits they tend to be centered in one of two nations. The East African Common Market fell apart because Kenya was enjoying the benefits of increased investment opportunity and there was really no way that Kenyans were able to compensate the Tanzanians for what the Tanzaians believed to be lost of investment opportunities. This is the type of problems facing economic integration of the Third World countries.

Following World War II, Europe's position diminished seriously. Empires were divested because of their cost and because of wider acceptance of national self determination. TheWorld War II had devastated the once powerful European economies. European political changes, however still of great significance, could rarely produce shock waves. Militarily, the postwar world was dominated by the United States and Soviet union. International politics was no longer Eurocentric. In reality, Western Europe had become the object of a power struggle between the United States and Soviet Union.

Western Europe faced not only rehabilitation, but also a perceived threat of Soviet invasion. As one Eastern European nation after another generally established communist governments, and as the Soviet Army remained quantitatively large and on station in Eastern Europe, Western European and the United States policy-makers concluded that the Soviet Union was bent on expansion, possibly even into Western Europe itself. At this point, however, both leaders began to wonder how the simultaneous economic and security challenges could be achieved. One way to achieve this according to Papp was through European economic integration. To quote Papp:

> One answer was through European integration. in September 1946, Winston Churchill urged that Franco-German reconciliation within "a kind of United States of Europe" be undertaken. To Churchill, such a reconciliation would create a political-economic counterbalance to Soviet power on the continent, would integrate French and German economies so that future conflicts between the two states would be rendered unlikely, and would lead in general to a more peaceful Europe.[5]

As a result of Soviet threat, United States offered Truman Aid and Marshall Plan as collective aid to European Recovery Plan. Two points must emphatically be made about the Marshall Plan. First, Marshall was not an American "giveaway" program. It was undertaken as much for American economic and security interests as for European Interests. Economically, a revived Europe would serve as a market for American products, and would be a productive avenue for surplus American capital. More market meant more sales, which in turn meant more jobs. Thus, United States Labor Union supported the proposal. Also, since productive investment meant more profit, so United

States business and financial interests further supported the policy.

Second, the Marshall Plan was predicated on European governments jointly studying their needs, jointly formulating a program to meet those needs, and jointly requesting requisite resources from the U.S. to execute their program. Winston Churchill's suggestion had itself been revitalized in a somewhat different and more comprehensive manner. The Marshall Plan was, in essence, the first step on the road toward European economic integration. As papp indicates:

> After Marshall's June 5 address, events proceeded slowly but relentlessly. On April 18, 1948, Western European states signed a treaty creating the Organization for European Economic Cooperation to administer Marshall Plan aid. That aid began flowing the same year. In May 1950, French Foreign Minister Robert Schuman proposed that a European Coal and Steel Community be created that would place all Western European coal and steel production under a common authority. The following year European states signed such a treaty. In June 1955, foreign ministers from West Germany, France, Italy, the Netherlands, Belgium, and Luxembourg decided to integrate Western European economies even more fully as a basis for future political unification. In March 1957, representatives from the same countries signed the Rome Treaties, which created the European Economic Community (EEC) and the European Atomic Energy Commission (EURATOM). In 1962, economic cooperation was extended to agriculture as well.[6]

In the case of West Africa, the ECOWAS was clearly launched in 1975 with the objective of establishing an economic union between its sixteen member countries. The economic goals and objectives of Economic Community of West African states were similar to those of the EEC. ECOWAS'S primary objectives include: to promote growth between and among member states by establishing a market large enough to provide the economies of scale necessary for effective production and to stimulate expanded trade and investment. Emerging firms could expand their production and trade in an ECOWAS market of over 162 million people and potential investors would be encouraged to create new firms to exploit that same market. Expanded trade in agricultural products was to be encouraged, but the establishment of ECOWAS was generally ameans   avenues of encouraging industrial trade and development.

Economic Community of West African states was to accomplish economic union in three sequent stages. At the first three year period, members would freeze their tariffs on goods eligible from intra ECOWAS trade. Within the second stage (eight year) period, members would eradicate their import duties on intra ECOWAS trade. During a Third stage, members would erect a common external tariff and eliminate other barriers to the free movement of services, goods, labor, capital, and technology between themselves.   At this point, however, an ECOWAS secretariat was created to coordinate ECOWAS activities and an ECOWAS Fund was set up to finance community-wide programs and to provide compensation to those countries suffering adverse economic consequences of integration.

However, ECOWAS has accomplished relatively few of its ultimate objectives so far.   Members of ECOWAS have supported measures to freeze and reduce tariffs on intra-ECOWAS trade but have failed to implement majority of these measures.   In 1981 all members of ECOWAS were to have introduced the harmonized customs and trade documents.   But, meanwhile, according to 1983 evaluation and assessment by the Economic Commission for Africa, no member country had done that.   Nor does it seem that member countries have started to reduce their tariffs on imports from other members. Also trade between member states has remained fragamentory at best.

Low performance on the part of ECOWAS has been of considerable concern to the majority of African leaders and policy makers that perceive the establishment of economic unions, specifically between Africa's small states, as important if the whole continent is ever to see the road of industrialization. As Lancaster puts it:

> The ECOWAS failure is especially painful as the EC, long the model for experiments in economic integration throughout the world and especially for ECOWAS, promises to make rapid progress in completing the integration of its own market. Why has ECOWAS failed while the EC has been successful? And what can be done to turn ECOWAS' failure into success? Discussions of the ECOWAS failure often point to the relatively short period of time it has existed, the economic problems, particularly the heavy debt burdens, of many member states, the passivity of the ECOWAS secretariat, and, above all, the "lack of political will" on the part of African leaders in implementing agreed integration policies. These are all very real problems, but they do not go far enough in explaining the disappointing performance thus far or what can be done to improve it in the future.[7]

Despite lack of political will among African leaders, there are also two major obstacles that distinguish ECOWAS from European Community which help to explain its lack of prosperity. First are the economic problems. The two major member states of the original EC-Germany and France had diversified economies with different economic strengths. During the late 1950s when the European Community was first formed, both nations anticipated immediate economic gains from reducing tariffs on trade between them. Germany expected to expand its manufactured goods exports to France and France looked forward to increasing its agricultural exports to Germany.

However, in the case of ECOWAS, the member states economies are similar to one another. West African countries produce and export generally primary goods, whereas they import manufactured goods. For this reason, they have relatively little or nothing to exchange with one another in the short-run, even if barriers to their trade are eradicated. The main benefits from economic integration to the member states of ECOWAS would come less from an immediate expansion in trade than from the new investment that, it is expected, will be encouraged by the establishment of an enlarge market. Also market size is the only factor affecting the future profits, and even not always the most essential one. Political and economic stability in the host nation specifically play a significant role in estimating for future profitability. Hence, the main benefits from economic or regional integration between LDCs including African states will eventually occurred only in the long-run, if at all.

The major difference between the EEC and ECOWAS is in the timing of potential costs and benefits. For EEC members the benefits are immediate. That benefits in some ways could offset the costs of integration. Whereas for ECOWAS member states, the benefits anticipated from economic integration may be realized in the long-run. For this reason, politicians rarely make decisions that carry immediate costs without the prospect of immediate profits as well.

In the case for West Africa, ECOWAS was established very much as a result of Nigerian diplomacy. The Nigerian government then lost some type of interest in ECOWAS and no major pressures on West African countries to join. The French government perceiving Nigeria's effort at regional integration as a deliberate act to deprive it of its economic gains from the francophone and therefore discouraged the francophone countries from participating actively. Also, there was a good deal of skepticism between some francophone nations as to whether they really wanted to involve into any economic or monetary union with Nigeria, since they view Nigeria as sub-imperialist nation. So, in reality the ECOWAS experiment has had pressures quite different from EEC.

What need to be done is an urgent question that demands an urgent answer. One major possibility might simply be to jointly identify an area in the ECOWAS region in which integration might be easily promoted. The European could provide some financing and/or stimulate investment. Sometimes some compensatory financing for nations that could not have immediate benefits from integration to get integration experiment moving in West Africa.

In the early 1987 the European Economic Community unanimously ratified the United Single European Act, committing its members to complete the integration of the European Common Market by the end of 1992. The accomplishment of the objectives of the act is believed to reduce the costs of production and trade and hence boost economic growth and employment in the EEC, promote research and development of a size and sophistication that would permit the EEC members to compete with Japan and the United States in advanced technologically markets; and improve the competitive strength and bargaining power of the EEC on global economic interactions.

It is not clearly define at present what economic and socio-political implications of completing European Economic Community market will have on the rest of international community, including the 16 nations of West Africa (Benin, Cape Verde, the Cote' d'lvoire, Ghana, Liberia, Guinea, Guinea Bissau, Burkina Faso, Gambia, Mauritania, Mali, Nigeria, Niger, Senegal, Sierra Leone and Togo). Much will be determined by the type of community-wide policy measures governing external economic relations that will be adopted as the remaining barriers to the free mobility of goods, services, capital, and labor among EEC members are eliminated. In the first place, these changes could provide incentive and/or encouragement for renewed endeavors at economic integration by the ECOWAS; since we know that the very idea of a West African regional integration economically was born from the EEC. The European Economic Community has long served as a model for economic and regional integration in Economic Community of West African states and elsewhere in Africa. The success of European Economic Community in near completing its economic and regional integration can provide reassurance to those struggling to promote regional integration in West Africa and Africa in general that their objectives are realizable in the long-run. The European Economic Community's experience can further provide lessons and insights for Africans on how they might overcome the problems to their integration endeavors. The European Economic Community now includes 12 active member states and a total population of 320 million. These member states already have common external tariffs and have eliminated internal tariffs. EEC member countries also have a common agricultural policy, which hopes to ensure community wide prices and markets for agricultural products. Meanwhile, nontariff barriers to trade in goods and services, and regulations on the mobility of capital, labor, technology, and entrepreneurship still continued. To complete the EEC market, nontariff barriers and obstacles to the free mobility of goods, services, capital, labor, and technology must be eradicated. Such barriers according to Lancaster include:

Varying technical specifications and standards for traded commodities, different qualifications for individuals providing professional services, differing tax regimes, and physical controls at borders to govern the movement of people and goods. Special trading arrangements between Community members and foreign countries, including 1,000 other goods and services must also be eliminated. In most cases, individual country arrangements will be replaced by EC-wide arrangements of some kind. Completing the EC market does not involve changes in the common agricultural policy, nor at this point, the establishment of a monetary union among EC member states. Progress thus far toward achieving the goals of the Single European Act includes ratification of the act itself and the adoption of roughly 100 out of the 300 regulations necessary to completing the EC market. Decision making on these regulations is based on qualified majority voting , an important change from the system of unanimous voting used in EC decision making in the past. The most contentious regulations have yet to be passed. These include elimination of border controls, harmonization of taxation, and external trade policies.[8]

It is essential to note that all said and done, Europe is still far from complete integration in an economic and political sense. Table 16:1 indicates some of the other diversities that remain in

Western European Countries. Some political progress toward unity also has taken place. The most remarkable single political step took place in 1979 when the first direct elections for the 410 member European Parliament were held. Inspite of this, there is no serious consideration of movement toward European political entity.

Intended Implications

A total completion of European Economic Community market is expected to produce the following results:

> •To lower the costs of production for EC industrial firms by providing the economies of scale associated with larger markets and by reducing the costs of trading associated with physical and bureaucratic barriers to trade, such as internal customs clearances at borders. •To lower the prices of goods and services traded by encouraging greater competition among producers of similar goods throughout the EC. •To promote research and development in high technology, large-scale production lines, which can only occur efficiently in large markets. •As a result of these benefits, to increase investment, employment, and growth in the EC. According to the EC Commission, removing nontariff barriers within the EC could produce as much as a 7 percent increase in Gross Domestic Product, five million new jobs, and a 4.5 percent decrease in consumer prices over the medium term.[9]

Lancaster in his work identifies three main uncertainties with European Economic Community endeavors to complete its market. First, will the EEC in reality be able and willing to agree on the difficult changes necessary to complete the market? There are already some serious concerns on the part of some nations, for instance, Great Britain, about the security effects of eradicating frontier regulations. France and Denmark have indicated some concerns about harmonizing taxes if and when such harmonization would lead to a fall in government revenues. Secondly, what will be the economic implication of elimination of nontariff barriers? One major short-run consequence may be a

TABLE 16:1
SELECTED STATES OF WESTERN EUROPE: GENERAL CHARACTERISTICS

Country	Sq.Km. X 10^6	% in Agriculture	Total (mil.)	Growth Rate %	Literacy Rate %	Ethnic Groups	Religion	Annual Bil.$	Per Capita	Type and Characteristics
Austria	.084	20	7.6	.1	98	German 99	Catholic 85 Protestant 6	118.1	15,573	Federal republic, officially nonaligned but Western-oriented
Belgium	.031	28	9.9	.1	98	Flemish 55 Walloon 33	Catholic 75	155.0	16,690	Constitutional monarchy; NATO member
Denmark	.043	61	5.1	.1	99	Danish 93	Lutheran 97	101.3	19,780	Constitutional monarchy; NATO member
Finland	.337	8 arable	5.0	.3	100	Finn 94	Lutheran 97	87.7	17,678 0	Republic; officially non-aligned but careful not to displease USSR
France	.547	34	56.0	.3	99	French 90	Catholic 90	939.2	16,800	Republic; very independent-minded; works with NATO but military forces not integrated
Greece	.132	29	10.0	.6	95	Greek 98	Greek Orthodox 98	34.9	3,544	Presidential parliament; NATO member
Italy	.301	50	57.6	.2	93	Italian 93	Catholic 99	814.0	14,200	Republic; many political parties from many instable coalition governentment; NATO member

TABLE 16:1 CONTINUED

Country	Sq. Km. X 10⁶	% in Agriculture	Total (mil.)	Growth Rate %	Literacy Rate %	Ethnic Groups	Religion	Annual Bil.$	Per Capita	Type and Characteristics
Netherlands	.401	70	14.8	.5	99	Dutch 99	Catholic 40 Protestant 31 Unaffiliated 24	223.3	15,170	Constitutional monarchy; NATO member
Norway	.324	3 arable	4.2	.3	100	Germanic 95	Lutheran 94	82.6	19,768	Constitutional monarchy; NATO member
Spain	.505	41	39.4	.5	97	Spanish 95	Catholic 99	288.3	7,390	Parliamentary monarchy; newest NATO member
Sweden	.450	7 arable	8.4	.1	99	Swedish 88	Lutherna 94	116.5	13,897	Constitutional monarchy; officially nonaligned but Western-oriented
Switzerland	.041	10 arable	6.6	.3	99	German 65 French 18 Italian 10	Catholic 49 Protestant 48	111.3	16,900	Federal republic; officially nonaligned bu Western-oriented
United Kingdom	.244	29 arable	57	.2	99	English 82 Scottish 10	Anglican 47 Catholic 9	758.4	13,329	Constitutional monarchy; NATO member
West Germany	.249	30 arable	61.0	.0	99	German 98	Catholic 45 Protestant 44	1,120.0	18,370	Federal republic; NATO member

SOURCE: CIA, The World Factbook 1989 (Washington: U.S. Government Printing Office, 1989, extracted from Daniel S. Papp work for understanding (New York: Macmillian publishing company, 1991).

shift in the demand for goods and services from higher cost, less competitive national producers to lower cost producers in other EEC member states. However, if the higher cost producers are unable to increase their productivity and compete as normal, they will be forced to go out of business. It is further expected that completing the EEC market could have a depressing implication on employment and economic activity in specific areas in the short-run. This, however, could lead to a drop in the demand for imports (including products imported from West Africa) in those areas. Meanwhile, there is little or no expectation that diverse economic implications of this kind will last for a long time.

Thirdly, what will be the implication of completing the EEC market on the rules and regulations governing the community's external trade zone? That is the main issue of great expectation to the majority of international community. Majority of foreign nations and their governments fear that internal nontariff barriers and single-nation trade agreements will be replaced with higher nontariff barriers to imports from outside the European Economic Community market.

EARLY MOTIVES AND PROBLEMS OF
REGIONAL CO-OPERATIVE ARRANGEMENTS

Regional integration can be defined as any interstate interaction with less than universal participation developed to meet some common and urgent need. The need according to OLantunde Ojo can be political, economic, military, or it may be of social, technical or residual public desire.[10] However, it is important to mention that regional integration is not a new concept in Africa. During the colonial administration, cooperative agreements abounded between regions governed by each colonial master. For instance, the Royal West African Frontier Force met a regional military need, the West African Customs Union met a regional economic need. What is the different is the brain behind regional cooperation at that time. In the case of Africa during the colonial rule, the motive for cooperation or cooperative arrangements was capitalist interest, the cooperative agreement providing the colonial master's administrative convenience and fiscal needs or protecting their trading companies' monopoly and profits.

After the achievement of political independence in the 1960s, African states began to struggle by developing new patterns and/or techniques of continental and regional cooperative arrangements. Their endeavors have sometimes resulted in what Green and Krishna identified as a "creative destruction" of the colonial agreements or their changes to meet the continental needs and aspirations.[11] Henceforth, the West African Currency Board and the West African Airways Corporation were abolished and replaced with national institutions. The primary motive in the post-colonial struggle for regional cooperative agreements or regional integration has been economic. As professor Jalloh clearly indicates:

> A motivating factor was consciousness of the small size of most of the countries involved and the realization of many of them that without joining others in large groups, they faced serious obstacles in promoting their economic development. In this, they were particularly influenced by the creation and success of the EEC. The reasoning was that if even major countries like France and Germany felt the need for regional integration, such a need was even greater for far smaller and underdeveloped countries.[12]

Also politico-security goals and objectives reinforce the economic motive behind the post-colonial endeavors at regional integration. OLatunde Ojo further observes:

> Small, economically and militarily weak, and politically insecure, the new states needed to present a collective front against the rest of the world, particularly the most developed part of it, in order to break down dependencies, political control and inferior status and to arrest the balkanization of Africa. There was also a defensive motive, arising from fear of larger and more powerful neighbors.

Thus the Union Douaniere et Economique de l'Afrique Centrale (UDEAC) was formed in part out of fear of the economic threat from Nigeria and Zaire and OCAM was partly inspired by fear of Ghana and the Casablanca bloc. The Communaute' Economique de l'Afrique de ol'Quest, (CEAO), was formed 'to counterbalance Nigeria's political and economic weight, in particular, check her attempts to organize a larger economic community'.[13]

Regional or cooperative arrangements and unity for collective self-reliance have been at the heart of African International relations since 1960. Therefore, Pan-Africanism, as an ideology and as a movement on the African Continent, was predicated on cooperation, unity, and solidarity. The struggle to establish new methods of post-colonial, continental and regional cooperative agreements was, in a true sense, an aspect of struggle to institutionalize Pan-Africanism.

It is essential to indicate at this point that the very concept of a West African regional integration economically was born from the EEC and ECA. Again, despite the fact that ECOWAS advocated for economic unity, the idea of an African unity in general should be credited to the Organization of African Unity which in itself took off from the idea of Pan-Africanism first profounded by Sylvester Williams in 1900.

In most entities or integrative endeavors, the gain to be received from this effort becomes the motivating factor that is always considered by the prospective members of such integration. Meanwhile, all integrative endeavors by all dependent economies such as those of West African countries have many variables which work against the successful accomplishment of such integration goals. Integration is a concept that works toward economic and political self reliance of the integrated group. This however runs contrary to neo-colonial interest since most West African states are linked by the history of colonialism to foreign powers to whom they still depend on for their economic, political, and military stability. For this reason, therefore, the colonial powers would do everything possible to thwart the goals of such an integrative endeavor.

The linguistic and cultural diversity of member nations can also constitute a hindrance towards all integration effort. If this statement holds true, then the obvious conclusion would seem that the ECOWAS community with its multiplicity of cultures and languages would experience too much problems in realizing her ambitions.

The level to which economic integration can be accomplished depends largely on the existing circumstances before the integrative endeavor. This, according to Carol Lancaster, has been identified by as size-power homogeneity of the states working for integration, the rate of transactions among them, the extent to which each state shows a pluralistic socio-political structure, and the degree of complimentarily of elite values existing within the proposed union.

Insecurity is another variable that influences the psychology of group behavior. A nation could misperceive the action of another as threatening to her existence and, therefore, generate disruptive indicators to integration. Furthermore, another factor which is necessary to mention here is the degree to which member nations can agree to the laws of the community is dependent on the enforcement mechanisms of the regional group. Also, previous experience indicates that international law, whether of the globe, continent or region is susceptible to national interest. This is because most countries are seen blatantly violating international laws when their national interests are seriously at stake.

The size of the regional institution and its degree of industrial development again determine the management ability of such an organization in the management of her internal crises and/or problems. ECOWAS being a regional organization with the largest number of members in the world when compared to her level of managerial development gives a projective image of the future of ECOWAS.

Imperialistic competition has both prevented and spurred regional integration in West Africa. There is no single doubt for example, that the initial hesitation of the majority of Francophone countries in rallying around Economic Community of West African states was based on their fear of possible French political and economic sanctions. Majority of these nations if not all, depend on France for internal and external defence.

Also, the Anglophone states considered their political and economic relationships with Western Europe and North America stronger than to support ECOWAS. Therefore, one can see how the perception of interdependence with a non-regional actor has intended to prevent West African regional economic integration. On the contrary, the perception of dependence on the imperialistic nations and increasing awareness of its dangers according to Ojo , were a major driving force behind Nigeria's commitment to the creation of ECOWAS in 1975 and behind the agreement by other West African countries to institute the organization. As Ojo comments:

> The reality of increasing economic, and indirect political, dependence on foreign powers and their multinational corporations and the implications for overcoming underdevelopment was a major factor in the North-South confrontation at the sixth special session of the UN General Assembly in 1974 as well as in the ACP-EEC negotiations. The mutual suspicion between France and Nigeria noted in our discussion of CEAO, the continuing French support for that organization and the general French anti-Nigerian and anti-Anglophone proclivity hardened Nigeria's resolve to make ECOWAS a reality. It was hoped thereby to thwart France, reduce its influence and curtail Francophone dependence on France. Because relationships between France and Francophone states are much more formally and alaborately structured than relationships between Britain and Anglophone Africa, the French presence constitutes the bulwark of Western imperialism in West Africa. On balance, then, the integrating impact of non-regional actors may be said to be significantly stronger than their disruptive role, thus supporting the theory that the existence of strong non-regional actors tends to persuade the regional actors to co-ordinate and harmonize policy more intensively.[14]

One of the major reasons for the division between Francophone and Anglophone nations in Africa was the links that most Francophone nations had with the European Economic Community. When the European Economic Community was established in 1957 with the signature of the Treaty of Rome, France argued that special trade preferences and arrangements should be given to its colonies. Inspite of the reluctance of the other members of the European Economic Community, France succeeded in adding section of the Treaty of Rome that provided for the eventual creation of a free trade area between the six founding fathers of the European Economic Community (Italy, Netherlands, Belgium, France, Laxembourg, and West Germany) and their colonies in Africa.

However, after most of French colonies achieved political independence in 1960s, these arrangements were renegotiated, leading to the general compromise of the first "Yaounde Convention" in 1963. With this term, export products from the eighteen associated African states, with the exception of agricultural goods included within the European Economic Community's Common Agricultural Program, were granted preferential and free access to the European Common Market. On this ground, a European Development Fund was created to provide financial assistance from the six member countries to the African partners. In reward, the African partners were obliged to grant tariff preferences to the six member of the EEC.

At this point, however, Anglophone nations were seriously suspicious of the agreements perceiving the "reverse" preferences demanded by the Francophone countries as a new ways of perpetuating neocolonialism, new imperialism and dependence relations. The relations with the European Economic Community, hence, reinforced the Francophone-Anglophone structural division and were a stumbling bloc for intra-African cooperation.

In summary, it would be pertinent to say that the extent to which ECOWAS would achieve her regional integration goal, would depend on if it can overcome all the obstacles indicated above. It is also necessary to mention here that the striking influence at all endeavors of regional integration is self interest or the gains that can accrue to individual member states by being members of such an integrated entity.

POST-COLONIAL ATTEMPTS TO REGIONAL CO-OPERATION IN AFRICA

Before the formation of the Economic Community of West African States, there were numerous attempts at the formation of a West African Union similar to that of the now ECOWAS. One of such efforts in the early 1960s was the idea to institutionalize the concept of Pan-Africanism by Kwame Nkrumah of Ghana who proposed the formation of a Continental Union Government or, at least a political union of West Africa. The proposal was seriously rejected by then Prime Minister of Nigeria, Tafawa Belewa who generally proposed the formation of a regional economic integration which would give fundamental growth in stages in economic, scientific, and technological development. The Nigerian government believed that if economic integration preceded a political union, it would provide for the establishment of a common market. This fundamental difference in views between Nigeria and Ghana, as to whether a political union or an economic integration was more appropriate for the region, left the issue of regional integration for future research in Africa.

As the concepts of integration was gaining ground, there were serious debates within the Nigerian Parliament against and for the establishment of the proposed regional integration by Balewa. The Nigerian government and policy makers argued that integration would reduce Francophone West African nation dependence on France and would increase Nigeria's bargaining power with Europe in their economic relations. They also contemplated that without integration, Nigerian markets were still very fragile to sustain large scale and diversified export and import substitution industries necessary to stimulate economic growth and development.

In view of this, the United Nations Economic Commission for Africa gave its own support to the creation of ECOWAS. In the mid 1960s, they divided Africa in regions for the purpose of economic development. Meanwhile, West African region had fourteen member states in their organization. By October 1966 and April-May 1967, the ECA called specialized meetings in Niamey, Niger and Accra. The first meeting was for discussion about the projected economic association of these states and the second was for the signing of an article of agreement of the then proposed Economic Community of West Africa States, and also for the formation of an interim Council of Ministers.

At this point, however, the Interim Council of Ministers met in Dakar in 1967 and prepared the grounds for an eventual meeting of the heads of state for April 1968 in Monrovia. This summit resulted in the creation of a West African regional entity, although it was attended by only nine members who signed the protocol. During the summit, Nigeria and Guinea were selected to study and report on areas of priority for cooperation between members. By 1969, they had concluded their study and their report recommended cooperation in the areas of: education, trade, transport and communication, cultural exchange and information, energy and heavy industries, research and health.

Nigeria henceforth favored functionalism, the concept that co-operation in non-controversial regions results in the acquisition of knowledge and skills which spill over to make cooperation in politically sensitive regions possible.[15] Furthermore, Nigeria was imbued with the idea of struggle for economic and political power. In West Africa, Nigeria has hegemonic power, but inAfrica as a whole it truly had competitors, such as Zaire and Egypt. The fear of Nigerian hegemonic influence in West Africa therefore, was one of the major reasons for Nkrumah's persistence on immediate United African States. The conflict over the proper method and scope of African unity created a power struggle between Ghana and Nigeria which eventually became a struggle for leadership in West Africa. The struggle was expanded to include the rest of Africa as Nkrumah embarked upon his nucleus unions and engaged in subversive operations against weaker African countries. Ojo has this to say:

> He succeeded only in creating the Casablanca bloc. Nigeria, for its part, sought support for its position in diplomatic fora such as the conferences of Independent African States in Monrovia (1961) and Lagos (1962). Most Francophone states were wary of Nigeria's position but their opposition to Nkrumah's position and personal ambition was strong enough for them to endorse the Nigerian position as the lesser of two evils. Thus emerged the Monrovia bloc. But Francophone wariness of Nigeria's position in particular and of co-operation with the Anglophones in general led to their forming of the Brazzaville group within the Monrovia bloc. To the extent that the divisions among these blocs formed the stuff of inter-African relations in the early 1960s.[16]

The concept of political unity in Africa was laid to rest with the creation and development of the Organization of African Unity. Many scholars and intellectuals on African international relations argued that the OAU was not created to bring about African unity; thus the strong objections by most of the framers to it being called the Organization For African Unity. Therefore the Organization's name has to be changed to the Organization of African Unity. However, under the effort of those countries which supported functional co-operation and coordination and with the help of the United Nations General Assembly resolution as well as independent endeavors of the Economic Commission For Africa, it became clearly accepted that for the purpose of economic co-operation and development, Africa should bedivided into five economically viable sub-entity. These countriesinclude: (1) East Africa (from Tanzania, Kenya to Ethiopia);

West Africa (from Nigeria to Ghana); North Africa consists of
Egypt to Algeria); and Southern Africa (from Zambia to
Angola).

Integration or co-operative efforts and institutions centered
around these regions. Meanwhile, a number of mini-schemes
inherited from the colonial period continued and others grew in
direct response to divergent political and ideological philosophies
and needs. At the same time, the search persisted for viable
region-wide complement. As of date, only in West Africa do we
have a region -wide institution-ECOWAS. But West Africa
however has the largest number of mini-schemes. For instance,
In 1979 alone there were more than thirty inter-governmental or
semi governmental institutions with a predominant West African
membership. The large majority of mini-schemes are concerned
with economic growth and development, thus underlining the
reality that the motivation for regional cooperation has been
economic.

THE PROBLEMS OF FUTURE ECOWAS

Having briefly commented on the internal and external influences
that predated the birth of ECOWAS, at this point, it becomes
necessary to mention the members who finally constituted the
ECOWAS group. These include Mali, Cape Verde, Upper
Volta, Togo, Benin, Ivory Coast, Ghana, Cameroon, Niger,
Nigeria, Guinea, Gambia, Liberia, Guinea Bissau, Sierra Leone
and Senegal. The treaty that gave birth to this multilateral
community aimed to achieve:

> to promote cooperation and development in all fields of economic
> activity particularly industry, transport, telecommunications,
> energy, agriculture, natural sciences, commerce, monetary and
> financial, and social and cultural matters, to raise the standard
> ofliving of its people, increase and maintain economic stability,

foster relations among members.[17]

In the same direction, the community will, by stages ensure among other things: abolition of nontariff barriers on trade among members; the elimination between member states of custom duties and similar charges; free movement between members of person, services and capital; harmonization of agricultural policies and promotion of common projects in the member states, especially in marketing, research and agro-industrial enterprise; a common customs, tariff and commercial policy toward third countries; harmonizing economic and industrial policies of members and eliminating disparities in development; joint development of transport, communication, energy and other infrastructural facilities; harmonization of monetary policies; establishment of a fund for cooperation, compensation and development and other activities to further the aims of the committee.[18]

Now the time has come to review some of the major problems and issues facing ECOWAS as an independent organization, we discovered that finance has been a serious problem ECOWAS has encountered since its inception. Realizing the strategic role that finance plays for effective running of an organization, it becomes evident that ECOWAS is not doing perfect, judging from her perpetual state of acute finance. Uka Ezenme in his article on "plenty of words but little action" in West African magazine of November 19, 1984, argued that financial contributions of members show a random pattern. His results show that by April 30, 1981 only one nation had paid any of its contributions to the operational budget of the Executive Secretariat for 1981. In 1980, only seven nations contributed to the Organization. Seven members had, as of that time, not settled their 1979 contribution, three their 1978 contribution and one country had not paid her contribution for 1977. This brings the total outstanding areas for these states to $13,133.[19] The conclusion that one would be left with is that members of the ECOWAS community have not fully committed themselves to the institution. No organization can do well without enough finance. To keep the organization going, sometimes the management is forced to look for funds elsewhere, and in most cases, from foreign countries. This in itself is ironic since perpetuating West African dependence on foreign countries has no place for reconciliation with the institutional objective of self reliance and/or political autonomy.

The lack of implementation of the community's decisions at national levels for the large majority of decisions is a very serious problem facing the ECOWAS. Between 1978 and 1979, for example, when the first protocol was signed by the authority of ECOWAS, a total of eleven protocols have been signed but ratification of these protocols by individual member states have been very slow. About six members have ratified none of the protocols.[20] People start to wonder at this point whether all this are signs of downfall of the institution.

In our own view, this is another indication of lack of total commitment to the community by member nation. The main reason for the formation of ECOWAS is to remove, to a certain degree the dependency status of most West African nations. The performance after five years of the formation of ECOWAS showed that it would be impossible for West African countries to remove from themselves the status of dependent relations. This position can be supported from the data on trade pattern between West African states and the EEC on imports and exports. See table 16:2, 16:3, and 16:4 respectively.

Table 16:2 indicates quite simply the position of the former colonial powers as trading partners of the new African Countries. Of the states indicated in table 16:2, for twenty-three, nearly half of the total, the former colonial power was the largest single market for their exports. In addition, nine African states looked to the former colonial power as their second largest market. As for imports, table 16:3 indicates that the majority of the Africanstates-Thirty-five or 81 percent of the total drew the

TABLE 16:2
ECOWAS EXPORTS TO THE EEC (MILLIONS OF $US)

ECOWAS MEMBERS	EXPORTS TO EEC: 1981	1982	1983	1984	1985	1986	1987
BENIN	15	14	35	98	141	109	74
BURKINA FASO	24	23	8	30	34	52	69
CAPE VERDE	2	2	2	1	1	3	6
GAMBIA	14	17	30	26	12	14	37
GHANA	333	334	366	197	255	331	411
GUINEA	200	176	202	273	272	272	323
GUINEA-BISSAU	10	11	8	9	6	5	4
IVORY COAST	1499	1278	183	1476	1783	1952	1805
LIBERIA	352	356	38	317	429	502	624
MALI	47	68	69	82	59	62	58
MAURITANIA	274	196	89	192	157	194	190
NIGER	212	233	233	179	173	28	369
NIGERIA	6665	6759	6939	7714	7975	4127	3120
SENEGAL	190	261	288	258	219	271	315
SIERRE LEONE	136	75	73	83	106	121	126
TOGO	129	99	83	120	106	144	18
TOTAL ECOWAS IMPORTS FROM EEC:	10101	9902	9992	11055	11729	8375	7647

TABLE 16:3
TOTAL IMPORTS FROM EEC

ECOWAS MEMEBERS	1981	1982	1983	1984	1985	1986	1987
BENIN	302	276	206	83	197	242	234
BURKINA FASO	170	88	129	102	134	221	214
CAPE VERDE	54	56	57	49	55	86	93
GAMBIA	59	54	54	49	62	88	102
GHANA	459	306	604	257	327	427	509
GUINEA	199	81	81	196	208	253	298
GUINEA-BISSAU	26	34	39	34	41	33	43
IVORY COAST	1211	1081	108	822	927	187	1260
LIBERIA	150	122	153	146	550	350	258
MALI	132	1786	181	179	224	243	240
MAURITANIA	268	272	236	232	136	205	234
NIGER	245	210	89	153	190	184	192
NIGERIA	11294	8461	4720	3523	3747	3154	2906
SENEGAL	532	491	530	441	426	490	720
SIERRE LEONE	142	101	60	67	69	93	95
TOGO	258	244	175	172	228	326	339
TOTAL ECOWAS IMPORTS FROM EEC:	15528	12213	8490	6585	7521	7562	7737

SOURCE: IMF Direction of Trade Statistics, 1988.

TABLE 16:4
Official Development Assistance from the EEC to West Africa
(Millions of $US)*

COUNTRY	1984	1987
Benin		
EEC	37.6	76.6
World	77.6	135.7
Burkina Fasco		
EEC	86.4	88.3
World	188.6	283.1
Cote d'Ivoire		
EEC	112.7	233.4
World	127.8	253.7
Gambia		
EEC	38.9	94.6
World	132.2	214.0
Guinea (Bissau		
EEC	25.2	36.4
World	55.2	104.4
Liberia		
EEC	21.3	22.2
World	133.2	78.4
Mali		
EEC	209.7	178.6
World	320.3	364.5
Mauritania		
EEC	50.5	89.2
World	175.0	177.7
Niger		
EEC	83.5	133.3
World	81.0	348.0
Nigeria		
EEC	13.8	33.3
World	33.0	69.3

TABLE 16:4 CONTINUED

Senegal		
EEC	155.2	317.
World	368.0	642.
Sierra Leone		
EEC	18.8	32.
World	60.8	68.

*Figures show disbursements of total ODA from EEC to West Africa.
Source: OECD, Geographical Distribution of Financial Flows to Developing Countries, Paris, 1989.

largest proportion of their imports from their former colonial powers.

According to *Economist*, in 1980 2.73 percent of the total West African export and 3.79 percent of import went to other countries in the region when compared to 88.65 percent and 82.15 percent respectively, to the industrialized countries. Intra-West African trade was dominated by food items, handicrafts and petroleum.[21] ECOWAS's continued dependence on the western countries and their institutions would generally affect its behavior towards West Africa regionalism and this obviously a problem to the survival of the Organization.

Also, the members of ECOWAS in reality, depend largely on their primary products for revenue from export. Their individual leaders want to achieve immediate industrialization and economic development; it however implies that for national economic interest and their domestic political support, leaders of West African states pursue national goals as opposed to striving for regional dynamics. It becomes not surprising why most ECOWAS member states show a lack of commitment toward the proper functioning of this regional cooperation.

Another serious problem for ECOWAS that need to be indicated in this research is the diversity of currencies for the West African countries. Senghor of Senegal describes this as a niggling "very complex exchange controls" that had hurt earlier efforts to create a West African economic union.[22] Because the

Francophone West African states use the France CFA in contrast to their Anglophone states, there is bound to be delays in payment caused seriously by the inconvertibility of their currencies. This further imposes a problem to ECOWAS members.

Furthermore, another important issue which should not be overlooked in this research is the fact that ECOWAS' operation or activities is influenced by competition amongst member states. This is so true of members colonial economic structure. As we indicated earlier, most ECOWAS countries produce few and similar products which compete amongst themselves for the foreign market, foreign technology and foreign financial assistance. It is also a reality that revenue from tariffs vary in importance to member states. To many, this is a main source of revenue which makes member states quite unwilling to implement most decisions taken to eliminate tariffs on trade amongst member states. All these factors again have negative impact to the integration scheme of ECOWAS.

Again, one of the problems to be considered as a possible threat to the proper functioning of the ECOWAS community is the issue of frequent changes in government in West African nations. Specific instances are the most recent ones involving Dow of Liberia, Flight Lt. Jerry Rawlings of Ghana, General Babangida of Nigeria and the recent change in government in the Sudan. This change in government, some through unconstitutional means might bring to power leaders whose ideological perspectives are inconsistent with the purpose for which ECOWAS is established.

The creation of a tribunal to enforce laws affecting disagreement amongst member states is another source of tension among the ECOWAS community. Past experience of nation states in regard to international law indicates that in most instances, when the laws passed by international organizations do not favor individual nations, the nation involved violate these laws seriously because they know that there exists no enforcing mechanism to take punitive action against them. This is not peculiar to ECOWAS alone. Other international organizations like the United Nations, O.A.U., O.A.S., O.E.C.D., E.E.C. and many others faced the same problem. However, this does not rule out the fact that such deliberate violation of organizational laws constitutes a big problem for the ECOWAS community.

According to the United Nation's Economic Commission for Africa report on ECOWAS *West Africa* November 1984, it was believed that one of the major problems of ECOWAS is the multiplicity of inter-governmental economic organizations in the sub-region. As of when it was reported, it pointed out that there were about thirty-two of such organizations involving the sixteen members of ECOWAS in various combinations with some countries belonging to as many as sixteen while others as few as four. Since their economic objective might differ from their strategy, the end result is the highlight of their historical differences and consequently dissipating of energy and a lot of overlapping activities.

THE CONSEQUENCES OF EUROPE 1992 ON ECOWAS

In order to understand the dynamic nature of Europe 1992 on ECOWAS, it becomes necessary to review economic links between the sixteen member states of ECOWAS and the EEC. However, economic and trade relations between ECOWAS and EEC posses the following characteristics according to Lancaster:

> The EC remains the major trading partner of most of the West Africa 8, amounting to over half of the total exports of many of those countries.
> At the same time, the total value of West African trade with the EC has fallen over the past several years as the volume of West

and as prices for commodities exported by West African countries have dropped.

Reliance on the EC as an export market has diminished over the last decade for almost all countries of West Africa (with Nigeria as the major exception).

The vast majority of the exports of the West African 8 to Europe are primary products, including cotton, coffee, iron, ore, timber, fish, fruits and vegetables, phosphate, and petroleum.[23]

Although accurate statistical data on private direct and portfolio investment by the European Economic Community in ECOWAS are not available, but certain things are visible from recent statistics on overall investment in these states as well as from past data on private flows by source. In West Africa, private direct and portfolio investment had remained unchange or even falling in 1980s. During the same period, the only nation in West Africa that experienced an increasing change in private flows is, Guinea, where changes in major and/or official government policies encouraging private, direct investment have stimulated foreign interest. Majority of the private, direct and portfolio investment within ECOWAS member states had come from EEC, with Britain, Germany and France as the main investors. This is more likely to remain unchange, although Japanese investment in West Africa has been growing; the United States still remains a minor investor except in some areas in Nigeria and Liberia.

With reference to concessional aid, the European Community including the European Development Fund (EDF) and aid from individual European Community member nations constituted the largest source of foreign aid for all but two of the ECOWAS member states in 1987.[24] Lancaster further provides the overall historical links between EEC and ECOWAS in this way:

> Statistics cannot capture fully the extent of economic links between West Africa and the EC. All West African countries, plus 50 other African, Caribbean, and Pacific (ACP) countries are part of the Lome Agreement with the EC, which provides preferential access to the EC market for certain exports from developing country

members of the agreement and for financial and technical
cooperation among ACP countries and the EC. Negotiations are just
getting underway on the fourth Lome Agreement. Finally, seven
West African countries-Benin, Burkina Faso, the Cote d'Ivoire,
Mali, Niger, Senegal, and Togo-are members of the Union
Monetaire Ouest Africaine (UMOA), one of only three monetary
unions that exist today among independent countries. (The other two
are the monetary union among five central African countries and
France and the land area between Lesotho, Swaziland, and the
Republic of South Africa.) With a common currency tied to the
French franc, these countries enjoy particularly close monetary and
financial links with that country.[25]

In conclusion therefore, trade and economic relations between
the members of ECOWAS and the EEC still remain very close.
The European Economic Community still remains ECOWAS'S
main export market and the major source of foreign aid.
However, in the area of trade, ECOWAS dependence on the
European Community market is steadily declining in real term.
How then is the completion of the EEC market likely to influence
these relationships?

In the long run members of ECOWAS will want to become
producers and exporters of manufactured products. If this
happens, the European Community market will be of an
important asset for them. If new controls or regulations
(including health, trade or technical specifications) governing
imports of textiles and other light manufactures indicate to be
more restrictive than those recently in place, the EEC market
may be even more difficult to penetrate than at present time.
That may possibly discourage further investment in
manufacturing for export from ECOWAS to the EEC.

Also, in terms of short run implication, the elimination of
internal, nontariff barriers to trade in goods and services between
and among EEC member states may not have any major
consequence on the sixteen member states of ECOWAS.
Majority of ECOWAS exports to the EEC market are
primaryproducts not directly affected by the changes in nontariff

barriers. ECOWAS is more likely to be affected by any arrangements or agreements resulting from the Urguay Round of GATT tariff negotiations, which may reduce the margin of preferential treatment enjoyed by the members of ECOWAS to the EEC under the Lome Arrangement. Although, there are certain areas where changes, as yet unknown, associated with completing the EEC market could affect ECOWAS'S interests and should remain a major and serious concern to these states until those changes are established. For example, the following questions as (1) what EEC-wide agreements will replace current bilateral agreements governing imports of textiles, bananas, footwear, and other products similar in nature that members of ECOWAS now export or might be able to export to EEC in the near future?; Will European Economic Community wide agreements be more or less restrictive than those recently encountered by West African Exporters?;How will European Economic Community policy measures on immigration impact on ECOWAS?; Will Europe 1992 have more restrictive immigration controls than already available to different nations?; What European Economic Community-wide agreements will be put in place to govern health standards and technical specifications governing imports from overseas?; What changes will EEC member states likely to make in their export credit programs as they reach near completion of their market? Since there are already reports on the need to unify export credit measures and the possibility of establishing a EEC-wide export credit agency. How will any of these changes affect access by ECOWAS member states to export credits from the EEC?; and finally if in the short run economic effect of completing EEC market is recessionary, how will that influence the EEC demand for the primary good imports from ECOWAS?

The major changes leading to "United Europe 1992" may further have consequences for the flow of investment to the members of ECOWAS. However, if completing the EEC marketencourages increased investment in Europe, there may be a smaller flow of investment to the members of ECOWAS in the future. Complete elimination of nontariff barriers between and among EC could well put additional pressures on member countries to move toward monetary union. Bearing in mind that it will be difficult, for instance, to operate monetary compensation agreements on intra-EEC trade in agricultural products, this will seriously affect agricultural product exports to EEC from ECOWAS. In reality, each step toward economic integration tends to increase additional pressures for yet further steps. If there should be a tendency toward forming monetary union within EEC members, the question of how to handle the Union Monetaire Ouest Africaine will seriously arise.

The economic changes brought by a completion of EC market by 1992 promise to be of major significance, both for Europeans and the rest of the global community. Since many details of the changes needed to accomplish the objectives of the Single European Plan are not certain, ECOWAS should seriously monitor some of these proposed changes very closely and ensure that their views and interests are taken into consideration.

THE FAILURE AND IRRELEVANCE OF CONVENTIONAL THEORY TO INTEGRATION AMONG AFRICAN STATES

Kadar has argued that the concept of integration by means of the market cannot even be progressed rationally if the economic environment is characterized by the general backwardness of market interactions.[26]   For this reason, therefore, economic integration strategies in African states must be geared to the specific characteristics of the economies involved.   Market-oriented integration based on orthodox economic theory may well (and indeed has been) either disfunctional or largely inefficientin the African context.

Even if markets in Africa and other less developed countries were effectively developed for western style integration, other variable factors would limit its effectiveness. Conventional theory believes that greater benefits will obtain from regional economic integration when (1) existing foreign trade is small relative to domestic production, and (2) a relatively large amount of trade is conducted with prospective integration partners prior to bloc formation. These conditions are generally the reverse of those typically found in African states, whose foreign trade is usually large relative to domestic production and whose intragroup trade is usually a very minor component of total trade. Therefore, economic integration or regional cooperation schemes based on the conventional wisdom may be at worst positively dangerous for African states. This theoretical concept of economic integration is irrelevant in reality because less developed countries including African states, depend largely on the exportation of primary goods and hence on the global markets, and integration is unlikely except in the very long run to affect essentially the volume of resources allocated to the production of such products. This is strictly very harmful since the imports of African states consist of mainly of intermediate products and finished manufacturers, which majority African countries produce either not at all or very inefficiently, so that they cannot compete successfully against the exports of industrialized capitalist countries, even assuming some degree of protection.

Consequently, it is in this context that we discover that the rationale for economic integration between and among African states does not lie in static benefits to be realized from changes in the existing pattern of trade or from the exploitation of comparative advantage based on existing pattern of production. Instead, the rationale for economic integration between and among African states is based on perspective benefits from rationalizing the emergent structure of production of the creation of regional markets on the more fundamental problems of these states (including the need to increase the opportunities for profitable investment by both domestic and international firms, and the need to mobilize unemployed resources). In reality, it is the drive to industrialize that is the main economic motivation for regional cooperation or economic integration among African states, and this shared motivation differentiates regional and/or economic integration in Africa from that among Western World. Integration is hence perceived as an integral part of development policy rather than as a logical consequence of development once accomplished.

Furthermore, given the high priority industrialization and development as objectives of regional integration among African states, one must address the issue of great disparities in the development levels of member states under such circumstances, reliance mainly on market mechanisms would be detrimental to the less developed members, for economic activity and the gains of integration would tend to concentrate in the relatively developed member states. Hence, economic integration endeavor between and among less developed countries of Africa specifically include the planned allocation of scarce resources and investment activities, with unilateral benefits and concessions extended to the less developed member states. Specific compensatory measures have involved preferential treatment in regard to taxes, tariffs, capital flow, and income distribution. However, none of these policies to date has been successful in substantially stimulating industrialization and development between and among African regional groupings.

Also, it is important to note that the existing pattern of trade relations have prevented economic or regional integration among African states. For example, the success of Western European integration has been based in part on the historically developed higher level of regional division of labor already existing when integration was launched in Western Europe. At that time, members were already conducting around one-third of their foreign trade with one another. When integration schemes were launched in Africa, however, the ratios of trade among members were 8 percent for the Communaute Economique de l'Afrique de l'Ouest, 6 percent for the Mano River Union and only 5 percent for the Economic Community of West African States. Hence, existing trade patterns tended strongly to support regional and/or economic cooperation in the European Economic Community, but to undermine it in Africa. Under these circumstances, the immediate welfare benefits from the allocative consequences of integration are small.

However, given the existing trade patterns, the only viable integration arrangement among African states is one which complement, rather than substitutes for, a strategy of more active participation by the less developed countries of Africa in the global economy. Economic integration or regional cooperation is hence perceived as a means of removing external barriers to industrialization and development through the deepening of import substitution on a regional level. Particularly in Africa today, economic integration methods must explicitly be designed to ameliorate the serious balance of payments problems. To be sure, the strategy of import substitution clearly changes the composition rather than the quantity of hard-currency imports (by replacing imports of good that can be produced within the region with those of capital and intermediate goods). Also a balance of export promotion with import substitution must be accomplished, because Western Markets for African exports are a crucial element of debt minimization.

In the final analysis, the continuing economic and financial crisis in Africa during the 1980s surely creates conditions unfavorable to regional and/or economic integration. Between 1981 and 1985 intraregional trade among less developed countries in the Western Hemisphere declined by 28 percent in value, generally because of import austerity measures and because the heavily indebted nations were forced to shift their exports away from regional arrangements towards convertible currency markets. In conclusion therefore, the severity of the situation has perhaps convinced many in Africa that regional economic integration is the only viable alternative to the continental problems. Thus, there has been a renewed effort in Africa for regional economic cooperation.

NOTES

1. Paul Marer and John M. Montias, eds., *East European Integration and East-West Trade* (Bloomington: Indiana University Press, 1980), pp. 2-38. For further analysis on regional integration, see the work by Anne Daltrop, *Political Realities: Politics and The European Community* (New York: Longman, 1990). Erast B. Haas, *Beyond the Nation-State* (Standford University Press, 1969). Michael Hodges, *European Integration* (New York: Penguin, 1972). Emile Novel, *Working Together: The Institutions of the European Community*, Office for Official Publications of the European Communities (London, James Currey, 1980). C. C. Twitchett, *A Framework For Development: the EEC and ACP* (London: Allen Unwin, 1981). See also James Barber, *"Trade Union in the Community"* in the European Economic Community: Work and Home (London: Open University, 1974). James Barber and Bruce Reed (ed), *"Transnational Political Forces"* in European Community Vision and Reality (London: Croom Helm, 1973).

2. Carol Lancaster, "Completing the European Market" ed in Olesegun Obasanjo *The Impact of Europe in 1992 on West Africa* (New York: Crane Russak, 1990) p. 26.

3. Ibid.

4. Ibid., p. 27.

5. Daniel S. Papp, *Contemporary International Relations: Framework For Understanding* (New York: MacMillan Publishing Company, 1991) p. 298.

6. Ibid., p. 29.

7. Lancaster, p. 36.

8. Ibid., pp. 29-30.

9. Ibid.

10. OLantunde Ojo, *African International Relations* ed. (New York: Longman, 1987).

11. Green and Krishna, *Economic Co-operation in Africa: Retrospect and Prospect*, (London: Oxford University Press, 1967).

12. Abdul Aziz Jalloh, "Recent Trends in Regional Integration in Africa," Nigerian *Journal of Internal Affairs*, 1980 p. 72.

13. Ojo, p. 143.

14. Ojo, p. 180.

15. Ernst Haas, *The Uniting of Europe* (California: Stanford University Press, 1958). Bela Balassa, *The Theory of Economic Integration* (Homewood ILL: Richard D. Irwin, 1961). Jack Barnouin, "Trade and Economic Cooperation Among Developing Countries," in *Finance and Development* (1982). See the analysis and funcitonal approach in the explanation of European Community by Ali M. ElAgraa, *International Economic Integration* (New York: St. Martin's Press, 1982) Fritz Machlup, *A History of Thought on Economic Integration* (New York: Columbia University Press, 1977). David Morawetz, *The Andean Group: A Case Study of Economic Integration Among Developing Countries* (Cambridge, Mass.: MIT, Press, 1974).

16. Ojo, p. 144.

17. *West Africa* (May 15, 1978), p. 1005.

18. Ojo, *African International Relations*. Larry Willmore, "Trade Creation, Trade Diversion and Effective Protection in the Central American Common Market," *Journal of Development Studies* (1976). Kenneth Swiltzer, "The Andean Group: A Reappraisal," *Inter American Economic Affairs* 27 (Spring 1973). Saleh M. Nsouli, "Monetary Integration in Developing Countries" *Finance and Development* (1981). R. J. Hersley, "Industrial Organization and Economic Development," *Economic Internationals* (August - November 1978). M. I. Little, "Import Controls and Exports in Developing Countries", *Finance and Development* (September 1978). Martin Cave and Paul Hare, *Alternative Approaches to Economic Planning* (New York: St. Martin's Press, 1981). Peter Drucker, "Multinational Corporation and Developing Countries: Myths and Realities" *Foreign Affairs* Feb. 1974).

19. *Economist*, October 16, 1981.

20. *West Africa*, May 16, 1980.

21. *Economist*, July 21, 1980.

22. Ibid., p. 43. See G. C. Abangwu, Systems Approach to Regional Integration in West Africa *Journal of Common Market Studies* (1975). Olajide Aluko, *Ghana and Nigeria 1957-1970: A Study in Inter- African Discord* (London: Collins, 1976). Andrew Axline, Underdevelopment, Dependence, and Integration: The Politics of Regionalism in the Third World, *International Organization* (1978). Ernst Haas, "The Study of Regional Integration: Reflections on the joy and anguish of pre theorizing," in Leon N. Lindberg and Stuart A. Scheingold (eds) *Regional Integration: Theory and Research* (Cambridge, Mass: Harvard University Press, 1971). Wood Hazel Arthur (ed) *African Integration and Disintegration* (London, Oxford University, 1967).

23. Lancaster, p. 31.

24. Ibid.
25. Ibid.
26. Bela Kadar, *Problems of Economic Growth in Latin America* (London: Hurst and Co., 1980), p. 127.

CHAPTER 17

Conclusion: The Future Characteristics Of Africa Toward The Twenty-First Century?

Writing a conclusion for this text is a difficult task, for its objective is to introduce the subject, to identify and explain the relationships, to expose political and economic dilemmas, to demonstrate policy prescriptions based on alternative theoretical perspectives, and eventually, we believe, to stimulate further analysis, explanation, interpretation and research. Instead of attempting to put together and integrate the most essential points analyzed in earlier chapters, we just provide discussion on the major and important characteristics of the field of African political economy that have significant impact on scholarly analysis and policy making.

By every indication, Africa continent is in a position of profound economic, political, ideological, and social crisis. Growth rates have decreased rapidly since 1970s in every sector and have overstripped or matched by increasing population growth rates. Also, food production per capita has declined over the two decades by up to 19 percent in some nations and by 8 percent over the entire continent. Industrial growth rates have been generally very minimum or even negative as businesses dependent on scarce foreign exchange for intermediate and raw materials imports have had to break down. Furthermore, foreign exchange rates have become very scarce as export revenues have decreased or even negative. Meanwhile, the resultant rises in balance of payments deficits have led to massive borrowing from industrial nations and their financial establishments. As the majority of less developed countries have moved their pattern and structure of exports away from dependence on primary goods, African states have made little or no success in this arrangement. While borrowing has increased to finance payments deficits, the burden of servicing the debt has also increased rapidly.

In addition, the severe drought which has seriously affected majority of this zone at different periods during the last two decades has in reality reduced food production and resulted in the deaths of millions through hunger, starvation and/or malnutrition. This has caused a severe strain on the balance of payments as food imports have had to be risen. Meanwhile, the main causes of Africa's economic predicament and the nature of efficient and/or effective solutions are not really as clear and are the subject of general debate. Even the International Monetary Fund (IMF) and the International Bank for Reconstruction and Development (IBRD) have been forced to agree that Africa's economic crisis is not mainly the product of shortcoming in macroeconomic policies but also of `a little success in export structure' and of prolonged drought.[1] The main issue that stands at the front of the debate is the degree to which International Monetary Fund stabilization measures and the World Bank structural adjustment market liberalization and incentive measures result in the continuation of this less success export structure and excessive vulnerability to the condition of the wider international economy.

Moreover, accelerating food insecurity has been a disturbing characteristic of the economic malaise in African Political economy. The evidence is more fragmentary and less robust than could be believed, but there is reason to assume that the number of people without enough to eat, on minimal nutritional standards, is increasing absolutely and relatively. However, this hunger indicates every possible sign of becoming worse unless important and counter measures are put into operation.

Between 1965 and 1970, the average annual production growth of major food crops in African economies has increased by 1.6 percent, but the population has increased by 2.8 percent. Therefore, food production has consistently lagged behind population growth now for over twenty-seven years, food production per capita has been decreasing at an annual rate of 1.2 percent. In these situations, it is not surprising therefore that food imports into African continent have been accelerating by more than 8 percent per year. A critical evaluation of measures prescribed by these two international institutions requires an accurate view of what has caused the global depression, recession or crisis and what the system is between African states and the International economy.

Also, the increasingly crude form neocolonialism, neo-imperialism and external economic dependency have attempted to override the relatively more subtle mechanisms in which capitalist, industrialized countries determine the course and/or direction of economic development or underdevelopment in the less developed countries including African states. In the case of Africa, the continuing dependence of most nations on export markets for raw materials, sometimes controlled by those purchasing for the large food and mineral consuming industrial corporations, is the major form of external hegemony. Again, the need for capital investment, foreign economic assistance, and capital borrowed on the commercial money and financial markets, are essentially ways by which the unequal interdependent relation of advanced capitalist economies of accumulation and African suppliers of primary commodities is affirmed.

Meanwhile, this is not the time to enter into a discussion of development and underdevelopment theory. Some discussion of this type will be found somewhere in this book. At this point, however, it is generally certain that the character or structure of internal class relations and the balance of political forces within the ruling class play a major role in determining and/or shaping the degree to which external economic interests are well maintained in African political economy. Furthermore, in Africa, as elsewhere in the less developed countries, the military and its civilian political arrangements play a serious and dominant role in the process of reinforcement of, or resistance to external economic hegemony. The major ways of receiving military equipment from one or other major power bloc, and/or even on the private market, will particularly affect the character and structure of external economic interactions. Also, the relationships between national and foreign capital and between foreign capital and the internal state, behave as a mechanism for continued external economic control. It is not generally true or false that foreign capital's acceleration has prohibited the growth and development of African economy. However, what seems to have been evident has been the relative strength of the local, state and its capability to support capital accumulation.

In Africa today, Internal structural arrangement and acts of nature have compounded by declining global economic relations. These variable factors have been responsible for accelerating the problems that now constitute the current economic and social crisis in many Africa states. Among the countries classified by the United Nations as "the least less developed countries, two-thirds are in Africa. As compared with other less developed countries, social and economic indicators of development, such as gross national product, per capita annual income, health, standard of living condition, and literacy rate have shown continuously weak result in this part of the world. Economic growth rates in Africa in the 1970s averaged 4.5 percent as compared with 6.7 percent recorded by Latin America. Average per capita income in 1988 was $604 as compared with $999 for Asia and $2,154 for

Latin America.[2]

The economic and financial position of the majority of African countries declined heavily in the mid-1970s and early 1980s. The annual rate of economic growth in the non-oil African economies, which reached 6.9 percent in 1974 and 5.8 percent in 1976, fell to less than 2.5 percent in 1977-1980 and to only 1.3 percent in 1981, a rate strongly lower than the 3 percent annual rise in population, leading to a major decline in real per capita income. At this point, their combined external current account deficit increased seriously, rising from $4.9 billion in 1973 to 14.1 billion in 1981, or from an average of about 10 percent specifically.[3] In order to finance these large and growing deficits, majority of African nations depended on foreign borrowing which was facilitated in the second half of the 1970s, by relatively easy access to external sources of funding. For this reason, the enormous borrowing combined with the rapid increase in interest rates resulted in an unprecedented debt crisis in most African nations. The weakening in economic development and the enormous external payments imbalances were exacerbated by an intensification of inflationary pressure. The average annual rate of inflation in the non-oil African countries seriously increased persistently from 10 percent in 1973 to over 20 percent during 1977-1983.[4] Again, the main consequence of external variable factors was compounded by ineffective and/or inefficient domestic demand management and structural programs. These in reality, contributed to the worsening in the balance of payments position of Africa economies.

Despite the economic and social crises encountered by the majority of African states, the African society is characterized by a tremendous political vitality. Although, the very problems that African states have encountered since former independence have generated experimentation with current forms and direction. We believe that the political economy choice approach that we haveaddressed in this text has provided readers with an idea that grasps the diversity of contemporary African political economy. Our theoretical and conceptual framework is far from deterministic. However, knowing the severe limitations under which most African states operate, we have simply emphasized that alternative theoretical models exist. Policy measures have led not only to increasingly different forms of government but also to different economic arrangements and establishments of relations with international actors. Therefore, it is naive if not misleading to speak in generalized fashions about Africa as if it were a single group, when in reality there are many Africans.

One thing is very true; that is the ideal traditional society much engendered by orthodox theorists of modernization or political development, has no room in contemporary Africa. African society has, for many years been penetrated by foreign traders for centuries, leaving few regions untouched by external influences. The concept and idea of economic differentiation and class formation have taken long before former independence. Despite economic problems in the last decade and a half, these trends are likely to persist in the remainder of the twenty-first century.

Also, the field of development in Africa is in disarray. One of its most essential sub-fields development economics has entered into a major crisis because of both empirical and normative difficulties. At this point, however, empirical difficulties occurred due largely to the failure to correctly predict which nations would develop and which would not; normative difficulties occurred because the emphasis of economic development studies expanded from an exclusive focus on growth to include questions of distribution and equity.

The question that need to be asked is what are the future expectations that the African economy will become more effective and/or efficient? There is small hope that essentially increased resources will become available: if the continent is to improve its ability for policy measure implementation, then existing resources must be utilized more productively and consistently.

The existence of domestic and transnational nongovernmental actors reduce the decisional latitude of African governments to the extent that they must be responsive to the demands of these entities. Since developments in the international economic and political system have widespread implications for domestic interests within African states, the governments are likely to be subject to extensive and conflicting pressures regarding appropriate policy postures. Therefore, the existence and increasing operation of global non governmental actors means that some developments in the African political economy are beyond the control of individual African states. We discussed in Chapters 5 and 6 how African states are concerned about the capability of multinational corporation to circumvent or ignore their policies. The problem is exacerbated by the fact that African governments have had difficulty developing effective or efficient multinational intergovernmental organizations to try to regulate and/or counter balance the effective maneuvers of such institutions. Many people believe that one of the reasons why African economies have been inefficient is that the implementation of policy-making is influence by sectional interests. How can the penetrative capability of African economies be accelerated while decision-making processes are opened to closer public criticism. Also, general optimism that military administrations would be able to resist pressures from various interest groups soon disappeared as it became evident that the soldiers were as divided as the wider societies from which they were raised.

Further, we do not claim to have made an exhaustive study of all the formidable challenges the economies of Africa might encounter in the period ahead. In reality, we have not dealt with global political concerns. Meanwhile, throughout our analysis we have been ambiguous of the consequences of some powerful trends which could have a profound influence on the capacity of the economies of Africa to meet the challenges and seize the opportunities of the twenty-first century. Therefore, because of the inevitable time frames in economic and social processes, there is an urgent need for early policy measure if these opportunities are to be exploited and undesirable results reduced.

There is a great certainty that African state will have to live with great interference by the International Monetary Fund and the World Bank. What will be likely relationship between these international institutions and African states? Will external institutions become essential catalysts in forcing policy change in Africa or will their operations invoke resistance from governments seeking to assert their sovereignty? Some believe that external institutions can be of major assistance while others are not. An argument is sometimes made that external agencies can be of major help to nations and governments that wish to introduce reform measures yet lack the domestic encouragement to do so. For this reason, the World Bank and the IMF have taken on the role of an international state mechanism, regulator of balance of payments equilibrium, consultant of financial equilibrium, examiner of African states' economic policies and coordinator of international economic measures, all generally influenced by the prevailing monetarist, perspective and orientation.

It is in the attaching of conditionalities to the granting of Fund balance of payments support, World Bank structural adjustment loans, or primarily the seal of respectability, that these international financial organizations have come in for considerable criticism in Africa. It is truism that lending organizations should want to lend in the climate of optimism that there is a very good chance that the loans will be repaid with interest, it is the universal policy prescriptions subscribed rather than the principle of conditionality itself, which have come under serious attack in Africa.[5]

NOTES

1. International Monetary Fund Annual Report, Washington, DC, 1982, p. 69. Peter Lawrence, *World Recession and The Food Crisis in Africa* (London: James Currey, 1986). Gerald Helleiner, *Africa and The International Monetary Fund* (Washington, D.C.: IMF, 1986). William C. Olson, *The Theory and Practice of International Relations* (New Jersey: Prentice Hall, 1987). Paul Cammack, David Pool and William Tordaff, *Third World Politics: A Comparative Introduction* (Baltimore: The Johns Hopkins University Press, 1993). See an indepth analysis done by Robert E. Gamer, *The Developing Nations: A Comparative Perspective* (Dubuque, Iowa: Win C. Brown Publishers, 1988). Jean F. Bayart, *The State in Africa: The Politics of the Belly* (New York: Longman, 1993). Robert J. Art and Robert Jervis, *International Politics: Enduring Concepts and Contemporary Issues* (New York: Harper Collins Publishers, 1992).

2. *International Monetary Fund Work Economic Outlook*, 1986. David Blake and Robert Walters, *The Politics of Global Economic Relations* (New Jersey: Prentice Hall, 1987). Peter Blackhum, "The Year of the IMF?" *Africa Report* No.6, (1986). Michael Boddie "Africa, the IMF and the Third World" New Nigeria, (March-April 1983). See also *International Monetary Fund Annual Report* 1988, 1990 Washington, D.C.: IMF, (1990). Geral Helleiner, *Africa and the International Monetary Fund* (Washington, D.C.: IMF, 1986).

3. Ibid., p. 103.

4. Helleiner, *Africa and the International Monetary Fund.*

5. Anunobi, *The Implications of Conditionality: The International Monetary Fund and Africa.* Helleiner, *Africa and the International Monetary Fund.* See the work by Peter Lawrence, *World Recession and the Food Crisis in Africa* (London: James Currey, 1986). Aderanti Adepoju, *The Impact of Structural Adjustment on the Population of Africa* (London: James Currey, 1993). Simon Commander, *Structural Adjustment and Agriculture: Theory and Practice in Africa and Latin America* (London: James Currey, 1989). Anne O. Krueger, *Economic Policy Reform in Developing Countries* (Cambridge, Mass.: Blackwell, 1992). Allan Roe, *Instruments of Economic Policy in Africa* (London: James Currey, 1992).

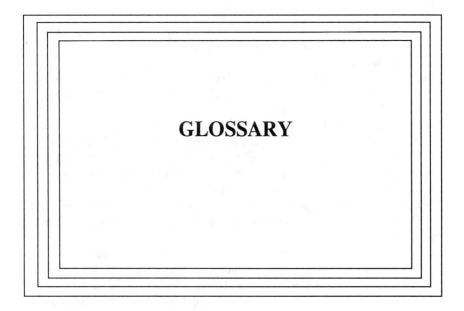

GLOSSARY

Absolute Advantage   This term refers to a country's ability to produce a product more cheaply than another country can. This concept was first developed by a classical British economist, Adam Smith in his book called *The Wealth of Nations*

Accountable   Subject to giving account. A government is suppose to be accountable to the voters if it conducts elections in which opposition candidates are free to compete.

Advanced Capitalism   An economic system characterized by private ownership but with serious function played by the government. Most industrialized countries such as the United States, Great Britain, Canada, Japan, Germany, and the like are classical examples of advanced capitalism.

African Development Bank   This concept refers to a regional bank created in 1963 to help independent African States through the provision of loans and technical assistance to further industrialization and development.

Anarchy   A condition without government, as in international relations, where no governmental authority exists and operates above the level of each sovereign nation-state.

Appropriate Technology   This term refers to a technology that is appropriate for existing factor endowments. For instance, a technology using a higher degree of labor relative to other factors of production in a labor-supply economy is clearly more appropriate than one that utilizes smaller labor proportions relative to other factors of production.

Autarky   A condition or policy of trying to make a nation-state economically self sufficient, not at all dependent on trading or any other foreign economic relations.

Authoritarianism   Describes a political government that is not assessable to the masses. It also refers to autocratic regime that seeks specifically to prevent and suppress political opposition but does not attempt to shape and control most structures of social life, such as religion, education, arts, economic relationship and organization.

Authority   Legitimate power, the right to give commands that people believe they have a moral obligation to obey; power derive from one's position.

Autocracy   Literally "self authorized rule". Any political system or institution in which rulers are not subject to enforceable legal rules or limited by other governmental organizations, free elections, or freely expressed public opinion. Classic examples are authoritarian and totalitarian governments.

Balance of Power   Shows a condition of equilibrium among sovereign states or alliances, a general equality of globally relevant power that governments of affected states sometimes accept. Often used to label policy of trying to establish or maintain such an equilibrium condition.

Balance of Trade   The difference between merchandise exports and imports.

Basic Political Rights   For democracy to function well, these basic rights must be provided to all citizens: freedom from arbitrary arrest and punishment, freedom of public expression, freedom of association and assembly, freedom to participate in fairly conducted competitive elections.

Bicameral   This refers to a legislative body made up of two different houses. In contrast, a single-house legislative body is unicameral.

Bipolarity   A balance of power concept in which two opposing independent nation-states are so much more powerful than their allies or any other nation-states that the two states competition polarizes structures and dominates the global arena. The classic example is U. S. - Soviet relations since the Second World War.

Black Market   This concept refers to a market in which sellers illegally sell to buyers at higher than legally mandated prices.

Bourgeoisie   Refers to the capitalist class - owners of means of production: land, labor, capital and technology in any capitalist society. This term is common among Marxist Scholars.

Brain Drain   The emigration of highly qualified, educated and skilled professional and technical manpower from the less developed to developed countries.

Bretton Woods System   A fixed exchange rate regime that functioned for most of the industrialized non-communist world in the Post World War II period until 1971.

Buffer Stocks   The stocks of products held by countries or international institutions that is used to subsidize or moderate the products' price fluctuation.

Calorie Supply   (Daily per Capita) Calculated by dividing the calorie equivalent of the available food supplies in a given country by its total population.

Capital   Capital is defined as wealth set aside for further production of wealth. This may mean, the amount of money it takes to start a business and to purchase production equipment and inventory.

Capital Accumulation   Increasing a country's stock of real capital (that net investment in fixed assets). This allows an increase in the production of capital goods at the expense of consumer goods.

Capital-Intensive Technique   A more capital-using process of production; that is one utilizing a greater amount of capital relative to other factors of production such as labor or land per unit of output.

Capitalism   This concept refers to an economic system by which the means of production: land, labor, capital and management are being controlled by the few private individuals who called themselves capitalist or bourgeoisie.

Cartel   A combination in restraint of trade, generally at the global level. An organization designed to maintain monopoly control over some aspect of international market. Organization of Petroleum Exporting Countries (OPEC), European Economic Community (EEC), Economic Community of West Africa States (ECOWAS) are specific examples.

Charismatic Authority   Individuals' subscribing to a leadership simply because they believe that he or she has extraordinary personal qualities that command their obedience, such as access to divine or ultimate truth, or heroic military capabilities.

Class System   A system of social stratification in which social status is determined by the family into which a person is born and subsequent socioeconomic achievements. Mobility between classes is possible.

Coalitions   Groups whose members cooperate with one another to realize common political ends.

Coalition Government   Central of the executive (primistership, cabinet positions etc.) within a parliamentary system by two or more distinct parties working together, dividing up leadership positions and cooperatively running the government.

Coercion   The use or threat of severe sanctions by power wielders against those whose action and behaviors they want to control. This is a form of political power which the dominant states use against the weaker ones.

Collectivism   An emphasis on collective objectives as opposed individual objectives.

Command Economy   An economic system where the allocation of resources, including determination of what goods and services should be produced, and in what quantity, is planned by the government.

Common External Tariff   Tariff imposed by member states of a customs union, common market regional cooperation's, regional organizations or economic community on imports from non-members.

Common Law System   This refers to a system of law based on tradition, precedent, and custom. When law courts interpret common law, they do so with regard to these characteristics.

Common Market   This concept refers to a group of countries committed to (1) removing all barriers to the free flow of goods. Services and factors of production between each other and (2) the pursuit of a common external trade policy.

Communism   This refers to a political ideology based on the writings of Marx and Lenin. It emphasizes class conflict and calls for the overthrow of capitalism, the disintegration of the capitalist class (the bourgeoisie) and the creation of a centrally planned economic system based on socialist principles. Democracy is to be replaced by a dictatorship of the proletariat, which the communist also refer to as "true democracy".

Comparative Advantage   This is the term developed by David Ricardo which states that countries should specialized in the production of those commodities in which they have the greatest comparative advantage and least comparative cost over the others. This concept emphasizes the greater relative advantage that a nation has in producing one type of commodity rather than another. The doctrine of comparative advantage is that each country should produce most sufficiently and import the rest from other countries in order to facilitate international trade.

Comprador   Thus concept refers to a local or domestic labor recruiter or purchasing agent employed by an international monopolies for the exploitation of his or her citizens.

Concessional Loan   This term refers to a credit extended in terms that are more favorable to the borrower than are available on the money markets.

Conditionality This concept generally refers to the requirement or policies imposed by the International Monetary Fund that a borrower nation undertake fiscal, monetary and global commercial reforms a condition to receiving a financial assistance for balance of payments disequilibrium.

Constituency This concept refers to a body of people grouped together for the primary purposes of elections and representation. The body of people to whom a representative is accountable. More specifically, a body of supporters who elect their representatives based on goodwill and trust.

Corporation This is a business owned by stockholders. A corporation is a legal entity with many of the rights, duties, and powers of a person, but separate from the people who own and manage it.

Coup d'etat This refers to illegal seizure or extension of power by an office holder. Now, it includes any forceful overthrow of an existing government whether by members of its own military forces or by armed revolutionaries it simply refers to a relatively bloodless seizure of power, usually by military leader, generally common in Africa and other Third World Nations.

Culture This is a set of beliefs, attitudes, values and ideas shape human behavior.

Customs Union This term refers to a form of economic integration in which two or more countries agree in principle to free all internal trade while levying a common external tariff on all non member countries.

Debt-Equity Swap This concept generally refers to a strategy or mechanism used by indebted Third World Countries to reduce real value of external debt by exchanging equity in domestic firm (stocks) or fixed interest obligations of the government (bonds) for private foreign debt at large discount.

Debt Renegotiation Changing the terms of existing loans, mainly by extending repayment dates without necessarily increasing the nominal interest rates.

Debt Service This concept specifically refers to the sum of interest payments and repayments of principal on external public and publicly guaranteed debt.

Debt Service Ratio Ratio of interest and principal payments due in a year to export receipts for that year.

Deflation This concept refers to a general decline in the price level of goods and services. This is the opposite of inflation.

Demand Demand is defined as the quantities of goods and services which individuals are willing and able to but at various prices over a given time period.

Democracy This term simply means government of the people for the people and by the people. To put it differently, it means a political system which calls for a government that is responsive and accountable to the people. In the modern world, the term democracy means constitutional, representative government in which top decision makers are elected in open and competitive elections, with almost all adults allowed to vote. It also requires effective protection of fundamental political rights and liberties and effective restraints on government officials.

Demography The Social Science that studies characteristics of human populations.

Dependency Theory This is a theoretical scheme which concerns economic relationships between the industrialized capitalist societies (examples U.S., Britain, Japan, France, Germany etc.) and the less developed countries (such as all African countries except South, all Asian Countries except Japan and all South American Countries), the claim being that the relationships are unequal and biased against the latter.

Devaluation of Currency This concept generally refers to a lowering of the official exchange rate between one country's currency and those of other countries.

Developing Countries These are countries predominantly in Africa, Asia and Latin America, whose per capita incomes and standards of living are far below those of other countries, but whose population growth rates are among the highest in the world.

Development This term usually refers to the process of improving the quality of all human lives which are measured in terms of per capita, standard of living and poverty.

Dictatorship This refers to a form of government in which one person or a small clique has absolute control of political authority. This form of control is often associated with the military government.

Division of Labor Division of duties among the workers such that each one engages in duties that he performs most efficient. Division of Labor promotes specialization thereby increases output at least cost per unit of factor of production. It has its theoretical and historical origins in Adam Smith's *Wealth of Nations*.

Dominance A condition of dominance exist when a country or group of countries have much greater power in making decisions affecting other vulnerable or dependence countries in international economic issues such as commodity price etc.

Economic Commission for Africa (ECA)   This is a regional branch of the United Nations system stationed in Addis Ababa, Ethiopia, and devoted to the analysis and evaluation of economic developments and trends in African countries.

Economic Commission for Latin America (ECLA)   This concept refers to a regional branch of the United Nations System stationed in Santiago, Chile, and designed to the regular publication of technical and statistical analyses of economic changes in Latin America.

Economic Community   Economic Union of nations attempting to coordinate monetary and fiscal measures as a strategy toward a common currency. This takes place in addition to maintaining a common external tariff and similar commercial measures and to removing restrictions on trade within its members.

Economic Community of West African States (ECOWAS)   This is an economic community, established in 1975, of 15 West African countries. This include 5 English, 1 Portuguese and 9 French with a total population of over 150 million. Now it has 16 members.

Economic Growth   This concept refers to an increase in an economy's capacity to produce goods and services as manifested by rising real gross domestic product and increasing standards of living

Economic Integration   The general elimination of economic barriers between countries. Forms of integration include currency unification, open immigration, free trade, political unification, customs union, coordination of monetary and fiscal policy and the like.

Economic Plan   This concept usually refers to a written document containing government policy decisions on how national resources shall be allocated among different uses in order to achieve a larger rate of economic growth over a specified time period.

Egalitarianism   A doctrine emphasizing the concept of human equality. Equality of opportunity. Equal treatment.

Elasticity   This concept refers to the degree of responsiveness to changes in price evident in demand schedules and supply schedules.

Elimination   This concept refers to a political strategy which involves getting rid of competitors or supposed threats, temporarily or permanently, legitimately or illegally, nonviolently or violently.

Elite   A minority with special characteristics or status giving them leadership. This term means in African context those nationalistic bourgeoisie who allied with international capital for the exploitation of its citizens and country. They are forced, to collaborate with foreign capital and erect an authoritarian government around a popular leader because they lack the economic power to secure their domination in any other way.

Enclave Economies   Those type of economies found among less developed
    countries in which there exist small pockets of economically
    developed areas (sometimes due to the presence of colonial or foreign
    business engaged in mining and plantation.

Equity   The rights or claims against the assets of a firm, shows how the
    assets have been financed.

Ethnic Group   A basic group of human social groups characterized by unity
    of race and cultural identity.

European Economic Community (EEC)   A European economic federation
    (common market) created under the Treaty of Rome in 1957 with a
    view to eradicate interstate tariffs within the federation in order to
    increase the volume of trade currently, there are twelve members of
    European Economic Community.

Export This concept refers to a domestically produced goods or services that
    are sold in another foreign country.

Export Promotion   Strong governmental efforts to expand and/or increase
    the volume of a country's exports through export incentives and other
    measures in order to create more foreign exchange and improve the
    current account of its balance of payments.

Exchange Rate   This term refers to the number of units of a currency
    required to purchase a unit of a foreign currency which is
    determined by the forces of demand and forces of supply in the
    foreign exchange market.

Federalism   This term refers to territorial institution of governmental
    authority; divided between a central government and a number of
    state governments, so that government at each level has some
    activities on which it makes final decision. It simply means, a
    division of power between federal and state government.

First World   This concept refers to the now economically advanced
    industrialized states of Western Europe, North America, Australia,
    New Zealand and Japan. These were the first nations to experience
    sustained and long term economic growth and development.

Fixed Exchange Rate   This concept refers to a regime of currency
    exchange where the rate at which one currency is converted into
    another fixed rate.

Floating Exchange Rate   This concept refers to the rate of exchange that
    fluctuates according to the international demand and supply for the
    currency.

Foreign Aid   This is defined as the global transfer of public funds in the
    form of loans or grants either directly from one government to
    another (bilateral assistance) or indirectly through the avenues of
    international institutions such as the World Bank or the International
    Monetary

Fund (Multilateral assistance).

Foreign Reserves The total value (generally expressed in U.S. dollars) of all gold, dollars, and special drawing rights held by a nation as both a, reserve and a fund from which global payments can be made.

Free Trade This concept refers to trade in which commodities or products can be imported and exported without any trade barriers such as tariffs, physical quotas, etc.

Free Trade Area This term refers to a form of economic integration in which there exists free internal trade among member states but each member is free to levy different external tariffs against non member countries.

General Agreement on Tariff and Trade (GATT) International Treaty that committed signatories to lowering barriers to the free flow of goods across domestic boundaries.

Gerrymander The drawing of the boundary lines of an electoral district in a seemingly capricious way to maximize the political strength of one party or racial group and to minimize the strength of another.

Government This concept, in general, means any set of political rules, or offices, whose occupants assume the principal responsibility for governing within a given social grouping. Some refer to it as a social contract between the people and government.

Grant This concept refers to an outright transfer payment usually from one country to another (foreign aid). That is, a gift of money or technical assistance which does not have to be repaid.

Gross Domestic Investment This comprises the outlays for additions to the fixed assets of both the private and public sectors plus the net value of inventory changes.

Gross Domestic Product (GDP) This concept measures the total final outputs of goods and services produced by the nation's economy that is, within the nation's boundary by residents and non-residents, regardless of its allocation between foreign and domestic claims.

Gross National Product (GNP) GNP is defined as a total market value of all final goods and services produced by a given economy in a given period of time, preferably one year.

Group of 7 These are the seven leading industrialized capitalist countries of the First World (U.S., Canada, France, Great Britain, West Germany, Italy and Japan.

Group of 77 This concept refers to a loose coalition of over 100 countries, particularly developing countries, originally formed by 77 nations at the United Nations Conference on Trade and Development (UNCTAD) in 1964, to express, protect and engender their collective self interests in the International Economic System.

Imperialism   This concept refers to a process by which empires, or unequal political relationships between peoples, are created, maintained and sometimes extended. An empire is a political structure in which a dominant people rule over subordinate political entities, usually overseas. Lenin describes imperialism as the highest stage of capitalism. Imperialism is also defined as a policy aimed at a reversal of the order of power, or as any relationship between a powerful and a weak state. Imperialism in an overall sense means a political domination for economic exploitation.

Import This concept refers to a foreign-made good or service that is purchased domestically.

Import Quota   This term refers to a specific limit placed on the number of units of a product that may be imported into a country.

Import Substitution   This concept usually refers to a deliberate attempt to replace major consumer imports by promoting the emergence and expansion of local or domestic industries such as shoes, textiles, etc. This involves the use of protective measures such as tariffs, quotas and other trade barriers to provide infant industries.

Income Inequality   This is the existence of disproportionate distribution of total national income among households whereby the share going to rich persons in a nation is far greater than that receiving by poor people. This is very common in LDCs due largely to the differences in the amount of income derived from ownership of property or as a result of differences in earned income.

Income per Capita   Total gross national product of a nation divided by the nation's population. Per capita income is sometimes used as an economic indicator of the levels of living and development.

Industrialization   This concept generally refers to the process of building up a nation's ability to process raw materials and to manufacture goods for consumption or further production.

Infant Industry Arguments New industries in developing states must be temporarily protected from international competition to help them reach a position where they can compete on world markets with the business of developed states.

Infant Mortality   This is the deaths among children between birth and one year of age. The infant mortality rate measures the number of these deaths per 1,000 live births.

Inflation   This term is defined as too much money in circulation buying too few goods.

Integrated Rural Development   This concept refers to the broad spectrum of rural development activities including small farmer agricultural progress; the provision of physical and social infrastructure; the development of rural non farm industries; and the ability of the rural section to withstand and improve and/or accelerate the pace of these improvement at a future date.

Interdependence Interrelationship between economic and non economic variables. In international relations, it means the situation in which one country's welfare depends to varying degrees on the decisions and policies of another country.

Interest Rate This concept refers to the amount that a borrower mast pay a lender over and above the total amount borrowed.

International Bank for Reconstruction and Development (IBRD) Otherwise known as the World Bank; it is an international financial institution owned by it's 150 member nations and stationed in Washington, D.C. Originally, World Bank was established to give lender over and above the total amount borrowed.

International Development Association (IDA) This term refers to an International body created in 1960 to help the World Bank in its endeavors to accelerate and promote economic development of the global community of nations by providing additional capital on a low interest rates (soft loans).

International Financial Corporation (IFC) This concept refers to a global financial organization that was created in 1956 to assist the World

International Monetary Fund (IMF) This concept refers to an international bank that helps stabilize the international monetary system by monitoring exchange rates and making short-term loans to members with balance of payments disequilibrium.

Investment This concept refers to that portion of national income or expenditure reserved for the production of capital or investment goods over a period of time. There are two major forms of investment;
gross investment refers to the total expenditure on new capital goods, while net investment refers to the additional capital goods produced in excess of depreciation and replacement.

Laissez faire This term is defined as a governmental hands-off policy in economic matters. A policy that respects the freedom of individuals in economic issues, allowing them to do more or less at their will. This policy assumes the private ownership of property and the profit motive.

Legitimacy A government is said to be legitimate to the degree that it is worthy of support or to the degree that the people consider it worthy of support.

Liberalism A political philosophy which emphasizes the liberty or freedom of individual. Some liberals perceive the state as the principal threat

Others see the state as an instrument for enhancing liberty by protecting the individual against restraints stemming from private individuals.

Life Expectancy at Birth   This concept shows the number of years newborn children would live if subject to the mortality risks occurring for the cross-section of population at the time of their birth.

Life Sustenance   Those fundamental goods and services such as food, clothing, and shelter that are necessary to sustain an average human being at the bare minimum level of living.

Literacy Rate   This is define in terms of the percentage of population aged 15 and over able to read and write. This term is sometimes used as one of the many social and economic indicators of the state of development within a given nation.

Malnutrition   This concept usually refers to a state of ill-health resulting from an inadequate diet - usually measured in terms of average daily protein consumption.

Market Economy   This concept refers to a society in which the operation of the market determines economic behavior and decision making.

Marxism-Leninism   An official ideology of the Soviet Union and of other communist countries and movements. This ideology combines Marx's emphasis on alleged scientific knowledge of the inevitable direction of historical development with Lenin's Vanguard revolutionary party that claims a monopoly of ideological truth and seeks to create and maintain its total control over society.

Medium of Exchange   This is one of the basic functions of money which makes exchange of goods and services easier in international market by eliminating the need for a barter system.

Mercantilism   This concept refers to an economic philosophy which advocates that countries should simultaneously encourage exports and discourage imports.

Modernization   This concept refers to development of money based exchange system, sizable industrial sector, specialization of jobs and functions, and proliferation of specialized institutions. Politically, this term had little meaning. Some refer it to basic authority on a non traditional claim to legitimacy; developing a specialized modern-type bureaucracy, creating effective mass political parties, and creating a system of relatively peaceful and orderly leadership succession.

Money   This concept refers to anything that is generally accepted as a medium of exchange for the settlement of debt.

Monopoly   A market structure in which one party or individual has sufficient control over a product or service to dictate the price at which it becomes available. Competition at this point, is completely absent.

Multinational Corporation (MNC) This is a global or transnational corporation with headquarters in one country, but branch offices in a wide range of different countries. Examples of such corporations are Coca-Cola, General Motor, Exxon, etc.

Nationalism The belief that all members of the nation should be politically united, usually within a given nation-state; and all members of the nation should be loyal primarily to it. Also, alternatively nationalism may be clearly an anti imperialist ideology.

Official Development Assistance (ODA) This consists of net disbursements of loans or grants made at concessional financial negotiations by official agencies of the members of the Development Assistance Committee of the Organization for Economic Corporation and Development (OECD) and members of the Organization of Petroleum Exporting Countries (OPEC) with the primary aim of promoting economic growth and development.

Oligopoly This concept refers to a market structure in which a few large producers sell smaller but not identical products to many small buyers.

Opportunity Cost In production process, the real value of resources used in the most desirable alternative. For instance, the opportunity cost of producing an extra unit of manufactured good is the output of, say, food that must be for gone as a result of transferring resources from agricultural to manufacturing operations.

Plan Implementation The practical carrying out of the objectives set forth in the development plan.

Political Science The disciplined, scholarly study of ideas, behavior, institutions, and policies related to politics, public and government.

Politics A struggle between two or more actors seeking political power, or a competition between two or more actors again, seeking for political power.

Population Increase This concept generally refers to the rate at which a given population grows over a period of time.

Power The ability of one actor to shape or influence the behavior of another actor. The act of control. To put it differently, the ability and capability to exert force on others.

Price Discrimination The practice of selling the same good or service to two or more customers at different prices.

Privatization This concept refers to the preponderance of private ownership of means of production -land, labor and capital. It may mean selling public assist (businesses) to private business interests.

Profit   Sales revenues less all production and other costs, the return to the owners for undertaking the risk inherent in operating business.

Profit Maximization   This refers to the maximum dollar value of output (sales revenues) for the minimum dollar value of input (costs and expenses).

Protectionism   This concept refers to the practice of shielding domestic industries from international competition through the use of various trade barriers.

Raw Materials   Industrial products that are inexpensive, unprocessed items that become a physical part of the product the firm is producing, inputs from which the firm makes its products.

Real Income   This is the income that a household or firm receives in terms of the real goods and services it can buy. To put it differently, it is simply what money income can buy, or money income adjusted by some price index.

Repatriation   Sending profits from an international company back to the country of origin rather than leaving them in the country in which they were earned.

Scarcity   In economics, the concept referring to a situation which arises when there is less of goods and services than people would like to have if it were free. The quantity of goods and services are scarce relative to individuals' desire for them because the nation's resources used in their production are themselves scarce.

Self Determination   This concept refers to the right of a nation or individual to determine for itself what its relationship to other nations or peoples should be.

Sovereignty   A state is sovereign when it is independent of the control of any other state. It is subject to international law but supreme over its own domestic law.

Stabilization Policies   A coordinated set of mostly restrictive monetary and fiscal policies aimed at reducing inflation, cutting budget deficits, and improving the balance of payments. See the International Monetary Fund conditionality.

Stages of Growth   This theory of development is associated with the American economic historian W. W. Rostow. According to Rostow in order to achieve development a nation must passes five states: the tradition, (2). the precondition, (3). take off state, (4). the drive to maturity stage, and (5). the stage of high mass consumption.

Structural Adjustment Loans   These are loans by the World Bank designed to foster structural adjustment in the less developed countries by supporting policies to remove excessive governmental controls, allowing factor and product prices to better reflect scarcity values, and encouraging market competition.

Subsidiary Corporation This term refers to a corporation in which the majority of the firm's common stock is owned by another company. This is very common among multinational corporations.

Trade Creation This concept refers a situation in the theory of customs Unions that, occurs when, following the formation of the union, there is a shift in the geographic location of production from higher cost to lower cost member countries.

Trade Deficit This concept refers to a situation in which total imports exceed total exports.

Trade Diversion This occurs when the creation of a customs union causes the locus of production of formerly imported goods to shift from a lower cost non member country to a higher-cost member country.

Trade Surplus This concept refers to a situation in which total exports exceed total imports.

Underdevelopment This concept generally refers to a situation in which there are persistent low levels of standard of living in addition to the following features: absolute poverty, low rates of economic growth, low per capita income, low consumption levels, high death rates, poor health standards, high birth rates, vulnerability to and dependence on international economies.

United Nations Conference on Trade and Development (UNCTAD) This is a body of the United Nations whose primary goal is to accelerate global trade and commerce with a particular reference to trade and balance of payments problems of the Third World. The First Secretary General of UNCTAD was Raul Prebisch of Latin America.

Wealth Wealth is defined as any thing material, non material, monetary or non monetary, desire by man, scarce in relations to demand, but has the ability to satisfy any monetary valuation.

Welfare State A state that seeks to promote welfare by relatively direct means, regulating behavior and providing benefits in a major way.

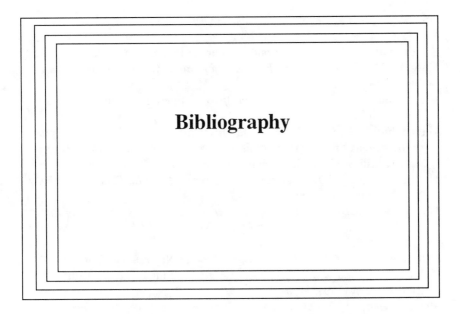

Bibliography

Abiola, B.M. *The History of West Africa.* (Ibadan: Ibadan University Press, 1971.

Abooja, Krishna. "Development Legislation in Africa." *The Journal of Development Studies* April (1966).

Adedeju, Adebayo. Economic Commission for Africa and Africa's Development, 1983-1008: A Preliminary Perspective Study. Addis Ababa, ECA, 1983.

Adelman, Inn. "Beyond Export Led Growth." *World Development,* Oxford, Vol. 12, No. 9 (September 1984).

Adeoye, Oyebola. *Modern Economics of West Africa.* Ibadan: Board. Publications Limited, 1970.

Adepoju, Aderanti. *The Impact of Structural Adjustment on the Population of Africa.* London: James Currey, 1993.

Africa, No. 49 (September, 1975).

Africa Analysis No. 1 (11 July 1986).

African Continental Bank of Nigeria. "Balance of Payment Report From Second Tier Foreign Exchange Market." *Lagos News* December 1987.

African Development Vol. 10, No. 3 (March 1976).

African Economic Digest, London, (23 March 1984).

African Market. "Nigerian's Shh! Devaluation." *New Africa* (September 1986).

African Review. (December 1980).

African News. (February 1985).

Africa South of the Sahara. London: Europe Publication, 1983.

Ainly, E. M. *The IMF: Past, Present and Future.* Cardiff: University of Wales Press, 1979.

Ake, Claude. *A Political Economy of Africa.* Nigeria: Longman Nigeria Limited, 1981.

Akeredolu-Ale, E. O. "Private Foreign Investment and the Underdevelopment of Indigenous Entrepreneurship in Nigeria, " *Nigeria Economy and Society.* Edited by William Gavin, London: Res Collins, 1976.

Akin, Marbogurije. *The Development Process: A Spatial Perspective.* New York: Holmes & Meier, 1981.

Akinsanya, Adeoye. *Economic Interdependence and Indigenization of Private Foreign Investment: The Experience of Nigeria and Ghana.* New York: Praeger, 1983.

Akinsanya, Adeoye A. "State Strategies Toward Nigerian and Foreign Business," *The Political Economy of Nigeria.* edited by I. William Zartman, New York: Praeger, 1983.

Alfred, Helen, ed. *The Bretton Woods Agreement and Why It Is Necessary.* Citizens Conference on International Union, 1944.

Ali, Shaukat. *Nation Building, Development and Administration: A Third World Perspective.* Lahore: Aziz Publishers, 1979

Allan, Roe. *Instruments of Economic Policy in Africa.* London: James Currey, 1992.

Almond, Gabriel A. and Bingham G. Powell. *Comparative Politics: A Developmental Approach.* Boston: Little Brown and Company, 1966.

Aluko, S. A. and Ijere, M.O. "The Economics of Mineral Oil." *Nigerian Journal of Economic and Social Studies,* Vol. 7. (1965).

Amin, Samir. *Imperialism and Unequal Development.* New York: Monthly Review Review Press, 1976.

_____. Self Reliance and the New International Economic Order. Monthly Review, (July-August 1977).

Amin, Samir. *Accumulation on a World Scale: A Critique of the Theory of Underdevelopment.* (volumes), New York: Monthly Review Press, 1974.

Amin, Samir, "Development and Structural Change: The African Experience, "The Widening Gap: Developing in the 1970s. edited by Barbara Ward, J. D. Runnals, and Lenore D. Anjou, New York Columbia University Press, 1971.

Anunobi, Fredoline O. *The Implications of Conditionality: The IMF Africa* MD: UPA, 1992

Apter, David E. *The Politics of Modernization.* Chicago: The University of Chicago Press, 1967.

Arnold, Guy. *Modern Nigeria.* London: Longman Group, 1977.

Arrighi, G. and J. Saul *Essays on the Political Economy of Africa*. New York: Monthly Review Press, 1972.

Awolowo, Obafemi. *The People's Republic*. Ibadan: Oxford University Press, 1968.

_____. The Autobiography of Chief Obafemi. Ibadan: Cambridge: Cambridge University Press, 1960.

Awolowo, Obafemi, "A Presidential Candidate Address at an Emergency meeting of the Action Group, Ibadan, October 12, 1957", cited in Chibuzo A. Ogbuagu, "The Nigerian Indigenization Policy: Nationalism or Pragmatism?" *African Affairs* (April, 1983).

Ayida, A. A. and Onitiri, H.M.A. eds. Reconstruction and Development in Nigeria. Ibadan: Oxford University Press, 1971.

Balabkins, Nicholas. *Indigenization and Economic Development: The Nigerian Experience*. London, England: Jal Press, 1982.

Baran, Paul A. *The Political Economy of Growth*. New York: Monthly Review Press, 1957

Beckford, George. Persistent Poverty: Underdevelopment in Plantation Regions of the World. New York: Oxford University Press, 1971.

Belassa, Bela. Trade Liberalization Among Industrial Countries. New York: McGraw-Hill, 1967.

Bello, V. I. "The Intentions, Implementation Process and Problems of the Nigerian Enterprises Promotion Decree (No. 4) 1972" In Nigeria's Indigenization Policy, Proceedings of the 1974 Symposium Organized by the Nigerian Economic Society. Ibadan: The Caxton Press, 1975.

Bennett, A. Leroy, International Organizations: Principles and Issues. 3rd Ed., Englewood Cliffs, NJ: Prentice Hall Inc., 1984.

Berger, Manfred. Industrialization Policies in Nigeria. Munich: Weltforun Verlag, 1975.

Berman, Bruce J. "Clientellism and Neocolonialism: Center periphery Relations and Political Development in African States". Studies in comparative International Development (Summer, 1974).

Bienen, Henry and V. P. Diejomaoh. (eds.) The Political Economy of Income Distribution in Nigeria. New York: Holmes and Meier, 1981.

Black, C. E. The Dynamic of Modernization. New York: Harper Row, 1976.

Black, Stanley W. Exchange Policies for Less Developed Countries. Princeton, New Jersey: Princeton University press, 1976.

Blake, David H. and Walters, Robert S. The Politics of Global Economic Relations. New Jersey: Prentice Halls, Inc., Englewood Cliffs, Third Edition, 1987.

Blake David H. "Government, Politics and the Multinational Enterprises,

"International Business-Government Affairs: Toward an Era of Accommodation. Edited by John Fayerweather, Cambridge, Mass.: Ballinger Publishing Company, 1973.

Block, Fred. The Origins of International Economic Disorder. Los Angeles: University of California Press, 1977.

Boddewyn, J. "The External Affairs Functions in American Multinational Corporations," International Business Government Affairs: Toward an Era of Accommodation. edited by John Fayerweather, Cambridge, Mass.: Ballinger Publishing Co., 1973.

Brandt, Willy. Independent Commission on International Issues North-South: A Program for Survival. Cambridge, Massachusetts: MIT Press, 1980.

Brown, Welt M. World Without National Policies Ruling the Waves. Princeton, New Jersey: Princeton University Press, 1976.

Brown, Robert and Cummings, Robert J. The Lagos Plan of Action vs. the Berg Report. Washington, DC: Howard University Press, 1984.

Buhari, Muhammadu. "Budgeting for Recovery." West African Magazine (April 1984).

Burns, S.A. History of Nigeria London: University of London Press, 1969.

Callaway, Barbara. "The Political Economy of Nigeria," *The Political Economy of Africa*. Edited by Harris Richardson, New York: John Wiley and Sons, 1975.

Camps, Murian. Collective Management: The Program of Global Economic Organizations. New York: McGraw-Hill, 1981.

Caporaso, James A. "Dependence, Dependency, and Power in Global System: A Structural and Behavioral Analysis." *International Organization*. 32 (1978).

Caporaso, James A. "Dependency Theory: Continuities and Discontinuities in Development Studies," *International Organization* 34, No. 4 (Autumn, 1980).

Cardoso, Fernado H. and Faletto, Enzo. *Dependency and Development in Latin America*. Mexico: Siglo Veintiuno, 1979.

Cavangh, John and Obadia, Cynthia. *From Debt to Development*. Washington, DC: Institute for Policy Studies, 1985.

Caves, Richard E. and Jones, Ronald W. *World Trade and Payments*. Boston: Little Brown and Company, 1981.

Central Bank of Nigeria Annual Reports and Economic and Financial Review, Various Issues posted Prices from *United Nations Monthly Bulletin of Statistics*, (November, 1976).

Central Bank of Nigeria. *Annual Report*: Lagos (1972 and 1974).

Central Bank of Nigeria. *Annual Report: Various Issues Complied in 1980,*

Lagos: 1981.

Cervenka, Zdenek. *The Nigerian Civil War, 1967-1970* Frankfurt: Bernard and Graefe Inc., 1971.

Chimeka, Uchem I. *The Evolution of Nigerian Exchange Rate.* Ibadan: Ibadan University Press, 1984.

Chase-Dunn, Christopher, "The Effects of International Economic Dependence on Development and Inequality: A Cross-National Study." *American Sociological Review* 6 (1975).

Chikelu, B. P. O. "Aims and Objectives of Indigenization Scheme". *Management in Nigeria*, (September, 1976).

Clairmonte, Frederick. *Economic Liberalism and Under-Development.* Bombay: Asian Publishing House, 1960.

Clark, Colin. *The Economics of 1960.* London: MacMillan, 1942.

Clark, Paul G. American Aid for Development. New York: Praeger Publisher, 1972.

Cline, W. and Weintraub, S. *Economic Stablization in Developing Countries.* (Washington, DC: Brookings Institute), 1981.

Clower, Robert W. *Growth Without Development.* Evanston, Illinois: Northwestern University Press, 1966.

Cockcroft, James. Frank, A. G. and Johnson, Dale. *Dependence and Underdevelopment: Latin American Political Economy.* New York: Doubleday and Company, Inc., 1972.

Coleman, J. S. *Nigeria: Background to Nationalism*, Berkley and Los Angeles: University of California Press, 1963.

_____. "The Political Economy of Indigenization: The Case of the Nigerian Enterprises Promotion Decree." *Quarterly Journal of Administration.* 9 (1975).

Committee for Economic Development. *Strengthening the World Monetary System.* New York, 1973.

Conway, Margaret M. and Frank B. Feigert. *Political Analysis: An Introduction.* Boston: Allyn and Bacon, Inc., 1976.

Cooper, Richard N. "Trade Policy is Foreign Policy". *Foreign Policy* 9 (Winter, 1972-73).

Daly, D. J. Globerman, S. Tariff and Science Policies: *Application of Model of Nationalism.* Toronto: University of Toronto Press, 1976.

Damanchi, Ukandi G. *Nigerian Modernization: The Colonial Legacy.* New York: The Third Press, 1972.

_____, "Nigerian Development Paths," *Development Path In Africa and China.* Edited by Ukandi G. Damachi, et al., Boulder, Colorado: Westview Press, 1976.

Danielson, Albert L. *The Evolution of OPEC.* New York: Harcourt Brace Jovanovick, 1982.

Dean, Edwin. *Plan Implementation in Nigeria 1962-1968.* Ibadan: Oxford University Press, 1972.

Desch, Michael C. *When the Third World Matters: Latin America and United States.* Grand Strategies. Baltimore: The Johns Hopkins University Press, 1993.

Deutsch, Karl. "Theories of Imperialism and Neocolonialism," *Testing Theories of Economic Imperialism.* Edited by S. J. Rosen and J. R. Kurth, Lexington, D.C. Heath, 1974.

Dos Santos, Theotonio. "The Structure of Dependence." *American Economic Review,* 60 (May, 1970).

_____. "The Crisis of Capitalism," *Latin American Perspective,* 3 (Spring, 1976).

Dudley, Billy. *Instability and Political Order: Politics and Crisis in Nigeria.* Ibadan: Ibadan University Press, 1973.

Dye, T. *Politics, Economics and the Public Policy Outcomes in the American States.* Chicago: Rand McNally, 1966.

Duvall, Raymond D. "Dependence and Dependencia Theory: Notes Toward Precision of Concept and Argument". *International Organization* 32, No. 1 (Winter, 1978).

Eckes, Jr. *A Search For Solvency.* Texas: Austin University Press, 1982.

Eckstein, H. "The Critical Case Study," *Handbook of Political Science.* edited by F. L. Greenstein and N. W. Polsby.

Eicher, Carl. *Growth and Development of the Nigeria Economy.* East Lansing: Michigan State University, 1970.

Eisenstadt, S. N. *Protest and Change.* Englewood Cliffs, New Jersey: Prentice-Hall, 1966.

Ejofor, Pita N. O. "Multinational Corporations As Agents of Imperialism" In B. O. Oribonoje, and O. A. Lawal (eds.), *The Indigence for National Development.* Ibadan: Oribonoje Publishers, 1976.

Eleazu, Uma. *Federation and National Building.* Elms Court, Devon: Arthur Stockwell, 1977.

Erb, Guy F. and Kallab, Valerianna. eds. *Beyond Dependency: The Developing World Speaks Out.* New York: Praeger, 1975.

Esseks, John D. "Economic Dependence and Political Development in New States of Africa." *Journal of Politics,* 33 (1971).

Eten, Inyang. "Indigenization for Lumpen-Bourgeois Development in Nigeria," *Path to Nigerian Development.* edited by Ikwudiba Nnoli, Enugu, Nigeria, Fourth Dimension Publishers, 1981, pp. 217-243.

Evans, Peter. *Dependent Development.* Princeton: Princeton University Press, 1979, p. 49.

Ezera, K. *Constitutional Developments In Nigeria.* London: Cambridge University Press, 1960.

Federal Republic of Nigeria. Annual Abstract of Statistics. Lagos Federal

Economic Development.

Federal Republic of Nigeria. *Economic and Statistical Review.* Government Press, Lagos: 1980.

Federal Office of Statistics. *Second National Development Plan: A Review of First National Development Plan,* Lagos, 1975.

Federal Ministry of Economic Development. *First National Development Plan (1962-1968): Sectoral Distribution,* Lagos, 1965.

Federal Ministry of Economic Development. *Third National Development Plan: 1975-1980,* Vol. 1 Lagos: The Central Planning Office, 1979.

Feinberg, Richard and Kallab, Valeriana. *Adjustment Crisis in the Third World.* Washington, D.C.: Overseas Development Council, 1984.

Feit, E. *The Armed Bureaucrats: Military Administrative Regimes and Political Development.* Boston: Houghton Mifflin, 1973.

Fesler, J. W. "The Case Method in Political Science," *Essays on the Case Method in Public Administration* edited by E. A. Bach, New York: International Institute of Administrative Sciences, 1962.

First, R. *The Barrel of a Gun: Political Power in Africa and the Coup d'Etat.* Allen Lane, The Penguin Press, 1970.

Flint, J. E. "Economic Change in West Africa in Nineteenth Centruy," *History of West Africa.* Edited by J. G. A. Ajayi and M. Crowder, London: Longman, 1974.

Foxley, Alejandro. *Latin American Experience in Neo-Conservative Economics.* Berkeley: University of California Press, 1983.

Frank, Andre Gunder. *Capitalism and Underdevelopment in Latin America.* New York: Monthly Review Press, 1969.

Frank, Andre Gunder. *Latin America: Underdevelopment or Revolution.* New York: Monthly Review Press, 1970.

Frey, Bruno S. *Modern Political Economy.* New York: John Wiley and Sons, 1978.

Furtado, Celso. *Obstacles to Development in Latin America.* New York: Doubleday, 1970.

Galbraith, J. K. "The Need For Foreign Investment." *Newswatch* Fall (1975).

Galtung, John. "A Structural Theory of Imperialism. *Journal of Peace Research* 8 (1971).

Gardner, L. C. *Economic Aspects of New Deal Diplomacy,* Madison: University of Wisconsin, 1964.

Gardner, Richard and M. L. Kan, M. *In the Global Partnership.* New York: Praeger, 1968.

Gee, Wilson. *Social Science Research Methods.* New York: Appleton Centruy Crofts, 1950.

Ghai, Dhanam P. "Concepts and Strategies of Economic Independence." *The Journal of Modern African Studies,* 1 (1973).

Gilpin, Robert. *U. S. Power and the Multinational Corporation: The Political Economy of Foreign Direct Investment.* New York: Basic Books, Inc., 1975.

Girman, Norman. *Corporate Imperialism: Conflict and Expropriation.* New York: Monthly Review Press, 1980.

Goulet, Dennis. *Economic Development in the Third World.* New York: Longmans, Inc., 1981.

Green, Reginald H. "Political Independence and the National Economy: An Essay on the Political Economy of Decolonization," *African Perspectives: Papers in the History, Politics, and Economy of Africa Presented to Thomas Hodgkin* Cambridge: Cambridge University Press, 1970.

Green, Reginald and Seidman, Anne. *Unity or Proverty? Economic of Pan Africanism.* Baltimore: Penguin, 1969.

Griffin, Keit and Enos, J. L. "Foreign Assistance: Objectives and Consequences." *Economic Development and Culture Change* (1970).

Harris, Richard. *The Political Economy of Africa.* London: Halstead Press (Achenkman Publishing Company), 1975.

Hastedt, Glenne Knickrehm, Kay. *Dimensions of World Politics.* New York: Harper Collins Publishers, 1991.

Hausman, W. H. *Managing Economic Development in Africa.* Cambridge, Massachusetts: M.I.T. Press, 1963.

Haynes, Jeff. "Debt in Sub-Saharan Africa: The Local Politics of Stabilization." *African Affairs* 86 (July 1987).

Hayter, Teresa. *Aid as Imperialism.* England: Pengui, 1972.

_____. *Aid: Rhetoric and Reality.* London: Plato Press, 1985.

Helleiner, Gerald. *Peasant Agriculture, Government and Growth in Nigeria.* Homewood, Illinois: Irwin, 1966.

Herbert, Obudozie. *Nigeria: From Dependency to Development.* Ibadan: University of Ibadan Press, 1986.

Hobson, J. A. *Imperialism: A Study.* Michigan: Ann Arbor, 1965.

Hopkins, A. G. *The Creation of a Colonial Monetary System: The Origins of the West African Currency Board.* Ibadan: University of Ibadan Press, 1975.

_____. *The Currency Revolution in South-West Nigeria.* Ibadan: University of Ibadan Press, 1983.

Holt, P. M. and Daly, M. W. *A History of the Sudan: From the Coming of Islam to the Present Day.* New York: Longman, 1988.

Huntington, Samuel P. *Political Order in Changing Societies..* New Haven: Yale University Press, 1968.

Igbozurike, Martin. *Problem Generating Structure In Nigerian's Rural Development.* New Haven: Yale University Press, 1976.

International Bank for Reconstruction and Development. *The Economic*

Development of Nigeria. Baltimore: The John Hopkins Press, 1955.

Iwayemi, Akin. "The Military and the Economy," *Nigerian Government and Politics Under Military Rule.* Edited by Oyeleye Gyediran, New York, St. Martin's Press, Inc., 1979.

Jackson, Steven. Bruce, Russett. Duncan, Sydal. David Sylvan. "Conflict and Coercion in Dependent States." *Journal of Conflict Resolution,* 12 (December, 1978).

Jodice, David A. "Sources of Change in Third World Regimes for Foreign Direct Investment, 1968-1976." *International Organization* 34 (Spring, 1980).

Johnson, Harry G. *Economic Nationalism in Old and New States.* Chicago: University of Chicago Press, 1967.

Johnson, J. J. *The Role of Military in Underdeveloped Countries.* Princeton: Princeton University Press, 1962.

Kamarck, Andrew. *The Economics of African Development.* New York: Praeger Publishers, 1972

Kaufman, Robert. Harry I. Chernotsky. Daniel, S. Geller. "A Preliminary Test of the Theory of Dependency." *Comparative Politics.* 3 (April, 1975).

Kegley, Charles W. and Wittkopf, Eugene. *World Politics: Trend and Transformation.* New York: St. Martin's Press, 1985.

Keynes, John M. *The General Theory of Employment, Interest and Money.* New York: Harcourt, 1936.

Kilby, Peter. *Industrialization in an Open Economy: Nigeria 1945-1966.* London: Cambridge University Press, 1967.

Kohlhagen, Steven W. "Host Country Policies and MNCs--The Pattern of Foreign Investment in Southeast Asia." *Columbia Journal of World Business* (Spring, 1977).

Krueger, Anne. *Economic Policy Reformation Developing Countries.* Cambridge: Blackwell, 1992.

Lagos, Nigeria, Chamber of Commerce and Industry. *Nigerian Business Review* (December 1981).

Lancaster, Carol. "Africa's Economic Crisis." *Foreign Policy* Vol. 52 (Fall 1983).

Landes, David S. "The Nature of Economic Imperialism. *Journal of Economic History* (December 1961).

Lenin, V. I. *Imperialism: The Highest Stage of Capitalism.* New York: International Publishers, 1970.

Leys, Colin. "What is the Problem about Corruption?" *Journal of Modern African Studies* 3 (1965).

Lewis, A. O. *Nigerian Exports: Problems, Prospects and Implications for Economic Growth.* Badapest: Center for Afro-Asian Research of The Hungarian Academy of Sciences, 1973.

Lichtheim, George. *Imperialism.* New York: Praeger Publishers, 1971.

Liedholm, C. ed. *Growth and Development of Nigerian Economy.* New York: East Lansing, 1970.

Long, Dianne. *The Other World: Issues and Politics in the Third World.* eds. New York: MacMillan Publishing Company, 1987.

Luckham, Robin. *The Nigerian Military: A Soiological Analysis of Authority and Revolt 1960-1967.* Cambridge: University Press, 1971.

Luxemburg, R. *The Accumulation of Capital.* London: Routledge, 1964.

Maboqunije, Akin L. *Urbanization in Nigeria.* London: University of London Press, 1969.

Macessiah, George. *The International Political Economy and the Third World.* New York: Praeger, 1981.

Magdoff, Harry. "Third World Debt." *Monthly Review* 37 (February 1986).

Magdoff, Harry. *The Age of Imperialism.* New York: Monthly Review Press, 1969.

Mahler, Vincent A. *Dependency Approaches to International Political Economy: A Cross-National Study.* New York: Columbia University Press, 1980.

Malthus, T. R. *An Essay on the Principle of Population or A View of Its Past and Present Effects on Human Happiness with an Inquiry into Our Prospects Respecting the Future Removal or Mitigation of the Evils Which it Occasions.* Homewood, Illinois: Richard D. Irwin, 1963.

Martin, Clara. "Home and Foreign Investments." *This Week.* July (1975).

Mars, J. "Extra-territorial Enterprises," *Mining Commerce and Finance in Nigeria.* edited by Margery Penham, London, 1948.

Marx, Karl. *Capital: A Critique of Political Economy.* Chicago: Henry Regnery, 1970.

May, Ronald S. "Direct Overseas Investment in Nigeria 1953-63: Some Aspect of Its Constitution and Contribution of Nigerian Economic Development." *Scottish Journal of Political Economy (1965).*

McGowan, Patrick J. "Economic Dependence and Economic Performance in Black Africa." *The Journal of Modern African Studies* 14 (1976).

Meier, Gerald M. ed. *Leading Issues in Economic Development.* New York: Oxford University Press, 1972.

Mill, John Stuart. *Principles of Political Economy.* New York: Augustus M. Kolley, 1909.

Morehouse, Ward. "Third World Disengagement and Collaboration: A Negotiated Transitional Option," *Mobilizing Technology for World Development.* edited by Jairam Ramesh and Charles Weiss, Jr., New York: Praeger, 1979, p. 74.

Mortime, Robert A. *The Third World Coalition in International Politics.* Boulder, Colorado: Westview Press, 1984.

Mummery, David R. *The Protection of International Private Investment: Nigeria and the World Community.* New York: Frederick A. Praeger Publishers, 1968.

Murray, Colin. "Latin America Experiment in Neoconservative Economics". *Journal of Development Studies.* Vol. 20 (August 1983).

Myint, H. "The Classical Theory of International Trade and the Underdeveloped Countries." *Economic Journal* (1958).

Myrdal, Gunnar. *Economic Theory and the Underdeveloped Regions.* London: Gerald Duckworth, 1957.

_____. *The Challenge of World Poverty.* New York: Vintage, 1970.

National Management Concerence. *Indigenisation and Economic Development.* Nigerian Institute of Management, Lagos, 1974.

Nelson, Joan M. *Aid, Incluence and Foreign Policy.* New York: MacMillan, 1968.

New Nigeria, 10 June 1984.

New Nigeria, 2 March 1985.

New Nigeria, 12 April 1985.

New Nigeria, 6 May 1985.

Nigerian Daily Times, 2 March 1984.

Nigerian Daily Times, 9 April 1984.

Nigerian Daily Times, 18 June 1984.

Nkrumah, Kwame. *Neo-Colonialism: The Last State of Imperialism.* New York: New York Publishers, 1966.

Nkrumah, Kwame. *Towards Colonial Freedom: Africa in the Struggle Against World Imperialism.* London: Panaf, 1962.

Nordlinger, Eric A. *Soldiers in Politics: Military Coups and Governments.* Englewood Cliffs, Prentice-Hall, Inc., 1977.

OAU, *Lagos Plan of Action for the Economic Development of Africa, 1980-2000.* Geneva: International Institute for Labor Studies for OAU, 1982.

O'Connell, James. "Political Integration: The Nigerian Case." In a Hazzlewood, ed.), *African Integration and Disintegration; Case Studies in Economic and Political Union.* London: Oxford University Press, 1967.

O'Connor, J. "The Uncanning of Economic Imperialism," *Imperialism and Underdevelopment: A Reader.* edited by R. I. Rhodes, New York: Monthly Review Press, 1970, p. 118.

Odetola, Theophilus O. *Military Politics in Nigeria.* New Brunswick, N.J.: Transaction Books, 1978.

O'Donnell, Guillermo A. *Modernization and Bureaucratic-Authoritarianism.* Berkely: University of California Press, 1979

Odumosu, O.I. *The Nigerian Constitution.* London: Sweet and Maxwell, 1963.

Ogbuagu, Chibuzo A. "The Nigerian Indigenization Policy: Nationalism or Pragmatism." *African Affairs* 2 (April, 1983).

Ogunsheye, A. "Experience and Problems of Indigenous Enterprises." *In The Proceedings of the Tenth Annual Conference of the Nigerian Institute of Management: Indigenisation and Economic Development.* Lagos NIM., 1972.

Ojo, Olatunde J. B. "Nigeria and the Formation of ECOWAS." *International Organization 34,* 4 (Autumn, 1980), 571-603.

Okarar, F.O. "The Nigerian Capital Market," in JK Onoh (ed.) *The Foundation of Nigeria's Financial Infrastructure.* London: Croom Helm, 1980.

Okafor, S.O. *Indirect Rule: The Development of Central Legislature in Nigeria.* Ikeja, Lagos: Thomas Nelson Nigeria LTD., 1981.

Okpau, Joseph. ed. *Nigeria: Dilemma of Nationhood.* New York: The Third Press, 1972.

Okubadejo, N.A.A. "Economic Development and Planning in Nigeria 1945-68." in T.M. Yesufu (ed.), Manpower Problems and Economic Development in Nigeria. Ibadon: Oxford University Press, 1970.

Olaloki, F.A. et al *Structures of the Nigerian Economy.* New York: St. Martin's Press, 1979.

Olaniyan, Richard. *African History and Culture.* New York: Longman 1992.

Olayide, S.O. *Economic Survey of Nigeria,* 1960-1975. Ibadan: Armolaran Publishing Co., 1976.

Oni, O. and Onimode, B. *Economic Development of Nigeria: The Socialist Alternative.* Ibadan: The Nigeria Academy of Arts, Sciences and Technology, 1975.

_____. *Imperialism and Underdevelopment in Nigeria.* London: Zed Press, 1985.

Onimode, Bade. "Imperialism and Multinational Corporations: A Case Study of Nigeria," *Decolonization and Dependency, Problems of Development of African Societies.* edited by Aguibou Y. Yansan, Connecticut: Greenwood Press, 1980

Oyebode, A. "National Participation and Control of Nigerian Economic Activities." Paper presented at the 15th Annual Conference of the Nigerian Association of Law Teachers, Lagos, University of Lagos, April 1977.

Oyejidi, T.A. *Tariff Policy and Industrialization in Nigeria.* Ibadan: Ibadan University Press, 1964.

Papp, Daniel S. *Contemporary International Relations: Frankworks for Understanding.* New York: MacMillan Publishing Co., 1991

Parenti, Michael "Imperialism: Third World Poverty" *The Third World Opposing Views.* San Diego, CA: Greenhaven Press, 1989.

Peter, Lawrence. *World Recession and the Food Crisis in Africa.* London: James Curry, 1986.

Prebisch, R. *The Economic Development of Latin America and Its Principal Problems*. New York: Lake Success, 1950.

Prebisch, Raul. *Toward a New Trade Policy for Development*. New York, London: Methuen, 1975.

Radwan, Dennis. *Land Policies and Farm Productivity in Sudan*. London: Hult Co. 1980.

Rhodes, Robert. *Imperialism and Underdevelopment: A Reader*. New York /London: Monthly review Press, 1970.

Richardson, Neil R. *Foreign Policy and Economic Dependence*. Austin: University of Texas Press, 1978.

Rimmer, Douglas. "Development in Nigeria: An Overview In H. Bienen and V. P. Diejomaoh, eds. *The Political Economy of Income Distribution in Nigeria*. New York: Holmes and Meier, 1981.

Robinson, Richard, "Dependence, Government Revenue, and Economic Growth." *Studies in Comparative International Development*, 12 (Summer, 1977), 3-28.

Robinson, Richard D. "The Engagement of Host Government Interest Upon the entry of Foreign Business." *International Business Affairs*. edited by John Fayerweather, Cambridge, Ballinger Publishing Company, (1973).

Rodney, Walter. *How Europe Underdeveloped Africa*. Washington, D.C.: Howard University Press, 1981.

Rostow, Walter W. *The Stages of Economic Growth: Non-Communist Manifesto*. Cambridge, Massachusetts: University of Cambridge Press, 1967.

Sathyamuirthy, T. V. *Nationalism in the Contemporary World: Political and Sociological and Perspectives*. London: Frances Printer, 1983.

Schatzl, L. H. *Petroleum in Nigerian Economy*. Ibadan: Ibadan University Press, 1973.

Schumpeter, Joseph. *Imperialism*. New York: Meridian, 1955.

Scott, James C. *Comparative Political Corruption*. Englewood: Cliffs, Prentice-Hall, Inc., 1972.

Schatz, Sayre P. *Nigerian Capitalism*. Berkeley: University of California Press, 1977.

Seidman, Ann Wilcox. *Planning for Development in Sub-Sahara Africa*. New York: Praeger Publishers, 1974.

Selltiz, Claire et al. *Research Method In Social Science Relation*. New York: Rhinehart and Winston, 1959.

Sharkansky, I. "Regionalism, Economic Status and Public Policies of American States," *Policy Analysis in Political Science*. edited by I. Sharansky, Chicago: Markham, 1970.

Shaw, Timothy and Fasehum, Orobola. "Nigeria in the World System: Alternative Approaches, Explanations and Projections". *Journal of Modern African Studies* 18 (December 1980)

Shaw, Timothy M. "Nigeria in the International System," *The Political Economy of Nigeria.* edited I. William Zartman, New York: Praeger Publishers, 1983, pp. 207-236.

Shen, T. Y. "Macro Development Planning in Tropical Africa: Technocratic and Non-Technocratic Causes of Failures." *Journal of Development Studies* 13 (July 1977).

Singer, Marshall. *Weak States in a World of Power: The Dynamics of International Relationships.* New York: Free Press, 1972.

Smith, Sheila. "Colonialism in Economic Theory: The Experience of Nigeria". *The Journal of Development Studies,* 15 (April, 1979).

Smith, Tony. "The Underdevelopment of Development Literature: The Case of Dependency Theory." *World Politics* 31, (January, 1979).

Sonaki, Olayinka. "Economic Dependence: The Problem of Definition." *Journal of Asian and African Studies* XIV (1979).

South Commission, The Challenge to South: The Report of the Commission New York: Oxford University Press, 1991.

Spengler, Joseph J. "John Stuart Mill on Economic Development," *Theories of Economic Growth.* edited by Bert F. Hoselitz, New York, Free Press, 1960.

Spero, Joan Edelman. *The Politics of International Economic Relations.* New York: St. Martin's Press, 1981.

Stauffer, Robert B. *National-Building in a Global Economy: The Role of the Multinational Corporation.* Sage Professional Paper, Beverly Hills, Sage Publications, Inc. 1973.

Stiles, Kendall and Akaha, Tsuneo. *International Political Economy.* New York: Harper Collins Publishers, 1991.

Suckow, Samuel. *Nigerian Law and Foreign Investment.* Paris, 1966.

Sunkel, Osvaldo, "Big Business and Dependencia." *Foreign Affairs* 50 (April, 173).

_____. "National Development Policy and External Dependence in Latin America." *Journal of Development Studies* 6 (1970).

Todaro, Michael. *Economic Development in the Third World.* New York: Longman Inc., 1977.

Tomori, S. and Fajana, F.O. Development Planning in F.A. Olaluki, et al., *Structure of the Nigerian Economy.* New York: St. Martin's Press, 1979.

Turner, T. "Multinational Corporations and the Instability of the Nigerian State." *Review of African Political Economy* Vol 5. (January 1976).

Turner, Terisa. "Commercial Capitalism and the 1975 Coup," *Soldiers and Oil--The Political Transformation of Nigeria.* edited by Keith Panter-Brick, New Jersey: Frank Cass and Co., Ltd., 1978.

U. S. Department of Commerce. "Foreign Economic Trade and Their Implications for the U.S. - Nigeria." *International Trade Administration* Washington, D.C., (January 1985).

U.S. Government Finance Statistics Yearbook. Washington, D.C.: IMF, 1977.

Vengroff, Richard. "Dependency and Underdevelopment in Black Africa: An Empirical Text." *Journal of Modern African Studies* 15 (1977).

Wallerstein, Immanuel. *The Modern World System-Capitalist Agriculture and the Origin of the European World-Economy in the Sixteenth Century.* New York: Academic Press, 1974.

Walter, James. *The Political Economy of Nigeria: Problem of Technology dependency.* New York: Praeger, 1980.

Ward, Barbara. et al. "Economic Imperialism and Its Aftermath," *Legacy of Imperialism.* edited by Barbara Ward, Pittsburgh: Chatham College, 1960.

Whitaker, C. S. *Politics of Tradition: Continuity and Change in Northern Nigeria.* Princeton: Princeton University Press, 1970.

Whitehead, John. "The African Economic Crisis." *Current Policy U.S. Department of State Bureau of Public Affairs* No. 157, (October 1985).

Wilber, Charles K. *The Political Economy of Development and Underdevelopment.* New York: University of Notre Dame, 1988.

World Bank. "Accelerated Development in Sub-Saharan Africa: and Agenda For Action" *African Review* (16 May 1982).

World Bank. *World Tables,* Washington, D.C., 1976.

World Bank. *World Tables, 2nd Edition,* Washington, D.C., 1980

World Bank. *World Development Report,* New York: Oxford University Press, 1983

World Bank. "World Development Report 1981: Accelerated Development in Sub-Sahara Africa," *African Red Family* 16 (May 1982).

World Bank. *World Tables,* 3rd ed., Vol. 2. Baltimore: John Hopkins University Press, 1983.

Yansana, U. *Decolonialization and Dependency: Problems of Development in Africa Society.* Westport, CT: Greenwood Press, 1980.

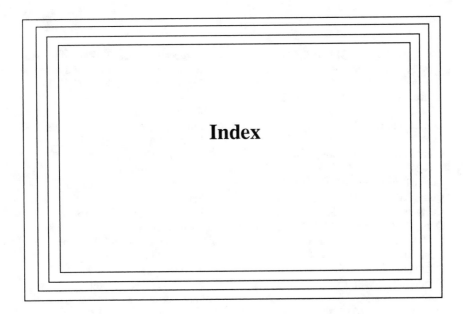

Index

AFRICA AFTER INDEPENDENCE